Teaching *and* Learning Languages

Teaching *and* Learning Languages

Selected readings from
Mosaic

edited by
Anthony Mollica

éditions **SOLEIL** *publishing inc.*

Cover Design: Frank Campion, Campion Marketing
Layout and Design: Anthony Mollica and Dennis Vanderwood

éditions Soleil publishing inc.

In Canada
P. O. Box 847
Welland, Ontario L3B 5Y5

In USA
P. O. Box 890
Lewiston, NY 14092-0890

Tel./Fax: [905] 788-2674.
Order Department: Fax 1-800-261-0833
E-mail: soleil@iaw.on.ca

ISBN 0-921831-65-X

Printed in Canada

Canadian Cataloguing in Publication Data

Main entry under title:

Teaching languages: selected readings from *Mosaic*

ISBN 0-921831-65-X

1. Language and languages – Study and teaching.
I. Mollica, Anthony, 1939-

P51.T422 1997   418'.0071   C98-932454-0

Table of Contents

Preface

The first issue of **Mosaic** appeared in the Fall of 1993. It was meant to be an unpretentious publication devoted to the professional development of teachers of Heritage/International languages – languages taught in elementary schools after school hours or on Saturday mornings. It immediately became evident, however, that *all* language teachers were interested in a "reader-friendly" publication which combined both theory and practice.

We did a massive mailing – publishing some 25,000 copies of the first issue – reaching selected teachers, consultants, and supervisors in both Canada and the United States. Frankly, we were surprised at the enthusiasm which the issue generated. Today, as we enter the fourth year of publication, **Mosaic** can boast of having almost 2,400 subscribers in North America alone.

We are fortunate to have had – and we hope that the trend will continue! – authors who successfully combine theory and practice and who write articles readily accessible to all readers. The fact that the first three volumes of the publication contain sufficient practical and theoretical articles to compile a book speaks highly not only for the Authors but also for the journal in which they published.

The request to put a number of selected articles from **Mosaic** in book form came from two colleagues from Erindale College, University of Toronto, Professors Charles Elkabas and Michael Lettieri, who are teaching a course on "Introduction to Second-Language Teaching." They felt that in the absence of a specific textbook, these articles would serve their purpose and form the basis for the course. As Editor, I was delighted to accede to their request and hence, *Teaching Languages. Selected Readings from* **Mosaic.**

The book was enthusiastically received and a handful of Canadian and American Faculties of Education adopted it as a textbook for their teacher-education courses.

It soon became apparent that several other excellent articles which subsequently appeared in **Mosaic** should be included in any future edition of *Teaching Languages*. It also occurred to us that the readings provided in the first edition did not only focus on *teaching* but also on *learning*. Hence, the new title, *Teaching and Learning Languages. Selected Readings from* **Mosaic.**

Selecting the articles to be included has been a painful *embarras de choix*. We regret that several other excellent contributions had to be omitted because of space restrictions. Their absence from the current "Table of Contents" does not diminish their value and their contribution to language teaching and learning.

Two articles which appeared in the first edition, namely, Peter Heffernan's "Sociopolitical Awareness, Intercultural Sensitivity, and the guage Teacher," and W. Jane Bancroft's "Another Language Teaching Approach: Dhority's Acquisition Through Creative Teaching (ACT)" have been replaced by two contributions by the same authors: "Promoting the Development of Strategic Competence in the Language Classroom"by Heffernan and "Non-Verbal Communication: How Important is It for the Language Teacher?" by Bancroft.

Selected from the first five volumes of **Mosaic,** these forty-seven practical and theoretical chapters, written by distinguished North American second-language scholars, are invaluable professional readings for both beginning and seasoned teachers.

The selections in *Teaching and Learning Languages*
recognize the importance of language teaching and learning

> (Mollica, "Language Learning: The Key to Understanding and Harmony"; Runte, "Surviving the Perils of Politics: The Language Classroom of the Next Century"),

acknowledge the important role of the student and teacher and the parent

> (Mollica and Nuessel, "The Good Language Learner and the Good Language Teacher: A Review of the Literature and Classroom Applications"; Ralph, "Motivating Parents to Support Second-Language Programs"),

identify students' anxiety and offer practical suggestions for studying

> Cankar, "Study Skill Suggestions for Students of Foreign Language Classes"; "Ten Way to Cope with Foreign language Anxiety"),

discuss classroom environment

> (Evans-Harvey, "Climate Setting in Second-Language Classrooms"; Heffernan, "Promoting the Development of Strategic Competence in the Language Classroom"),

provide practical teaching techniques which will assist teachers in their day-to-day teaching activity

> (Chastain, "Planning for Instruction"; Mollica, "The Lesson Outline", "Classroom Expressions", "Questioning Strategies"; Richards, "Questioning in the Language Classroom," "Discipline in the Language Class"; Papalia, "Classroom Settings"; Bell, "The Challenge of Multilevel Classes"),

highlight the partnership between home and school

> (Antonek, Tucker and Donato, "Interactive Homework: Creating Connections Between Home and School"),

identify the fundamentals of second-language teaching

> (LeBlanc, "The Fundamentals of Second-Language Teaching"),

focus on the teaching of a specific point of grammar

> (Maceri, "Reducing Stress in the Foreign Language Classroom: Teaching Descriptive Adjectives Through Humour"; Mason, "Mnemonic for Mastering the Imperfect and the Irregular Future in French, Italian and Spanish"),

propose vocabulary expansion

(Mollica, Schutz and Tessar, "Focus on Descriptive Adjectives: Creative Activities for the Language Classroom"; Howlett and Péchon, "French in Disguise"),

emphasize the fun element in language teaching

(Danesi and Mollica, "Games and Puzzles in the Second-Language Classroom: A Second Look"),

identify methods and approaches to language teaching

(Doggett, "Eight Approaches to Language Teaching"; Danesi and Mollica "Conceptual Fluency Theory and Second-Language Teaching"),

assess the neuroscientific interest of second-language educators

(Mollica and Danesi, "The Foray into the Neurosciences: Have We Learned Anything Useful?"),

suggest **caveats** *with print and non-print materials*

(Hammerly, "What Visual Aids Can and Cannot Do in Second Language Teaching"),

evaluate visuals in the classroom

(Hammerly, "A Picture is Worth 1000 Words and A Word is Worth 1000 Pictures"),

offer suggestions for creative activities

(Mollica, "A Picture is worth 1000 words... Creative Activities for the Language Classroom"; Nuessel, "Postage Stamps: A Pedagogical Tool in the Language Classroom"),

focus on three of the language skills:

speaking

(Valette, "The Five-Step Performance-Based Model of Oral Proficiency"),

reading

(Krashen, "Immersion: Why Not Try Free Voluntary Reading?"; Constantino, "The Effects of Pleasure Reading"; Valette, "Four Approaches to Authentic Reading"),

writing

(Nuessel and Cicogna, "Teaching Writing in Elementary and Intermediate Language Classes: Suggestions and Activities"; Besnard, Elkabas, and Rosienski-Pellerin, "Students' Empowerment: E-mail Exchange and the Development of Writing Skills"),

as well as on culture and body language

(Wilcox, "Gestures and Language: Fair and Foul in Other Cultures"; Bancroft, "Nonverbal Communication: How Important is It for the Language Teacher?"),

discuss the importance of evaluation

(Ralph, "Teaching to the Test: Principles of Authentic Assessment for Second Language Education").

and conclude with background information on North American cultural festivities

(Mollica, "Teaching Culture in a North American Context: An Introductory Note", " Thanksgiving"; Mollica, Séguin, Maiguashca, Valenzuela, "Halloween"; Lewin and Riesenbach, "Hannukka"; Onyschuk, "Ukrainian Easter"; Luo, "The Chinese New Year"; Mollica, Séguin and Valenzuela, "Valentine's Day"; Mollica and Sterling, "Mother's Day/ Father's Day".)

I should like to express my gratitude to the above colleagues for permission to reproduce the articles included in this anthology. Whatever success these readings will enjoy belongs to them.

Anthony Mollica

1 Language Learning: The Key to Understanding and Harmony

Anthony Mollica

Teachers, parents and researchers can give a long list of advantages to be derived from studying a second language.

The incorrect translation of a word may have very well been responsible for the death of over 200,000 people. Towards the end of the Second World War, the United States had offered Japan an opportunity to surrender. The Japanese reply contained the word *mokusatsu* which means "withholding comment pending decision." Through mistranslation, the verb *mokusatsu* was rendered as "ignore." As a result, the allies believed that the ultimatum had been flatly rejected and President Truman ordered the use of the atomic bomb. I don't know whether the story is true or not, but it certainly is a good language anecdote...

Gaffes

Less tragic examples abound: *The Wall Street Journal* reported that General Motors was puzzled by the lack of enthusiasm the introduction of its Chevrolet Nova automobile aroused among Puerto Ricans. The reason was very simple. *Nova* means *star* in Spanish, but when spoken it sounds like *no va* which means "it doesn't go." GM quickly changed the name to Caribe and the car sold nicely.

Linguistic and cultural gaffes made by translators or by non-native speakers have often been a source of chagrin. One recalls the embarrassment President Carter faced when the interpreter stated that the President "lusted" for Polish women. A more recent situation reported by the Canadian Press, involved Jean Drapeau, a former mayor of Montreal. At the end of a speech during a tour of China, the Mayor urged his audience "to beat up your brother when he is drunk." A glance at M. Drapeau's French text, however, showed that he never advocated such violence! What he had said in French was "Il faut battre le fer pendant qu'il est chaud."

Richard Lederer's "Lost in Translation" List

In his book, *Anguished English,* Richard Lederer (1987) identifies a number of incorrect translations which may very well lead to communicative... incompetence!

Teachers wishing to turn these mistranslations into a language activity can ask students to re-write them to convey the meaning intended.

In a Tokyo hotel:

It is forbidden to steal towels please. If you are not person to do such thing is please not to read this notis.

In another Japanese hotel room:

Please to bathe inside the tub.

In a Bucharest hotel lobby:

The lift is being fixed for the next day. During that time, we regret that you will be unbearable.

In a Leipzig elevator:

Do not enter lift backwards, and only when lit up.

Posted on a Belgrade hotel elevator:

To move the cabin, push button for wishing floor. If the cabin should enter more persons, each person should press a number of wishing floor. Driving is then going alphabetically by national order.

In a Paris hotel elevator:

Please leave your values at the front desk.

In a hotel in Athens:

Visitors are expected to complain at the office between the hours of 9 and 11 a.m. daily.

In a Yugoslavian hotel:

The flattening of underwear with pleasure is a job of the chambermaid.

In a Japanese hotel:

You are invited to take advantage of the chambermaid.

In a lobby of a Moscow hotel across from a Russian Orthodox monastery:

You are welcome to visit the cemetery where famous Russian and Soviet composers, artists, and writers are buried daily except Thursday.

In an Austrian hotel catering to skiers:

Not to perambulate the corridors in the hours of repose in boots of ascension.

On a menu of a Swiss restaurant:

Our wines leave you nothing to hope for.

On the menu of a Polish hotel:

Salad a firm's own make: limpid reed beet soup with cheesy dumplings in form of a finger' roasted duck let loose' beef rashers beaten up in the country people's fashion.

In a Hong Kong supermarket:

For your convenience, we recommend courteous, efficient, self-service.

Outside a Hong Kong tailor shop:

Ladies may have a fit upstairs.

In Bangkok dry cleaner's:

Drop your trousers here for best results.

Outside a Paris dress shop:

Dresses for street walking.

In a Rhodes tailor shop:

Order your summers suits. Because is big rush, we will execute customers in strict rotation.

From the *Soviet Weekly:*

There will be a Moscow Exhibition of Arts by 15,000 Soviet Republic painters and sculptors. They were executed over the past two years.

In an East African newspaper:

A new swimming pool is rapidly taking shape since the contractors have thrown in the bulk of their workers.

In a Vienna hotel:

In case of fire, do your utmost to alarm the hotel porter.

A sign posted in Germany's Black Forest:

It is strictly forbidden on our black forest camping site that people of different sex, for instance, men and women, live together in one tent unless they are married with each other for that purpose.

In a Zurich hotel:

Because of the impropriety of entertaining guests of the opposite sex in the bedroom, it is suggested that the lobby be used for that purpose.

In an advertisement by a Hong Kong dentist:

Teeth will be extracted by the latest Methodists.

A translation sentence from a Russian chess book:

A lot of water has been passed under the bridge since this variation has been played.

In a Rome laundry:

Ladies, leave your clothes here and spend the afternoon having a good time.

In a Czechoslovakian tourist agency:

Take one of our horse-driven city tours – we guarantee no miscarriages.

Advertisement for donkey rides in Thailand:

Would you like to ride on your own ass?

On the faucet in a Finnish washroom:

To stop the drip, turn cock to the right.

In the window of a Swedish furrier:

Fur coats made for ladies from their own skin.

On the box of a clockwork toy made in Hong Kong:

Guaranteed to work throughout its useful life.

Detour sign in Kyushi, Japan:

Stop: Drive Sideways.

In a Swiss mountain inn:

Special today – no ice cream.

In a Bangkok temple:

It is forbidden to enter a woman even a foreigner if dressed as a man.

In a Tokyo bar:

Special cocktails for ladies with nuts.

In a Copenhagen airline ticket office:

We take your bags and send them in all directions.

On the door of a Moscow hotel room:

If this is the first visit to the USSR, you are welcome to it.

In a Norwegian cocktail lounge:

Ladies are requested not to have children in the bar.

At a Budapest zoo:

Please do not feed the animals. If you have any suitable food, give it to the guard on duty.

In the office of a Roman doctor:

Specialist in women and other diseases.

In an Acapulco hotel:

The Manager has personally passed all the water served here.

In a Tokyo shop:

Our nylons cost more than common, but you'll find they are best in the long run.

From a Japanese information booklet about using a hotel air conditioner:

Cooles and Heates: If you want just condition of warm in your room, please control yourself.

From a brochure of a car rental in Tokyo:

When passenger of foot heave in sight, tootle the horn. Trumpet horn melodiously at first, but if he still obstacles your passage then tootle him with vigour.

Cultural Meaning

Our ability to communicate effectively is dependent upon our skill in using language. But it is important not only to teach communication but also "cultural" meaning of words. *Language and culture are inseparable.* To teach one means to teach the other. Authors of second-language textbooks must not only identify the *denotation* of words, but also, where necessary, the *connotations* of those words and idioms. Where words seem to correspond lexically in their denotation, they may well diverge considerably in their connotation or the emotional association they arouse. While *bread* and *le pain* may correspond lexically in their denotation, they certainly do not correspond in their connotation. *Bread* is often found in a plasticized wrapping and is soft. The French *pain* brings markedly different association to mind! As a recent publication stressed,

> Both at home and abroad, the linguistic skills that students need to communicate with speakers of other languages must be accompanied by knowledge about the culture. For example, students need to know not only words to use in greetings but also how to vary greetings according to the time of day, the social context, the age of the individual, and so forth, as well as what gestures to use, such as shaking hands or bowing. (College Entrance Examination Board 1986:22).

It is a widely-accepted notion, then, that language skills must be taught integrally with cultural knowledge.

Heritage/International Languages in the Curriculum

Education in Canada falls under provincial jurisdiction. Each province or territory has its own ministry of education and is autonomous, although funds in some cases are channelled to the provinces from the federal government coffers. This is, in fact, the case for the expansion of both official languages, English and French as second languages.

Most, if not all, provinces recognize only two languages for study at the elementary level: English and French. All other languages generally fall under the category of Heritage Languages in English-speaking provinces and as *langues d'origine* in Quebec. Although only English and French are recognized as the official languages of instruction, Ontario has recognized the use of another language with a group of students in the classroom to acculturate them in either official language. The teaching of Heritage Languages is consistent with Canada's political ideology: the United States stresses the "melting pot," Canada favours the "multicultural mosaic."

Recent newspaper reports show that there is a political backlash not only for French but also to the cultural mosaic of which Canada is justifiably proud. Ethnic communities must not simply be passive observers of events but also take more than an active interest in issues which affect them. If ethnic groups are to keep their roots and not become entirely assimilated, a dispassionate, objective campaign on the preservation of one's ethnic identity must be fought at both the provincial and national level.

The campaign to encourage and promote the learning of Heritage Languages must be fought objectively and not emotionally, educationally and not politically. My solution appears to be simplistic and I will readily agree that it is difficult to separate objectivity from emotions, or politics from education. Nevertheless, I feel that information about the advantages of learning a second or third language should be widely circulated in order to enlighten politicians and the general public on the values of Heritage Languages.

If Heritage Language programs are under attack, perhaps it is because the average person sees the introduction and the expansion of a Heritage Language as part of the maintenance of an ethnic group's identity and Canadian taxpayers, already overburden, do not feel that they should support the preservation of the language for the various ethnic groups. We must change this perception and emphasize the educational values of Heritage Languages. Certainly, the current term, Heritage Language, is not very appropriate in the current political situation and every effort should be made to change the term to International Languages, a term already used in other provinces. *(Editor's Note:* The Ontario Minister of Education changed the term "Heritage Languages" into "International Languages – Elementary" in 1994.)

The Value of Language Learning

Teachers and parents are quick to recite a whole litany of advantages and benefits to be derived from studying second or more languages:

✓ Second-language students perform better in English than non-second language students.

✓ A second language helps students gain greater insight into their own culture.

✓ The self-concept of second-language students is significantly higher than that of non-second-language students.

✓ Studies have shown positive correlation between the study of a second language and the creative functioning of learners.

✓ A working knowledge of other languages is important for research.

✓ Reading skills are shown to be transferable from one language to another.

✓ Second-language learners have larger vocabulary.

✓ Today's students are career-oriented, and they must not overlook jobs that require second languages. The knowledge of a second or third language increases employment opportunities.

✓ The knowledge of the language of the region or country being visited, makes travelling more fun and more enjoyable.

Wilga Rivers (1968:8-9) identifies six classes of objectives for the study of another language:

✓ to develop the student's intellectual powers through foreign- language study;

✓ to increase the student's personal culture through the study of the great literature and philosophy to which it is the key;

✓ to increase the student's understanding of how the language functions and to bring him, through the study of a foreign language, to a great awareness of the functioning of his own language;

✓ to teach the student to read the foreign language with comprehension so that he may keep abreast of modern writing, research, and information;

✓ to bring the student to a greater understanding of people across national barriers by giving him a sympathetic insight into the life and ways of thinking of the people who speak the language he is learning;

✓   to provide the student with skills which will enable him to communicate orally, and to some degree in writing, with speakers of another
language and with people of other nationalities who have also learned
this language.

During a keynote address at the annual conference of the Ontario
Modern Language Teachers' Association, Veronica Lacey (1993), Director
of Education for North York, Ontario, stressed that,

> Learning a language is far more than an intellectual, cognitive challenge. It is a
> means to grow and mature through the experience of other cultures. It gives
> breadth and depth to our personalities. It allows us to approach problems
> differently because we have experienced different worlds; it allows us, as Proust
> says, to see with new eyes.

Endorsements for learning languages have come from thousands of
writers or politicians. Napoleon is reported to have said, "The man who
knows two languages is worth two people" and the German novelist-
dramatist Goethe, "A man who is ignorant of foreign languages is ignorant
of his own."

Pam Goossen (1994:5), a trustee with the Toronto Board of Education,
is convinced that

> an exposure to international languages in elementary school classrooms
> constitutes an important part of a forward looking up-to-date educational system.

Roseann Runte (1995:9), President of Victoria College, University of
Toronto, stresses that

> Language is more than grammar. It is more than a way of structuring thought. It
> is a way of signifying our deepest feelings, our most sincere beliefs. Each time I
> learn a word which has no translation into another language, I feel that I have
> discovered a rare gift, a new idea, a fresh insight.

And, elsewhere, Runte (1996) concludes,

> If we want that part of our country which is humane and tolerant to continue on
> into the future, we need to educate the next generation to be tolerant, to be open.
> What better way to do this than through learning languages?

Edwin Ralph (1995), an associate professor of Education at the University of Saskatchewan, points out that

> Recent global events have emphasized the critical importance of multinational
> communication. Growing trade and commercial relationships among European
> nations, among the Pacific rim countries, and among our own North American
> partners – plus the potential to forge further links between/among these larger
> international blocs – signal that people skilled in various languages will be required
> to help expedite these communicative relationships.

Even UNESCO's (United Nations Education, Science, and Culture
Organization) report on *Our Creative Diversity* (1996), as quoted by Runte
(1996), notes the importance of language learning. The "observable advantage of bilinguals" is that they are "more used to switching thought patterns
and have more flexible minds," Their knowledge of language(s) makes
them more familiar with "different, often contradictory concepts" and this,

in turn, makes bilinguals or multilinguals more "tolerant than monolinguals, and more capable of understanding sides of an argument."

And the list of endorsements could continue.

But all these reasons can fall under four major objectives for studying a second language, as outlined by Jan Amos Komensky, known as "Comenius," Czech writer and humanist (1592-1671),:

Political:

to serve the nation's interests.

Cultural:

to know the culture of other people for one's own personal enrichment.

Practical:

to be able to communicate in the language of the foreign speaker.

Educational:

to sharpen the mind and to shape the personality of the learner.

Heightened Abilities

The Canadian researchers, Elizabeth Peal and Wallace E. Lambert (1962), repeatedly pointed out that learning more than one language heightens the learners' ability to call into play a variety of learning configurations which will otherwise have been limited. "Figuring out" the sound system and grammatical rules in more than one language seems

- to increase the learners' ability to organize perceptions of reality,
- to recognize concepts in several different forms, and
- to solve complex linguistic and cultural problems.

   Raymond Aron said,

   I have always felt that the ability to speak freely in two different languages provides us with a kind of personal freedom that no other means can provide. When I speak English or German, I don't think the same way as I think in French. This frees me from feeling like a prisoner of my own words (as reported in Mollica, 1984).

While the practical and educational values of learning two or more languages are readily recited what is not as well known is that, as psychological research has now documented beyond any doubt, learning another language brings about a whole series of psychological and affective benefits as a bi-product to the practical ones.

Myth

Before going into the kinds of research which pertain to this statement, it is perhaps useful, and probably necessary, to dispel a long-held myth about foreign language teaching, a myth which Marcel Danesi, a professor at the University of Toronto, in several studies has called the "neurological space myth." Essentially, this was a myth which was generated by research on bilingual children during the 1930s, 1940s and 1950s in the United States and which was connected to the socio-cultural variables rather than psychological ones. The subjects of study were always from lower class backgrounds which did not stress the learning of languages in the home. Nevertheless, this research generated the impression that the learning of another language, or the retention of the mother tongue as a second language, was detrimental to overall cognition because it was believed, or was hypothesized, that the brain had only so much space in it for language. To put another code into the brain, it was argued, would take away from the space the dominant language needed to be able to function and to operate normally in school environments.

This myth has now been debunked by whole series of neurological studies which show the exact opposite; that the insertion of another code into the brain, either in the primary ages during childhood or in the secondary ages during adolescence and adulthood, brings with it a re-organization of neurological linguistic operation so that, in fact, what another code does in the brain helps the brain to function more globally, more holistically and more completely than it otherwise would. Canadian researchers such as Wallace E. Lambert and G. Richard Tucker (1972), Jim Cummins and Merril Swain (1986) as well as many others have documented this phenomenon in several of their studies.

Social Convergence

In a study, done a decade ago, B. McLaughlin (1984) observed that the research in Canada provides evidence that "bilingual education leads to a more liberal and enlightened perception of other ethnic groups." Similarly, the research done by Jim Cummins and Merrill Swain (1986) of the Ontario Institute for Studies in Education finds that Heritage Language programs, for example, promote inter-ethnic cohesion by allowing ethnically diverse children an opportunity to adapt gradually to a new psycho-cultural way of living. By generating a favourable attitude to one's ethnic identity and background, these programs tend to produce what may be called a "social convergence" effect; that is, they promote cross-cultural understanding by inhibiting a natural tendency to reject cultural modes that might be perceived as being "different."

Other Worlds

In learning a second language, the students acquire new modes of thought, new ways of behaviour. They begin to understand those new modes and new ways. Understanding leads to acceptance. Acceptance leads to tolerance and diversification of one's world view. As I recently claimed in a slogan, "Monolingualism *can* be cured!" because it is, in a way, a type of cognitive disease. Monolingualism constrains. Monolingualism lessens our viewpoint and our *Weltanschauung*, the personal philosophy of the world. Learning other languages cannot help but diversify and broaden the point of view. Therefore, once we've come to see another person's point of view, we accept the other person. By accepting the other person, we accept that person's culture. Accepting another culture leads to increased tolerance and harmony and, ultimately, to peace in the world. This, after all, was the contention Alfred Korzybysky (1933), the founder of general semantics. The science and theory of general semantics was based on the view that knowing how other people talk is knowing how they think, how they behave, and this knowledge will lead to acceptance.

Language and Unity

This conclusion contradicts the waving placards of demonstrators against Canada's 1988 Official Languages Act: "One language unites, two languages divide." I am firmly convinced that only when the study of either official language or of Heritage/International Languages is depoliticized and the learning of languages is accepted for its own intrinsic value, will we be able, in my opinion, to have linguistic peace and harmony in this country.*

References

College Entrance Examination Board. 1986. *Academic Preparation in Foreign Language. Teaching for Transition from High School to College.* New York: College Entrance Examination Board.

Cummins, J. and Swain M. 1986. *Bilingualism in Education.* London: Longman.

Danesi, Marcel. 1988. "The Utilization of the Mother Tongue in the Educational Experience of the Minority Language Child: A Synopsis of Research." *Multiculturalism,* 11: 6-10.

Goossen, Tam. 1994. "Should International Languages Be Part of the School Curriculum?" *Mosaic,* 1, 3: 19.

Korzybski, A. 1933. *Science and Sanity: An Introduction to non-Aristotelian Systems and General Semantics.* Lancaster: Science Press.

Lambert, W.E. and G.R. Tucker, 1972. *Bilingual Education of Children: The St. Lambert Experiment.* Rowley MA, Newbury House.

Lacey, Veronica. 1993. "Modern Languages: Recognizing their Relevance." Keynote address at the Spring Conference on the Ontario Modern Language Teachers' Association. March. Mimeo.

Lederer, Richard. 1987. *Anguished English. An Anthology of Accidental Assaults Upon Our Language.* Charleston, NC: Wyric and Company.

McLaughlin, B. 1984. *Second-Language Acquisition and Childhood.* Hillsdale, NJ: Lawrence Earlbaum Associates.

Mollica, Anthony. 1984. "Student Exchanges: Getting to Know One Another." *Dialogue, A Newsletter on the Teaching of English and French as Second Languages,* 3 ,1(November) 1-12. Toronto: Council of Ministers of Education, Canada.

Peel, Elizabeth and Wallace E. Lambert. 1962. "Relationship of Bilingualism to Intelligence." *Psychological Monographs,* 76 (whole issue).

Ralph, Edwin G. 1995. "Motivating Parents to Support Second Language Programs." *Mosaic,* 2, 4: 17.

Rivers, Wilga. 1968. *Teaching Foreign-Language Skills.* Chicago, IL: University of Chicago Press.

Runte, Roseann. 1995. "Learning Languages in the Context of Canada's Many Cultures." *Mosaic,* 2, 4: 8-11.

Runte, Roseann. 1996. "Surviving the Perils of Politics: The Language Classroom of the Next Century." *Mosaic,* 3, 2: 1, 3-7.

*Mollica *et al.* have published, through éditions Soleil publishing inc., a series of 18"x24" posters identifying reasons for promoting/encouraging the study of languages.

CS-001 Why *you* should learn a second lan- guage

CS-002 Non knowledge of a second language?

CS-003 Why learn a modern language?

CS-004 Important benefits of second language learning

CS-005 Why learn French in Canada?

CS-006 Why learn a Heritage Language?

CS-007 Why learn French?

CS-008 Why learn German?

CS-009 Why learn Latin

CS-010 Why learn Italian?

CS-011 Why lean Spanish?

Caption-only posters:

LP-001 Monolingualism *can* be cured!

LP-002 French. Don't leave *school* without it!

LP-003 Italian. Don't leave *school* without it!

LP-004 Languages. A golden opportunity!

Editor's Note: This is a revised, expanded, and up-dated version of Anthony Mollica, "Language Learning: The Key to Understanding and Harmony," *Language and Society/Langue et société,* 26, Spring 1989. Published by the Office of the Commissioner of Official Languages. It is reprinted with permission of the Minister of Supply and Services, Canada, 1989.

The current article includes sections from Anthony Mollica, *"Traduttore, traditore!* Beware of Communicative Incompetence!" *Mosaic,* 3, 1(Fall 1993), pp. 23-24

Reprinted from: Anthony Mollica, "Language Learning: The Key to Understanding and Harmony," *Mosaic,* 1, 1 (Fall 1993), pp. 1, 3-5.

2 Motivating Parents to Support Second Language Programs

Edwin G. Ralph

Based on an assumption that second language teachers provide the key motivating force facilitating this parental support, this paper presents several successful strategies – grounded both in second-language teachers' actual experiences and in related action-research – which have been shown to enhance parental support for school second-language programs.

The nineties are witnessing a growing societal demand for increased involvement by parents and the community in the improvement of education. Recent social, political, economic, and ecological events, worldwide – which often receive instantaneous exposure because of the advancement of global communication systems – have combined to exert pressure upon the educational establishment to become more effective, accountable, open, and collaborative with respect to the public they serve (Simpson, 1994).

Gone are the days when educators could "sidestep" demands from parents or could deflect societal pressure by arguing: "We are the trained professionals in education, parents are not. Just let us alone to do our jobs: we will teach your children what they need to know." Today's educators, on the other hand, are becoming increasingly pro-active in their deliberate solicitation of family involvement in education and are, as well, welcoming wider community participation by business, industry, and other agencies (Brandt, 1994).

Background and Rationale

The rationale supporting increased family and community involvement in schooling generally – and in second-language education specifically – rests upon three key assumptions. Although these foundational premises are not necessarily new nor profound, they have recently regained prominence – particularly in the light of the tenuous balance currently existing between the desire for international cooperation among nations, on the one hand, and the dangers of global competition, on the other.

The first assumption is rooted in the fundamental purpose of schooling in society. Schools were initially established by Western nations to be service agencies accountable to the families and citizens who financed them. The latter paid taxes to be used for the purpose of providing education for their children. Logically, then, those who pay for such educational services should have the right to be involved in examining the results of the enterprise, and in requiring improvements if necessary.

Traditionally, this involvement was secured in North America by several means:

- the election of representative school boards who set educational policy for groups of schools in a district;
- the establishment of school-division wide citizen advisory groups to provide school trustees with "grassroots input" about education from the community;
- the establishment of parent-teacher associations at each school; and
- other *ad hoc* committees set up from time to time, to provide information or to present concerns on educational matters to governing bodies at various levels.

In this paper, "second-language education" has a much wider scope than English-as-a-second-language (ESL), and French-as-a-second-language programs (FSL). Although the term includes ESL and FSL programs of all types, it also encompasses the so-called "modern languages" and the Heritage/International languages, as well as the First Nations languages.

With respect to second-language education in Canada over the past few years, the groups just described have pressured school districts in many regions to make policy-changes in favour of providing a variety of language-learning programs (See, for example, Ralph, 1979). In fact, it would be fair to say that – as a group – the parents of children in Canadian second-language programs, particularly those whose children are enroled in the various immersion options across the Nation, would tend to rate higher in "being motivated" about these school programs, than would comparable groups of parents whose children are not in these second-language programs. This is so because of the unique phenomenon in Canada that is unlike the experience in most parts of the world where people learn two or more languages, as a routine. In Canada, parents who choose immersion programs for their children must face several issues, some of which are:

- Will they and their children be stigmatized for "breaking neighbourhood ties" by sending pupils to centralized immersion schools?
- Will they be labelled as "elitist" because of this decision (and because of often receiving "free" bus transportation to and from the immersion schools that are often a distance away)?
- Will their children's scholastic achievement suffer, in their first language? in their second language? in the other subjects?
- How will parents ever know if they have made the right decision?

In short, because these parents, as a group, have riskèd "daring to be different", they will naturally tend to form a close-knit, supportive group, who become highly motivated in seeing their children succeed and thus will support the school program.

A second assumption underlying the principle of encouraging parental and community support for second-language programs is rooted in the fundamental biological/psychological basis of parenting. Parents care for their children, and they are ultimately the most important influence in their children's lives. While it is true that the make-up of the traditional family has recently shifted (Pawlas, 1994), it is equally true that the vast majority of parents, from all types of family units, are interested in being involved in assisting in their children's school experiences, but are often not sure of how to go about it (Elam, Rose, Gallup, 1993; Epstein, 1993).

For example, Canter (1991) reports that in a recent poll, only 25% of parents reported receiving systematic requests/instructions from teachers with respect to assisting in students' learning activities at school or at home. In order to help remedy this situation, he consequently suggests – on the basis of his research in this area – that educators must capitalize on this ready parental desire to help, and that schools should initiate specific efforts to "turn parents into partners". The key to gaining and maintaining this support is effective teacher communication that expresses to parents a genuine interest in having *every* student succeed, and that treats the parent the way the teacher – if a parent – would want to be treated by her/his child's own teacher (Canter, 1991).

One of the clearest examples of organized parental involvement in second-language education has been the growth of Canadian Parents for French (CPF) over the past 20 years (Sloan, 1989; Maclsaac, 1990; Morissette, 1992). CPF, now numbering more than 18,000 members throughout Canada's 10 provinces and two territories, has been recognized as "the most successful educational lobby in history" (Hood, 1989)). This parental organization has been a major factor in exerting pressure:

(a) to increase access to improved FSL instruction (both core and immersion programs) for children in all regions of Canada;

(b) to promote para-educational activities for these students (e.g., FSL exchanges, trips, weekends, camps, media/materials, and interactive experiences); and

(c) to call for improved governmental second-language services for minorities in Canada.

A key result of CPF's efforts is that the current generation of Canadian school children ranks as the most bilingual in Canada's entire history (Maclsaac, 1990); and what is equally as notable, is that 90% of a recent survey of CPF members indicated that they would provide their children with the same FSL experiences, again, if they had the opportunity (Morissette, 1992). This association has not only demonstrated a consistently organized and powerful voice in presenting parental and community concerns to educational policy-makers, but have been influential in helping establish and/or modify second-language policies/practices for individual schools and school districts.

In the United States, a comparable organization called "Advocates for Language Learning" (ALL), is a similarly powerful parental group that supports second-language school programs (Antonek, Tucker, and Donato, 1995). Erlich (1987), the founder of ALL, indicates – as does CPF – that immersion programs provide ideal means for children to learn a second language within regular school programs.

Another more recent example illustrating the increased importance of parental and community involvement in education on a broader front was the 1994 announcement by United States Secretary of Education, Richard Riley, of the formation of a nation-wide partnership among the U.S. Department of Education, the 45-member National Coalition for Parent Involvement in Education, and several prominent parent, religious, business, civic and community-based organizations (U.S. Department, 1994). This coalition is directly linked to one of the 8 National Education Goals recently enacted by the U.S. government as part of the *Goals 2000: Educate America* Act, which is to promote partnerships that will increase parental involvement and participation in the activities of the school.

These examples illustrate the underlying fundamental assumption with regard to parental support that is backed by 30 years of research: "Greater family involvement in children's learning is a critical link to achieving a high-quality education and a safe, disciplined learning environment for every student" (U.S. Department, 1994, p. 1).

A third foundational premise underlying the need for family and community support of students' learning is that the classroom teacher is the key source in initiating and upholding the school-home relationship. Although government legislation, school-board policy, and school-site expectations are all needed to promote school-community bonding, it is essentially the responsibility of the teacher – and mostly through her daily interactions and relationships with students during the routines of school-life – to nurture and sustain this relationship. Parents promptly learn from their children – often even before the "September Open-House" is held – what the teacher is like (whether or not such an "assessment" is accurate). According to their children's descriptions, reactions, and opinions of the teacher's work, conduct, and attitude at school, the family's perceptions and views of the teacher and the program are soon formed, and the teacher's reputation becomes firmly established. Whether positive or not, this perception becomes relatively difficult to change. In fact, one director of education from a school district in Western Canada (on the basis of his 25 years' experience in education) recently advised a group of teacher-interns embarking on a job-search for their first teaching position that:

> If parents think you are effective as a teacher, then they will readily forgive you if you make a blunder – even a serious one! However, if they don't like you – on the basis of what their kids, and others, say about you –you will have an uphill struggle... You have to show that you really – not superficially care for their children... (Johnson, 1994).

Effective Ways to Involve Parents/Communities

Using the above rationale as a conceptual framework, I draw upon three sources from which to derive some specific practices that have proven successful in encouraging families and community to support second-language education. The three sources are:

1. responses both from practising and from retired educators (many in second-language education) (Ralph, 1994b);
2. recent findings reported in the related educational literature (Danesi, 1993; Mollica, 1993); and
3. my own 30 years' experience in education (as second-language teacher, second-language program coordinator, school principal, career counsellor, president/director of a publishing firm marketing second-language instructional materials, college/ university professor, and supervisor of teacher-interns).

In many countries, government legislation and policy at both federal and provincial (or state) levels – together with local school district and individual school-site policies, regulations, and procedures – have all been combined to establish overall guidelines for second-language education. However, in recent years, the traditional top-down, hierarchical governance and administration of education has been displaced by: trends toward increased collaboration among stakeholders; more empowerment of school-based personnel to participate in decision-making and policy-formation that affects them; and transformational leadership, whereby administrative and supervisory tasks are shared among *all* professionals.

In the light of these reforms, and based on the assumptions undergirding quality parental cooperation, what specific practices have been shown to promote the involvement of the family and the community in second-language programs? Several practices are presented below. It should be noted, again, that even though some of these initiatives may be externally legislated, or bureaucratically mandated by various educational officials, it is the second-language teachers, themselves, who are key determinants in the degree of lasting success of these efforts.

Orientating Parents to Second-Language Programs

Several effective projects and programs that effectively link parents and the community to second-language programs have been reported. One initiative that invariably motivates parents and the school community – particularly in the case of immersion schools (or immersion programs within regular schools) is an "Orientation Evening" or "Open House" typically held early in the school year. At such sessions, school-based personnel describe the second-language program, answer parents' questions and allay their concerns about the program. Presentations on such topics as "Why Learn a second language?", or "What A Quarter-Century of Research Findings Tell Us About second-language Program Options" prove very valuable in clarifying misconceptions and/or re-assuring parents that they have made sound decisions in enroling their children in particular programs.

With respect to the "Why Learn a second language?" topic, I have found in my experience as a teacher of second-language and a coordinator of second-language programs in a Western Canadian school district, that I was able to help defuse certain criticisms and fears of parents, students, and the community by first of all clearly articulating opponents' doubts about a specific second-language program, and then by deliberately refuting these misconceptions, one by one, using the well-established research results for second language programs. Furthermore, at these meetings, I was able to describe and clarify the strengths and comparative limitations of the various second-language program-options (i.e., early, intermediate, and late immersion; extended programs; and core and conversational courses) (Ralph, 1981).

Several current writers have synthesized the rationale supporting the study of a second language (Danesi, 1993; Mollica, 1993; Ralph, 1982, 1994a). A particularly valuable resource for this topic is Mollica's (1990) "The Clipboard Series" of eleven poster-size visuals presenting valid, practical reasons for learning a second language (e.g., Spanish, Italian, or Heritage Languages).

A technique I found to be particularly effective in this vein was to present these concrete benefits of being bi-or multi-lingual to students and parents. Stating the following advantages proved to be a powerful means either to reduce negative attitudes or to bolster parent/student commitment towards various second-language programs:

(a) in general, people who know more than one language have a certain mental enrichment or cognitive stimulation about their personalities, not observable in comparable groups of monolinguals;

(b) bilingual/multilingual individuals' scores on psychological tests (both verbal and non-verbal) are as a rule higher for divergent thinking skills and diversified reasoning processes, than are similar scores for monolinguals;

(c) people who know more than one language typically get to know their mother tongue better than do comparable groups of monolinguals

(d) bi- or multi-linguals, compared to their unilingual peers, tend to have a more socially relaxed and at ease reaction to meeting others from different cultures;

(e) they are generally less provincial, stereotypic, prejudiced, and biased in their views of other cultures or individuals, than are similar groups of monolinguals; and

(f) compared to unilingual peers, bilinguals as a group, enjoy more pragmatic benefits, such as being more disposed to travel to other countries overseas, and having access to wider job and career opportunities, because of their second-language abilities (Ralph, 1982, 1994a).

Furthermore, providing parents with attractive, concise print materials outlining the second-language program, its expectations, and its activities (and a time-schedule for these activities) – in the form of brochures, newsletters, and bulletins is typically well-received (Canter, 1991).

Capitalize on "Current Practicalities"

Recent global events have emphasized the critical importance of multinational communication. Growing trade and commercial relationships among European nations, among Pacific rim countries, and among our own North American partners – plus the potential to forge further links between/among these larger international blocs – signal that people skilled in various languages will be required to help expedite these communicative relationships. For example, because of expanding free-trade among Canada, Mexico, and the US on our continent, Spanish will no doubt become increasingly important, here.

With respect to the pragmatic benefits of knowing an second language, educators currently involved in Ukrainian language programs could especially use to their advantage in promoting the second-language program the recent events that have developed in Canada/Ukraine relations. For example, the 1994 visit to Canada by Ukraine's President Leonid Kuchma (Roberts, 1994) could be used by teachers to enhance the status of the study of Ukrainian in Canada. Not only did the two nations form an accord to increase their trade partnership, but Canada has agreed to share commercial and business information and to provide consultants in areas of Ukraine's economic growth, investments, and scientific/technological/environmental concerns. During this visit, Canadian Prime Minister Chrétien noted that Ukrainian settlers helped to develop Western Canada a century ago, and now it is Canada's turn to reciprocate by assisting Ukraine to develop its newly acquired democracy and free-market system. He stated:

> We are the best country to benefit from Ukraine, because we can offer a lot of Canadian experts who speak Ukrainian... We are the best country to take advantage of the economic growth that will eventually come in Ukraine ("Canada Giving," 1994).

Kuchma later visited Western Canada, home of thousands of citizens of Ukrainian descent. He attended the G7 meeting in Winnipeg, and later met with Saskatchewan's Premier Romanow, himself of Ukrainian ancestry. The two discussed establishing business and government ties to help Ukraine in the areas of energy, agriculture, and health care.

One interesting incident that second-language teachers could use a motivator for senior students and/or parents occurred near the end of this Kuchma-Romanow visit. The President invited the Premier to visit Ukraine, but jokingly advised that he would need to improve his Ukrainian first (Smart, 1994). Teachers could use this actual event to alert students that if native speakers of a language (even key politicians) need to work at ameliorating their linguistic skills, then second-language learners should not feel discouraged if their performance seems slow at times! These recent events graphically represent realistic possibilities for students of Ukrainian to pursue in order to prepare themselves to take advantage of future career opportunities. They will be able to use their bilingualism to assist the two nations in the fields of government, business, industry, labour, and education relations.

Such a pragmatic goal has also been recently highlighted by another Saskatchewan initiative involving the Ukrainian language (McMahen, 1994). In order to help Ukraine improve its schools and teaching since its 1991 independence, a joint initiative has been undertaken by representatives the Saskatchewan Teachers of Ukrainian (the only provincial association for teachers of this language in Canada), the Saskatchewan Department of Education, and the University of Saskatchewan. This project has established a growing number of educational exchanges (of teachers, professors, students, and administrators) between the two countries. During the past three years there has been a 1991 joint education conference in Ukraine, a 1992 student exchange, a sharing of resource materials, Saskatchewan educators' visits to Ukraine in 1993, Ukrainian officials' visits to Saskatchewan schools, and a second joint educational conference in Ukraine in 1994. All of these activities – and potential future developments – have combined to bolster the image of Ukrainian second-language education in Western Canada.

Building Bridges for Students' Second-Language Growth

Although a school's annual "Open House", "Back-to-School Night", or "Meet/Greet Treat" in September are basic means in attracting parents, additional ways have been recently reported to enhance these activities. Research by Epstein (1993) and Canter (1991), for instance, suggests that the school – through its individual teachers – must not only introduce but continue clear and interesting communication links with each family. Some of these initiatives are:

(a) "introductory letters" to parents in August to present briefly the teacher and the second-language program, and to invite them to the first September meeting;

(b) a short form sent to parents on which they are asked to describe "What the teacher should know about my child" (e.g. his/her likes/dislikes, academic strengths/limitations, pertinent background/experiences);

(c) occasional "positive" notes/memos/telephone calls home *throughout* the year to support, or acknowledge a child's particular performance/improvement/contribution in second language;

(d) specific teacher requests for parental assistance in: helping a child with a particular second-language homework project; being a classroom guest to share with students a unique expertise/skill/trip concerning second-language; or filling out a brief check-list indicating the tasks/events/projects regarding second-language, in which the parents would be willing to assist during the school term; and

(e) invitations to assist children, individually or in groups – at home or at specific times at school – in practising their second-language skills (conversing, reading/listening to reading, and writing).

An excellent example of how interactive homework strategies are currently being used to promote home-school collaboration is the work reported by Antonek, Tucker, and Donato, 1994; 1995) related to a K-5 Japanese Foreign Language in the Elementary School (FLES) program in Pittsburgh. The researchers found that the majority of parents completed and appreciated an assigned amount of interactive homework with children. It was also found that even though the parents had not studied the target language, themselves, prior to this project, they welcomed the teachers' initiatives as helping:

> [...] them to understand, to participate in, and to support their children's learning experiences [...] They provided a valuable tool for enriching the partnership between home and school that has seemingly been ignored (Antonek, Tucker, and Donato, 1995, p. 9).

Although it is generally believed that this last initiative (i.e., parents helping children learn at home) is a common occurrence, recent research suggests just the opposite! Devlin-Scherer and Devlin-Scherer (1994) discovered in a study examining the 5779 tasks assigned over a 4-year period by 10 school boards in Vermont, less than 2% of those tasks dealt with parent involvement – and not one of these tasks dealt with assisting student learning at home. Both Canter (1991) and Riley (U.S. Department, 1994) believe that schools in the 90s must help remedy this problem by implementing such projects as:

(a) recommending families to undertake a family learning project (e.g., to go on a "Walk 'n Talk", listing [using second language] 10 things that they saw/heard/smelled/felt);

(b) providing parents with brief but specific guidelines/tips for guiding children in their completion of [second-language] homework assignments (and having the parents, the student, and the teacher to sign a follow-up document as the student finishes it); and

(c) reinforce children's successful [second-language] achievements (and parents' assistance towards these) with short, genuine, and positive communications – by note, telephone, or in person

With respect to Ukrainian-as-a-second-language programs, second-language teachers of Ukrainian, themselves, have found that having parents/grandparents, or other interested community-members who know the language, to take on tutor roles – either as occasional guests, or on a semi-regular basis at school has proved to be a powerful "win/win/win" motivator for all participants. That is,

(a) the visitors feel like worthwhile contributors to the second-language program;

(b) the students are permitted to practice their language skills with "authentic" speakers; and

(c) the teachers sense "a warm glow of satisfaction" from facilitating these successful experiences.

Involving Parents in Cultural Projects

As well as participating in linguistic activities with students, parents have been effectively involved with cultural activities and promotions in the second-language program. (In fact, this article contains several suggestions actually made by the conference attendees during a brainstorming session which I conducted as part of my presentation at the STU 1994 Conference in Saskatoon). Teachers of Ukrainian report high volunteer-rates by families of students for such projects as assisting teachers and their classes in:

(a) preparing traditional Ukrainian meals;

(b) helping or conducting cultural musical and/or dance programs;

(c) teaching/guiding special art projects; and

(d) providing assistance for Christmas Eve and Easter ceremonies (e.g., see Onyschuck, 1994).

A recent example that generated substantial parent and community interest in Ukrainian culture, in a non-Ukrainian school district where no Ukrainian second-language programs existed, occurred with one of my teacher-interns. The intern, who is of Ukrainian descent, and who is a skilled performer in a Ukrainian dance-troupe, was invited to have the sixth grade class, with whom he was working during his internship, to learn and perform a traditional Ukrainian dance-routine at the school's annual pre-Christmas, "Community Cultural Program". Not only did the teacher-intern and his students practice, prepare, and present an outstanding performance, but the reaction from the rest of the student body, the school-staff, the dancers' parents, and the "fullhouse" audience from the surrounding community was highly supportive.

This case reinforces the underlying theme of this present article: the teacher is the key agent to solicit parental involvement. In this case, the entire school community was positively disposed toward the Ukrainian culture by a single teacher, who through his own enthusiasm, motivated the students – and consequently their parents and the community at large.

Such teacher motivation is clearly essential – but insufficient – to achieve success in garnering continued community support for second-language programs. Indeed, to rouse parental motivation, initially, is one thing, but to sustain it over time it requires what effective teachers have always practised: persistence. creativity, and respect! My experience in establishing and maintaining parental and community support for second-language education has been consistent with what other educators and researchers have repeatedly confirmed (Brodkin, 1992; Canter, 1991, Epstein, 1993), and that is: teachers should deal with all second-language students as they would want their children to be treated if they were in that particular program.

References

Antonek, J., Donato, R., and Tucker, G. 1994. "Japanese in elementary school: Description of an innovative Pittsburgh program." _Mosaic, 2, 2: 5-9_

Antonek, J., G. Tucker, and R. Donato. 1995. "Interactive homework: Creating connections between home and school." *Mosaic*, 2, 3: 1-10.

Brandt, R., ed. 1994. "The new alternative schools." *Educational Leadership*, 52, (September): 1.

Brodkin, A. 1992. Parents and schools: Working together. *Instructor*, 101, 5: 6-7.

"Canada giving $50 million in help to Ukraine." 1994. *The Star Phoenix*, (October 25), p. C4.

Canter, L. and Associates. 1991. *Parents on your side*. Santa Monica, CA: Lee Canter and Associates.

Danesi, M. 1993. "Literacy and bilingual education programs in elementary school: Assessing the research." *Mosaic*, 1, 1: 6-12.

Devlin-Scherer, R. and W. Devlin- Scherer, W. 1994. "Do school boards encourage parent involvement?" *Education*, 114, 4: 535-541.

Ehrlich, M. 1987. "Parents: The child's most important teachers." In J.M. Darcey, ed., *Commitment and collaboration*. Middlebury, VT: Northeast Conference on the Teaching of Foreign Languages.

Elam, S., L. Rose and A. Gallup. 1993. "The 25th annual Phi Delta Kappa/ Gallup poll of the public's attitudes toward the public schools." *Phi Delta Kappa*, 75 (2, 1371 52.

Epstein, J. 1993. "Make parents your partners." *Instructor*. 102 (8, 52-53.

Hood, Sarah. 1989. "The need for excellence in French language teaching." *Language and Society/Langue et société*, 27, pp. 19-20

Johnson, R. 1994. "*Information for interns seeking teaching positions: views from a director of education*." Presentation to teacher-interns at Internship Seminar #3, (October 26. McLurg High School, Wilkie, Saskatchewan.

Maclsaac, J. 1990. "The Commissioner speaks to Canadian Parents for French: Good news for the 90s." *Language and Society/Langue et société*, 33, 14.

McMahen, L. 1994. "Saskatchewan-Ukraine educational exchanges booming." *Saskatchewan Bulletin*, 61 3: 6. (Available from the Saskatchewan Teachers' Federation, Saskatoon.)

Mollica, Anthony, *et al.* 1990. "The Clipboard series", Posters. Welland, Ontario: *éditions Soleil publishing inc.*

Mollica, Anthony. 1993. "Language learning: The key to understanding and harmony." *Mosaic*, 1, 1: 1, 3-5.

Morissette, B. 1992. "Canadian Parents for French: 15 years later." *Language and Society/Langue et société*, 41, 17-18.

Onyschuck, T. 1994. "Teaching culture in a North American context: Ukrainian Easter." *Mosaic*, 1, 3:, 21-22.

Pawlas, G. 1994. "Homeless students at the school door." *Educational Leadership*, 51, 8: 79-82.

Ralph, E. 1979. *French-programming policy issues in a school jurisdiction: A case study.* Unpublished doctoral dissertation, University of Manitoba, Winnipeg.

Ralph, E. 1981. "*Immersion: Questions and answers*." Presentation at Parents' Orientation Meeting, Assiniboine South School Division, Winnipeg, Manitoba. Mimeo.

Ralph, E. 1982. "The unmotivated second-language learner: Can students' negative attitudes be changed?" *The Canadian Modern Language Review/La revue canadienne des langues vivantes*, 38 (3, 493-502.

Ralph, E. 1994a. "Middle and secondary L2 teachers: Meeting classroom challenges via effective teaching research." *Foreign Language Annals*, 27, 1: 89-103.

Ralph E. 1994b. "On assembling the pieces: What do retired educators tell us?" *Action in Teacher Education*, 16, 2: 62-72.

Roberts, D. 1994. "Ukraine gets life line from G7." *The Globe and Mail*, (October 28), pp. B1, B4.

Simpson, J. 1994. "The future of society is knowledge, and schools are at the centre." *The Globe and Mail*, (November 4), p. A20.

Sloan, Tom. 1989. "Canadian Parents for French: Two Provinces," *Language and Society/Langue et société*, 26 (spring): 34-36.

Smart, S. 1994. "Premier, Ukrainian president discuss economic links." *The Star Phoenix*, (October 27), p. A8.

U.S. Department of Education. 1994. "Riley urges families to get involved in children's learning." *Goals 2000 Community Update*, 17, 1: 4.

Editor's Note: Portions of this paper formed the basis of an address to the Saskatchewan Teachers of Ukrainian annual convention in Saskatoon, November 3, 1994.)

Reprinted from: Edwin G. Ralph, "Motivating Parents to Support Second-Language Programs." *Mosaic*, 2, 4 (Summer 1995), pp. 1, 3-7.

3 Surviving the Perils of Politics: The Language Classroom of the Next Century

Roseann Runte

A response to critics of education, a justification for our mission as language teachers, and some practical suggestions for partnership in today's changing social, technological, and economic context.

In the eighth century, the Chinese philosopher Han Yu said that for one who sits at the bottom of a well, the sky appears small. Today, ill-informed people make the wrong decisions for what could actually be the right reasons. How could this happen? Have we fallen to the bottom of the well? Have we lost our perspective?

It is said that a little knowledge is a dangerous thing. Too little can prove fatal. Unfortunately for all parties: the unknowing knowers and their unintended victims. This is the first peril that education suffers and that we, as educators, must survive. Everyone knows everything about education. Even if they only walk their dogs across our schoolyard or our campus, people consider themselves experts on education and offer suggestions, not to mention criticisms. And even if they never learned a second language, they can tell us just where we are going wrong. Furthermore, the general public is buttressed in its wise ignorance by the stock of horror stories which we have all heard. These tales include children who graduate and cannot read or count. Anyone who cannot find a job can blame the educational system. And, of course, there are the drop-outs whom we did not serve well.

But what about all the success stories? One problem is that educators concentrate on the process of educating and do not take the time for public relations. But even if we did, would we succeed? Newpapers do not usually print "feel good" stories. As the late former Canadian Prime Minister Diefenbaker once said, "Nobody wants to read about the lost dog who came home." Is there another way for us to escape this peril? I certainly hope so.

The second peril we face today is cutting fever. I think we should counter with a case of "Hey Fever": let's simply say: "Hey, let's stop. When does a short-term economic gain become a long-term economic loss?" I am reminded of an occasion on which I tried to save money on the hairdresser and cut my hair myself. It seemed quite simple. I took a bit off one side and then the other. Alas, it then seemed uneven. By the time I finished, I had to purchase a hat. Well, there are no hats which can cover the serious problems we can cause when we get carried away with the scissors and the education budget. Unfortunately the result of a good education is largely invisible. People are improved. Society is improved. The economy is improved. But how do you measure it? Education takes a long time, and as people are educated, they will make other changes in the social fabric and economic conditions so that one can hardly isolate and link the cause and the effect. We can, however, see drastic results in underdeveloped nations where making education available to women ended up changing the population growth rate significantly. We can also see the effect of education in developed nations. For example, in France, the University of Grenoble is considered responsible for having brought economic prosperity to that region, and the same is true for the corridor around MIT, Harvard and Boston University. The Silicon Valley also owes its existence to the level of education of the population in the region. We know the effect of education on individuals. We can remember Mitterand (1991) saying that Europe is the key to the Future and that Education is the key to Europe. We should, in particular, recall that Luc Ferri (1991) said that learning a second language is an authentically revolutionary process of aspiration. It is a method of social equalization on a global level. If Canadians do not participate, we will be the intellectually colonized, the verbally handicapped citizens of the world, and we will negotiate ourselves out of a future which will belong to those who have mastered the intellectual processes of learning.

Now for the politics of the matter. That quintessentially Canadian quality of modesty and self-doubt can be charming, and lead, as the late Robertson Davies has noted, to "a decency incarnate" or perhaps an "unbearable simplicity" (p. 180). However, exaggerated doubt leads also to fear and we all recall that Emerson said in his *"Essay on Thoreau," (1937)* that "there is nothing so much to be feared as fear itself" (Vol. III, p. 402). There are several kinds of fear. There is, for example, fear of change. Some of that comes from common sense. The feudal lords in Europe once supposedly called for the peasants to produce two harvests a year so that the taxes would increase. The peasants sent a message to the lords that they would accept the proposal as long as the lords would change the constitution of a year from twelve months to twenty-four. There are some things which cannot and should not change. Yet there are others which can and should change and which cause, in this fashion, concern and indeed fear. Some parents think that they never spoke a second language, so their children do not need to do so. Some people are really afraid of what they do not know. I remember once translating for some people who were convinced that I was leaving something out. They actually thought that there were remarks directed at them and that I was politely omitting them. They were afraid of what they did not understand. Some parents have told me that they were afraid that they would lose their children, at least partially, to a world to which they had no access. Some spouses do not want their wives or husbands to continue their education or to become immersed in a new language and culture from which they would be excluded.

Some people are afraid of differences. They fear other cultures. These are the stereotypical "meat and potatoes" kind of people who make fun of others who eat quiche, vegetables or foods from different cultures. "Why," the 'meat-and-potatoes' types say, "can't *they* simply learn to speak English?" The point is that *they* do and then *they* know more, are intellectually enriched and may even be better off economically. Mark Twain said, in *Pudd'nhead Wilson's Calendar*, that "cauliflower is nothing but a cabbage with a college education." There are people who are afraid to try cauliflower – or broccoli, for that matter. It is a political menu as well as a cultural one. It is unfortunate because a varied diet is enjoyable, and we all know that cauliflower is good for one's health.

Then there is the fear that there is simply too much to learn out there, and we should limit ourselves to the basics. The rest of the subjects are costly frills and tax the poor students' brains. The problem is the definition of basics. What level will we accept and what subjects? Should a student learn only to add up to a certain amount because they will never have more dollars or see more stars at once than that? Should a student learn to speak in only one language? At one point I dreamed of how lovely it would be to be an English Professor. How much more basic could you get? I would never have to justify my job. But colleagues in the English Departments assure me that they are equally assailed by the back-to-basics bug. Why bother with literature – just stick to plain English. Skip the poetry. Everyday prose will do. Let me give you three examples of everyday prose I picked up in magazines in the last week or so. Here is a newspaper headline about a strike vote: "More than 100% of the workers participated." (Is this a mathematical problem or a problem in expression?) This was in a children's magazine: "Grandmother told the story of Mr. Brown's goat, sitting in the living room knitting." (Talented goat, that one!) And from a Church Bulletin: "Next month, we are organizing a white elephant sale. We are counting on you to bring all your old things you don't need any more – books, knickknacks, clothes, and of course, your husbands."

The basics simply do not suffice. One needs more than vocabulary and grammar. One needs logic, rhetoric and metaphor. One needs examples and references. Alonso de Ercilla y Zuñiga (1852) said, "no hay más difícil bien mirado que conocer un necio si es callado" (Canto 17) and Francis Bacon (1626) gave the English equivalent when he wrote that "silence is the Virtue of Fools" (p. 36). But elections are won by people who know how to speak. Treaties are negotiated by people who know how to talk. Trade deals are composed by people who know how to write. And the future belongs to those who communicate best.

People also have a great fear of falling – the falling dollar. They worry about the costs of education. I worry about the costs of cutting education.

Some educators have attempted to respond to these fears with the politics of promise. They have stated, and correctly, that the better educated people are the ones who get the jobs. They have shown that bilingual and trilingual people have greater flexibility and ability to find employment even in a difficult job market. I have even permitted myself to reminisce about wanting to drop Latin. My mother said, "No, do not drop the course, you never know but someday it might be useful." The first time I applied for a job in a secondary school the Principal told me that he would love to hire me, but that the job required teaching Latin as well as French. Well, I got the job thanks to my mother and my Latin prof. But, you will rightly note that Latin is no longer taught in most secondary schools. However, I assure you that if my mother were sending me to school today, not thirty years ago, I would be taking Japanese or Chinese or Russian or Arabic.

There is an inherent danger in promising jobs as the hope for an educated people. I see the merits of this promise, but it creates a chain that can hobble us. Education should be for more than jobs. It should be for life, for society, to create good citizens. We should be teaching languages not only to help the economy but also to promote communication and under-standing, to build a society in which peace will be the common coin. We should be educating people for a society in which I can talk about the values of peace and tolerance, in which I can talk about values which cannot be easily economically factored, and be considered strong and not weak.

Now we are bedeviled with another problem. It is the immediacy of politics and the impatience of a society which cannot wait for results. The time factor is against us. Profound changes take a long time. It is not like legislating a law. You can legislate the wearing of seat belts and then count the accidents and measure the damages. This can be done between elec-tions. However, in the case of education, we are talking about generations. We have not yet discovered the instant, miracle formula to educate people. French Immersion has only been around for about 20 years and we have already condemned it because not everyone uses the second language every day or at work. I do not drive my car every day. I do not see people about to condemn cars – and that might be good for the environment! In education some results cannot be measured. How can we know how many wars have not been fought? Mark Twain once said in "The Facts Concerning My Recent Resignation" that there is only one difference between violence and education: they are both very effective agents of change (p. 241). Violence just happens to be faster. Perhaps Twain's alternative provides the argument we need for taking the time. It is using fear again, but this time, for a positive end.

The context for education has been changing and is undergoing change even as we speak. This should not faze us as language teachers. We have faced change repeatedly. I know of almost no other area of teaching which has undergone such radical changes. Every five years at least we discover new methodologies, and new equipment to assist us in teaching and our students in learning. We have been through the audio-lingual revolution, we have moved through *Suggestopedia* to Asher's *Total Physical Response*, and we have gone from total immersion to partial immersion, late and early, and so on. Thus, I feel certain that language teachers have what it takes to succeed in a context of change.

The first change we face is the privatization of education, the viewing of education as a business. This is a change we must work to reverse. The profit model is different from the service model. A friend of mine was a teacher in Toronto, and we were walking down the street when a young man came up and hugged her and thanked her for all she had done for him. He had been in her class nine years before. She remembered his name. She recalled the difficulty he had experienced and how she had, in her words, "gone to bat for him" because she knew him and was in a position to judge his potential. Well, today, with bigger classes and more classes, with an emphasis on using gadgets and distant-learning devices, how will we know our students? They will still need us. The profit/business notion simply does not calculate the human investment which we need to make – which is the reward of good teachers and the reward for society. Students are not customers or consumers. They are partners in the learning experience *not* the learning enterprise, please). Students cannot expect to purchase knowledge. They must invest themselves in the process of education. The results depend on their efforts. I have had students come in to me on the first day of class and ask me what they can expect to know after my course. The answer is that they can expect only what they are willing to commit to the educational process themselves. I cannot learn for them. I can present information in an interesting fashion, logically, and orally, in writing and with repetitions and various forms of reinforcement. But unless they come with open minds and work at it, they will not take anything away from the class. This point about partnership is one half of my answer to the public relations issue. If students are seen as responsible for what they learn, as responsible as the teachers, then we can all share the blame for the failures of education, as well as the glory for those success stories. Once, when I was at Glendon College, York University, a young woman graduated who had spent the last two years of her university life in hospital. The newspapers reported her courage to have pursued her education from her hospital bed. I wrote the newspapers that they had only half the tale. The other half was the faculty who had gone to the hospital to give her the courses and who had done so without seeking extra pay or praise. They deserved as much applause. The point is that without the focus on the student's effort, my letter would never have been published.

The view of education as a business also encourages educational institutions to seek partnerships with the business community. There are work-study programs and similar ventures which are touted as the solutions to all our problems. They may be the solution for some problems and for some individuals. However, they may force unnatural partnerships. Perhaps the best partnership we may seek is with the parents. Now, I know there are Parent-Teacher Associations. The last time I went to a parent-teacher night the teachers were nervous. They were loudly criticized by a few vociferous parents who felt that their progeny were not receiving the grade, the attention, or whatever that they should. They were blaming the teacher. Other parents were nervous at not understanding what was going on and were too shy to ask. But let us think back to those parents who do not understand another language, who want to help their children, but who do not know how

One of my colleagues announced to me last week that her eight-year old daughter said that she should do all her homework alone from now on. The parent felt hurt, shut out. Perhaps she was not up on the methods used in that classroom, but working together is good for the family. My friends in Europe study as a family for their children's exams. My best friend is taking English lessons at night to be able to assist her son. I think that would be the ideal: for the students, the teachers and the parents to be partners in the educational experience. How we should achieve this requires thought. However, one idea for language teaching is the Saturday program the *Alliance française* put on in Halifax. Parents went with their children on Saturday mornings. University students were hired to play with the children in the target language while the parents studied with the teacher, doing the week's lessons in an hour. The parents could then assist their children, be familiar with the problems they experienced, not be alienated or isolated. This might be considered. We have courses on birthing, but then we leave parents to educate their children without much help from infancy until they come to school. Even then, we do not help them know what they can do to assist in the learning process. And indeed, they can be helpful. We definitely need all the help we can get. Now, you are thinking, "the parents will teach the children incorrect information, thought processes, logic and conclusions." But the chances are, they won't if *we* teach the parents. I think we need to open a whole range of programs for the parents to assist us in providing the education we would like to offer the young leaders of tomorrow. Rather than complain about the education children receive outside the school, which is, let's face it, a longer time than they spend in school, let's do something to improve it. Now, we only need to persuade governments that they will save money by investing in this unlimited partnership! We need parent tutorials. If parents are to be tutors, then they also need tutoring. It might be an inexpensive way to provide additional schooling for our students, to bring families closer together and to integrate parents into the community and into the process of learning. I think we should be writing parents' manuals as well as teachers' guides. I think we should make of education a cooperative endeavour in which we all play a rôle, an adventure in learning that goes beyond the walls of the school and the few hours we spend with our students.

I think education will be more and more international and that foreign educational businesses will be marketing more and more their products in Canada. I think that those who are involved in education for a profit have profit as their first motive. I think our first motive should be the child. I think as well that education for profit benefits principally the well-off in society and that offering them additional advantages ends up increasing the differences between rich and poor, intellectual haves and have-nots. I see however, a great pressure by parents to have children's schooling enriched and a need for the children to be supervised when both parents are working and do not have the time for the educational partnership I have recommended earlier. There are also cases where parents cannot participate in the educational process. I think that in this case, we are going to have to look at school boards running summer learning camps for all students and after-school classes. I think university students would make excellent volunteers, along with senior citizens and people who have retired early and have the free time. Now, I know that organizing volunteers can be trying and time-consuming. However, I truly believe that the effort will be worthwhile. Until we have all the pseudo-educational experts learning and actively involved, we will be the subject of criticism. Until we use every resource at our disposal, we will be deemed too costly, and until we all become partners in education, we will never benefit from the advantages of a partnership where everyone shares common goals.

I believe that C. E. Ritchie (1991), the former Chair of the Bank of Nova Scotia, was right when he said that "we have to focus this country's talents and energies on the real challenge from the growing number of countries in Asia, Europe and even in Latin America, that have really gotten their act together." He saw education as the way to meet that challenge. He even focused on the humanities and on language learning. George Borrow (who was a writer and not a banker) (1842) spoke of the limitations of translation which is at best an echo (pp. 358ff.). And we know already that to bargain, we need to be able to speak. This is even more true when it comes to selling. To sell, you need to speak the language of the purchaser. The other day a woman stopped me in the grocery and asked if I knew where the napkins were. I sent her to the display of serviettes. As I was leaving, I met her at the checkout with a package of diapers. And to think, we both spoke the same language!

In the days of my grandmother's youth, it was a big trip for people in Ontario to go to Niagara Falls. Now people fly all over the globe. Two centuries ago Thomas Paine said, in *The Rights of Man*, that he had no passion save that of humanity.

All mankind were his brethren (p. 413). He felt he was a world citizen, even if he would never see but a small part of the world. In like vein, H.G. Wells (1920) said, "Our true nationality is mankind" (p. 750). If we are to develop international understanding, we certainly must be able to communicate. I might well have a Ph.D., but when in a country where I do not speak the language, I am reduced to pantomimes. I feel exactly like the idiot I must closely resemble. And errors can be fatal. Captain Cook and his crew landed on the shores of British Columbia several centuries ago in a month without the letter "R". The natives tried to tell them not to eat the shellfish, but they did and were poisoned by the red tide. Successful communication would certainly have saved some of Captain Cook's crew and it would certainly go a long way to solving some of the problems in the war in Eastern Europe, to name but one contemporary example of strife. This sounds as if it is far from our own realities. It is not. I know someone with a peanut allergy who loves life enough to learn "peanut" in every language possible. And, if we want that part of our country which is humane and tolerant to continue on into the future, we need to educate the next generation to be tolerant, open. What better way to do this than through learning languages?

Another revolution in education lies in the technology. We have new tools: the Internet and interactive videos, for example. Now they are accompanied by two dangers. The first is posed by those who believe that they can save small fortunes by investing in machines and reducing the human effort and cost. The second is our own problem. We have now at our disposal an opportunity to educate secretly, without their knowing what is happening, a whole generation. Television happened and we lost a magnificent opportunity to use TV as an educational tool. Granted, it is not an entire loss, but *Sesame Street* does not make up for hours of cartoons. And our belated attempts to produce classes of talking heads on shoestring budgets on television and to compete with Disney are pretty poor, we must admit. With the Internet and transmission of visual images by telephone cables, we have a blank highway and we can invent signs, places to stop and to learn. We have to get busy! We should not forget that the Standing Committee on the Status of the Artist reported to Parliament (1989) that culture was the ninth largest manufacturing industry in Canada, the 4th largest employer, earning 12 billion dollars profit in 1985. This will not pass unnoticed, and we can be sure that for-profit organizations will soon be producing all sorts of materials to fill the electronic airwaves. In Gabriel García Márquez's *One Hundred Years of Solitude*, (1970),the people in the mountain village are afflicted with a terrible disease which causes them to lose their memories. They realize their affliction and carefully label every-thing and write out instructions on how to use things so that they will be able to function once they have lost their memories. The irony was that they also forgot how to read. Some people say that our society is losing the ability to read and write. I disagree. I think that with computers we are and will be writing more. Unlike the people in Márquez's village, we have the capacity to write our future. The written word is not simply a guidepost to the past, but a key to discovery, to the future, to a new society, to new worlds.

Northrop Frye (1982) once wrote that the only crystal ball we have is our rear-view mirror (p. 190). He meant that our future is known to us only though analogy with the past. Thus, he thought our ideas of the future would be coloured by the same prejudices and narrowed by the very ignorance which currently is ours. Yet this is a very passive and rather pessimistic view. I prefer the outlook of Cervantes who wrote, "Cada uno es hijo de sus obras"(We are each the result of our own works) (1949, Vol. I, p. 43). A similar statement was made, perhaps more poetically and even more optimistically, in the 15th century by a Japanese writer, Moritake (1977) who said, "a fallen blossom returns to its branch. It is a butterfly." And Dante went right to the heart of the matter: "considerate la vostra semenza fatti no foste a viver come bruti ma per seguir virtute e conoscenza" – "we are not born to live as animals but to strive for virtue and knowledge" (p. 141). Believing in the perfectibility of humankind is not the same as believing in perfection. Education is one tool, perhaps the only tool we possess, to push beyond the boundaries set around us by ignorance. H.G. Wells (1920) said that "human history is a race between education and catastrophe" (p. 458). Let us hope that education wins and that we are able to create a new society, a better civilization, one in which not only the philosophers declare themselves citizens of the world and brothers to all, but one also where all citizens share the basic rights, freedoms and privileges which make peace and human happiness possible.

We have all heard that the classroom of the future may not be a space at all. It may be in a living room or living rooms, in a shopping mall or business. The students might be of varying ages studying individually in the time convenient to them. The equipment used for teaching might be some gadget we have not even imagined yet. And we are supposed to prepare for this? Well, yes. And I think the best beginning is to ask what we would like. What would be ideal? I do not like learning in isolation. I would like to ensure that there is dialogue and always some kind of community of learners. I would like the technology to be humanized, not just user-friendly but permitting interpersonal communication. I would like the programs to be well-resourced. I would like to have the best technology and know how to use it. I would, of course, like willing learners. I would like to see us be able to devote some time to thinking about the future and some resources to train teachers for the future. For to what end do we speak about the future, if we have neither the time nor the ability to do something about it?

This will doubtlessly be a hard sell in the present economic times. However, if families and students are our partners, we will have considerable support, and perhaps the resources will come. Perhaps we will be able to realize a few of our dreams. It is too important not to try. The possession of a better future is one goal for which we all can and must strive. And education is the only path to the future.

I conclude with a little story of my summer holiday. I went rafting down the Tatshenshini and Alsek Rivers to where they join the Pacific Ocean. I knew I was going to be rowing so I worked out in the gym on a rowing machine for several months before leaving, to be sure I had the strength and endurance necessary.

But when I got in the boat, I discovered that the problem was not actual strength. It was the same problem I have when I try to imagine the future. First of all, I was looking in the opposite direction to where I was going. Since I could not see the rocks, tree trunks and icebergs which we were in danger of hitting, I needed to rely on my partners in the raft to steer me clear of these obstacles. I needed to understand their messages – when Mary said "left", it meant that I should row on the right. On the other hand, when Peter said "left", he meant "row harder on the left." I had to learn which side was starboard to catch the instructions of others. The second problem was to coordinate our efforts. We had one set of long oars and four paddles. We learned that we could quickly get into difficulties if we all tried to solve the same problem at the same time. If we all leaned left, we could dump the raft over, and if we all rowed on the left to avoid one rock, there would certainly be another not too far to the right. Well, behind the oars and looking backwards, I felt a bit like Northrop Frye looking in the rear view mirror. However, there was a difference. I had no mirror – l had only the voices of my friends. And we navigated the rough waters by teamwork. Each one saw part of the danger. Each one did part of the work. Each one called out to me the future as he or she perceived it. Perhaps we can go beyond the individual prejudices of our pasts, beyond the limitations of our own experiences and imaginations by sharing and working together. Perhaps it is indeed through partnerships that we can take our educational system that one step further so that the future of our children will be better than our own.

As language teachers we work in communication, in changing attitudes, in teaching openness to other cultures. Our very jobs are sharing, and we work in close partnership already with other teachers, students and technicians. There is no reason for us not to be leaders in forging the partnerships of the future, and in choosing our own partners. I look forward to learning about the history You will be making.

References

Alighieri, Dante. 1932 (printing). *The Divine Comedy.* New York: Random House.

Bacon, Francis. 1626. *Apothegemes: New and Old Collected by the right Honourable Francis Lord Bacon.* London: H. Barret and R. Whitaker.

Borrow, George. 1842. *The Bible in Spain.* London and Glasgow: Collins.

Cervantes Saavedra, Miguel de. 1949. *The Adventures of Don Quixote.* New York: Viking.

Davies, Robertson. 1967. *Marchbank's Almanach.* Toronto: McClelland and Stewart.

Emerson, Ralph Waldo. 1937. *The Works.* New York: Tudor Publishing.

Ercilla y Zuñiga, Alonso de. 1852. *La Arancuna, poema.* Madrid: Gaspar.

Ferri, Luc. 1991. Cited in Plenary Address to the Association of Universities and Colleges of Canada by the Rector of the University of Paris. Queen's University, Kingston, Ontario.

Frye, Northrop. 1982. *Divisions on a Ground: Essays on Canadian Culture.* Toronto: Anansi.

García Márquez, Gabriel. 1970. *One Hundred Years of Solitude.* Trans. Gregory Rab. London: Cape.

Mitterand, François. 1991. Cited in Plenary Address to the Association of Universities and Colleges of Canada by the Rector of the University of Paris Queens University, Kingston, Ontario).

Moritake, Arakida. 1977. *Mortitake senku chu / Iida shoiichi hen.* Edited by Akashi Toshiyo *et al.* Tokyo: Furukawa Shobo.

Paine, Thomas. 1969. *The Complete Writings.* Edited by Philip S. Foner. New York: Citadel Press.

Report to the House. Status of the Artist. 1989. Ottawa: Queen's Printer, Canadian Government Publishing Centre.

Ritchie, C.E. 1991 "Canada in a Competitive World: Challenges and Solutions." Address to the 159th Annual and Special Meeting of the shareholders of the Bank of Nova Scotia, Halifax, 1991.

Twain, Mark (Samuel Celements). (1992). *Collected Tales, Sketches and Essays, 1852-1890.* New York: Literary Classics of the U.S.,Inc.

Wells, H.G. 1920. *An Outline of History.* London: George Newnes Ltd.

Editor's Note: The text is the keynote address delivered by the Author at the Annual Conference of the British Columbia Association of Teachers of Modern Languages, Vancouver, BC, October 1995

Reprinted from: Roseann Runte, "Surviving the Perils of Politics: The Language Classroom of the Next Century." *Mosaic,* 3, 2 (Winter 1996), pp. 1, 3-7.

4 The Fundamentals of Second-Language Teaching

J. Clarence LeBlanc

As second-language teachers do we agree on the fundamentals of our profession? Clarifying this question would help many beginning as well as seasoned teachers – not to mention curriculum developers and textbook authors. The article offers a number of elements for readers' consideration.

In sports, when a team is not winning, the coach often tells the players to get back to the fundamentals. Unlike many sports truisms, this one makes sense. Unless the fundamentals of an activity are mastered, respectable performance is impossible. One can hardly imagine a hockey player who skates poorly, or a ball player who can't throw, having much success no matter what other skills they might possess. What would we think of a coach who would make such athletes practice fancy manoeuvres that are beyond their level of development? Is there a lesson here for second-language teachers? What are the fundamentals of our activity? How well do we ensure their development before we take the students beyond them? Why do so many students, particularly in regular French (as opposed to Immersion or intensive programs)[1] seem to know so little after many years of second language study? They have been exposed to many aspects of the language but have retained little. Had they even learned one important function and notion per day, they would now have a considerable repertoire, enough for at least basic communication.

Before exploring the fundamentals of second-language teaching, mention must be made of another list that is even more vital to successful second-language teaching, the *working conditions* necessary for effective teaching and learning to take place (LeBlanc, 1990). It would include:

- a reasonable class size
- administrative support for the program at the school, district and province/state levels
- appropriate curriculum materials
- competent teachers who believe in what they do
- parental and societal valuing of language learning.

Without these conditions, discussion of in-class considerations is almost pointless. Without support, even good teachers can only struggle for so long before becoming exhausted and gradually losing focus. Decision-makers who fail to provide the conditions necessary for success in a school program should be fired for incompetence or better still, arrested for stealing (education) from children.

When existing conditions make successful teaching next to impossible, steps must be taken to improve the situation. Teachers, who are often isolated as individual employees of a bureaucratic system, have considerable power if they act in concert through their provincial/state language associations. Complaining in the staff-room may relieve stress but it does not improve conditions in the classroom. Professional associations can, and should, play a large role in educating decision-makers about the conditions necessary for an effective program. They could, for example, create a commission of experts to list reasonable conditions for effective second-language teaching, publish it widely, monitor how closely the schools or system meet them, and perhaps publish a yearly report card. At a more aggressive level they might research and publish the average class sizes in second-language classes attended by civil servants and business executives and compare the results with average second-language classes. For their own good and that of their students, teachers must be active members of their professional associations.

Assuming, then, that the system will provide at least reasonable conditions and support to the front-line staff who teach the students, I suggest that the following are fundamentals of second-language teaching.

Motivating Students

William Glasser (1990), the noted education theorist, makes the interesting observation that "being an effective teacher may be the most difficult job of all in our society" (p. 14). His rationale is that while many tasks are difficult, they involve no inherent resistance; patients want the doctor to cure them, clients want lawyers to defend them. The wood does not resist the carpenter, and the piano does not resist the musician. But...

> teachers are people managers, and most everyone will agree that students as workers seem to be the most resistant of all to being managed (Glasser, 16).

Yet he also believes that students have an inner sense of what is quality work and that they can be encouraged to produce at that level. Managing thirty or so students (each a complex individual with a myriad of needs), and motivating them as learners, are basic teacher functions. Teachers require great skill, empathy, knowledge, organization, time, and supporting school and societal climates. Experience helps as well. While it is presumptuous to write about motivating students in one paragraph, my experiences in the classroom led me to the following beliefs:

- Students won't care until they know the teacher cares... about the subject and about them.
- On the first day of class teachers must sell their subject as useful to the students; otherwise why should they bother learning it? It is a challenging but essential task for which there are , fortunately, many supporting materials. Lacey (in Mollica, 1993) stressed that

a language is far more than an intellectual cognitive challenge. It is a means to grow and mature through the experience of other cultures. It gives breadth and depth to our personalities. (p. 4).

Mollica (1993) identifies a number of reasons for the value of second-language learning and concludes that

only when the study of languages is depoliticized and the learning of languages is accepted for its own intrinsic qualities, will we be able to have linguistic peace and harmony... (p. 5).

Danesi (1993), in an article on the role of more than one language in literacy acquisition, points out that

The bilingual learner has access, therefore, to more than one way of processing information, and this cannot help but diversify and enhance the child's overall cognitive capacities.

Ralph (1995) stressed the "financial" advantages to language learning:

Recent global events have emphasized the critical importance of multinational communication. Growing trade and commercial relationships among European nations, among Pacific rim countries, and among our own North American partners – plus the potential to forge further links between/among these larger international blocs – signal that people skilled in various languages will be required to help expedite these communicative relationships.

Runte (1995) aptly points out that

Language is much more than grammar. It is more than a way of structuring thought. It is a way of signifying our deepest feelings, our most sincere beliefs. Each time I learn a word which has no translation into another language, I feel that I have discovered a rare gift, a new idea, a fresh insight... (p. 9).

Learning languages promotes interdisciplinarity and the ability to think in a creative fashion. It promotes creativity and discovery. Languages teach us new ways of seeing things, new perspectives (p. 10).

Today our students face many problems: change and instability, violence and lack of meaning, fragmentation and loss of identity. Communication, creativity and unity are the solutions to these problems, and they are all found in and promoted by the learning of languages (p. 11).

She asks

If we want to be part of a country which is humane and tolerant to continue on into the future, we need to educate the next generation to be tolerant and open. What better way to do this than through learning languages? (Runte, 1996a: 7).

Even UNESCO in a report favours the preservation of Languages (see Runte, 1996b:18).

The "observable advantage of bilingual over monolinguals" is that they are "more used to switching thought patterns and have more flexible minds." Their knowledge of language(s) makes them more familiar with "different often contradictory concepts"and this, in turn, makes bilinguals or multilinguals more "tolerant than monolinguals, and more capable of understanding an argument."

And even Canadian Parents for French (1995), a national association devoted to the promotion of French as a second language has produced a video in which young people laud the acquisitions of a second or even third language (reviewed by Runte, 1996c:23).

Teachers must remind the students regularly that they are working for themselves, their own futures. Why should they get up in the morning and go work for teachers?

If the Coleman Study correctly concluded that the most important determinant of academic success is a willingness to defer gratification, i.e., to work now in order to have something later, students must learn how to do this. The finding of "deferred gratification" as a major determinant of success was a bit of a surprise. The expectation had been that school facilities, programs, etc. would largely explain the difference between "successful" students and less successful ones. Deferred gratification ought to be taught at home, but when it isn't, teachers must fill the gap, as usual. Students should learn to set short-term, intermediate and ultimate goals, and experience sequential success in meeting them.

Teachers must foster a climate where the focus is on the students, individually and collectively, not on the teacher or textbook (Evans-Harvey, 1993). I recommend "reverse onus" teaching, whereby students are made aware that they are the *raison d'être* of the system and that teachers help them acquire skills and knowledge. Off-task students are seen as disrupters of their own and other students' learning, not of the teacher. It creates a different dynamic *vis-à-vis* collaborative goal setting and behavioural expectations.

The classroom atmosphere must be so focussed on learning that risk taking and errors are almost stress free. Teachers should emphasize to students that not knowing something and making mistakes are central to learning. If students knew everything, they would not need the teachers who would then be unemployed. Students should also understand that most errors are smart, not dumb, because they involve logical inferences. For example, students who say

"Je suis 13 ans vieux"

in French are not saying something stupid; they are applying a correct syntactical structure from English. Much can be learned from such "mistakes" when students are taught that they are "smart mistakes."

Learning should be done in a context of "fun and games" as often as possible. Students are still children; they can learn without always knowing they are doing so. What involves more genuine communication than playing a game in the target language? Moreover, we know that second-language learning often involve attitudes and prejudices. When children have fun, they often forget that they "hate" the second-language (Danesi and Mollica, 1994).

Teaching in the Target Language

Many practices in education are matters of opinion, but the results of others have been demonstrated beyond discussion. One of these is the inefficacy of teaching a second language in the mother language. For decades in Canada, French as a second language was taught by the grammar-translation method with all real communication being in English. Most of its former students are living proof of its failure. "I can read it," they say, "I understand some, but I can't speak it." Dissatisfaction with that state of affairs, in an officially bilingual country, led to the creation of "immersion" classes, the communicative approach, the multidimensional curriculum, and [Canada's] National Core French Study (NCFS). The latter development is explained in some detail later. The NCFS's key conclusion was that second-language teaching should aim first and foremost at imparting communicative skills for real-life purposes.

With the proper introduction and attitude, students can be motivated to use the target language from the start. In fact, its use stimulates interest and motivation. Students want to communicate, and if the second language must be the medium of communication in that class, so be it. It has been said that "immersion" programs are not immersion at all since even the most intensive of them only involve a small fraction of the students' daily life. Nevertheless, immersion works because its key article of faith is target language use. Essentially, regular second-language classes should also be "immersion" during the class period. Of course these students would benefit from a more significant exposure to the language than one short period per day. A five-month intensive introduction has been proposed by some as a desirable common experience for all Canadian children, after which they could opt for immersion or regular French. Perhaps it will happen some day, but whatever the format, second language teachers who wish to be successful must quickly and systematically make the target language the norm in their classroom.

In a lead article published in *Dialogue*, Stern (1983a: 4) stresses that the teaching of Core French (i.e. "regular") requires a diversified approach. He points out that

> In the last few years a new view of language acquisition has resulted partly from research on second langauge learning and partly from the immersion experience. It underlines the fact that a language cannot be learned by formal practice alone. Much of it is learnt best in the process of doing something else.

Calvé (1985:278) echoes similar sentiments when he states that

> Ce n'est qu'en communiquant qu'on peut apprendre à communiquer.

Mollica (1985:490) wonders whether we are

> [...] truly fulfilling our task to teach students to communicate. Are we providing the classroom environment which encourages communication. How much English is *really* spoken in the French classroom? While in immersion classes we insist on French being the language for communication and are careful not to deviate from this norm, in the Core French class we appear to have adopted the slogan of the Commissioner of Official Languages: "English or French. It's your choice."

He suggests that teachers audiotape their lesson and listen to the recording to determine:

• How much time we spent trying to get the class's attention

- How much time we spent speaking English
- How much time we spent speaking French
- How much time was left for our students to speak French. (p. 490).

The Language Management System

Second language teachers are regularly urged to teach in the target language, but when faced with a class that doesn't understand even the most rudimentary elements of the language they often dismiss the advice as unrealistic. Yet, little progress can be made in a language that isn't used for (real) classroom communication. So, *how* does one teach in a language not understood by the students? Many theorists promote an aural phase when the students hear the second language, its sound and cadence, for a period of time. They begin by processing and understanding, and then reach a readiness stage, a desire to speak. Whether one subscribes to that approach or not, when it is time for students to speak perhaps my Language Management System may be useful (LeBlanc, 1994). Used systematically, this mechanism allows a teacher to use the target language in class from the outset. Its key assumption is that the FIRST need anyone has when faced with a second language is acquiring the tools to cope with the linguistic situation itself. If they don't understand those strange French sounds, for example, the phrase "Je ne comprends pas." effectively sends the ball back to the other side of the court. While that could be accomplished with the traditional physical gestures, other language management tools such as "Comment dit-on ... en français?" and "Que veut dire le mot...?" are most effectively conveyed verbally. (See chapter 13, "Classroom Expressions" by Mollica in this volume.)

One of the most effective devices to develop teacher respect for the fundamentals, and empathy for the students' predicament, is a training session in which teachers become students of a language that they don't know at all, Mandarin or Russian, for example. They quickly experience what it is to have a person make unfamiliar sounds at you, then act as if you are stupid for not understanding right away and not assimilating strange structures after only one or two repetitions. Very early on, the students should be taught the verbal tools to slow the teacher down, to make him or her use basic vocabulary and to re-use words or functions a reasonable number of times in meaningful contexts. That is how the first language is learned, and how other languages are learned as well. The Language Management System is intended as a mechanism that students use to survive the initial phase of second language learning, then to acquire more language.

The Concept of Interlanguage

While the concept of interlanguage, the rudimentary form of language that concentrates exclusively on the message, is very simple, most theorists feel it has an important place in language development. It involves saying, for example, "Me hungry, where restaurant please," in any language. Language teachers all spoke that way as babies, and nearly all would use interlanguage spontaneously in a foreign environment, yet many make little room for it in the classroom. They forget that beginning students are at the baby stage in second language learning and that the classroom is a foreign environment for students. The active encouragement or tolerance of interlanguage in the classroom has been a matter of considerable debate, but in my view it has a place among second-language teaching's fundamentals. Some will point to the fossilized errors so endemic to immersion students, but that is more related to how long interlanguage should be tolerated rather than whether it is a normal first stage leading to more correct expression. As Chastain (1971: 316) points out,

> To learn a language, the students must reach a point at which they concentrate on *what* they are saying instead of *how* they are saying it, but often can not reach this point because the teacher places grammatical and phonological interruptions and stumbling blocks in their way. Language teachers tend to have an unwarranted obsession with perfection in their classroom. *They should remember that the initial goal is not native speech but the ability to communicate with the native* (italics mine).

And Grittner (1985:14) concurs that

> Teachers should apply the old adage "Practice makes perfect," in contrast to the tendency in the foreign language profession to say: "You've got to be perfect before you can practice." This means accepting errors as part of the learning process rather than making believe that they will not occur. Mistakes should be used to diagnose errors and prescribe remedial practice.

Le Vocabulaire fondamental

The basic building block of linguistic communication is the word. When one reads, hears, writes, or speaks a language, it is done by means of words used individually or organized in some fashion. Whether they are used on the strict basis of communication, as in the interlanguage discussed above, or according to sophisticated rules sanctioned by the Académie Française, for example, each utterance is made up of... words. Therefore, language learning is fundamentally about vocabulary learning. Indeed, when one visits a second-language class one sees the vocabulary that the teacher sets as priority for that particular group. One might, for example, visit a grade three second-language class and see large posters of fruits with each part, from the outer skin to the innermost pit, listed and the vocabulary being drilled. If these students ever become fruit buyers for a produce company, they are ready; they know all the vocabulary. But, are those the words they most need to learn at that point in their language development? I doubt it. And unless next year's teacher asks them about fruits, they will appear to know little of the language.

As Robert Galisson pointed out (cited in Nemni, 1985),

> Jusqu'à preuve du contraire, les mots restent bien utiles pour communiquer.

The point is that vocabulary is central to second language study and must be selected very judiciously. There are said to be more than half a million words in the French language, for example, and it is estimated that a university graduate knows perhaps fifty to sixty thousand words, and a high school student perhaps fifteen thousand. We also know that to be mastered, words must be reused often. (see Pellerin, 1996). How do we know which words should be prioritized? A most interesting research project was conducted by the Centre de Recherche et d'Étude pour la Diffusion du Français (CREDIF) and published in 1959 as Le Français Fondamental. Thousands of everyday conversations were recorded and word frequency lists were compiled. Naturally certain words appeared more often than others. The most basic words were organized a bit and it was deemed that with 1222 lexical words and 253 grammatical words (*Le Français Fondamental*), a person could function quite effectively in everyday life. The point for teachers is that the most basic words should be prioritized and re-utilized until they are assimilated by the students. Teachers should also teach the basic skill of circumlocution by which, if students don't know the exact word they want to say, instead of shutting down the communication they find a way to explain their meaning using the words they know.

Teachers can consult *Le Français Fondamental* or similar lists of basic words, but they can also create their own list by asking themselves if a word is an often used general one or a less used specific one. Another criterion for essential words are those needed to operate in the classroom. The vocabulary for classroom routines should be taught first and if, for example, the teachers want to play a game, the vocabulary and language functions needed to play should be taught beforehand. As soon as students have sufficient literacy skills to do so, the class-room vocabulary should be written in a special scribbler and reviewed regularly. It becomes their personal "dictionnaire fondamental."

Functions and Grammar

If vocabulary is important as the language's building blocks, and is organized in elemental fashion in interlanguage, we want to advance quickly to language forms that are like those that native speakers use. The question is, as usual... "How?" Most teachers itch to teach grammar for at least two reasons; they wince at the students' fractured structures and they personally relate to grammar because of their studies (which they chose because they liked to study language). But formal grammar is not what most beginning students need. Teachers should review the alternative view of language as evolved in The Threshold Level by a Council of Europe research group in 1975. It separates language in two basic components, the "functions", and "notions", as J. A. Van Ek (1976:6) explained:

> What people do *by means* of language can be described as verbally perform certain functions. By means of language people assert, question, command, expostulate, persuade, apologize, etc. etc. In performing such functions people express, refer to or - to use a more general term-handle certain notions.

Second-language teachers must initially think in terms of functions and notions (another word for "vocabulary") rather than in grammatical terms. If students want, for example, to perform the language function of asking permission to do something, let's provide the function rather than the grammar. Students should learn such functions as: "Est-ce que je peux aller...?" and the notion "aux toilettes" without learning to conjugate completely the irregular verbs involved. Teachers and students should think in terms of developing and   expanding their repertoire of functions and notions. For the time and place of grammar, teachers might start by reviewing the theories of Stephen Krashen (1995) and Krashen and Terrell (1983) and the debates they stimulated, the Language Syllabus of the National Core French Study, and innumerable articles on the issue.

The National Core French Study

The National Core French Study[2] was created by the Canadian Association of Second-Language Teachers (CASLT) and supported by government, to meet the challenge of making regular (Core) French effective. The proposal for such a study was first outlined in a keynote address given by the late H.H. Stern (1983) on "French Programs in Canada: How Can We Improve Them?", at the annual CASLT convention held in Winnipeg, Canada. The project was originally chaired by Stern himself and, after his death, by Raymond LeBlanc. A strong cadre of second-language experts were enlisted and participated in various capacities. A central research group, supported by six task groups and schools committees, fleshed out Stern's multidimensional model for restructuring second-language teaching.

A five-year, seven-volume, national study cannot be fairly summarized in one paragraph. There exists an excellent synthesis written by Raymond LeBlanc (1990), and a comprehensive summary published as a special issue by *The Canadian Modern Language Review/La Revue canadienne des langues vivantes* (1990) that can easily be accessed. In the proverbial nutshell, the National Core French Study proposed that second language teaching integrate four aspects of language, each described in a separate syllabus:

- language
- communicative-experiential
- culture, and
- general language.

Two other work groups addressed the important questions of testing and teacher education. These are all part of the total package, six fundamentals, if you will. While each report contains a chapter on classroom approaches, the project was more geared to providing a blueprint for second-language teaching in Canadian schools. We are much gratified that ministries and publishers have accepted the basic concepts and are integrating them in their latest materials. In spite of the name, it is generally accepted that the principles of the multidimensional approach are equally valid for immersion teaching. Teachers who consult the study will find themselves better equipped to understand and deliver the latest programs.

Opportunity for oral testing

"Ok, students, take your pencils and paper and we'll see how well you speak the second language you have been studying." That doesn't seem reasonable but it is often what we do. How we test is very important because it is the ultimate motivator for many students. "Does it count?" they ask. However, to test orally there must be conditions in place that allow it. Asking teachers to give up most of their noon hours and preparation time to interview students individually is simply unreasonable. There are many things teachers can do in class to test orally, including monitoring a few students each day, having student presentations, mastery teaching, having students tape certain answers, etc. If your school is fortunate enough to have a language lab, it can make oral testing a breeze, especially at the middle and secondary levels. As well, aural comprehension tests can be administered to the entire class, and they should be part of any quality curriculum material. For oral testing beyond that, teachers will need assistants or release time.

A comprehensive package of field-tested testing instruments for the intermediate level is now available through the Canadian Association of Second Language (see address in Note 2.) It should provide a theoretical base and accessible materials for ensuring that testing is closely related to communicative teaching.

Conclusion

Second-language teaching in the public school context is a very demanding occupation. Reviewing and applying the fundamentals is no panacea, but it offers perspective and helps define the conditions for success. Once these are in place, second-language teaching can be a most stimulating task. Unlike other subjects, where teachers must follow a curriculum closely, communicative-experiential teaching allows teachers to discuss events and issues, play games, undertake projects, watch TV, listen to music, etc. Granted, most of these activities are conducted in a *vocabulaire fondamental*, but a great deal of variety is still possible. Second-language teachers who master the fundamentals of their profession can derive much satisfaction from effectively introducing students to a new language and culture.

Notes

1. In Canada, French is the main second language taught in schools due to the bilingual nature of the country. The regular second-language course, typically one class period per day up to 12 years in all other provinces and territories (except in Ontario up to 13 years), is called Core French. This involves a minimum of 40-minute daily classes. More intensive programs, involving up to 100 per cent of the school day in the initial years and lesser percentages at the middle and high school levels are called "Immersion" where the language of instruction for subjects is in French.

2. The materials related to the National Core French Assessment Project may be purchased from
    The Canadian Association of Second Language Teachers (CASLT)
    176 Gloucester St., Suite 310
    Ottawa, Ontario, Canada K2P 0A6
    E-mail: caslt@istar.ca

References

Calvé, Pierre. 1985. "Les programmes de base: des principes à la réalité." *The Canadian Modern Language Review/La Revue canadienne des langues vivantes*, 42, 2: 271-287.

The Canadian Modern Language Review/La Revue canadienne des langues vivantes. 1990. Vol. 47, 1. The entire issue is dedicated to the National Core French Study.

Canadian Parents for French. 1995. *Proud of Two Languages.* Ottawa, Ontario: Canadian parents for French. Video. 14 min., 52 sec. Reviewed by Runte (1996c).

Chastain, Kenneth. 1971. *The Development of Foreign Language Skills.* Philadelphia, PA: The Center for Curriculum Development, Inc.

Council of Europe. 1975. *The Threshold Level in a European Unit/Credit System for Modern Language Learning.*

Danesi, Marcel. 1993. "Literacy and Bilingual Education Programs in Elementary School: Assessing the Research." *Mosaic*, 1, 1: 6-12.

Danesi, Marcel and Anthony Mollica. 1994. "Games and Puzzles in Second Language Teaching: A Second Look." *Mosaic*, 2, 2: 13-22.

Glasser, William. 1990. *The Quality School: Managing Students Without Coercion.* New York: Harper Perennial Press.

Evans-Harvey. 1993. "Climate Setting in the Second-Language Classroom." *Mosaic*, 1,2:1,3-5.

Grittner, Frank. 1985. "What Language Teachers Should Do to Improve Instruction." *Indiana Foreign language Teachers Association News*, (Fall): 14-15. The article was published originally in *Information* (1984), Wisconsin, 11, 3: 19.

Krashen, Stephen D. 1985. *The Input Hypothesis.* London: Longman.

Krashen, Stephen D. and Tracy Terrell. 1983. *The Natural Approach: Language Acquisition in the Classroom.* Oxford: Pergamon.

Lacey, Veronica. 1993. "Modern Languages: Recognizing their Relevance." Keynote address at the Ontario Modern Language Teachers' Association. Mimeo. Quoted in Mollica (1993).

LeBlanc, Clarence. 1990. "Administrative Conditions for Effective FSL Programs." *The Canadian Modern Language Review/La Revue canadienne des langues vivantes*, 46, 4: 783-787.

LeBlanc, Clarence. 1994. The "Language Management System." In "A Touch of... Class!" *The Canadian Modern Language Reviews/La Revue canadienne des langues vivantes*, 52, 2: 331-335.

Mollica, Anthony. 1993. "Language Learning: The Key to Understanding and Harmony." *Mosaic*, 1, 1: 1, 3-5 (1993). An expanded version the above article. An expanded and revised version was also published in Anthony Mollica, ed., *Teaching Languages. Selected Readings from Mosaic.* Welland, ON: éditions Soleil publishing inc., 1997. Pp. 1-10.

Nemni, Monique. 1985. "Les maux des mots." *The Canadian Modern Language Review/La Revue canadienne des langues vivantes.* 41, 6: 1020-1040.

Pellerin, Suzanne. "L'enseignement du vocabulaire en FLS niveau universitaire (débutant)." In R. Furgiuele and N. Naiman, eds., *The Converging of Two Visions: the Learning and Teaching of French and English as Second Languages at the University Level.* Toronto: Canadian Scholars' Press, p. 55, 104-105, 161-162.

Ralph, Edwin G. 1995. "Motivating Parents to Support Second Language Programs." *Mosaic*, 2, 4: 1, 3-7.

Runte, Roseann. 1995. "Learning Languages in the Context of Canada's Many Cultures." *Mosaic,* 2, 4: 8-11.

Runte, Roseann. 1996a. "Surviving the Perils of Politics: The Language Classroom of the Next Century." *Mosaic,* 3, 2: 1, 3-7.

Runte, Roseann. 1996b. "UNESCO Report favours Preservation of Languages." *Mosaic,* 3, 4: 18.

Runte, Roseann. 1996c. "A Review of Proud of Two Languages. Video produced by Canadian Parents for French. *Mosaic,* 4, 1: 23.

Stern, H. H. 1983a "And Cinderella may yet go to the Ball: A personal view of the past, present and future of core French." *Dialogue. A Newsletter on the Teaching of English and French as Second Languages.* 2, 1: 1-4. Toronto, Ontario: Council of Ministers of Education, Canada.

Stern, H. H. 1983b. "French Core Programs across Canada: How can we Improve Them?" *The Canadian Modern Language Review/La Revue canadienne des langues vivantes,* 39, 1: 34-47.

Van Ek, J. A. 1976. *The Threshold Level for Modern Language Learning in Schools.* London: Longman.

Reprinted from: Clarence LeBlanc, "The Fundamentals of Second-Language Teaching," *Mosaic,* 5, 1 (Fall 1997): 1, 3-8.

5 The Good Language Learner and the Good Language Teacher: A Review of the Literature and Classroom Applications

Anthony Mollica and Frank Nuessel

What are the characteristics of the good language learner? Knowledge of these traits can help the good language teacher create a classroom environment that will facilitate second-language learning.

The Good Language Learner

Nearly twenty-five years ago, in an important article, Stern (1975: 316) summarized the following ten learning strategies associated with the good language learner:

1. A personal learning style or positive learning strategies;
2. An active approach;
3. A tolerant and outgoing approach to the target language and empathy with its speakers;
4. Technical know-how about how to tackle a language;
5. Strategies of experimentation and planning, with the object of developing the new language into an ordered system and of revising the system progressively;
6. Constantly searching for meaning;
7. Willingness to practise;
8. Willingness to use the language in real communication;
9. Self-monitoring and critical sensitivity to language use; and
10. Developing the target language more and more as a separate reference system, and learning to think in it.

In the same year as Stern's (1975) article, Rubin (1975: 45-48) published an article on the same topic entitled "What the 'good language learner' can teach us." In that essay, Rubin enumerated the following seven strategies employed by the good language learner:

1. The good language learner is a willing and accurate guesser.

2. The good language learner has a strong drive to communicate, or to learn from communication. He [sic] is willing to do many things to get his message across.

3. The good language learner is often not inhibited.   He is willing to appear foolish if reasonable communication results. He is willing to make mistakes in order to learn and to communicate. He is willing to live with a certain amount of vagueness.

4. In addition to focussing on communication, the good language learner is prepared to attend to form. The good language learner is constantly looking for patterns in the language.

5. The good language learner practises.

6. The good language learner monitors his own speech and that of others. That is, he is constantly attending to how well his speech is being received and whether his performance meets the standards he has learned.

7. The good language learner attends to meaning. He knows that in order to understand the message, it is not sufficient to pay attention to the grammar of the language or to the surface form of speech.

Subsequent Research
on the Good Language Learner

Various follow-up studies on the good language learner have appeared since the publication of the initial essays by Rubin (1975) and Stern (1975). In their comprehensive review of this topic, Naiman, Fröhlich, Stern, and Todesco (1978: 25; cited in Stern 1983: 406), state that good language learners

> take advantage of potentially useful learning situations, and if necessary create them. They develop learning techniques and strategies appropriate to their individual needs.

These same researchers further observe that good language learners

> demonstrate that, contrary to popular belief, language success is not so much attributable to an 'innate' gift,' as to a conscious effort and constant involvement.

Reiss (1985: 512) pointed out that Rubin's (1975) and Stern's (1975)

> strategies are eminently plausible, but unfortunately empirical data supporting them is not available.

Reiss (1985: 513) also points out that if the term "strategy" is defined as a "conscious approach used by an individual to facilitate learning" then Rubin's strategy no. 3 [see item # 3 in the previous section] 'the good language learner is often not inhibited' is not a strategy but a personality variable.

Based on her own research on the good language learner, Reiss (1985: 518) concluded that

> the good language learner may or may not be inhibited. He [sic] is fairly comfortable with ambiguity. He uses a variety of strategies, including monitoring, inferencing, and practising. He pays attention to form and meaning. He likes to communicate and enjoys learning a   foreign language. Above all, the good

language learner is an *active* participant in the conscious-learning process. The word "active"' is of great significance because the successful language learner is constantly processing information whether called upon or not. Even when silent, he is active mentally and thus becomes a *silent speaker*. This may well explain why the successful language learner need not necessarily be an extrovert. He may not volunteer or take chances on errors "aloud" but this does not stop him from practising silently. This silent speaking is the cornerstone upon which many other strategies are built. Once a student is "speaking silently" he is ipso facto practising, inferencing, looking for meaning, etc.

As a means of ascertaining the specific attributes that second-language instructors deem pertinent to successful second-language learning, Lalonde, Lee, and Gardner (1987: 16) summarize a study by Naiman, Fröhlich and Stern (1975) by observing that

> teachers most often characterize the good language learner as being meticulous (perfectionistic), mature or responsible, and self-confident, as exhibiting classroom behaviours of attentiveness, active participation, and regularity in completing homework, and in demonstrating good memory, a good ear for sound, and general all-around ability.

These same researchers (Lalonde, Lee, and Gardner 1987: 28) provided an exhaustive examination of the extant research on the relationship between personality traits and second-language achievement. The purpose of their research project was to determine if there was agreement by teachers on the personality traits and classroom behaviours of the successful language learner. The results indicate that teachers, in fact, agree on a cluster of personality characteristics and behaviours demonstrated by the good language learner. Nevertheless,

> no evidence of a relationship was found between these personality traits and classroom behaviours.

In their study, Lalonde, Lee, and Gardner (1987: 23) found that teachers identified three classroom behaviours as significant for the good language learner. In this regard, these researchers state that

> teachers perceived the good language learner to be an individual who actively vocalizes corrections, speaks out regardless of making mistakes, and focuses on getting an idea across in the second language.

They further state that (see also Politzer 1983)

> the finding of only three behaviours being identified as important for good language learners could be due to the fact that teachers only relate to the communication aspects of second-language learning.

The Learner's Role

In her summary of strategies exhibited by the good language learner, Cook (1991: 80) suggests the following:

1. Find a learning style that suits you.
2. Involve yourself in the language learning process.
3. Develop an awareness of language both as system and communication.
4. Pay consistent attention to expanding your language.

5. Develop the L2 as a separate system.

6. Take into account the demands that L2 learning imposes.

Classroom Applications of Research
on the Good Language Learner

The extant research on the good language learner by Lalonde, Lee, and Gardner (1987) reveals two important points:

- There are certain personality variables that play a role in good language learning
- Good language learners display specific learning behaviours.

It is the latter aspect that has a direct classroom application, since strategies employed by this group are explicit learnable behaviours that may be acquired by any student enrolled in a language class. This language-learning or language-acquisition conduct involves both the instructor and the learner. The second-language teacher can teach students how to change inappropriate and ineffective learning. Such behaviour modification may help to improve the learner's strategies. Likewise, the learner must make a conscious effort to adapt the second-language learning demeanour that will be most helpful in acquiring another language.

The Instructor's Role in Developing
Good Language Learners

In her article on the unsuccessful language learner, Reiss (1983: 265) concludes that instructors can help "less successful students increase their level of competency." In this essay, Reiss referred to Rubin's (1975) study on the good language learner and also addressed two other factors involved in the problems of the unsuccessful language learner, namely, personality and cognitive style variables.

In particular, Reiss states that teachers can:

1. inform students honestly of the task of learning a language, the work involved, and the rewards to be gained;
2. create the kind of classroom climate in which students feel comfortable and involved;
3. aid students in developing certain cognitive styles helpful in language learning by assigning tasks such as   those suggested by Omaggio and Birckbichler [1978];
4. help students develop the art of inferencing by making them aware of clues for intelligent guessing;
5. personalize language instruction whenever feasible in order to motivate students to express themselves readily;
6. ask students to monitor each other's speech and thus take an active part, not only in learning, but also in teaching;
7. seek out opportunities for students to use the language outside the classroom;

8. present all material in a meaningful manner and, in turn, expect students to attend to both structure and meaning from the outset;
9. ask successful language learners to serve as informants regarding strategies, techniques, and study skills; and
10. encourage slow students to experiment freely until they find their own particular learning style.

As a concluding note, we highly recommend the following books on strategies employed by the good language learner:

1. O'Malley, J. M. , and A. U. Chamot. 1990. *Learning Strategies in Second Language Acquisition*. Cambridge: Cambridge University Press.
2. Pimsleur, Paul. 1980. *How to Learn a Foreign Language*. Boston, MA: Heinle and Heinle.
3. Stevick, Earl W. 1989. *Success with Foreign Languages: Seven Who Achieved it and What Worked for Them*. New York: Prentice Hall.
4. Wenden, Anita and Joan Rubin. 1987. *Learner Strategies in Language Learning*. New York: Prentice-Hall.

The Good Language Teacher

The good language teacher has a pivotal role in the second-language learning/acquisition task. The good language teacher at every educational level (elementary, secondary, and post-secondary) engages in behaviour and activities designed to provide an environment conducive to the acquisition and appreciation of a second language and its culture.

The good language teacher fulfills numerous important roles both in and out of the classroom that facilitate optimal second-language learning opportunities. The following summary specifies many of those varied and distinct roles:

Out-of-Class Roles
- Researcher
- Planner
- Manager
- Advocate
- Organizer
- Evaluator
- Communicator

In-Class Roles
- Teacher
- Motivator
- Evaluator
- Facilitator
- Innovator
- Communicator
- Disciplinarian

The roles enumerated above indicate that the good language teacher must dedicate a considerable amount of time outside the classroom to engage in activities that will maintain and enhance his/her professional status in terms of competency, fluency and proficiency. There is, of course, some overlap in the roles both in and out of class, namely, those of evaluator and communicator.

This provides teachers-in-training, neophyte teachers, experienced teachers, and people charged with evaluating the performance of second-language teachers with an overview of the professional development and behaviour exhibited by the good language teacher.

The following sections outline the ways in which the good language teacher maintains and enriches his/her professional status. The good language teacher must dedicate a significant part of his or professional life to the various roles specified above, because this person literally lives the profession of language teacher inside and outside the classroom.

1. Professional training and preparation
  a. Personal library
  b. Professional organizations
  c.   Professional journals
  d. Professional meetings
  e. Pedagogical textbooks
  f. Library usage
  g. Professional travel
  h. Methodology
  i. Oral proficiency training
  j. Instructional trends and developments
  k. Instructional techniques and strategies
  l. The lesson plan and outline
  m. Activities for student use during the brief classroom absence of the good language teacher.

2. The four skills and cultural comprehension
  a. Listening comprehension
  b. Speaking proficiency and performance
  d. Reading
  c. Writing techniques and strategies
  e. Stages of presentation of materials for the four skills and cultural comprehension
  f. Cultural comprehension
  g. Vocabulary acquisition
  h. Homework.

3. Instructional materials
  a. isual materials
  b. Pedagogical graphics
  c. Visual aids
  d. Audio materials
  e. Language teach

4. Assessment and evaluation
    a.   Assessment of students
    b.   Self-assessment
    c.   Peer review
    d.   Professional testing.

5. Classroom environment
    a.   Reduction of second-language anxiety
    b.   Maintenance of classroom discipline
    c.   Improvement of student study skills
    d.   Activity-appropriate classroom seating
    e.   Sponsorship of language organizations.

Professional Training and Preparation

Obvious as it may seem, the good language teacher is enrolled in, or has graduated from an accredited post-secondary institution. At the elementary and secondary level, this means that the good language teacher enrolls in appropriate accredited second-language pro-grams and obtains the professional provincial or state credentials and certification required to engage in licensed instruction in the geographical area in which he or she seeks employment. In addition to these requirements, the good language teacher also willingly engages in related voluntary activities. This section outlines some of the out-of-class professional development carried out by the good language teacher.

a. Personal Library

The good language teacher builds a personal library of professional resources. The following constitute a core of basic resources that ought to appear in every good language teacher's home library:

1. Bilingual dictionary
2. Dictionary in the target language
3. Grammar of the target language
4. Current textbooks used in the field
5. History of the target language
6. Popular literature (magazines, newspapers, comic books)
7. Collection of proverbs in the target language.

b. Professional Organizations

The good language teacher joins professional language organizations and associations to keep abreast of current trends and issues in second language education. Consult Appendix A ("Selected Professional Organizations for Second-Language Teachers") for a list of associations to which many good language teachers belong. Moreover, the good language teacher belongs to local and provincial or state language organizations.

c. Professional Journals

The good language teacher subscribes to professional journals in order to remain current in the field. As Heffernan (1987:6) aptly wrote:

the language teacher [graduate] who never reads a professional journal and participates only minimally, if at all, in professional meetings, will stagnate. There is an onus on the profession in all areas to upgrade and keep abreast of current developments in his field.

Appendix B ("Selected Professional Journals for Second-Language Teachers") identifies a number of professional journals. Most, if not all, professional organizations (See Appendix A) have their own publication(s) which provide interesting and up-to-date professional news and information.

d. Professional Meetings

The good language teacher attends professional meetings on a regular basis to learn about innovations, and significant trends and issues in the profession. The organizations referred to in Appendices A and B sponsor annual professional meetings, with workshops and numerous sessions devoted to the scholarly study of literature, culture, pedagogy and methodology.

e. Pedagogical Textbooks

The good language teacher maintains, in his/her personal library, current textbooks in the target language designed for classroom usage. This part of the personal library allows the good language teacher to refer to other alternative presentations of materials for use in the classroom. In addition, such a collection of books allows the good language teacher to make informed decisions about the selection of a new textbook (see Nuessel 1991-1992 for an objective approach for the evaluation of pedagogical textbooks).

f. Library Usage

The good language teacher possesses a library card for the local public library and local or regional college or university libraries. The good language teacher becomes familiar with and utilizes local public and academic libraries to carry out research on specific projects. By visiting the local college and university libraries, the good language teacher can determine which professional organizations best serve his/her needs.

g. Professional Travel

The good language teacher visits, vacations or lives in the countries in which the target language is spoken. Information about such trips of varying duration is available in the advertising sections of professional journals or through the local college or university.

The good language teacher utilizes foreign travel as a means of gathering authentic materials for use in the classroom (Nuessel and Cicogna 1997 in press, Omaggio Hadley 1993: 82-3, 174-8, 383-94).

Rogers and Medley (1988: 468) define the notion of authentic materials as

language samples, either oral or written, that reflect a naturalness of form and appropriateness of cultural and situational context that would be found in the language as used by native speakers.

The following is a representative "shopping list" of such pedagogical resources:

1. Postage stamps at local philatelic shops
2. Samples of low denomination paper and metal currency at local numismatist shops
3. Recorded and published versions of popular songs and music (including folk music)
4. Advertisements from local shops and international companies, e.g., McDonalds®, etc.
5. Video cassettes of films in the target language and films originally in English with target-language dubbing
6. Video cassettes of television programs and commercials
7. Political announcements distributed in the streets
8. Newspapers and magazines (puzzle booklets, cartoons)
9. Popular icons of the target culture (*Astérix, Mafalda, Pinocchio*)
10. Books with collections proverbial language, humour, cartoons, tongue-twisters
11. Greeting cards
12. Business cards.

h. Methodology

The good language teacher knows the current teaching methodologies and selects one approach or devises an eclectic strategy that draws the best techniques from each approach.

Larsen-Freeman (1986) describes eight of the most prevalent teaching methods in current use. In a recent article, Doggett (1994) summarizes Larsen-Freeman's list in schematic format:

1. The Grammar-Translation Method
2. The Direct Method
3. The Audio-Lingual Method
4. The Silent Way
5. Suggestopedia
6. Community Language Learning
7. The Total Physical Response
8. The Communicative Approach.

Given the widespread acceptance of the proficiency movement and the subsequent incorporation of its strategies into pedagogical textbooks, it is likely that many instructors will elect to include elements of the communicative approach in their methodology (Omaggio Hadley 1993). Nevertheless, the good language teacher must review current methods and new strategies critically and incorporate the best elements of each methodology into his/her curriculum (Bancroft 1996).

i. Oral Proficiency Training

The good language teacher will also be familiar with the *ACTFL Proficiency Guidelines* (see Omaggio Hadley 1993: Appendix A, pp. 501-11). Moreover, the good language teacher will seek formal training in the Oral Proficiency Interview (OPI) through ACTFL (6 Executive Plaza, Yonkers, NY 108701-6801). The good language teacher will also recognize that the OPI is neither a theory nor a method, but rather a procedure for measuring what a second-language learner can do functionally.

j. Instructional Trends and Developments

The good language teacher keeps up to date with the major trends and issues in the field of second-language education. One of the most important recent developments is the standards movement. In fact, the important publication *Standards for Foreign Language Learning: Preparing for the 21st Century* (Standards 1996: 35-63; available from ACTFL) enumerates five goals which summarize the most significant developments in the profession, and now commonly referred to as the "Five C's":

1. *Communication:* Communicate in languages other than English.
2. *Cultures:* Gain knowledge and understanding of other cultures.
3. *Connections:* Connect with other disciplines and acquire new information.
4. *Comparisons:* Develop insight into the nature of language and culture.
5. *Communities:* Participate in multilingual communities at home and around the world.

k. Instructional Techniques and Strategies

The good language teacher keeps well informed with innovations and new ideas and developments in instructional materials for use in the classroom. This means that the good language teacher reads the current literature in the field, consults with colleagues about their successful strategies, and attends conferences and workshops to learn about meaningful innovations.

l. The Lesson Plan and the Lesson Outline

The good language teacher carefully plans for and organizes materials for classroom instruction. Chastain (1994: 16; 1988, chapter 12) notes that lesson preparation involves three aspects:

1. Pre-planning analysis,
2. Textbook adaptation, and
3. Lesson planning.

With regard to the specific aspects of lesson planning, Mollica (1994a: 14) proposes that a lesson outline include the following components:

1. Theme or topic
2. Aims and objectives
3. Warm-up period
4. Materials needed by
   a. Teacher

     b. Students

  5. Presentation

  6. Application

  7. Summary

  8. Assignment

  9. Evaluation

 10. Teacher's references

 11. Motivation.

m. Provision for Temporary Classroom Absence of the Good Language Teacher

The good language teacher also prepares several packets of lessons for substitute teachers in the event of an absence due to illness or emergency, or for attendance at a professional conference. These packages should be easy to locate by the substitute teacher. Moreover, such materials should be self-contained and designed to be completed or viewed by students within one class period. These packets may include the following items:

1. A selection of guided essays (Nuessel and Cicogna 1993 and 1994b).
2. A packet of problem-solving activities (Cicogna, Danesi and Mollica 1992, Mollica and Danesi 1994).
3. Video tapes with material that relates to the cultural content of the curriculum.

The Four Skills and Cultural Comprehension

The good language teacher devotes an appropriate amount of time to the four skills, including the so-called active skills (speaking and writing) and the receptive skills (listening and reading). Following are some recommendations concerning the presentation of these skills together with activities.

a. Stages of Presentation of Materials for the Four Skills and Cultural Listening Comprehension

The good language teacher recognizes that planning activities for the introduction and practice of the four skills (see section on lesson planning above) is very important. The following format will help the good language teacher to present these activities to help insure success:

1. Pre-activity Stage

a. Provide information appropriate to the actual activity, e.g., vocabulary, grammatical structures, cultural data (geography, history, and so forth)
b. Ask questions to assist students in anticipating the activity stage.
c. Ask students to summarize what they have learned.
d. Model the activities.

2. Activity Stage

a. Introduce the activities.
b. Practice the activities individually and in pair or group formats.

3. Post-Activity Stage

  a. Apply the knowledge gained in the activity stage to novel situations.
  b. Assess the activities to determine if students have learned the salient points, or to determine if they have developed the appropriate skills to demonstrate their knowledge of the topic.

b. Listening Comprehension

The good language teacher develops materials and adapts textbook materials that enhance listening comprehension (Davis and Rinvolucri 1988, Karsenti 1996, Krashen 1995b, Rost 1990, Rubin 1994; see also questioning techniques and strategies Mollica 1994b Richards 1995). To this end, the good language teacher will develop and utilize authentic materials that focus on different categories of listening experiences (Rost 1990 11; see chart below).

Categories of Listening Experiences	+
Type of listening:	*General purpose:*
Transactional listening	learning new information
Interactional listening	recognizing personal component of message
Critical listening	evaluating reasoning and evidence
Recreational listening	appreciating random or integrated aspects of event

c. Speaking Proficiency and Performance

The good language teacher introduces classroom activities that facilitate oral communication. Valette (1994) provides a five-step model to accomplish this goal:

  1. *Guided observations:* Listening to the spoken word.
  2. *Guided analysis:* Learning how the language works.
  3. *Guided practice:* Building the skills.
  4. *Simulated performance:* Participating in guided conversations and role play (see Di Pietro 1987 for his excellent Strategic Interaction Method).
  5. *Performance:* Speaking in real-life situations.

Implicit in this recommendation is the presumption that the target language will be the exclusive medium of communication during the class time. Moreover, the good language teacher provides students with opportunities to use the target language outside the classroom through language clubs, language houses, language tables, and travel to areas where the target language is used.

d. Reading

The good language teacher incorporates diverse reading activities into the second-language curriculum. Grellet (1981: 4-5; cf. Munby 1978 as Grellet's source) notes that the following components are involved in developing an effective reading a text:

1. Recognizing the script of a language.
2. Deducing the meaning and use of unfamiliar vocabulary.
3. Understanding information that is stated explicitly.
4. Understanding implications not explicitly stated.
5. Understanding relationships within sentences.
6. Understanding relationships between parts of a text through cohesive devices both grammatical and lexical.
7. Identifying the main idea from the supporting detail.
8. Distinguishing the main idea from the supporting detail.
9. Extracting main points in order to summarize.
10. Understanding the communicative value and function of the texts.

A variety of activities may be utilized to facilitate the reading of novel texts in a class as discussed by Constantino (1995), Krashen (1989, 1995a, b), Mollica (1971), Swaffar, Arens, and Byrnes (1991), and Valette (1997).

e. Writing Techniques and Strategies

The good language teacher provides his/her students with opportunities to write. Writing tasks in the second-language course too often receive inadequate attention. The good language teacher recognizes that a writing assignment may be divided into achievable sub-components, and thus provides students with opportunities to engage in writing assignments that are feasible. In this regard, Hedge (1988: 21) points out that the act of writing consists of seven stages:

1. Initial motivation
2. Assembly of ideas
3. Planning and outlining
4. Note-taking
5. Preparation of a first draft
6. Revision and replanning of the initial draft
7. Formal presentation of the final product.

Several articles and books provide useful information and strategies for developing writing activities (Besnard, Elkabas, and Rosienski-Pellerin 1996, Hedge 1988, Laviosa 1994, Mollica 1995, Nuessel and Cicogna 1993, Raimes 1983).

f. Vocabulary Acquisition

The good language teacher employs a variety of strategies and techniques to enhance and enrich students' vocabulary.

Krashen (1989, 1995a,b) argues that voluntary free reading of authentic texts in the second language significantly enhances vocabulary acquisition and improves spelling in the target language.

The development of problem-solving activities such as crossword puzzles, word search materials, scrambled letters, word creation, tic-tac-toe, provide students with an interesting and amusing way of learning vocabulary (Mollica 1981, Nuessell 1992, Danesi and Mollica 1994).

Carter (1987) and Carter and McCarthy (1988) specify seven procedures for enhancing vocabulary acquisition:

1. Utilize techniques that evoke visual images and associations.
2. Focus on phonological patterns as a strategy for lexical retention.
3. Develop a notion of core versus peripheral vocabulary.
4. Encourage lexical amplification in more advanced classes through semantic grids.
5. Teach fixed and idiomatic expressions.
6. Encourage students to guess by using contextual clues for ascertaining the meaning of new vocabulary in oral or written formats.
7. Teach words in discourse to develop an appreciation of syntactic, semantic and pragmatic functions of lexical items.

In two excellent articles focussing on vocabulary, Maiguashca proposes a variety of activities for figurative language (1984) and offers an overview of the various developments that have taken place during the last twenty years in the area of vocabulary research within the field of second-language education (1993).

g. Cultural Comprehension

The good language teacher includes meaningful and authentic cultural content in the curriculum. With regard to this dimension of classroom instruction, Stern (1992) has enumerated ten goals for cultural learning in order of difficulty:

1. Knowledge of the cultural connotations of words and phases
2. Knowledge of how to behave in common situations
3. The development of interest and understanding of the second culture
4. Understanding of crosscultural differences
5. Understanding of intercultural institutions and differences
6. Research-projects
7. Development of an integrated view of the second culture
8. Ability to evaluate statements about the second culture
9. Development of an empathy toward a second culture and its people
10. Academic research on the second culture.

One very helpful strategy for developing and maintaining an interest in the target culture is to conduct a class survey to determine which cultural facets to study. Dechert and Kastner's study on culture (1989: 180-2) reveals that the following topics belong to the following general domains that are of greatest interest to students:

1. Everyday life
2. Tourist attractions and travel tips
3. History
4. Landscape and climate
5. Social and political structure
6. Culture
7. Technology
8. School system
9. Church and religion
10. Social structure and classes in society
11. Production
12. Demography

h. Homework

The good language teacher gives meaningful and creative homework assignments that reflect and reinforce classroom activities just discussed above. The assignment of such homework requires careful planning and effort so that such work is not just rote and tedious drudgery. In this regard, Antonek, Tucker, and Donato (1995: 1) discuss the innovative use of interactive homework that

> communicates to parents, *facilitates* classroom learning, and *mediates* the home/school relationship.

In today's world of institutional accountability, interactive homework in this type of school-home-parent communicative interaction and bridge-building strengthens important educational ties between the home and public institutions (Ralph 1995).

Instructional Materials

The good language teacher acquires over time a bank of appropriate instructional materials for use in the second-language classroom. This process is an ongoing and essentially lifelong task. The inventory should include published visual materials (posters, maps, etc.), teacher-created visuals, audio materials (recordings), and multi-media materials (computer software, CD-ROM, videos).

a. Visual materials

At a strictly theoretical level, Mollica and Danesi (1995; see also Danesi 1988) have demonstrated that the bimodal model of second-language instruction benefits the acquisition of a second-language by stimulating both hemispheres of the brain (Danesi 1987, Nuessel and Cicogna 1992: 291). In Danesi's (1987: 384-9) applications of this model to actual pedagogical situations, there are four key components for the classroom:

1. *Contextualization:* the appropriate environmental placement of an exercise to make it meaningful.

2. *Visualization:* the use of visuals (pictures, slides, overhead projections, film, interactive CALL [computer-assisted language learning] (Nuessel 1989, Smith 1987, 1989) and interactive TELL [technology-enhanced language learning; see below] (Bush and Terry 1997).

3. *Diversification:* the use of a wide range of learning activities.

4. *Personalization:* the direct inclusion of students in language learning activities.

b. Pedagogical Graphics

The good language teacher employs pedagogical graphics consistently when introducing grammatical structures with "in-house" materials developed. In this regard, Danesi (1983: 73-4) points out the importance of "pedagogical graphics" which he defines as:

> any symbol, figure, schema or chart (dots, lines, arrows, circles, braces, etc.) that can be used to enhance the presentation of a grammatical point; i.e., it is a visual device that can be utilized in conjunction with, or superimposed upon, target language data in order to highlight some structural feature, relationship or process.

There are three functions of pedagogical graphics:

1. They are time savers.
2. They are highly intelligible.
3. They enhance the learning of structure (Danesi 1983: 74-5).

c. Visual Aids

The good language teacher employs visual aids in the classroom setting in an appropriate manner. Hammerly (1995:12, 1994) defines visual aids as

> drawings, photos, graphics or models of a nonverbal nature used to facilitate (second-language) teaching/learning.

With regard to pictures, Wright (1989:2) notes that these graphics add to:

1. interest and motivation
2. a sense of context of the language
3. a specific reference point or stimulus.

Selected examples of visuals include the following:

1. Gestures (Kirch 1979, Nuessel 1985, Wilcox 1994)
2. Postage stamps (Nuessel 1996)
3. Pictures (Wright 1989)
4. Problem-solving activities and puzzles (Mollica and Danesi 1994)
5. Videos (Donley 1996b, Stempleski and Tomalin 1990).
6 Graphic materials in general (Mollica 1979a, Hammerly 1994, 1995, Mollica and Danesi 1994, 1995, Stevick 1986, Wright 1989).

d. Audio Materials

The good language teacher uses appropriate examples of authentic audio materials to introduce a variety of listening experiences in the classroom. This strategy includes the following possibilities:

1. Music and songs (Anton 1990, Karsenti 1996, Nuessel and Cicogna 1991).
2. Dictation activities (Davis and Rinvolucri 1988).

e. Language Teaching and Learning Technology

The good language teacher uses technology-enhanced instructional materials as appropriate (see Tremblay 1996 for a discussion of the use of the Internet). Bush (1997: vii) points out in the "foreword" to *Technology-Enhanced Language Learning* a decade ago Smith (1987, 1989) used the acronym CALL (= Computer-Aided Language Learning) to refer to the use of technology in second-language instruction. Today, however, that acronym has been replaced by the newer and more apt designation TELL (= Technology-Enhanced Language Learn-ing). As Bush (1997: vii) further states:

> the change in emphasis from *computer* to *technology* places direct importance on the media of communication made possible by the computer, which itself often remains unseen, rather than on the computer itself. For example, it is possible to observe present technological evolution and conclude from different perspectives that on the one hand the computer is becoming a television, or on the other that the television is becoming a computer. Furthermore, the computer makes possible the Internet, that intriguing network of networks that enables communications of all sorts that have only recently become imaginable.

TELL requires continuing teacher education and the wise investment of resources in appropriate equipment that will be useful for a reasonable length of time before it becomes obsolete. In the ever-changing technological environment, multimedia instruction involves the following significant issues (Pusack and Otto 1997: 6):

1. The combination of media types.
2. The dimension of control.
3. Aspects of help and guidance for interactivity.

Assessment and Evaluation

The good language teacher engages in periodic (formative) review and final (summative) review of his/her students to ensure that they have acquired the basic skills and knowledge associated with the study of a second language. The extent to which students succeed, i.e., demonstrate linguistic proficiency and cultural competency, is one measure of the good language teacher's effectiveness and competency.

At the same time, the good language teacher monitors his/her own performance to determine the effectiveness of specific activities and projects in the classroom. Finally, the good language teacher undergoes periodic professional review (most likely once a year) by his/her peers who will make additional, objective judgments about teaching performance and effectiveness, or through standardized tests of proficiency.

a. Assessment of Students

The good language teacher regularly assesses students in a fair and reasonable fashion to determine the effectiveness of classroom instruction in the four skills (listening, speaking, reading, writing) and cultural comprehension. This facet of instruction involves the use of a variety of assessment instruments to determine the retention of classroom content at various intervals in the course (formative evaluation) and at the end of the course (summative evaluation).

Specific suggestions for such assessment may be found in Boyd (1978), Nuessel (1991),Ralph 1994).

b. Self-Assessment

The good language teacher evaluates his/her own progress in the instructional task. Perhaps the most effective approach to this process is the use of the Glossodynamic Model first discussed by Roback (1955). As applied to second-language teaching, the Glossodynamic Model involves the following stages (Titone and Danesi 1985: 167):

1. Familiarize (yourself).
2. Adapt.
3. Try out.
4. Adjust.
5. Evaluate.

c. Peer Review

The good language teacher also participates in assessment of his/her teaching effectiveness through peer review of classroom performance and materials (syllabus, handouts, and related materials). Moreover, the good language teacher also has his/her instruction rated by students with an official teaching rating instrument. These forms of evaluation allow the good language teacher to retain the positive elements of instruction, change the less than effective pedagogical strategies, and eliminate ineffective teaching practices.

d. Professional Testing

The good language teacher undergoes professional testing to assess his/her linguistic proficiency. Lewin, Flewelling, and Gagné (1996) discuss a number of existing tests for second-language teachers.

Classroom Environment

The good language teacher seeks to provide a classroom environment that maximizes teaching effectiveness by reducing those problems that most often contribute to ineffective language learning (Evans-Harvey 1993): anxiety (Donley 1996a, Horwitz and Young 1991, Maceri 1995), poor study habits (Cankar 1996), discipline problems (Richards 1994), and activity-appropriate seating arrangements (Papalia 1994).

a. Reduction of Second-Language Anxiety

The good language teacher helps students to reduce their anxiety over learning a second language. One helpful strategy includes the distribution of Donley's (1996a reproduced in the current issue of *Mosaic*) list of ten ways to cope with foreign language anxiety (see also Horwitz and Young 1991, Maceri 1995).

b. Maintenance of Classroom Discipline

The good language teacher maintains an orderly classroom. In this regard, Richards (1994) advises the following plan of action:
1. Prevent possible problems.
2. Head off problems.
3. Discuss the consequences of serious misbehaviour.
4. Seek help for a crisis situation.

c. Improvement of Student Study Skills

Another way in which the good language teacher enhances effective second-language learning is to discuss with students effective study skills (see Cankar 1996 reproduced in this current issue of *Mosaic*).

d. Activity-Appropriate Classroom Seating

The good language teacher is attentive to seating arrangement in the classroom. Different types of second-language activities require different seating arrangements (Papalia 1994). The choice of classroom seating arrangements is directly related to the type of activity that occurs in the classroom (choral work, individual work, paired activities, group activities).

e. Sponsorship of Language Organizations

The good language teacher sponsors language organizations outside of the classroom. Language organizations, especially those affiliated with national organizations, are one effective way of maintaining and expanding interest in a second language outside the classroom. Such organizations may engage in a number of activities designed to promote the use of the language outside of the classroom:
1. Development of exhibits in public locations (libraries, commercial enterprises) to inform people of the numerous benefits associated with learning another language.
2. Sponsorship of language tables at meal time where the target language is the sole medium of communication.
3. Invitation of speakers who will provide lectures or talks in the target language.
4. Promotion of a language house at post-secondary institutions where the target language is the sole medium of communication, e.g., a section of a college or university dormitory.
5. Plans for work/study trips to a geographical area where the target language is spoken (Hershberg and Van Fleet 1987).
6. Scheduling and planning for a teacher-guided educational trip to a location where the target language is spoken.
7. Memberships in honour societies affiliated with national organizations.
8. Awards for academic achievement by students from the national headquarters.

✔	The Good Language Teacher: Activity Performance Checklist	
	Activity:	What: Where: When: Why:
	1. Professional Training and Preparation	
	a. Personal library	
	b. Professional organizations	
	c. Professional journals	
	d. Professional meetings	
	e. Pedagogical textbooks	
	f. Library usage	
	g. Professional travel	
	h. Methodology	
	i. Oral proficiency training	
	j. Instructional trends and developments	
	k. Instructional techniques and strategies	
	l. The lesson plan and outline	
	m. Provision for Temporary classroom absence	
	2. The Four Skills and Cultural Comprehension:	
	a. Stages of presentation of materials	
	b. Listening comprehension	
	c. Writing techniques and strategies	
	d. Speaking proficiency and performance	
	e. Reading	
	f. Vocabulary acquisition	
	g. Cultural comprehension	
	h. Homework	
	3. Instructional materials:	
	a. Visual materials	
	b. Pedagogical graphics	
	c. Peer review	

d.	Professional testing	
4.	**Classroom Environments**	
a.	Reduction of second-language anxiety	
b.	Improvement of student study skills	
c.	Maintenance of classroom discipline	
d.	Activity-appropriate classroom seating	
e.	Sponsorship of language organizations	

Conclusions

A review of the literature on the good language learner reveals certain conduct and personality traits associated with that type of learner. The good language teacher may utilize information about the behavioural characteristics of the good language learner to point out to the less successful language learner specific strategies for achieving second-language success.

This article enumerated those aspects of the good language teacher's teaching behaviour, administration, communication, and professional activities that contribute to a profile of a good language teacher. In particular, we examined the domains of professional training and preparation, the development of the four skills and cultural comprehension in the classroom, the creation of appropriate instructional materials, the assessment of student and teacher performance, and the building of a positive classroom environment where effective teaching and successful learning may take place.

A more specific purpose of our attention to the good language teacher is to inform teachers-in-training and neophyte teachers of their professional expectations. Finally, supervisors and administrators who evaluate a second- language teachers are provided with an objective and professionally-oriented set of guidelines to carry out such assessments.

References

Allen, V. F. 1983. *Techniques in Teaching Vocabulary.* Oxford: Oxford University Press.

Anton, Ronald J. 1990. "Combining Singing and Psychology." *Hispania*, 73: 1166-1170.

Antonek, Janis L., G. Richard Tucker, and Richard Donato. "Interactive Homework: Creating Connections between Home and School." *Mosaic*, 2, 3: 1-10.

Bancroft, W. Jane. 1996. "SALT for Language Acquisition." *Mosaic*, 3, 3: 16-20.

Besnard, Christine, Charles Elkabas, and Sylvie Rosienski-Pellerin. 1996. "Students' Empowerment: E-mail Exchange and the Development of Writing Skills." *Mosaic*, 3, 2: 8-12.

Boyd, J. Alvin. "Evaluating the Active Communication Skills: Writing." *The Canadian Modern Language Review/La Revue canadienne des langues vivantes*, 34, 4:735-745. Trans. into French with the title of "L'évaluation des habiletés de communication: écrire," in Pierre Calvé et Anthony Mollica, réds, *Le français langues seconde: des principes à la pratique*. Welland, Ont.: The Canadian Modern Language Review, 1987, pp.385- 397

Bush, Michael D. 1997. "Foreword." In Michael D. Bush and Robert M. Terry eds.,. *Technology-Enhanced Language Learning*. Lincolnwood, IL: National Textbook Company, pp. vii-ix.

Bush, Michael D. and Robert M. Terry, eds. 1997. *Technology-Enhanced Language Learning*. Lincolnwood, IL: National Textbook Company.

Cankar, Paul. 1996. "Study Skill Suggestions for Students of Foreign Language Classes." *The Forum of Phi Sigma Iota*, 18, 1: 11-12. See Chapter 8, in this volume.

Carter, Ronald. 1987. *Vocabulary: Applied Linguistic Perspectives*. London: Allen and Unwin.

Carter, Ronald and Michael McCarthy. 1988. "Developments in the Teaching of Vocabulary: 1945 to the Present Day." In Ronald Carter and Michael McCarthy, eds., *Vocabulary and Language Teaching*. London: Longman, pp. 39-59.

Chastain, Kenneth. 1988. *Developing Second-Language Skills: Theory and Practice*. 3rd ed. San Diego, CA: Harcourt Brace Jovanovich.

Chastain, Kenneth. 1994. "Planning for Instruction." *Mosaic*, 2, 1: 16-17.

Cicogna, Caterina, Marcel Danesi, and Anthony Mollica, eds. 1992. *Problem Solving in Second-Language Teaching*. Welland, ON: éditions Soleil publishing, Inc.

Constantino, Rebecca. 1995. "The Effects of Pleasure Reading." *Mosaic*, 3, 1: 15-17.

Cook, Vivian. 1991. *Second Language Learning and Language Teaching*. London: Edward Arnold.

Danesi, Marcel. 1983. "Pedagogical Graphics in Second-Language Teaching." *The Canadian Modern Language Review/La revue canadienne des langues vivantes*, 40,1: 73-81.

Danesi, Marcel. 1987. "Practical Applications of Current Brain Research to the Teaching of Italian." *Italica*, 64: 77-92.

Danesi, Marcel. 1988. "Neurological Bimodality and Theories of Language Teaching." *Studies in Second Language Acquisition*, 10: 13-31.

Danesi, Marcel and Anthony Mollica. 1994. "Games and Puzzles in Second-Language Teaching: A Second Look." *Mosaic*, 2, 2: 13-22.

Davis, Paul and Mario Rinvolucri. 1988. *Dictation: New Methods, New Possibilities*. Cambridge: Cambridge University Press.

Dechert, Christiane, and Peter Kastner. 1989. "Undergraduate Student Interests and the Cultural Content of Textbooks for German." *The Modern Language Journal*, 73, 2: 173-191.

Di Pietro, Robert J. 1987. *Strategic Interaction: Learning Language through Scenarios*. Cambridge: Cambridge University Press.

Doggett, Gina. 1994. "Eight Approaches to Language Teach-ing." *Mosaic*, 1, 3: 8-13.

Donley, Philip M. 1996a. "Ten Ways to Cope with Foreign Language Anxiety." *The Forum of Phi Sigma Iota*, 18, 1, 13. See Chapter 9, in this volume.

Donley, Philip M. 1996b. "Using Video to Promote Critical Thinking." *The Forum of Phi Sigma Iota*, 18, 2, 10.

Evans-Harvey, Cher. 1993. "Climate Setting in Second-Language Classroom." *Mosaic*, 1, 2, 1: 2-5.

Evans-Harvey, Cher. 1994. "Planning for Effective Teaching: The Unit Plan." *Mosaic*, 2, 2: 10-12.

Garrett, Nina. 1991. "Technology in the Service of Language Learning: Trends and Issues." *The Modern Language Journal,* 75, 1: 74-101.

Giroux Collins, Rosemarie. 1994. "Group Work: From Process to Product." *Mosaic,* 2, 1: 6-9.

Grellet, Françoise. 1981. *Developing Reading Skills: A Practical Guide to Reading Comprehension Exercises.* Cambridge: Cambridge University Press.

Hammerly, Hector. 1994. "A Picture is Worth 1000 Words and a Word is Worth 1000 Pictures." *Mosaic,* 1, 4: 13-17.

Hammerly, Hector. 1995. "What Visual Aids Can and Cannot Do in Second Language Teaching." Mosaic, 2, 3: 11-18.

Hedge, Tricia. 1988. *Writing.* Oxford: Oxford University Press.

Heffernan, Peter J. 1987. "Core French Teacher's Continuing Professional Development: Balancing the Ideal and the Real." *Dialogue,* 5, 1:1,5-8.

Hershberg, David, and James A. Van Fleet. 1987. "Work Exchange Programs: Achieving More for Less." *The Modern Language Journal,* 71, 2: 174-179.

Horwitz, E. K. and D. J. Young. 1991. *Language Anxiety: From Theory and Research to Classroom Applications.* Englewood Cliffs, NJ: Prentice Hall.

Karsenti, Thierry P. 1996. "Bringing Songs in the Second-Language Classroom." *Mosaic,* 3, 4: 10-15.

Kirch, Max S. 1979. "Non-Verbal Communication across Cultures." *The Modern Language Journal,* 63, 416-23.

Krashen, Stephen. 1989. "We Acquire Vocabulary and Spelling by Reading: Additional Evidence for the Input Hypothesis." *The Modern Language Journal,* 73, 4: 440-464.

Krashen, Stephen. 1995a. "Immersion: Why Not Try Free Voluntary Reading?" *Mosaic,* 3, 1: 1, 3-4.

Krashen, Stephen. 1995b. "The Reading/Listening Library." *Mosaic,* 2, 4: 20.

Lalonde, R. N., P. A. Lee, and R. C. Gardner. 1987. "The Common View of the Good Language Learner: An Investigation of Teachers' Beliefs." *The Canadian Modern Language Review/La revue canadienne des langues vivantes,* 44, 1: 16-34.

Larsen-Freeman, Diane. 1986. *Techniques and Principles in Language Teaching.* Oxford: Oxford University Press.

Laviosa, Flavia. 1994. "The Writing Process of Italian as a Second Language: Theory and Practice." *Italica,* 71, 4: 484-504.

Lewin, Louise, Janet Flewelling, and Antoinette Gagné. 1996. "Meeting the Challenge: The Creation of a Communicative Test for Evaluating the Proficiency of Second-Language Teachers." *Mosaic,* 4, 1: 9-14.

Maceri, Domenico. 1995. "Reducing Stress in the Foreign Language Classroom: Teaching Descriptive Adjectives through Humour." *Mosaic,* 2, 4: 21-2.

Maiguashca, Raffaella Uslenghi. 1984. "Semantic Fields: Towards a Methodology for Teaching Vocabulary in the Second-Language Classroom." *The Canadian Modern Language Review/La revue canadienne des langues vivantes,* 40, 2: 274- 97.

Maiguashca, Raffaella Uslenghi. 1993. "Teaching and Learning Vocabulary in a Second Language: Past, Present and Future Directions." *The Canadian Modern Language Review/La revue canadienne des langues vivantes,* 50, 1: 83-100.

Mollica, Anthony, 1971. "The Reading Program and Oral Practice," *Italica,* 48, 4: 522-544. Reprinted in Antony Mollica, ed., *A Handbook for Teachers of Italian.* Toronto: Livingstone, 1976, pp. 75-96.

Mollica, Anthony. 1978. "The Film Advertisement: A Source for Language Activities." *The Canadian Modern Language Review/La Revue canadienne des langues vivantes*, 34, 2: 221-243.

Mollica, Anthony. 1979a. "Print and Non-Print Materials: Adapting for Classroom Use." In June K. Phillips, ed., *Building on Experience – Building for Success*. Skokie, IL: National Textbook Co., pp. 157-198.

Mollica, Anthony. 1979b. "*A Tiger in Your Tank*: Advertisements in the Language Classroom." *The Canadian Modern Language Review/La Revue canadienne des langues vivantes*, 35, 4: 691-743.

Mollica, Anthony. 1981. "Visual Puzzles in the Language Classroom." *The Canadian Modern Language Review/La Revue canadienne des langues vivantes*, 37, 3: 582-622. Trans. into French with the title of "Casse-tête visuels dans la salle de classe," in Pierre Calvé et Anthony Mollica, réds, *Le français langues seconde: des principes à la pratique*. Welland, Ont.: The Canadian Modern Language Review, 1987, pp. 267-300.

Mollica, Anthony. 1992a. *A Picture is Worth... 1000 Words! Book 1*. Welland, ON: éditions Soleil publishing inc. With Teacher's Guides in English French, German, Italian, Portuguese and Spanish.

Mollica, Anthony. 1992b. *A Picture is Worth... 1000 Words! Book 2*. Welland, ON: éditions Soleil publishing inc. With Teacher's Guides in English French, German, Italian, Portuguese and Spanish.

Mollica, Anthony. 1994a. "Planning for Successful Teaching: The Lesson Outline." *Mosaic*, 1, 3: 13-15.

Mollica, Anthony. 1994b. "Planning for Successful Teaching: Question-ing Strategies." *Mosaic*, 1, 4: 18-20.

Mollica, Anthony. 1995. "Creative Writing: Poetry in the Language Classroom." *Mosaic*, 3, 1: 18-20.

Mollica, Anthony, ed. 1997. Teaching Languages: *Selected Readings from Mosaic*. Welland, Ontario, Canada: éditions Soleil publishing, inc.

Mollica, Anthony, and Marcel Danesi. 1995. "The Foray into the Neurosciences: Have We Learned Anything Useful? *Mosaic*, 2, 4: 12-20.

Munby, John. 1978. *Communicative Syllabus Design*. Cambridge: Cam-bridge University Press.

Naiman, N., M. Fröhlich, and H. H. Stern. 1975. *The Good Language Learner*. Toronto: Institute for Studies in Education.

Naiman, N., M. Fröhlich, H. H. Stern, and A. Todesco. 1978. *The Good Language Learner*. Research in Education Series No. 7. Toronto: The Ontario Institute for Studies in Education.

Nuessel, Frank. 1985."Teaching Kinesics through Literature." *The Canadian Modern Language Review/La revue canadienne des langues vivantes*, 41, 1014-19.

Nuessel, Frank. 1989."The Role of CALL in Second-Language Education." *Language Teaching Strategies*, 4: 3-12.

Nuessel, Frank. 1991."Foreign Language Testing Today: Issues in Language Program Direction." In Richard V. Teschner, ed., *Assessing Foreign Language Proficiency of Undergraduates*. Boston:° einle and Heinle, 1-20.

Nuessel, Frank. 1991-1992."Criteria for the Objective Evaluation of Pedagogical Textbooks." *Language Teaching Strategies*, 5-6: 41-51.

Nuessel, Frank. 1996. "Postage Stamps: A Pedagogical Tool in the Second Language" Classroom." *Mosaic*, 3, 2: 12-17.

Nuessel, Frank and Caterina Cicogna. 1991. "The Integration of Songs and Music into the Italian Curriculum." *Italica*, 68, 473-86.

Nuessel, Frank, and Caterina Cicogna. 1992. "Pedagogical Applications of the Bimodal Model of Learning through Visual and Auditory Stimuli."In Jeanette Beer, Charles Ganelin, and Anthony Julian Tamburri, eds., *Romance Languages Annual 1991*, Vol. III. West Lafayette, IN: Purdue Research Foundation, , pp. 289-92

Nuessel, Frank and Caterina Cicogna. 1993. "Teaching Writing in Elementary and Intermediate Language Classes." *Mosaic*, 1, 2: 9-11.

Nuessel, Frank and Caterina Cicogna. 1994a."Strategies for Teaching Vocabulary in the Elementary and Intermediate Italian Classroom." *Italica*, 71, 4: 521-547.

Nuessel, Frank and Caterina Cicogna. 1994b. "Writing in the Elementary and Intermediate Italian Class: Theory, Practice, and Assessment." In Jeanette Beer, Charles Ganelin, and Ben Lawton, eds., *Romance Languages Annual 1993*. West Lafayette, IN: Purdue Research Foundation, pp. 265-71.

Nuessel, Frank and Caterina Cicogna. 1997 (in press). "The Integration of Authentic Cultural Materials into the Elementary Italian Curriculum." *Romance Languages Annual 8*.

Omaggio Hadley, Alice. 1993. *Teaching Language in Context*. 2nd ed. Boston: Heinle and Heinle.

Omaggio, A. and D. Birckbichler. 1978. "Diagnosing and Responding to Individual Learner Needs." *The Modern Language Journal*, 62, 336- 345.

O'Malley, J. M. and A. U. Chamot. 1990. *Learning Strategies in Second Language Acquisition*. Cambridge: Cambridge University Press.

Papalia, Anthony. 1994. "Planning for Effective Teaching: Papalia's Classroom Settings."*Mosaic*, 1, 3: 16.

Pattison, Pat. 1987. *Developing Communication Skills: A Practical Handbook for Language Teachers, with Examples in English, French and German*. Cambridge: Cambridge University Press.

Politzer, Robert L. 1983."An Exploratory Study of Self-Reported Language Learning Behaviours and Their Relationship to Achievement." *Studies in Second Language Acquisition*, 6, 1: 54-68.

Pusack, James P. and Sue K. Otto. 1997. "Taking Control of Multimedia." In Michael D. Bush and Robert M. Terry, eds., *Technology-Enhanced Language Learning*. Lincolnwood, IL: National Textbook Company, pp. 1-46.

Raimes, Ann. 1983. *Techniques in Teaching Writing*. Oxford: Oxford University Press.

Ralph, Edwin. 1994. "Teaching to the Test: Principles of Authentic Assessment for Second-Language Education." *Mosaic*, 1, 4: 9-13.

Ralph, Edwin. 1995. "Motivating Parents to Support Second-Language Programs." *Mosaic*, 2, 4: 1-7.

Reiss, Mary-Ann. 1981. "Helping the Unsuccessful Language Learner." *The Modern Language Journal*, 65, 2, 121-128.

Reiss, Mary-Ann. 1985. "The Good Language Learner: Another Look." *The Canadian Modern Language Review/La revue canadienne des langues vivantes*, 41, 3: 511-523.

Richards, J. 1976. "The Role of Vocabulary in Teaching." *TESOL Quarterly*, 10, 77-89.

Richards, Merle. 1994. "Discipline in the Language Class." *Mosaic*, 2, 1: 14-15.

Richards, Merle. 1995. "Planning for Successful Teaching: Questioning in the Language Classroom." *Mosaic*, 2, 3: 21-22.

Roback, A. A. 1955. "Glossodynamics and the Present Status of Psycholinguistics." In A. A. Roback, ed., *Present-Day Psychology.* . New York: Philosophical Library, pp. 897-912

Rogers, Carmen, and Frank W. Medley, Jr. 1988. "Language with a Purpose: Using Authentic Materials in the Foreign Language Classroom." *Foreign Language Annals,* 21, 5: 467-88.

Rost, Michael. 1990. *Listening in Language Learning.* London: Longman.

Rubin, Joan. 1975. "What the 'Good Language Learner' Can Teach Us." *TESOL Quarterly,* 9, 41-50.

Rubin, Joan. 1994. "A Review of Second Language Listening Research." *The Modern Language Journal,* 78, 2: 199-221.

Seelye, H. Ned. 1984. *Teaching Culture: Strategies for Intercultural Communication.* Lincolnwood, IL: NTC Publishing.

Smith, Wm. Flint, ed. 1987. *Modern Media in Foreign Language Education: Theory and Implementation.* Lincolnwood, IL: National Textbook Company.

Smith, Wm. Flint, ed. 1989. *Modern Technology in Foreign Language Education: Applications and Projects.* Lincolnwood, IL: National Textbook Company.

Standards for Foreign Language Learning: Preparing for the 21st Century. 1996. Yonkers, NY: ACTFL.

Stempleski, Susan, and Barry Tomalin. 1990. *Video in Action.* Englewood Cliffs, NJ: Prentice-Hall.

Stern, H. H. 1975. "What Can We Learn from the Good Language Learner?" *The Canadian Modern Language Review/La revue canadienne des langues vivantes,* 31, 4: 304-318.

Stern, H. H. 1983. *Fundamental Concepts of Language Teaching.* Oxford: Oxford University Press.

Stern, H. H. 1992. *Issues and Options in Language Teaching.* Oxford: Oxford University Press.

Stevick, Earl W. 1986. *Images and Options in the Language Classroom.* Cambridge: Cambridge University Press.

Stevick, Earl W. 1989. *Success with Foreign Languages: Seven Who Achieved and What Worked for Them.* New York: Prentice Hall.

Swaffar, Janet K., Katherine M. Arens, and Heidi Byrnes. 1991. *Reading for Meaning: An Integrated Approach to Language Learning.* Englewood Cliffs, NJ: Prentice-Hall.

Titone, Renzo, and Marcel Danesi. 1985. *Applied Psycholinguistics: An Introduction to the Psychology of Language Learning and Teaching.* Toronto: University of Toronto Press.

Tremblay, Roger. 1996. "Professional Development Via the Internet: A Proposal." *Mosaic,* 4, 1: 3-8.

Valette, Rebecca. 1994. "The Five-Step Performance-Based Model of Oral Proficiency." *Mosaic,* 2, 2: 1-4.

Weinrib, Alice. 1997. "A Sampling of Information Sources in Second-Language Pedagogy." *Mosaic,* 4, 3:20-21.

Wenden, Anita, and Joan Rubin. 1987. *Learner Strategies in Language Learning.* New York: Prentice-Hall.

Wilcox, Joanne. 1994. "Gestures and Language: Fair and Foul in Other Cultures." *Mosaic,* 2, 1: 10-13.

Wright, Andrew. 1989. *Pictures for Language Learning.* Cambridge: Cambridge University Press.

Appendix A
Selected Professional Organizations

The American Association for Applied Linguistics (AAAL)

7630 West 145th Street, Suite 202, Apple Valley, MN 55125 USA. Publication: Applied Linguistics. Membership: $40.00, $20.00 student. Tel.: (612) 953-0805, Fax: (612) 891-1800.

The American Association of Teachers of Esperanto (AATE)

S-ino Dorothy Holland, 5140 San Lorenzo Drive, Santa Barbara, CA 93111-2521 USA. Publications: *Quarterly Bulletin of the American Association of Teachers of Esperanto, Internacia Pedagogia Revuo*. Membership: $25.00 individual: $15.00 new member.

The American Association of Teachers of French (AATF)

Professor Fred M. Jenkins, 57 E. Armory Ave., Champaign, IL 61820 USA. Publication: *The French Review*. Membership: $45.00 individual, $17.00 student. Tel.: (217) 333-2842, Fax: (217) 333-5850

The American Association of Teachers of German (AATG)

112 Haddontowne Court # 104, Cherry Hill, NJ 08034-3662 USA, Publications: *Die Unterrichtspraxis, The German Quarterly*. Membership: $35.00. Tel.: (609) 795-5553, Fax: (609) 795-5592.

The American Association of Teachers of Italian (AATI)

Professor Pier Raimondo Baldini, Treasurer, Department of Foreign Languages, Arizona State University, Tempe, AZ 85287-0202. Publication: Italica, AATI Newsletter. Membership: $35.00 individual; $40.00 joint. Tel.: (608) 262-3941, Fax: (608) 265-3892.

The American Association of Teachers of Slavic and East European Languages (AATSEEL)

Gerard L. Ervin, Executive Director, 1933 N. Fountain Park Drive, Tucson, AZ 85715 USA. Publication: *Slavic and East European Journal*. Membership: Administrators, full and associate professors $40.00, assistant professors, instructors and lecturers $30.00, secondary school teachers $25.00, students, emeriti and unemployed $20.00. Tel.: (520) 621-9765, Fax: (520) 621-9765

The American Association of Teachers of Spanish and Portuguese (AATSP)

Dr. Lynn A. Sandstedt, Executive Director, AATSP, Fraiser Hall-Room 8, University of Northern Colorado, Greeley, CO 80639. Publications: Enlace, Hispania. Membership: $30.00 individuals; $15.00 student (maximum three years). Tel.: (970) 351-1090, Fax: (970) 351-1095.

The American Council on the Teaching of Foreign Languages, Inc. (ACTFL)

6 Executive Place, Yonkers, NY 10701-6801, USA. Publications: *ACTFL Newsletter, Foreign Language Annals*. Membership: $65.00 regular domestic member; $45.00 new teachers-domestic only; $25.00 student or retired member. Tel.: (914) 963-8830, Fax: (914) 963-1275.

Canadian Association of Second Language Teachers/L'Association canadienne des professeurs de langues secondes (CASLT/ACPLS)

176 Gloucester St., Suite 310 , Ottawa, Ontario K2P 0A6. E-mail: caslt@istar.ca

The Chinese Language Teachers Association (CLTA)

Professor Madeline Chu, 1200 Academy Street, Kalamazoo College, Kalamazoo, MI 49006 USA. Membership: $50.00. Tel.: (616) 337-7001, Fax: (616) 337-7251

Computer Assisted Language Instruction Consortium

Professor Eleanor Johnson, 014 Language Center, Duke University, Box 90267, Durham, NC 27708-0267 USA. Publication: *CALICO Journal*. Tel.: (919) 660-3180, Fax: (919) 660-3183

The Modern Language Association of America (MLA)

10 Astor Place, New York, NY 10003-6981 USA. Publications: *PMLA* (= Publications of the Modern Language Association of America), *MLA Newsletter, MLA International Bibliography* (5 volumes, annual). Membership: Variable, individual membership based on annual salary. Tel.: (212) 475-9500, Fax: (212) 477-9863

National Council of Secondary Teachers of Japanese (NCSTJ)

Professor Stephanie Wratten, PO Box 2744, Kirkland, WA 98083-2744 USA. Publication: *Oshirase*. Tel.: (718) 519-2773, Fax: (718) 519-2793.

Teachers of English to Speakers of Other Languages (TESOL)

1600 Cameron Street, Suite 300, Alexandria, VA 22314-2751 USA. Publications: *TESOL Matters, TESOL Quarterly*. Tel.: (703) 836-0074, Fax: (703) 836-7684

Appendix B
Selected Professional Journals

Athelstan Newsletter on Technology and Language Learning

2476 Bolsover, # 464 ,Houston, TX 77705 USA. Subscription: $10.00.

The Canadian Modern Language Review/La revue canadienne des langues vivantes

University of Toronto Press, 5201 Dufferin Street, North York, ON (Canada) M3H 5T8. Subscription: $26.00 in Canada and USA

The Modern Language Journal

The University of Wisconsin Press, 114 North Murray Street, Madison, WI 53715 USA. Subscription: $25.00; student subscriptions $25.00 for two years, non-renewable.

Mosaic. A Journal for Language Teachers

P.O. Box 847, Welland, Ontario, CANADA L3B 5Y5 or PO Box 890, Lewiston, NY 14092-0890 USA. Subscription: $12.00

System (An International Journal of Educational Technology and Applied Linguistics)

Elsevier Science Customer Support Department, PO Box 945, New York, NY 10010. Subscription: $289.00

Studies in Second Language Acquisition

Cambridge University Press, 110 Midland Avenue, Port Chester, NY 10573. Subscription: $50.00 individual (Available to members of the American Association for Applied Linguistics at a reduced rate).

Reprinted from: Anthony Mollica and Frank Nuessel;, "The Good Language Learner and the Good Language Teacher: A Review of the Literature and Classroom Applications," *Mosaic*, 4, 3 (Spring 1997), pp. 1, 3-16.

6 Promoting the Development of Strategic Competence in the Language Classroom

Peter J. Heffernan

Research into what strategies work best in second language learning has much to offer the classroom practitioner

Overview of Learning Strategies Research

There exists a message embedded in dubious advertising appearing periodically in mainstream media beckoning the unaware to purchase language learning products with which they are guaranteed to learn a second language almost overnight, with limited or no effort and seemingly unconsciously. On the other hand, most teachers and learners of second languages are well aware that acquiring a new language takes considerable time, effort and focus, usually involving significant immersion in the target linguistic and cultural milieu combined with formal language/culture study at home and abroad.

Learners of other languages, like other learners, also vary tremendously in their predilections, predispositions and natural proclivities and abilities. Einstein-like, some students appear almost to have been born with scientific insight. Others produce works of visual art and interpret music apparently spontaneously and in the way of virtuosos. Language learning gurus, masters of dozens of languages, the current Pope John Paul II being one living example, have also been recorded in the annals of human history. Of course, talent counts for something in all such examples. Behind the façade of talent, though, there also exist strategies or approaches to learning which work much better than others and which account, most often much more than talent, for the seemingly easy success in learning of such individuals.

Twenty years ago, the Modern Language Centre of the Ontario Institute for the Study of Education in Toronto undertook research on the good second language learner (Naiman *et al.*, 1978). Like others in that period, such as Rubin (1975) and Stern (1975), this team of researchers attempted to find the response to these nearly mystical and elusive questions: "what makes the good language learner tick?" or "what can the good language learner teach us?." We mused: if only all our students could be like the good language learner!

There is no need to downplay the significance and contribution of this research activity. As Vandergrift (1995:88) aptly suggests:

It is here that the study of language learning strategies finds its roots.

Indeed, among its most important findings, one reads that one-size-fits-all does not work as language teaching methodology. Among outstanding adult language learners, for example, it was found that development of learning techniques and strategies appropriate to their individual needs was common to all. The idea of individualization was also supported for public school classrooms where students' preferred activities and likes and dislikes were made explicit. Regarding good language learners, Rubin's work suggests they are:

- risk-takers who are willing to try informed guesses and make and learn from mistakes,
- driven communicators,
- metalinguists willing to attend to form,
- faithful practitioners who search out means to try and use the target language,
- self-regulating monitors of their new speech, contrasting it routinely with their native standard, and
- social animals with their antennae out and attuned to social context variables.
- For his part, Stern identified ten learning strategies, as follows:
- *planning strategy:* a personal learning style or positive learning strategy,
- *active strategy:* an active approach to the learning task,
- *emphatic strategy:* a tolerant and outgoing approach to the target language and its speakers,
- *formal strategy:* technical savoir-faire of how to tackle a language,
- *experimental strategy:* a methodical but flexible approach, developing the new language into an ordered system and constantly revising it,
- *semantic strategy:* constant searching for meaning,
- *practise strategy:* eagerness to practise and learn by trial and error,
- *communication strategy:* willingness to use the language in real communication,
- *monitoring strategy:* self-monitoring and critical sensitivity to language use, and
- *internalization strategy:* developing second language more and more as a separate reference system and learning to think in it.

Cohen and Hosenfield (1981) have also strongly recommended the use of introspection and retrospection as important techniques in language learning. Moore's (1977), Rivers' (1979) and, more recently, Heffernan's (1992) writings are representative published examples of such introspections/retrospections.

The early work on identification of good language learning strategies, referred to above, spawned a plethora (Hosenfeld, 1976; Pimsleur, 1980; Reiss, 1985; Wenden and Rubin, 1987; Prokop, 1989; Stevick, 1989; Galloway and Labarca, 1990; O'Malley and Chamot, 1990; Oxford, 1990; Lawson and Hogben, 1996; Gu and Johnson, 1996; Robinson, 1997) of related research activity on

- personality and cognitive styles (e.g., Prokop *et al.*, 1982),
- learner characteristics (Lalonde, Lee and Gardner, 1987),
- so called 'general language education' (Hébert, 1990; Heffernan, 1990; LeBlanc, 1990),
- multiple intelligences (Gardner, 1993),
- brain hemispheric learning research (Sousa, 1995; 1998)
- and so forth in the 1980's and 1990's and has had a major and widespread impact on current curricula for second language teaching (e.g., Alberta Education, 1991). Vandergrift (1995) provides a quite thorough synthesis of this research and theoretical focus to the mid-1990's.

Towards An Understanding of Strategic Competence

What is being focussed on essentially is the development of a specific competence in language learning, which is most appropriately called strategic competence. This concept is far from being new. Canale and Swain (1980) described such a competence, above and beyond Chomskyan (1966) linguistic and Hymesian (1972) communicative or sociolinguistic and sociocultural competence, as being the knowledge of communicative strategies, that is strategies that second language learners intend to make use of in order to get meaning across in spite of their imperfect command of the language:

- paraphrasing,
- avoidance of difficulties,
- circumlocution,
- simplifications,
- survival skills or
- coping techniques
- and so on.

Vandergrift (1995:88) further refines our understanding of the meaning of strategic competence by the distinction he makes between learning and communicative strategies. As he suggests:

> Language learning strategies are deliberate, cognitive steps used by learners to enhance comprehension, learning and retention of the target language; they can be accessed for conscious verbal report... Language learning strategies focus on techniques used to learn a language."

Communicative strategies, in contrast, focus on techniques used to communicate in the target language. In reference to the above, the former help the learner to assimilate language knowledge and skills, the latter help to negotiate meaning between speakers. In keeping with this evolving conceptual development, it is proposed here that strategic competence is manifest by second language learners' ability to exhibit, overtly and explicitly, what and how they implicitly learn to learn so as to function efficiently, effectively and creatively in a second language. Admittedly, as Wenden and Rubin (1987) point out, while some learner strategies employed may be non-observable, it is anticipated that they may be identified by learners via conscious probing, reflection, recall, introspection and retrospection, inter alia (for more such techniques, see Rubin, 1981).

Classroom Implications of Learning Strategies Research

The burgeoning research activity outlined above which has led to a current focus on the development of strategic competence has correspondingly given rise to a veritable industry of workshops, articles and monographs on coping strategies in the language classroom: helping our students learn how to learn, multiple intelligences and the second language learner, matching second language learners and their dominant learning styles, and so forth. All of this is, in fact, quite desirable, worthwhile professional activity and focus. However, for beleaguered neophyte and experienced language teaching practitioners, short on time and thirsty for practicable, theoretically sound ideas, what is essential to be retained?

The answer, it seems, is not provided easily. Learning strategy researchers and theorists, with their findings, perhaps not unsurprisingly, muddy the waters. Nothing in life is simple. Politzer and McGroarty (1985:118), for example, found that

> good behaviours may be differentially appropriate for the various types of skills related to the purpose of second language study.

Different variables can affect the choice of language learning strategies:
*   achievement,
*   level of language learning,
*   years of language study,
*   nature and difficulty of the task,
*   motivation, goal of language study,
*   method of teaching,
*   ethnic or cultural background of the learner, and
*   gender.

Prokop *et al.* (1982) had earlier arrived at similar conclusions and warn against any dogmatic statements about language learners without taking into account all the background variables. Indeed, subsequent researchers (particularly Oxford, Nyikos and Ehrman, 1988; Ehrman and Oxford, 1989; 1990; Oxford and Nyikos, 1989) suggest teachers consider use of a personality test, such as the Myer-Briggs-type indicator or MBTI, the results which can serve as a signpost to describe personality traits and assign the preferred type of training for that personality type. A couple of adaptations of such learning style tests, originally developed for an Ontario ministerial publication (1996), are included in the appendices appearing at the end of this chapter.

Learning strategies research is very extensive. Oxford's exhaustive classification scheme, for example, consists of 60 language learning strategies incorporating every strategy cited in the voluminous language learning strategies literature. Additionally, the cautionary remarks noted above must be taken into account. Accordingly, the ideas which follow regarding how to promote the development of strategic competence in the language classroom are intended as tentative and exploratory only, though research-informed and reasonably grounded in evolving theory on the subject.

Classroom practitioners need to be aware that:

- Like linguistic and communicative competence, strategic competence can be developed through teaching and learning.
- Language learning strategies can become automatic through explicit instruction and convert to implicit linguistic knowledge [or procedural knowledge], thereby facilitating language competence (Vandergrift, 1995: 98).
- Less successful differ from more successful language learners in their more limited range of language learning strategies use and in their deployment of language learning strategies not always most appropriate to the task. Hence, what successful language learners intuit to a greater degree needs to be taught explicitly to weaker language learners.
- Notwithstanding weaker language learners' more limited repertoire of language learning strategies, like successful language learners, they do use, albeit not always most appropriately, different language learning strategies and are capable of describing the strategies they use. Their strategic competence can be enhanced through explicit instruction.
- Language learning strategies can be categorized in three groups, all of which warrant explicit classroom instructional focus - cognitive, socio-affective and metacognitive language learning strategies (Oxford, 1985; 1990; O'Malley and Chamot, 1990; Vandergrift, 1995). Some specific, representative examples of each category are repeating/imitating, matching, memorizing, making associations and applying knowledge from one's maternal language (cognitive); developing a positive attitude in using the language, taking risks, cooperating with peers or the teacher, asking questions for assistance or verification/clarification (socio-affective); and using selective attention, organizing one's learning, monitoring one's learning and evaluating one's own progress (metacognitive). These are described in more detail in Alberta Education (1991: 30-34) and Vandergrift (1995: 95).

Cognitive language learning strategies can be made operative, for example, in the following ways/contexts in the classroom:
developing sound pronunciation skills/habits

- imitation, mimicry
- building vocabulary - using the dictionary to determine the meaning of a word, activation of newly learned words, matching vocabulary words with pictures, using informed guessing to devise meaning of words similar in the mother tongue and target language.
- developing grammatical awareness/precision in use - making complete sentences from two column lists, matching sentences that have the

same meaning but are said or written differently, such as, "I have lots of books/I have many books."

- developing aural comprehension (listening) skills - contextual guessing, clumping together of known material so as to attend to the unknown, recognizing semantic patterns, using one's ability and experience to anticipate contextual elements, inferencing.
- developing oral production (speaking) skills -rehearsing an oral text produced by the students themselves or by others, using circumlocution or asking for help with a word or phrase (just as one would in one's mother tongue).
- developing reading comprehension skills -using contextual classes to assist in the comprehension of a text, skimming or scanning written texts for information (e.g., headlines, sub titles, keywords, italics), using one's knowledge about text genre to determine the type of text
- developing written expression skills -note-taking for future reference, transferring style features for forms of writing from the mother tongue that are appropriate to the target language.

Socio-affective language learning strategies might be made operative in ways such as the following:

- developing sound pronunciation skills/habits -openness by way of exposure to regional and other dialect varieties, understanding and accepting that approximative pronunciation patterns may not be understood and may be corrected or need to be repeated.
- building vocabulary - recognizing and accepting semantic differences and similarities across languages (e.g., cognates, 'faux amis').
- developing grammatical awareness/precision in use - openness to feedback, willingly entering activities with peers and the teacher which are designed to reinforce/develop automatisms in grammar patterns, seeking clarification/ verification regarding the grammaticality of a sentence.
- developing aural comprehension (listening) skills - tolerance of ambiguity, openness to cultural clues and patterns that might differ from those in the mother tongue, actively searching out opportunities to hear the target language spoken (e.g., radio and TV broadcasts, second-language clubs).
- developing oral production (speaking) skills -active participation in cooperative learning activities, participation in impromptu skits/debates, acceptance in self and others of pause, hesitations, backtracking and such as normal practices in oral discourse, actively searching out situations in which to use the target language.
- developing reading comprehension skills -tolerance of ambiguity, openness to cultural clues and patterns that might differ from those in the mother tongue, self-selecting outside class reading opportunities in the target language.

- developing written expression skills -openness to feedback, peer review, self-evaluation (using grids, for example).

Metacognitive language learning strategies might be promoted in the following ways:

- developing sound pronunciation skills/habits
- contrasting one's own approximative patterns of pronunciation with those of a native speaker role model, self-correcting.
- building vocabulary - paying attention to word formation, skillful use of dictionaries, vocabulary building using semantic maps.
- developing grammatical awareness/precision in use - conscious awareness of one's own errors.
- developing aural comprehension (listening) skills - going from getting the main idea (gist) to understanding specific details, hypothesizing, attending to key information in a text.
- developing oral production (speaking) skills -brainstorming, group problem-solving.
- developing reading comprehension skills -going from getting the main idea (gist) to understanding specific skills, attending to key information in a text/ using selective attention.
- developing written expression skills -discerning differing written styles/patterns in diverse written genres, note-taking.

Conclusion

Teachers ignore at their peril focusing on development of strategic competence among learners in their second language classroom. Considerable research demonstrates that language learning strategies vary in their usefulness and applicability dependent on such variables as: achievement, motivation, level of language learning, years of language study, method of teaching, nature and difficulty of the task, ethnic or cultural background of the learner and gender, among possible others yet to be identified. All the same, it is clear that all language learners, successful and less successful, use a variety of language learning strategies and are capable of describing them. Moreover, developing strategic competence enhances over time learner's linguistic and communicative competence. It is clearly the second language teacher's responsibility, given what is known at this time about cognitive, socio-affective and metacognitive strategies for language learning, to help students become cognizant of strategy use and subsequently apply this knowledge. Teachers can help both more and less successful students broaden their strategies repertoire (i.e., enhance their strategic competence) and, in particular, help weaker language learners learn to make choices of strategies use more appropriate to the task at hand.

It is likely that second language classrooms where teachers focus tentatively and carefully on the development of strategic competence, in addition to linguistic and communicative competence, will result also in less frustrated learners and more satisfied teachers. This seems a reasonable payback for some worthwhile, research-substantiated and theoretically-sound activity in the classroom.

Appendix

Kinaesthetic Learning Style	Auditory Learning Style	Visual Learning Style
tries things out, touches , feels, and manipulates	talks about what to do	looks around and examines situations
expresses feelings physically, jumping for joy, pushing, tugging, pounding	expresses emotion by shouting for joy, blowing up verbally, or varying tone, pitch, and volume	is less exuberant than the kinaesthetic/tactual learner
shows emotion through facial expression, staring when angry and beaming when happy	enjoys listening but cannot wait to get a chance to talk	thinks in pictures and detail
asks questions during and after a presentation	likes to recite information;	may be quiet
seems easily distracted	thinks in sounds and is easily distracted by sounds	can easily be distracted by visual disorder or movement
is a poor listener and loses interest in a long speech		may be impatient when asked to listen
stands very close to a person to whom he/she is listening or speaking	may mouth the words silently while reading	
	recalls lists of words better when they are presented orally	can recall lists of words better when they are presented visually
may start the day off looking neat and tidy but becomes dishevelled through physical activity		is neat in appearance
gestures while speaking		
may write neatly initially but loses that neatness as h/she runs out of space on the paper		has good handwriting
needs to write down words to determine if they "feel" right	uses a phonics approach in spelling	recognizes words by their configurations
	tends to remember names but forgets faces	has a vivid imagination
		likes to take notes

Questionnaire on Learning Styles

Teachers should present this questionnaire in a way that is not threatening to students and does not make comparisons among them. It is recommended that the teacher read the questions aloud with the students and clarify them if necessary.

Learning Styles Questionnaire

This is a questionnaire to help you find out how you learn best. There are no wrong answers.

Answer the following questions quickly. If you agree strongly circle A. If you sometimes agree, circle B. If you disagree, circle C.

A = strongly agree   B = sometimes agree C = disagree

1. Once I hear a song, I can recognize the tune the next time I hear it.   A B C
2. I recognize a voice on the phone very quickly.   A B C
3. I understand the person speaking if I watch him/her closely.   A B C
4. I enjoy watching others dance.   A B C
5. I pour and carry full cups easily and do not spill liquids.   A B C
6. When I climb stairs, I look ahead rather than at my feet.   A B C
7. I think a diagram or picture is better than an explanation.   A B C
8. Noises from the outside interfere with my ability to concentrate.   A B C
9. If an article is illustrated with pictures, it helps hold my interest.   A B C
10. When riding a bicycle, I can look to the side without turning the handlebars in the direction I am looking.   A B C
11. I can walk in the complete dark and not bump into anything.   A B C
12. When I dial a telephone number, I notice if there is an unusual ring.   A B C
13. I am very aware of the fine tuning and colour on the TV.   A B C
14. I decide that my hair needs washing by the way it feels.   A B C
15. I can easily remember faces.   A B C
16. I do well on a test if it is about information we have talked about in class.   A B C
17. Good sound quality is important to me when I listen to the radio or stereo.   A B C
18. I enjoy going barefoot and walking in sand or grass, if it is safe.   A B C
19. I can remember a license-plate number long enough to write it down an hour later.   A B C
20. The texture of the material is important to me when I buy clothes.   A B C
21. I would rather receive a phone call from a friend than get a letter.   A B C

Scoring the Questionnaire

If most of your answers to statements 5, 6, 10, 11, 14, 18, and 20 are A, you tend to learn by doing.

If most of your answers to statements 1, 2, 8, 12, 16, 17, and 21 are A, you tend to learn by listening.

If most of your answers to statements 3, 4, 7, 9, 13, 15, and 19 are A, you tend to learn by seeing.

If most of your answers are B in one of these three groups, that is probably your backup system.

If most of your answers are C in one of these groups, that is probably not the way you prefer to learn.

References

Alberta Education. 1991. *French as a Second Language Teacher Resource Manual.* Edmonton, Alberta: Alberta Education.

Canale, M. and Swain, M. 1980. "Theoretical bases of communicative approaches to second language teaching and testing." *Applied Linguistics*, 1, 1: 1-47.

Chomsky, N. 1966. "Linguistic Theory." In R.B. Mead Jr., ed., *Language Teaching: Broader Contexts. Northeast Conference on the Teaching of Foreign Languages: Reports of the Working Committees.* New York: MLA Materials Centre, 43-49.

Cohen, A. and C. Hosenfeld.1981. "Some uses of mentalistic data in second-language research." *Language Learning*, 31: 285-313.

Ehrman, M. and R. Oxford. 1989. "Effects of sex differences, career choice and psychological type on adult language learning strategies." *The Modern Language Journal*, 73, 1: 1-13.

Ehrman, M. and R. Oxford. 1990. "Adult language learning styles and strategies in an intensive training setting." *The Modern Language Journal*, 74, 3: 311-327.

Galloway, V. and A. Labarca. 1991. "From student to learner: Style, process and strategy." In D. Birckbichler, ed., *New Perspectives and New Directions in Foreign Language Education.* Lincolnwood, Illinois: National Textbook Co., 111-158.

Gardner, H. 1993. *Multiple Intelligences: The Theory in Practice.* New York: Harper Collins.

Gu, Y. and R. K. Johnson. 1996. "Vocabulary learning strategies and language learning outcomes." *Language Learning*, 46, 4: 643-679.

Hébert, Y., *et al.* 1990. *Syllabus formation langagière générale.* Ottawa, Ontario: Canadian Association of Second Language Teachers.

Heffernan, P.J. 1990. *National Core French Study: Summary Report/Étude nationale sur les programmes de français de base: Abrégé de l'Étude.* Ottawa, Ontario: Canadian Association of Second Language Teachers.

Heffernan, P.J. 1992. "Language learning remembered." *Alberta Modern Language Journal*, 29, 1: 16-19.

Hosenfeld, C. 1976. "Learning about learning: Discovering our students' strategies." *Foreign Language Annals*, 9: 117-129.

Hymes, D. 1972. "On communicative competence." In J.B. Pride and J. Holmes, eds., *Sociolinguistics: Selected readings.* Harmondsworth: Penguin Books, 269-293.

Lalonde, R.N., P.A. Lee, and R.C. Gardner. 1987. "The common view of the good language learner: An investigation of teachers' beliefs." *The Canadian Modern Language Review*, 44, 1: 16-34.

Lawson, M.J. and Hogben, D. 1996. "The vocabulary-learning strategies of foreign-language students." *Language Learning*, 46, 1: 101-135.

LeBlanc, R., *et al.* 1990. *National Core French Study - A Synthesis/Étude nationale sur les programmes de français de base - Rapport synthèse.* Ottawa, Ontario: Canadian Association of Second Language Teachers.

Moore, T. 1977. "An experimental language handicap (personal account)." *Bulletin of the British Psychological Society*, 30: 107-110.

Naiman, N., M. Frölich, H.H. Stern, and A. Todesco. 1978. *The Good Language Learner.* Toronto, Ontario: OISE.

O'Malley, J.M. and A.U. Chamot. 1990. *Learning Strategies in Second Language Acquisition.* Cambridge: Cambridge University Press.

Ontario Ministry of Education. 1996. *French for Communication.* Toronto, Ontario: Ministry of Education.

Oxford, R., M. Nyikos, and M. Ehrman. 1988. "Vive la différence? Reflections on sex differences in use of language learning strategies." *Foreign Language Annals*, 21, 4: 321-329.

Oxford, R. and M. Nyikos. 1989. "Variables affecting choice of language learning strategies by university students." *The Modern Language Journal*, 73, 3: 291-300.

Oxford, R. 1985. *A New Taxonomy of Language Learning Strategies.* Washington, DC: ERIC Clearinghouse on Languages and Linguistics.

Oxford, R. 1990. *Language Learning Strategies: What Every Teacher Should Know.* New York: Newbury House.

Pimsleur, P. 1980. *How to Learn a Foreign Language.* Boston, MA: Heinle and Heinle.

Politzer, R.L. and McGroarty, M. 1985. "An exploratory study of learning behaviours and their relationship to gains in linguistic and communicative competence." *TESOL Quarterly*, 19,1: 103-123.

Prokop, M., D. Fearon, D. and B. Rollet, 1982. *Second Language Learning Strategies in Formal Instructional Contexts.* Edmonton, Alberta: University of Alberta.

Prokop, M. 1989. *Learning Strategies for Second Language Users.* Queenston, Ontario: Edwin Mellen Press.

Reiss, M. 1985. "The good language learner: Another look." *The Canadian Modern Language Review*, 41: 511-523.

Rivers, W.M. 1979. "Learning a sixth language: An adult learner's daily diary." *The Canadian Modern Language Review*, 36: 67-82.

Robinson, P. 1997. "Individual differences and the fundamental similarity of implicit and explicit adult second language learning." *Language Learning*, 47, 1: 45-99.

Rubin, J. 1975. "What the good language learner can teach us." *TESOL Quarterly*, 9: 41-51.

Rubin, J. 1981. "Study of cognitive processes in second language learning." *Applied Linguistics*, 11, 2: 117-131.

Sousa, D. A. 1995. *How the Brain Learns.* Thousand Oaks, CA: Corwin Press.

Sousa, D.A. 1998. *Learning Manual for How the Brain Learns.* Thousand Oaks, CA: Corwin Press.

Stern, H.H. 1975. "What can we learn from the good language learner?" *The Canadian Modern Language Review*, 25: 9-21.

Stevick, E. 1989. *Success with Foreign Languages: Seven Who Achieved It and What Worked for Them.* New York: Prentice-Hall.

Vandergrift, L. 1995. "Language learning strategy research: Development of definitions and theory." *Journal of the CAAL/Revue de l'ACLA*, 17, 1: 87-104.

Wenden, A. and J. Rubin. 1987. *Learner Strategies in Language Learning.* Englewood Cliffs, N.J.: Prentice-Hall.

Reprinted from: Peter J. Heffernan, "Promoting the Development of Strategic Competence in the Language Classroom." *Mosaic*, 5, 4 (Summer 1998): 1, 3-8.

7 Nonverbal Communication: How important is it for the Language Teacher?

W. Jane Bancroft

Nonverbal communication in the language classroom can have dramatic results — not only on the students' liking for the subject but also in the cognitive domain. Research shows that the personality and expectations of the teachers, their gestures, tone of voice and facial expressions have an important effect on language acquisition.

The term "nonverbal" is commonly used to describe all events of human communication that transcend spoken or written words. Nonverbal communication is said by researchers to be important because of the role it plays in the total communication system, the tremendous quantity of information cues it gives in any particular situation, and because of its use in such fundamental areas of our daily life as politics, medicine, the arts, advertising, television, job interviews, courtship and education. It has been said, for example, that when we receive contradictory messages on the verbal and nonverbal levels, we are more likely to trust and believe in the nonverbal message. It is assumed that nonverbal signals are more spontaneous, harder to fake and less apt to be manipulated. (It has also been speculated that those who prefer nonverbal cues over verbal ones show a right-brain dominance.) Estimates have it that, in a normal two-person conversation, the verbal components carry less than 35 per cent of the social meaning of the situation; more than 65 per cent of the social meaning is carried at the nonverbal level.

Learning has a cognitive domain, an affective domain, and a psychomotor domain. The cognitive domain of learning deals with the attainment of knowledge and the acquisition of intellectual and analytical abilities and skills. The affective domain is concerned with teaching effects which have some "emotional overtone": student likes and dislikes, attitudes, values, beliefs, appreciations and interests. (The third domain, the psychomotor domain, emphasizes muscular or motor skills and is mainly concerned with the student's ability to reproduce a neuromuscular coordination task.) In most learning environments, attention is usually focused on the cognitive domain. The affective domain, centred around the creative of positive feelings, is, however, very important in the media age. The nonverbal as well as the verbal messages that teachers employ have an important effect on students' liking for the teacher, the subject matter, and the discipline area.

As was shown by Rosenthal in *Pygmalion in the Classroom* (1968), expectations can be transmitted nonverbally, and subtle nonverbal influences in the classroom can have dramatic results. According to Neill (1991: 79), enthusiastic instructors use more marked nonverbal signals, such as gestures and range of intonation, than would be normal in informal social interaction. (They also tend to give much more intense listening signals (Neill 1991: 87). Andersen and Andersen (1982) found that half of the variation in student liking for teachers was associated with the kind of nonverbal communication the teachers employed. Teachers who use positive gestures, eye contact and smiles produce interpersonal closeness, reduce psycho-logical distance, and have a positive impact on student performance. At the secondary and university levels, videotape studies suggest effective teachers convey more enthusiasm nonverbally than average or ineffective teachers. It has been found that effective language instructors of university courses make more use of nonverbal signals to focus student attention on important points, to demonstrate or illustrate points they are making, and to encourage students by approaching them. Average teachers are more likely to use directing or threatening signals or to show anxious signals (Neill 1991: 66).

According to Lozanov's Suggestopedia (1978, 1988), "double-planeness" is a very important factor in education. The teacher's body language and tone(s) of voice are instrumental in the educational process, as is the physical and social environment. The teacher should have the confidence and the artistic presentation skills of the trained actor. Attention should be paid to classroom design (wall colours, seating arrangements, etc.) as it has a definite influence on student participation, performance and learning in the classroom. So, too, does the "social environment", consisting of the staff of the educational institution.

According to Mark Knapp (1980: 4-11, 21), the theoretical writings and research on nonverbal communication can be divided into the following seven areas:
1. kinesics or body motion;
2. physical characteristics (including physique or body shape, general attractiveness, clothing);
3. touching behaviour or haptics (tactile communication is probably the most basic or primitive form of communication);
4. paralanguage (including voice qualities and vocalizations);
5. proxemics (the study of the use and perception of social and personal space);
6. artifacts (including the use of objects such as jewellery and cosmetics and other decorations that may serve as nonverbal stimuli);
7. the environment or environmental factors within which the interaction occurs.

An eighth category, oculesics, or the study of messages sent by the eyes, is another important area for nonverbal communication. The areas which are especially important for education in general and language teaching in particular are:

- kinesics
- paralanguage
- proxemics
- the environment and
- oculesics.

According to Knapp (1980: 98, 115), we initially respond much more favourably to those whom we perceive as physically attractive than to those who are seen as less attractive or ugly. Higher-ranked clothing is associated with an increase in rank, whereas lower-ranked clothing is associated with loss of rank. According to Dhority (1992: 56), the teacher's mode of dress is very important; appearance and dress are part of the total nonverbal stimuli that influence interpersonal responses between teacher and students. While tactile communication is considered by many to be the most effective form of communication, and while therapeutic methods employed to put individuals "in touch" with themselves and others continue to enjoy popularity, touching behaviour in today's society can – and increasingly does – elicit negative or hostile reactions. The use of haptics, therefore, puts teachers at risk.

Kinesics

Kinesics is communication that occurs via body movement, for example:

- gestures
- posture
- movements of the head and body
- facial expressions.

According to Ekman and Friesen (1969a), categories of nonverbal behavioural acts are:

- emblems
- illustrators
- affect displays
- regulators, and
- adaptors.

i) Emblems

These are stylized nonverbal acts or signs that have a direct or specific verbal translation or dictionary definition, usually consisting of a word or two or a phrase. They are usually produced with the hands, but they may also be produced by the face. There is general agreement among members of a culture or subculture on the verbal "translation" of these signals. Culture-specific emblems appear to be learned very much the way language vocabulary is learned, and they are usually performed with awareness and with an intent to communicate a specifiable message.

Because they originate within cultures, emblems may cause particular difficulties for the international traveller and for the foreign language student. The meaning the traveller has for a gesture may not be shared by the citizens of the host country. If one is to travel successfully and/or be truly competent in communication in a foreign language, one needs to learn the gestures (especially emblems) of the foreign country or culture (Wylie 1977). Emblems may also pose a problem in classes where a given language (say, English or French) is being taught as a second language to students of various cultures whose emblematic gestures are very different from those used by the instructor (Neill 1991: 134).

ii) Illustrators

These are nonverbal acts or signs that are intimately linked to spoken discourse and serve to illustrate (or amplify on) what is being said verbally. Illustrators are done primarily with the hands, but they can also be done with the head, the face, and the total body. Patterns of illustration appear to be learned in the family which, in turn, reflects the larger social or cultural pattern. Mediterranean peoples, for example, use more illustrative gestures than do Anglo-Saxons. In all, six major types of illustrators have been identified:

- pointers
- pictographs
- spatials
- kinetographs
- batons, and
- ideographs.

The pointer simply points to some present object in the sense of "I want that one." The pictograph draws a picture of the referent in the air. According to Neill (1991: 69), pantomiming, which is frequently used in the classroom – especially the language classroom – is allied to pictographs; it involves demonstrating an action with a standardized imaginary object. The spatials show size or depict a spatial relationship. The kinetographs recreate some bodily action. The batons are movements which accentuate or punctuate; they beat out the tempo of the verbal statement (e.g. "I really [gesture] mean it [gesture]"). Ideographs trace the flow of an idea. They tend to be rolling or flowing movements that help the receiver see the connection between ideas or the direction in which a line of thought is moving.

Many factors can alter the frequency with which illustrators are displayed. More illustrators are used, for example, in face-to-face communication than over an intercom; more illustrators are used in "difficult" communication situations when words fail or when the potential receiver is unable to comprehend the intended message. Individuals who are excited and enthusiastic display more illustrators than do those who are not. Research has shown that effective teachers who are involved with their ideas and who play a theatrical role in the classroom use a great many illustrative gestures (Neill 1991: 153). Suggestopedic teachers are trained to use gestures in their presentation of the lesson material and pantomime to suggest the meaning of new words in the foreign language (Bancroft 1975; Lozanov 1978, 1988).

iii) Affect Displays

These are nonverbal signs or sign patterns that display affective or emotional states. The face is the primary source of affect (i.e., it is considered the primary site for communication of emotional states); however, the body can also be read for global judgments of emotion. Affect displays can repeat, augment, contradict, or be unrelated to verbal affective statements. Affect displays are often not intended to communicate (i.e. they are involuntary), but they can be intentional.

Certain display rules – cultural and professional – are learned regarding facial expressions, although these rules are not always present at a conscious level of awareness when we use them. Although the face is capable of making hundreds of distinct movements and communicating many emotional states, those displays that have been uncovered by virtually every researcher since 1940 (and which are called primary affect displays) are:

- surprise
- fear
- anger
- disgust
- happiness
- sadness, and
- interest.

In addition to information about specific emotions, people also seem to judge facial expressions primarily along the following dimensions:

- pleasant/unpleasant;
- active/passive; and
- intense/controlled.

The face is a multi-message system, which can communicate information regarding one's emotional state(s) and personality as well as interest and responsiveness during interaction. It is a particularly important means of communication in the classroom. One of the most powerful (and most positive) cues is the smile on the face. A smile may temper a message that may otherwise be interpreted as extremely negative. A smile is one of the primary ways by which affiliativeness is communicated and may produce positive therapeutic effects in relationships. A teacher who smiles frequently communicates "immediacy"; i.e., warmth, closeness, spontaneity and enthusiasm (Andersen and Andersen, 1982) and, since smiles are reciprocal behaviours, invites smiles in return. Students at all levels are sensitive to smiles as a sign of positive interest and concern.

iv) Regulators

These are nonverbal acts or signs that maintain and regulate the give and take of speaking and listening between two or more interactants. They tell the speaker to continue, repeat, elaborate, hurry up, become more interesting; they give the other person a chance to talk; and so on. Familiar regulators associated with turn-taking include head nods, hand movements, and eye behaviour. Some of the behaviours associated with greetings and leave-takings may be regulators to the extent that they indicate the initiation or termination of face-to-face communication. Regulators seem to be on the periphery of our awareness and are generally difficult to inhibit. While they have an involuntary nature when we use them personally, we are very much aware of these signals when they are sent by others.

Head nodding is a kinesic behaviour that communicates "immediacy," especially when head nods are used by a listener to respond to a speaker (Andersen and Andersen, 1982). It is believed that in both primates and human beings, head nods originated as ritual bowing gestures which signal submission and approachability. Research indicates that head nods are approval-seeking behaviours and tend to be used to increase communication and friendliness. Head nods are used by effective classroom teachers to communicate warmth, spontaneity, and enthusiasm and to provide reinforcement to students. These nods provide a student with feedback that the teacher is listening to, and understanding his/her communication.

v) Adaptors

Adaptors are nonverbal markers that originate in the satisfaction of self needs, such as eating, cleansing oneself, rubbing tired eyes. Adaptors are not intended for use in communication as such, but they may be seen when a person is alone or they may be triggered by verbal behaviour in a given situation associated with conditions that occurred when the adaptive habit was first learned. (For the observer, the adaptor may have sign value; it may be an informative indicator of the performer's inner state.)

Ekman and Friesen (1969a) identified three types of adaptors:

- self-directed
- object-directed, and
- alter-directed.

Self-adaptors refer to manipulations of one's own body, such as holding and rubbing. These self-adaptors will often increase as a person's anxiety level increases. Alter-adaptors are learned in conjunction with our early experiences with interpersonal relations -giving to, and taking from another, attacking or protecting, establishing closeness or withdrawing. Object-adaptors involve the manipulation of objects and may be derived from the performance of some instrumental task - such as writing with a pencil. There may be a close link between body-touching and preoccupation with oneself, reduction of communicative intent and withdrawal from interaction. Teachers who use too many adaptors convey tenseness and uncertainty.

Some of the investigations of body movements and posture have examined various communication outcomes rather than specific types of nonverbal behaviour. These outcomes or communicative goals include:

1. attitudes of liking/disliking
2. status and power
3. deception.

According to Mehrabian (1972: 16-30), liking is distinguished from disliking, and positive attitudes from negative attitudes toward another or others by more forward lean, a closer proximity, more eye gaze, more openness of arms and body, more direct body orientation, more touching, more postural relaxation and more positive facial and vocal expressions. Insofar as kinesics is concerned, postural relaxation and open body positions communicate increased warmth or "immediacy." Folding one's arms and holding one's legs tightly together communicate defensiveness and coldness. The use of an arms-akimbo (hands on hips) position by a standing communicator is indicative of dislike. Teachers who are tense and anxious and who maintain closed body positions are perceived as cold, unfriendly and not very responsive; they communicate negative attitudes to their students. Andersen and Andersen (1982) found that more "immediate" college teachers demonstrate more relaxed body positions.

Other investigators have explored similar liking/disliking behaviours under the labels of "warm/cold." Warmth indicators include a shift of posture toward the other person, a smile, direct eye contact, and hands remaining still. A "cold" person looked around the room, slumped, drummed fingers, and did not smile. Warmth cues were effective in increasing verbal output from the other person.

Kinesic "immediacy" is also communicated through more gestural activity. Howard Rosenfeld (1966, 1967) found that smiles, head-nodding and a generally higher level of gestural activity characterized approval seekers. Mehrabian (1971) found that more hand and arm gestures per minute were a part of communicating greater affiliation with others. Andersen and Andersen (1982) found that more "immediate" college teachers employed more overall body movement. In contrast, as reported in Neill (1991: 33), uncertain teachers communicate their uncertainty to the class by "movements of escape," i.e., agitated, jerky movements, as opposed to the smooth movements of the confident individual. Some researchers believe that people who have very similar attitudes will share a common interaction posture, whereas non-congruent postures may reflect attitudinal or relationship distance. It has been shown that posture sharing (the extent to which teachers and students assume symmetrical body positions) has a positive effect on student-teacher rapport (Andersen and Andersen 1982). Generally speaking, we do communicate interpersonal attitudes of liking and disliking, warmth and coldness, persuasion and affiliation, through our body movements. Properly used gestures (especially expansive ones) communicate interest and warmth, not only in interpersonal interactions and therapy, but also in teaching. Gestures not only help the teacher to illustrate ideas, but also convey more enthusiasm for his or her subject area.

According to Knapp (1980: 138), Mehrabian's work provides us with information concerning the role of status in kinesic communication. Generally speaking, high-status or dominant persons are associated with less eye gaze, postural relaxation, greater voice loudness, more frequent use of arms-akimbo, dress ornamentation with power symbols, greater territorial access, more expansive movements and postures, and greater height and more distance. Teachers should be aware of research in this area and, while they should not strive to be too "authoritarian," they must, according to Lozanov (1978), play the dominant or leadership role in the classroom.

An increasing number of researchers are asking which nonverbal cues are linked to deception and/or convey a negative image. Nonverbal behaviours linked to deception and which are to be avoided by teachers include:

- higher pitch;
- less gaze duration and longer adaptor duration;
- fewer illustrators (less enthusiasm)
- more hand-shrug emblems (uncertainty);
- more adaptors (especially face play adaptors) and less nodding;
- more speech errors;
- a slower speaking rate; and
- less immediate positions relative to their partners (Knapp 1980: 140; Ekman and Friesen 1969b).

Nonverbal signals such as bodily signs of nervousness and vocal signs of stress may contradict speech, and leak information that the teacher is uncertain, has low expectations for, or limited interest in a particular student. Because of a lack of conscious awareness, emotions which a teacher would prefer to remain hidden may be revealed by "nonverbal leakage" (Neill 1991: 8). Teachers who wish to have a positive impact on their students should follow Lozanov's advice and consciously create a harmony between the verbal and nonverbal elements of their presentations in the classroom.

Oculesics

The study of messages sent by the eyes is called oculesics. Throughout history we have been preoccupied with the eye, its expression of human emotion, and its effects on human behaviour. Our fascination with the eyes has led to the exploration of almost every conceivable feature of the eyes (size, colour, position) and the surrounding parts (eyebrows, circles, wrinkles). One important area of research (and one that relates to pedagogy) is concerned with eye contact (mutual glances, visual interaction, gazing or the line of regard).

Gaze refers to an individual's looking behaviour, which may or may not be at the other person, whereas mutual gaze refers to a situation in which the two interactants are looking at each other, usually in the region of the face. Gazing and mutual gazing can be reliably assessed. What should be considered "normal" gazing patterns will vary according to the background and personalities of the participants, the topic, the other person's gazing patterns, objects of mutual interest in the environment, and so on. According to Knapp (1980: 185 ff.), gazing involves regulating the flow of

- communication
- monitoring feedback concerning others' reactions
- expressing emotions
- communicating the nature of the interpersonal relationship.

Gazing and mutual gazing is often indicative of the nature of the relationship between two interactants. With all other variables held relatively constant, it has been found that gazing and mutual gazing are moderate with a very high-status addressee, maximized with a moderately high-status addressee, and minimal with a very low-status addressee (Knapp, 1980: 188-89). Gaze is related to dominance in adults of both sexes (Neill, 1991: 39).

Eye contact communicates interested and friendly involvement with another/others. Generally speaking, we seem to gaze more at people we like (Mehrabian, 1972; Knapp, 1980: 189). Therapist warmth is related to more glances at patients. Extroverts seem to gaze more frequently than introverts and for longer periods of time, particularly when they are talking. A person who is trying to be persuasive will generally look more. We gaze more when we are interested in someone else's reaction and when we are interpersonally involved. Listeners seem to judge speakers with more gaze as more persuasive, truthful, sincere and credible. It has been found that speakers rated as sincere had an average of 63.4 per cent eye gaze, whereas those who were rated insincere had an average of 20.8 per cent (Knapp, 1980: 194).

Eye contact, then, is an invitation to communicate. Numerous researchers have shown eye contact and gaze to be important components of "immediacy." (For example, Argyle (1967: 105-116), found that perceptions of intimacy were, in part, a function of increased eye contact.) Eye contact performs an important monitoring function which communicates to others that one is "taking account of them," is available for, or open to communication, and/or is really involved in the discussion, once it begins.

Andersen and Andersen (1982) have found that eye contact is an important part of teacher "immediacy." Avoiding the gaze of the "audience" by constantly looking at one's notes conveys a lack of enthusiasm and a lack of competence. Teachers who use more eye contact can not only more easily monitor and regulate their classes (gaze is a feature of dominant behaviour), they can also communicate more warmth and involvement to their students. (Absence of visual attention is perceived as unwillingness to become involved; fixing the gaze on one or two individuals at the expense of others may be interpreted as favouritism). Greater eye contact increases the opportunity for communication to occur and enables the teacher to respond to the many nonverbal behaviours of students such as eye-closing, for example, a sign that the student is closing off incoming stimuli. Teachers should position themselves so that they can and do establish eye contact with every student in the class. It is probable that "immediacy" cannot be successfully communicated by a teacher in the absence of eye contact.

Paralanguage or Vocalics

Paralanguage (i.e., language alongside of language) deals with *how* something is said, as opposed to *what* is said; vocalics deals with the nonverbal elements of the human voice. Paralanguage or vocalics encompasses the range of nonverbal vocal cues surrounding common speech behaviour. According to Trager (1958), paralanguage has the following components:

  a) voice qualities (including such things as pitch range, rhythm, tempo, articulation, resonance);
  b) vocalizations (including vocal characterizers, vocal qualifiers and vocal segregates).

Vocal characterizers comprise such elements as

- laughing
- crying
- sighing
- yawning
- coughing
- groaning
- yelling
- whispering

Vocal qualifiers include

- intensity (over loud to over soft);
- pitch height (over high to over low) and extent (extreme drawl to extreme clipping)

Vocal segregates are related to the somewhat broader category of speech nonfluencies and include such things as "uh-huh," "um," "ah," and variants thereof.

Work on such topics as silent pauses and intruding sounds would also be included in this category.

Numerous research efforts have been aimed at determining whether certain personality traits are expressed in one's voice, and whether others are sensitive to these cues. Studies of content-free speech indicate that the voice alone can carry information about the speaker and his or her emotions, and that emotional meanings can be communicated accurately by vocal expression. (For example, affection can be conveyed by a soft, low, resonant voice speaking at a slow rate, with a regular rhythm, steady and slight inflection and slurred enunciation (Knapp, 1980: 217). Speakers vary in their ability to produce expressed emotion. Some people are more conscious of, and have more control over their expressive behaviour. Individuals who have a high degree of self-monitoring behaviour are better able to express emotions intentionally in both vocal and facial channels (Knapp, 1980: 215).

In addition to its role in personality and emotional judgments, the voice also seems to play a part in retention and attitude change; this has been primarily studied in the public speaking situation. Typical prescriptions for use of the voice in delivering a public speech include:

1. use variety in volume, rate, pitch, and articulation;
2. decisions concerning loud-soft, fast-slow, high/low or precise-sloppy should be based on what is appropriate for a given audience in a given situation;
3. excessive nonfluencies are to be avoided.

Nonfluencies and hesitations are likely to be interpreted by a listener as symptoms of stress and uncertainty; overuse may reduce the speaker's credibility, appearance of competence, and effectiveness.

It is clear that we can communicate various attitudes with our voice alone – for example, friendliness, hostility, superiority, submissiveness. Mehrabian and Williams (1969) conducted a series of studies on the nonverbal correlates of intended and perceived persuasiveness. Extracting only findings on vocal cues, the following seem to be associated with both increasing intent to persuade and enhancing the persuasiveness of a communication:

- more intonation
- more speech volume
- higher speech rate and
- less halting speech.

A speaker's perceived credibility may profoundly affect his or her persuasive impact.

Vocalic communication is an important nonverbal element in the classroom. According to Neill (1991: 74), effective teachers use more varied and more animated intonation than ineffective teachers who use more neutral intonation. Great importance is attached in Suggestopedia to the voice qualities and intonation(s) of the language teacher. In the presentation of the lesson, the teacher is expected to vary the pitch, loudness and tempo of his or her speech in the manner of a well-trained actor. During the "concert session," the voice has to be positioned correctly so that a soft, soothing, persuasive tone is achieved for the artistic reading of the lesson-text over a background of baroque music. In a series of studies it has been shown that interpersonal liking is, in large part, a function of vocal cues (as well as facial cues), rather than verbal/content ones. Voices which are expressive, enthusiastic and varied (particularly in pitch and tempo) seem to convey the greatest "immediacy."

Another vocal behaviour which communicates interpersonal "immediacy" is laughing. Considerable literature exists indicating that this vocal characterizer operates physiologically as a tension reducer and contributes to relaxation, especially during tense interactions. As reported in Andersen and Andersen (1982), an early study by Barr (1929) found that "good" teachers engaged more often in laughter, including laughing along with the class. According to Neill (1991: 90), effective teachers use a mixture of self-deprecating and pupil-directed humour. (Self-directed humour on its own is seen as weakness, pupil-directed humour alone as stern and/or sarcastic). It seems that teachers who are more willing to laugh with their students communicate more warmth and spontaneity to the class.

Vocal cues frequently play a major role in determining responses in human communication situations in general and in the classroom in particular. Vocal cues do not only concern *how* something is said; frequently (like other nonverbal cues), they *are what* is said. Teachers should pay heed to Lozanov's advice: there should be a harmony between the vocal message and the verbal message.

Environmental Factors

This category concerns those elements that impinge on the human relationship but are not directly a part of it. Environmental factors include the furniture, architectural style, interior decorating, lighting conditions, colours, temperature, additional noises or music and the like, within which the interaction occurs. Variations in arrangements, materials, shapes, or surfaces of objects in the interacting environment can be extremely influential in our lives and in the outcome of an interpersonal relationship as well as of a teaching situation.

Mehrabian (1976) argues (like Lozanov) that we react emotionally to our surroundings and that the nature of our emotional reactions can be accounted for in terms of how aroused (i.e., stimulated, active and alert) the environment made us feel, how pleasurable (or satisfied) we felt and how dominant (or submissive) we are made to feel. Environments that are novel, surprising, crowded and complex will probably produce feelings of higher arousal. According to Knapp (1980: 54-55), more intimate communication is associated with informal, unconstrained, private, familiar, close, and warm environments.

Each environment is made up of three major components:
1. the natural environment – geography, location, atmospheric conditions;
2. the presence or absence of other people; and
3. architectural and design features, including movable objects.

Insofar as the natural environment is concerned, temperature fluctuations and changes in humidity and barometric pressure have an impact on groups and individuals. According to scientific investigations, monotonous weather is more apt to affect one's spirits; seasonally one does one's best mental work in late winter, early spring and fall; and the ideal work temperature should be neither too high nor too low. Classroom temperature should be maintained between 66 degrees and 72 degrees Fahrenheit, according to Todd-Mancillas (1982), in order to assure optimal performance when students are engaged in mental and physical activities. During winter months, classroom humidity should not fall below 30 per cent or rise above 50 per cent, as humidity levels either above or below this range are associated with student illness and absenteeism. Serious effort should be made to provide air conditioning in the classroom during the summer months.

Other people can be perceived as part of the environment and will have an effect on one's behaviour. These people may be regarded as "active" or "passive" participants, depending on the degree to which they are perceived as "involved" in one's conversation (by speaking or listening). The presence of others may increase our motivation to "look good" in what we say or do, which may either be detrimental (information-distorting) or beneficial. Lozanov, as has been mentioned above, emphasizes the importance of the social environment, as well as the physical one.

Insofar as architectural and design features are concerned, a greater sense of well-being and energy has been found in rooms that are well-appointed or beautiful, as opposed to neutral or ugly (Maslow and Mintz, 1956; Mintz, 1956). Well decorated, attractive classrooms convey warmth and excitement to students, whereas a drab, depressing classroom suppresses student enthusiasm and spontaneity. To facilitate positive classroom interactions, educators should select and arrange in an aesthetically pleasing fashion furnishings and other artifacts which lend a pleasant ambiance to the learning environment. The presence of plants and art objects (as in suggestopedic language classrooms), as well as an appearance of neatness and the attractive arrangement of furniture, all have an impact on students' comfort level and performance. Students, where appropriate, should also be encouraged to contribute "art work" to the classroom (Todd-Mancillas 1982).

Studies have provided evidence on the impact of visual-aesthetic surroundings on the nature of human interaction in the following areas: colour, sound, lighting, movable objects, structure and design.

Colour

Findings from environmental research suggest that colours, in conjunction with other factors, influence moods and behaviour. Although optimal use of colour probably varies as a function of context and individual preference, according to Mehrabian (1976: 90), the most pleasant (and relaxing) hues are blue and green, and the most arousing hues are red, orange and yellow. There is a body of educational and design literature which suggests that carefully planned colour schemes have an influence on scholastic achievement. For younger students, classrooms should be painted warm colours, including yellow, peach and pink, while for older students (secondary school age and older), classrooms should be painted cooler colours, including blue and blue-green (Todd-Mancillas 1982). Lawrence Rosenfeld (1977) summarizes research done by Ketcham (in 1958) establishing empirical support for the proposition that learning is affected by variations in colour of classroom environments. Children's IQ scores can be dramatically affected by variations in classroom colour. Those playing in warm, bright-coloured rooms experience an IQ gain while the reverse is true for children playing in white, black or brown rooms. In addition, students feel more pride when attending schools with refurbished colour schemes. Todd-Mancillas (1982) suggests that, when it is not possible to repaint classrooms, every effort should be made by teachers to incorporate colour variations in the actual learning and testing materials.

Sound

The types of sounds and their intensity also affect interpersonal behaviour. A large enclosed space – such as an open classroom – creates a relatively hostile acoustic environment for the purposes of teaching (Neill 1991: 122), although carpeting can reduce the noise of impact from students' feet, the movement of furniture, etc. and partitions can attenuate noise levels. According to Mehrabian (1976: 49-51), music can have a strong and immediate effect on arousal level and pleasure. Generally speaking, the more pleasant the music, the more likely we are to engage in "approaching" rather than "avoiding" behaviour. According to Todd-Mancillas (1982), playing soothing music is one means of generating positive emotions and cooperative behaviour. The effect of slow, simple, soft and familiar sounding music is to lower our arousal levels while maintaining pleasure and eliciting an easygoing and satisfying feeling. Since there is a positive correlation between soothing music and the heightening of pleasant interactions, music helps to establish suitable class moods and counteract class boredom. In addition, according to Lozanov (1978, 1988) and Schuster and Gritton (1986), the use of suitable music in the classroom stimulates memory and memorization (of language materials, for example).

Lighting

Lighting also helps to structure our perceptions of an environment, and these perceptions may very well influence the types of messages we send. If we enter a room that has dim lighting, we may talk more softly and presume that more personal communication will take place there. Bright lights, on the other hand, are more apt to be arousing, add to initial discomfort in interacting with strangers, and thus lead to less intimate interaction. Whenever possible, in the classroom, ordinary reduced-spectrum fluorescent lighting should be avoided with either incandescent or full-spectrum fluorescent lighting used instead (Todd-Mancillas, 1982). In the atmosphere of fluorescent lighting, children experience significantly greater nervous fatigue, eye strain, anxiety, irritability, lapses of attention, hyperactivity, and decreased classroom performance. Many educators have expressed the belief that natural light sources are preferable to artificial light sources and that all classrooms should have windows, preferably ones that open. In any event, static lighting systems which disallow modification of light intensity or hues, regardless of the weather conditions or the classroom activity, and which make for marked contrasts between lit and unlit areas, are to be avoided. Individuals seek maximum control over their physical environment. When they are prevented from exercising this control, there is frequently a diminishing quality of their work and interpersonal relationships (Todd-Mancillas, 1982). Lighting in the classroom, as in the best restaurants, should be adjusted to minimize jarring harshness and to communicate a sense of comfort.

Movable Objects

Since the arrangement of certain objects in our environment can help structure the communication that takes place there, we often try to manipulate objects in order to bring about certain types of responses. The desk seems to be an important object in the analysis of interpersonal communication. Most classrooms have a desk separating the students and their teacher, and it has been shown that student-teacher relationships are affected by desk placement. (A desk can be not only a physical barrier but also a psychological one.) Researchers have labelled environments which separate communications as sociofugal and environments which bring communicators together as sociopetal (Andersen and Andersen, 1982). (Sociofugal classrooms include fixed seating in rows, teachers hidden behind podiums, and hard chairs for students). "Unbarricaded" professors have been rated by students as more willing to encourage the development of different student viewpoints, as ready to give individual attention to students who need it, and as less likely to show undue favouritism. Teachers who want to convey warmth and "immediacy" must ascertain if the classroom has physical (or psychological) barriers which reduce communication.

Structure and Design

Architecture can also have an affect, whether positive or negative, on human interaction. Like office buildings and dormitories, classrooms tend to be constructed from a standard plan; they are rectangular in shape with straight rows of chairs. Classroom seats are often permanently attached to the floor for reasons of tidiness and ease of maintenance. Most classrooms have some type of partition (usually a desk) that separates the teacher from the students. Overall classroom structure and design can have a definite impact on student-teacher behaviour.

Traditional row and column arrangements are appropriate in those instances where listening and note taking are the preferred instructional activities (Sommer, 1977). Modular arrangements are appropriate for facilitating multiple small group interactions, such as those that occur when students are divided into several small groups and all are working independently toward the resolution of a given problem (Todd-Mancillas, 1982). Sommer found that the odds of a student participating in class discussion are slightly greater for small classes. In seminar rooms, most participation comes from students who are seated directly opposite the instructor. In straight-row rooms, the following observations have been made:

1. students within eye contact range of the instructor participated more;

2. there was a tendency for more participation to occur in the centre sections of each row and for participation to decrease from the front row to the back (this tendency, however, was not evident when interested students sat in locations other than those that provided maximum visual contact with the instructor);

3. participation decreased as class size increased (Sommer, 1969, 1974).

It has been found that high verbalizers tend to select seats in the zone of participation more than low or moderate verbalizers (Knapp 1980: 67ff). As reported in Neill (1991: 113) high verbalizers are also likely to be the most dominant individuals. Central seats in university classes are the most strongly defended if someone else takes them during a break; the central group of students is also more committed to learning.

Since spatial distance, proximity and setting can have a great impact on human interaction and communication, teachers should consider arrangements that reduce the number of students who are seated behind other students. For purposes of encouraging discussion among the greatest number of students, a circular or horseshoe arrangement is preferred, with the instructor at the head. As in the original suggestopedic language class, this arrangement fosters interaction among the students, but also maintains the instructor as a moderator in control (Harrison, 1974: 153-54; Bancroft, 1975). Insofar as group interaction is concerned, the more visual information one has about other group participants, the more likely one is to engage in verbal exchanges with them (Todd-Mancillas, 1982). Teachers should also move around the classroom to establish contact with all their students. Environment influences our behaviour, but we can also alter environments to serve our own communication goals.

Proxemics

Proxemics is generally considered to be the study of our use and perception of social and personal space. The influence of architectural features on residential living units and on communities is of concern to those who study human proxemic behaviour. Our personal space orientation is sometimes studied in the context of conversational distance and how it varies according to sex, status, roles, cultural orientation and so forth. The term "territoriality" is frequently used in the study of proxemics to denote the human tendency to stake out personal territory – or untouchable space – much as do animals and birds in the wild.

Our use of space (our own and others') can dramatically affect our ability to achieve certain desired communication goals. In *The Hidden Dimension* (1966), Edward Hall identified three types of space:

- fixed-feature space, the type created by immovable walls and objects;
- semi-fixed feature space, created by large objects such as chairs and tables;
- informal space, the bubble of personal space individuals carry with them as they move from interaction to interaction.

He further classified informal space into four subcategories:

- intimate
- casual-personal
- social-consultative, and
- public.

Intimate distances (at least for Americans) range from actual physical contact to about 18 inches; casual-personal extends from 18 inches to 4 feet; social-consultative (for impersonal business) ranges from 4 to 12 feet; and public distance covers the area from 12 feet to the limits of visibility or hearing. Spatial relationships in cultures other than American, with different needs and different norms, may, however, produce different distances for interacting.

Distance is said to be based on the balance of approach and avoidance forces. Factors modifying the distances we choose include:

1. age and sex;
2. cultural and ethnic background;
3. topic or subject matter (pleasant topics attract);
4. setting for the interaction (lighting, temperature, noise and available space affect interaction distance);
5. physical characteristics of one's interaction partner;
6. attitudinal and emotional orientation (subjects choose closer distances when interacting with a "friendly" person);
7. characteristics of the interpersonal relationship (as status is associated with greater space or distance in our culture, those with higher status have more and better space and greater freedom to move about);
8. personality characteristics (closer distances are seen when people have a high self-concept, high affiliative needs, are low on authoritarianism and are "self-directed") (Knapp, 1980: 82 ff).

In addition to studying human spatial behaviour in overcrowded situations and in conversation, some researchers have examined such questions in the context of meetings or small groups – particularly with regard to seating patterns. The study of seating behaviour and spatial arrangements in small groups is known as small-group ecology.

It appears to be a cultural norm that leaders are expected to be found at the head or end of the table. Cooperation seems to elicit a preponderance of side-by-side choices in seating. Spatial orientation and seating selection are influenced by

- age and sex;
- motivation (as motivation for contact and conversation increases, persons want to sit closer to, or have more eye contact with another/others);
- introversion/extroversion (extroverts choose to "sit opposite" and disregard positions which would put them at an angle; introverts generally choose positions that keep them at a distance, both visually and physically) (Knapp, 1980: 90 ff).

It is clear that our perceptions and use of space contribute extensively to communication outcomes.

At least two proxemic cues are thought to signal warmth and spontaneity during communication and create a positive atmosphere in the classroom:

a) reduced or closer physical distance between teacher and students;

b) body angle of the teacher in the classroom.

Since researchers have found that communicators stand closer to people they like than to those they dislike, closer distances result in more positive attitudes and establish greater teacher/student contact and closeness in the classroom. Many teachers, according to Andersen and Andersen (1982), fail to establish much interpersonal closeness with a class because they remain physically remote. Standing at the front of the room or sitting behind a desk are all too common forms of teacher behaviour. In these "remote" positions, it is quite difficult for a teacher to develop a close relationship with a class, even if the teacher wants to develop such a relationship. Nervous, insecure teachers establish their "territory" around their desk, whereas confident teachers use the entire room and frequently move among their students. As reported in Neill (1991: 111), "itinerant" teachers are viewed as more encouraging and more supportive of students' ideas.

The second proxemic behaviour that signals closeness and warmth is body angle or body orientation. More "immediacy" is communicated when two or more interactants face one another (Andersen and Andersen (1982). Many teachers do not fully face their class when teaching. They hide behind desks, podiums and tables and often continuously write on the blackboard, with their backs to the students. Not only does this behaviour reduce the "immediacy" between teachers and their classes, it also removes any visual communication between the teacher and the class members. In this situation, the teacher cannot see behaviour problems, fails to receive any nonverbal communication from the students, and cannot field questions or comments. Experienced teachers learn to do most of their blackboard work before the class begins and spend the largest amount of their teaching time facing their "audience."

According to Knapp (1980: 231 ff), the ability to send and receive (encode and decode) nonverbal cues accurately is essential for developing social and professional competence. Effective senders of nonverbal signals are outgoing, active and popular. According to research findings, individual teachers (among other professionals) who were rated "excellent" at their jobs did well on the PONS instrument (the Profile of Nonverbal Sensitivity, developed by Robert Rosenthal, which measures nonverbal decoding ability). Much of the ability we have in sending and receiving nonverbal signals is derived from motivation, attitude, observation, and experience.

It is well established in the study of interpersonal communication that nonverbal behaviours can communicate feelings of warmth and positive emotions (Andersen and Andersen, 1982). Of the three domains of learning, nonverbal "immediacy" behaviours have their most powerful impact on affective learning. However, since affective learning influences cognitive achievement, the skilled use of nonverbal communication probably has positive effects on cognitive learning as well (Andersen and Andersen, 1982).

Students feel more positively disposed towards teachers who are skilled in the positive use of nonverbal communication. In fact, half of the variance in college student liking for an instructor could be accounted for by "immediacy" behaviours of the teacher (Andersen and Andersen, 1982). A study of college student preferences indicated that responding warmly to students was a major characteristic of an ideal teacher. In contrast, college students responded very negatively to a formal, "nonimmediate" instructor. Across many grade levels, it has been observed that creating a friendly atmosphere is one of the most important elements in establishing good teacher-student relationships.

"Immediate" teachers (i.e., those who are warm, spontaneous and friendly) also produce a more positive student attitude toward the course, the subject matter, and the educational institution. As reported in Neill (1991: 158), a nonverbally positive teacher is regarded by students as more effective. College students are more likely to enrol voluntarily in future classes in the same subject area when the instructor is "immediate." On the other hand, researchers found a greater percentage of students interested in dropping a class after a session with an instructor who was formal and "nonimmediate" (Andersen and Andersen, 1982).

Teacher "immediacy" is also associated with more class participation. A variety of experimental studies have consistently supported the finding that subjects in conditions with more "immediate" interactants are more likely to engage in greater amounts of verbal interaction. When college students were given a description of an instructor, 56 per cent of the students initiated interaction with the instructor when the latter was described as warm, while only 32 per cent initiated interaction when the instructor was described as cold (Andersen and Andersen, 1982).

Students are also more likely to engage in continued reading and studying when the teacher is "immediate." A strong relationship has been reported for secondary school students between affiliative behaviours of teachers and self-initiated work by students. A more "immediate" teacher is more persuasive. Andersen and Andersen (1982) found that students of more "immediate" teachers are more willing to engage in the communication strategies suggested in the course.

While some researchers suggest that a genuinely warm, positive attitude towards students is probably a prerequisite for a teacher to communicate "immediacy" successfully, others have found that teachers who were trained to be more enthusiastic did, indeed, develop more enthusiastic attitudes towards teaching (Andersen and Andersen, 1982). Nonverbal skills may be acquired (or improved upon) by observation and imitation of model-teachers, by self-observation and/or by specific training or instruction. Direct training approaches which focus on specific behaviours are considered more effective than indirect training, which aims to change more general personality attributes. According to Neill (1991: 157), effective direct training courses in nonverbal communication contain at least two of the following four elements: presentation of theory, training in discriminating nonverbal signals, modelling of the skills involved, and practice of the new skills with feedback. Since teacher "immediacy" behaviours have the potential to make the teacher and the learning environment more attractive to the student, it is important that all teachers have an awareness of, and skill in nonverbal communication. Clearly, knowledge of research in nonverbal communication is essential for the language teacher.

References

Andersen, P. and J. Andersen. 1982. "Nonverbal Immediacy in Instruction." In L.L. Barker, ed., *Communication in the Classroom*. Englewood Cliffs, N.J: Prentice-Hall, pp. 98-120.

Argyle, M. 1967. *The Psychology of Interpersonal Behaviour*. London: Penguin Books.

Bancroft, W.J. 1975. "The Lozanov Language Class." *ERIC Documents on Foreign Language Teaching and Linguistics*. 53 pp. in microfiche. ED 108 475.

Dhority, L. 1992. *The ACT Approach*. New York: Gordon and Breach.

Ekman, P. and W.V. Friesen. 1969a. "The Repertoire of Nonverbal Behaviour: Categories, Origins, Usage and Coding." *Semiotica*, 1: 49-98.

Ekman, P. and W.V. Friesen. 1969b. "Nonverbal Leakage and Clues to Deception." *Psychiatry*, 32: 88-106.

Hall, E.T. 1966. *The Hidden Dimension*. New York: Doubleday & Co.

Harrison, R.P. 1974. Beyond Words: *An Introduction to Nonverbal Communication*. Englewood Cliffs, N.J: Prentice-Hall.

Knapp, M.L. 1980. *Essentials of Non-verbal Communication*. New York: Holt, Rinehart and Winston.

Lozanov, G. 1978. *Suggestology and Outlines of Suggestopedy*. New York: Gordon and Breach.

Lozanov, G. and E. Gateva. 1988. *The Foreign Language Teacher's Suggestopedic Manual*. New York: Gordon and Breach.

Maslow, A.H. and N.L. Mintz. 1956. "Effects of Aesthetic Surroundings: I. Initial Effects of Three Aesthetic Conditions Upon Perceiving 'Energy' and 'Well-Being' in Faces." *Journal of Psychology*, 41: 247-54.

Mehrabian, A. and M. Williams. 1969. "Nonverbal Concomitants of Perceived and Intended Persuasiveness." *Journal of Personality and Social Psychology*, 13: 37-58.

Mehrabian, A. 1971. "Verbal and Non-verbal Interaction of Strangers in a Waiting Situation." *Journal of Experimental Research in Personality*, 5: 127-38.

Mehrabian, A. 1972. *Nonverbal Communication*. Chicago: Aldine-Atherton.

Mehrabian, A. 1976. *Public Places and Private Spaces*. New York: Basic Books.

Mintz, N. L. 1956. "Effects of Aesthetic Surroundings: II. Prolonged and Repeated Experience in a 'Beautiful' and an 'Ugly' Room." *Journal of Psychology*, 41: 459-66.

Neill, S. 1991. *Classroom Nonverbal Communication*. London: Routledge.

Rosenfeld, H.M. 1966. "Instrumental Affiliative Functions of Facial and Gestural Expressions." *Journal of Personality and Social Psychology,* 4: 65-72.

Rosenfeld, H.M. 1967. "Nonverbal Reciprocation of Approval: An Experimental Analysis." *Journal of Experimental Social Psychology,* 3: 102-111.

Rosenfeld, L. B. 1977. "Setting the Stage for Learning." *Theory into Practice,* 16: 167-73.

Rosenthal, R. and L. Jacobson. 1968. *Pygmalion in the Classroom.* New York: Holt Rinehart and Winston.

Schuster, D.H. and C.E. Gritton. 1986. *Suggestive-Accelerative Learning Techniques.* New York: Gordon and Breach.

Sommer, R. 1969. *Personal Space.* Englewood Cliffs, N.J: Prentice- Hall.

Sommer, R. 1974. *Tight Spaces: Hard Architecture and How to Humanize It.* Englewood Cliffs, N.J: Prentice- Hall.

Sommer, R. 1977. "Classroom Layout." *Theory into Practice,* 16: 174-75.

Todd-Mancillas, W.R. 1982. "Classroom Environments and Non-verbal Behavior." In L.L. Barker, ed., *Communication in the Classroom.* Englewood Cliffs, N.J: Prentice-Hall, pp. 77-97.

Trager, G.L. 1958. "Paralanguage: A First Approximation." *Studies in Linguistics,* 13, 1-12.

Wylie, L. 1977. *Beaux Gestes: A Guide to French Body Talk.* Cambridge, MA: The Undergraduate Press.

Reprinted from: W. Jane Bancroft, "Nonverbal Communication: How important is it for the Language Teacher?" *Mosaic,* 4, 4 (Summer 1997): 1, 3-12.

8 Study Skill Suggestions for Students of Foreign Language Classes

Paul Cankar

As a part-time instructor at Austin Community College I have had the opportunity to conduct Study Skills Workshops for students taking foreign language classes. In my workshops, I have focused mainly on three topics:

1. Tips on how to study effectively at home for the class;
2. How to benefit from in-class time; and
3. What many foreign language instructors expect from their students.

Here are some of the ideas and suggestions I have shared with students in the workshops.

Tips on how to study effectively at home for the class:

1. *Find an atmosphere which works best for you.*

   Study with friends or a study group vs. studying alone.

   Study at home vs. the library.

   Study with quiet vs. having music in the background or head-phones.

   Always have good lighting.

   Have ready supplies and reference materials (books, dictionary, pens, paper, etc.)

2. *Know exactly what it is you should be concentrating on.*

3. *Periodically reward yourself.*

   Don't feel guilty about taking a short break to have a snack, make a telephone call, watch the news, look at a magazine or the newspaper or watch a television program.

   By rewarding yourself during study sessions, you'll study for a longer period of time and you'll accomplish a lot more. Sometimes you need to get away from the material to clear your mind and/or relax. Or course, take breaks in moderation!

4. *New vocabulary words.*

   Learning new vocabulary is an important part of learning a foreign language. You might want to try a few of these ideas:

   Flash cards: Using index cards, write the word in the target language on one side and the English equivalent on the other.

   Lists: Using the vocabulary lists in your textbook, or those supplied by your teacher, cover the target language column. Begin at the top of the list, working your way down. At each English word, write and say its equivalent in the target language. Each time you miss a word, go to the top of the list and repeat the procedure.

Categorize: If the vocabulary lists aren't already in categories (such as nouns, adjectives, verbs - or -places, foods, etc.), you may want to group your new words into categories to help you learn them.

Colour: On your flashcards, use one colour for all masculine nouns and another colour for all the feminine nouns.

Sentences: Create sentences with the new words you want to remember.

Label: Label objects in your house or apartment.

Repeat: Repeat the new vocabulary words aloud.

Write: Write the new vocabulary words over and over.

Record: Record on tape the new words and their definitions.

Use context: Let the context help you. Use the phrase or sentence to help figure out the meaning of a new word or expression.

5. *Work with new verbs*: Learning and working with new verbs is an important part of learning a foreign language. You might want to try the following ideas:

   Use colour: On your flash cards (or any other method you choose) use certain colours for certain verb infinitive endings. The use of colour can also be incorporated into conjugating the verbs by using specific colours for specific subject-related endings.

6. *Keep up with the material.* Don't let things go by without looking at the book or supplementary materials, such as the workbook.

7. *Remember that you cannot cram the night before for a foreign language exam!*

8. *Get used to spending some time* **every day** *with your foreign language textbook.* Try to devote extra time on the weekends to studying. Since language learning is a gradual, continual process, you need to approach the material with steady, consistent study habits.

9. *If you have cable TV, watch some shows in the target language.* Don't worry about understanding everything that is said. Practise your listening skills concentrating on the rhythm and sounds of the language.

10. *Rent foreign films from the video store.* If possible, watch the films with other students.

11. Since language learning is a building process, *review past materials* while you're learning new materials.

12. *Don't think that you have to be perfect.* Set some short goals that are challenging but not unreasonable.

How to benefit from in-class time:

1. *Never feel embarrassed or afraid to ask questions.* If your teacher makes you feel uncomfortable, he or she has a problem - not you.

2. *Come to class prepared.* Read over the materials to be covered before coming to class.

3. *Listen attentively and pay special attention to points which the teacher refers to as "important or significant."*

4. *Sometimes, referring to your native language can be helpful, but at other times it isn't.*

   You'll often be faced with structures, vocabulary, sentence structure, etc., in the language that seem odd, even ridiculous. Keep an open mind and remember that you're dealing with a new language and its contents - not your native language.

5. *Don't feel awkward, silly or embarrassed about trying to pronounce the new language as your teacher does or as you hear it on tape.*

6. *When working in pairs or groups, speak in the target language, avoid going off task or reverting to English and chatting.*

   Take advantage of the time in class (with your classmates and teacher present) to work with the language.

7. *Listen for mistakes of your classmates.*

   Paying attention to their mistakes may help you avoid making them yourself.

8. *Paraphrase.*

   If you don't know the target language equivalent for a certain word, use other words to describe it or to get your point across. For example, if you couldn't remember the word for "party", you could say "a celebration with food and music." This is called circumlocution.

What many foreign language instructors expect from their students.

1. *Since teachers have different expectations, pay attention to what is in the class syllabus.*

   There are a variety of things which instructors may deem important: attendance, participation, no late homework or compositions, no make-up quizzes or tests, etc. Focus on what it is that your instructor expects from you and give it back to your instructor.

2. *Attend all classes, and be on time.*

   All instructors would love to have every student attend every class session. If for any reason you cannot attend class, notify your instructor before the class period.

3. *Come to class as well-prepared as possible.*

   This doesn't necessarily mean that you have the new material down completely, but that you have made an attempt to learn the material before coming to class.

4. *Since language is communication, try to get used to participating actively in class.*

   This involves answering questions when called on, volunteering answers, and asking questions when you don't understand something.

5. *Do the workbook activities and the lab book activities.* This involves taking time to go to the library and listening to (or borrowing copies of) the audio or video cassettes.
6. *Cooperate and be flexible with your instructor, and be supportive of your fellow classmates.*
7. *Keep the lines of communication open between you and your instructor.* For example, if you're having problems keeping up due to your heavy work schedule or you were "less than perfect" in class because you were up all night writing a paper, let your instructor know. Don't let your instructor draw false conclusions about you.*

*The article was originally published in *The Forum of Phi Sigma Iota*, 8, 1 (Spring 1996), p. 11-12. It is reprinted in *Mosaic* with permission of the Editor, Pennie A. Nichols-Alem.

Reprinted from: Paul Cankar, "Study Skill Suggestions for Students of Foreign Language Classes." *Mosaic.* 4, 3, (Spring 1997), pp. 18-19.

9 Ten Ways to Cope with Foreign Language Anxiety

Philip Donley

Although most of our readers do not suffer FLA (Foreign Language Anxiety), as tutors and teachers, many of us know people who do. Pass these helpful hints on to FLA afflicted students!

☐ Do you frequently feel nervous or apprehensive in your foreign language class?

☐ Do you often freeze when your instructor calls on you?

☐ Do you inexplicably go blank when taking a test in the foreign language?

☐ Do you dread your foreign language class so much that you are tempted to skip class or drop the course?

If you answered "yes" to one or more of these questions, you may suffer from foreign language anxiety.

If foreign language anxiety is a serious problem for you, you may want to use a few strategies to help you manage your anxious feelings. Ten coping strategies are listed below. Some of the strategies may be more effective for you than others, and you may find that certain combinations of strategies are especially useful for you. The right strategies to use are, of course, the ones that feel right and work best for *you*.

Coping strategies

1. *Discuss your feelings with other students.*

   You may feel more comfortable in your language class if you find out that other students empathize with your feelings.

2. *Tell your instructor how you feel.*

   Your instructor may be able to give you a different perspective on your learning experience. Also, your instructor may be much more understanding than you expect; remember, your instructor has probably been a language student too.

3. *Do something fun and relaxing.*

   Go for a walk, go to a movie, listen to your favourite music, participate in a sport. The possibilities are endless. Sometimes all you need do to alleviate your anxiety is to take your mind off your class for a few minutes or hours.

4. *Eat healthful food and get enough rest and exercise.*

If you haven't been taking care of your body, you may be especially susceptible to anxiety.

5. *Make sure you're prepared for class.*

You will probably feel less nervous while taking a test or when your instructor calls on you if you feel well-prepared. You may want to prepare an organized study and practice schedule for yourself.

6. *Attend every class.*

Learning a language is less stressful if you learn a little bit every day. If you skip class, you will miss important information and valuable practice. When you return to class and have to catch up with your classmates, you may feel anxious and overwhelmed.

7. *Keep your foreign language class in perspective.*

If you're doing poorly in one facet of the class, take some time to think of other parts of the class in which you *are* doing well. Also, remember that your life consists of more than your foreign language class. Remind yourself of those areas of your life in which you *do* feel relaxed and confident.

8. *Seek out opportunities to practise the foreign language.*

The more confidence you gain in using the language, the less apprehensive you will be about using it in class. You may want to build your skills by conversing with native speakers, practising with more advanced students, or writing a pen pal.

9. *Remember that errors are a part of language learning.*

Errors are a natural part of language learning. Even educated native speakers make errors occasionally, so don't expect yourself to be perfect. Don't be afraid to take a few risks in order to learn.

10. *Develop your own standards and rewards for success.*

While grades are important, what you learn is more important. Set reasonable learning goals for yourself, and reward yourself for small successes along the way.*

*The article was originally published in *The Forum of Phi Sigma Iota*, 8, 1 (Spring 1996), p. 13. It is reprinted in this issue of *Mosaic* with permission of the Editor, Pennie A. Nichols-Alem.

Reprinted from: Philip Donley, "Ten Ways to Cope with Foreign Language Anxiety." *Mosaic*, 4, 3 (Spring 1997): 17.

10 Climate Setting in Second-Language Classrooms

Cher Evans-Harvey

A positive classroom climate enhances language acquisition, but how do teachers create an atmosphere conducive to learning? This paper suggests ways of establishing a positive classroom climate.

Introduction

In recent years there has been a lot of discussion about effective schools. Three studies refer directly to the climate or culture within the school as having an impact on learning. Mark Holmes, Kenneth Leithwood and Donald Musella (1989) outlined the following characteristics of effective schools:

- strong leadership aimed at academic achievement,
- an academic climate of high expectations,
- regular monitoring of student achievement,
- a safe, orderly and pleasant environment.

J. Howard Johnston (1984) and his colleagues also found that:

> Effective schools emerge from a complex set of cultural and social factors that focus attention on academic performance, support academic growth in a manner consistent with the developmental stage of the youngster, and build an intellectual community that rewards and reinforces academic pursuits in its public rituals and in its private interactions. It is the creation of the culture [...] that will enhance student learning and produce long-term school improvements. (p. vii)

Johnston and Ramos de Perez (1985) also identified positive (not remedial) school environments as one of fourteen characteristics of effective schools. Although more information is available on school climate, very little has been written on classroom climate and on how to establish a positive, relaxed and happy climate that is conducive to learning. Language teachers are very aware that a positive classroom climate enhances language acquisition. Authors such as H. D. Brown (1987), Adelaide Heyde (1979), Marjorie MacKinnon (1988) and Moos and Tricket (1987) make reference to positive classroom climate enhancing second-language acquisition.

The purpose of this paper is:

- to clarify the meaning of classroom climate,
- to relate four aspects of school climate to the climate in language classrooms, and

- to suggest ways of establishing a positive climate in the language classroom.

Definition

Lawrence Lezotte *et al.* (1979) define climate as the norms, beliefs and attitudes reflected in institutional patterns and behavioral practices that enhance or impede student achievement. Borich (1988), in his commonly used text in teacher education programs, defines classroom climate as

> the atmosphere or mood in which interactions between teacher and students take place. Classroom climate, for example, will determine the manner and degree to which a teacher will exercise authority, show warmth and support and allow for independent judgement and choice. (p. 277)

Malcolm Knowles (1984), a leading theorist of adult education contends that

> There are seven elements or procedures which the teachers of adults have to consider. The first, and the prerequisite one, deals with establishing a climate that is conducive to learning. This means providing experiences in an atmosphere in the classroom, workshop or institute in which the learners feel respected and in which they feel secure, supported, non-threatened, collaborative rather than competitive, trusting of one another and trusting of the teacher, liked, cared about, cared for, comfortable, informal, relaxed. These conditions are more conducive to learning than their opposites: cold, aloof, rigid, one-way transmission, judgemental, competitive. Creating such a climate conducive to learning is a step not usually considered in traditional education. The students walk into the room and the transmission of content starts. No time is given to creating feelings of respect and trust. (p. 92)

Four Dimensions of Classroom Climate

J. Howard Johnston and Maria Ramos de Perez (1983), in their paper "Four climates of Effective Middle Level Schools" outlined four climates common to effective schools:

- the physical climate,
- the academic climate,
- the organization climate, and
- the social-emotional climate.

Discussion of the four climates with direct reference to language classrooms offers language teachers ideas for improving the climate in their classrooms.

Physical Climate

Although language teachers teach in a variety of settings that range from their own classrooms to makeshift facilities, they should work towards providing learning areas that are well-lit and bright. The area should be well-maintained, safe and clean. Furniture should be appropriate to the age of the children. The air temperature and ventilation should be considered. It should be visually appealing with pictures and posters of the target language as well as student work displayed in an attractive manner. Given good facilities and evidence that learning the language is valued, the classroom environment is enhanced.

Academic Climate

There are five features to consider in improving the academic climate.

1. *People talk about academics.*
   Language teachers should ask students questions about their academic performance and show their interest in student success. They should talk about strategies for learning languages and organizing materials. They should ask students to help them solve problems.

2. *Academic achievements are recognized and rewarded.* Language teachers should display student work in the classroom and in the halls. Achievement should be rewarded liberally. Smiles, encouraging words, stickers, happy-grams, certificates, medals, and graduation gifts for top students should be given for learning languages.

3. *Academics form the basis for leisure pursuits.* Language clubs provide students with the opportunity to socialize in the target language and explore the culture in cooperative projects. Inter-provincial and international exchanges and visits provide similar opportunities.

4. *Expectations are high but reasonable, and failure is tolerated.* Language teachers should be aware of the abilities and feelings of the students. They should ask students to demonstrate new skills without an audience, or practice with their peers in a small group setting.

5. *Teachers use time wisely.* Language teachers should provide for maximum engaged learning time by organizing activities that are intrinsically interesting, require active cognitive engagement and are at a level that will benefit the student.

Organizational Climate

Four characteristics of organizational climate within effective schools can be related directly to the language classroom.

In these schools there are few rules, but those that exist are clear reasonable and fair. In the classroom, rules such as respect yourself and others, cooperate, do your best and treat other people the way you would like to be treated indicate values that promote learning.

The Student Council plays a dual role of influencing school policy and securing opportunities for student participation in the events of the day. The language teacher should promote the activities and events organized for the language program, making sure that class representatives and the Student Council are aware of what is planned so they, in turn, can promote them in the school. Activities such as field trips, concerts by singers, musicians, actors or storytellers, special assemblies or invited guests will have a more positive impact if the students themselves are involved in the planning and promotion of these activities.

Another important feature of effective schools is the belief students hold that the school is responsive to their concerns and feelings. This is manifest in the language classroom. The teacher should talk to the students and be responsive to their concerns about learning the language, the type and difficulty of assignments and evaluation

Finally, with respect to organizational climate   in effective schools, Johnson and Ramos de Perez (1983) found that teachers make major decisions about curriculum, students, special events and finances. Language teachers should make decisions that promote the language program. Examples could be integrated units, decisions about which students would be placed in split grades, what special events could be planned for the year, how the language budget would be spent and whether fundraising activities would be appropriate.

Social-Emotional Climate

Johnston and Ramos de Perez (1983) found that the social-emotional climate has a profound effect on the life of the school, the academic quality of its programs and the effectiveness of the teachers and students. These characteristics will be discussed with direct application for a language classroom.

The classroom should be encouraging, welcoming, supporting and positive. Teachers should try to find the good in each student even though their strengths may not lie in language learning. Valuing student achievement in language learning as well as in other subject areas, in sports, dance, music or drama, helps students increase their self-esteem. Adelaide Heyde (1979), suggests that teachers really can have a positive and influential effect on both the linguistic performance and the emotional well-being of the student.

The classroom should be a secure place where students feel safe from physical, psychological and emotional harm. A classroom should have a high level of comfort where students feel free to take risks, make mistakes and learn with each other without fear of put-downs or being laughed at by their peers or criticized by the teacher.

Language teachers should anticipate student needs and fill them without fanfare. Attention should be given to grouping students, to adjusting curriculum for gifted and for disabled learners, to making each person feel like a valued and important member of the class. Attention to student needs is proactive as many disruptive situations can be prevented.

Classrooms should be trusting places. Students are trusted to make important decisions about their learning in terms of choices, behaviour and evaluation of their progress. Language teachers could build in choices of activities, assignments and presentations. They could include a self-evaluation component into the course as well as contracts for learning and comportment.

Finally, classrooms should be civil places. Teachers should emphasize excellence, reward achievement and offer students intellectual tasks that are appropriate for their development in a comfortable learning environment. The students would be relaxed, happy and friendly.

Johnston and Ramos de Perez (1983) conclude that climate affects the quality of schooling to a great degree and that the creation of a school culture is mostly dependent on the behaviour of the adults in the school. It follows, then, that the climate in the language classroom affects the quality of the language learning and that the creation of a positive climate is dependent on the behaviour of the language teacher.

What can language teachers do to create and promote positive climates in the classroom?

A key factor is to know the students well: their characteristics, interests, needs, aspirations, learning styles and expectations. Before the course starts, teachers should inform themselves of the characteristics of the students by reading *Observing Children* (Metropolitan Toronto Board of Education, 1980) or *Observing Adolescents* (Metropolitan Toronto Board of Education, 1984) or by checking ministry documents that have sections relating language learning to the developmental stage of the student.

- To discover student interests, teachers could distribute an interest questionnaire, or organize activities such as asking the students directly or having them create lists of interests.

- Learning about student needs deals with physical, intellectual and social needs. Teachers should find out if students have physical handicaps, learning disabilities or social disadvantages.

- Knowing the aspirations of the students provides the teacher with the means to motivate. Asking students, providing communicative activities dealing with aspirations, creating lists or drawing are strategies that help teachers discover what aspirations the students have.

- Knowing the way students learn is also of vital importance for the teacher to provide appropriate resources for the visual, auditory or kinaesthetic learners. Distributing a single learning styles questionnaire helps the students and the teacher become more aware of how they like to learn. The Canfield Learning Styles Inventory (1976) may be appropriate for older students.

- Finally, near the beginning of the course the teacher should ask each person, through private conversation or though written comments what they expect to learn from the course in order to adjust strategies and resources.

This is the background information a language teacher needs to know to maximize the learning. The next step is to implement activities that are positive and create trust such as:

1. Getting to know student names by memorization, name tags or seating plans.

2. Sharing personal information about yourself, your background, interests and aspirations. An easy way to do this is through activities such as *Getting To Know Me, A Personal Coat of Arms* or a *Class Book*.

   To organize *Getting To Know Me*, the teacher brings in a bag or box of personal items to share with the class such as a photograph of his or her family, a favourite novel, a stuffed animal representing the family pet, their favourite word (e.g. respect) or something humorous. The students are then invited to bring in items to share with others to introduce themselves. They can present individually in front of the class or within a small group.

To organize *A Personal Coat of Arms*, the teacher presents his or her family, shares personal interests, aspirations and preferred ways of learning. This is presented on a large sheet of graph paper cut in the shape of a coat of arms. Drawings, photographs or pictures from magazines can be used. The students are invited to prepare their own copy to present themselves to their classmates. If displayed in the classroom, they are visually attractive and provide information for communicative activities that help the students learn about each other. For example, "Who enjoys downhill skiing?" "Who wants to become a professional hockey player?" "How does Susan enjoy learning?"

To organize a *Class Book*, the teacher introduces himself or herself by reading a few short paragraphs about his or her family, personal interests, dreams or goals etc. Students are then invited to interview a partner, write a short paragraph, peer edit, produce the final copy and introduce their partner to the other students. The teacher then takes a picture of each student, glues it on the bottom of the page, laminates all the pages and assembles them in book form. This is more appropriate for students who are able to write in the target language. If any of these three activities are used at the beginning of the course, the teacher gets to know the students quickly, the students learn about each other and the teacher in a relaxed and friendly way.

3. Simple activities such as "Autographs", "Name Bingo" or "Introduce the person next to you" are also effective.

4. Distributing and discussing the course outline in detail -the objectives, the content, the process and the evaluation procedures.

5. Organizing simple communicative activities that stress the positive such as: discussing with a partner the best thing that has happened today, or the funniest thing that happened last week.

6. Working on building the individuals' self-esteem by having them identify their strengths, things they're good at, and nice things people have said about them.

7. Developing their appreciation of others by thinking and saying nice things about each other and by having them learn to give compliments to others when good things happen in the classroom.

8. Building team spirit by having them choose a name for their class or group to develop commitment and have a *sense of ownership and belonging*.

Many of these activities take only a few minutes of class time but help to establish a positive and effective climate in the classroom.

References

Borich, G. 1988. *Effective Teaching Methods*. Toronto: Merrill Publishing.

Brown, H. Douglas. 1987. *Principles of Language Learning and Teaching*. Englewood Cliffs, NJ: Prentice Hall Regents.

Canfield, A. and Canfield, S. 1976. *Canfield Learning Styles Inventory*. La Crescenta, CA: Humanics Media.

Heyde, A. 1979. *The relationship between self-esteem and the oral production of a second language*. Unpublished doctoral dissertation, University of Michigan.

Holmes, Mark, Kenneth Leithwood and Donald Musella, eds. 1989. *Educational Policy for Effective Schools*. Toronto: Ontario Institute for Studies in Education Press.

Johnston, J. Howard Glenn C. Markle and Maria Ramos de Perez. 1984. "Effective Schools." In J . H. Johnston and G.C. Markle, 1986, *What Research Says to the Middle Level Practitioner*. Columbus, Ohio: National Middle School Association. p. 9.

Johnston, J. Howard and Maria Ramos de Perez. 1985. "Four Climates of Effective Middle Schools". In *Schools in the Middle: A Report on Trends and Practices*. (January),p. 1. As quoted by Oppenheimer, 1990.

Johnston, J. Howard and Maria de Perez. 1983. "Four Climates of Effective Middle Level Schools." A Paper presented at the Middle School Invitational IV, Chicago. Mimeo.

Knowles, M. 1984. *The Adult Learner: A Neglected Species*. Houston, Texas: Gulf Publishing Co.

Lezotte, L., Douglas Hatheway, Stephen Miller, Joseph Pasalacqua and Wilber Brookover, 1979. *School Learning Climate and Student Achievement*. Centre for Urban Affairs, College of Urban Development and Institute for Research on Teaching. East Lansing, Michigan: Michigan State University.

MacKinnon, M. 1988. "Creating Environment for Learning." *University of New Brunswick Training Bulletin*, 1, 2. Fredericton: University of New Brunswick.

Metropolitan Toronto School Board. *Observing Children*. 1980. Toronto: Metropolitan Toronto School Board.

Metropolitan Toronto School Board. 1984. *Observing Adolescents*. Toronto: Metropolitan Toronto School Board.

Moos, R. H. and E. Trickett. 1987. *Classroom Environment Scale Manual*. Second Edition. Palo Alto: Consulting Psychologists Press, Inc.

Oppenheimer, Jo. 1990. *Getting It Right: Meeting the Needs of the Adolescent Learner*. Toronto: Federation of Women Teachers' Associations of Ontario.

Reprinted from: Cher Evans-Harvey, "Climate Setting In Second-Language Classrooms," *Mosaic*, 1, 2:(Winter 1993), pp. 1, 3-5.

11 Planning for Instruction

Kenneth Chastain

Adapting textbooks and preparing lesson plans require innumerable decisions. Planning for instructionis not easy. Plans that are appropriate to the students and that are well organized require considerable forethought, time, and energy. How do teachers select the explanations, the exercises and the activities and put them in the order that will be the most effective? Upon what bases do teachers make these choices?

Introduction

Planning for instruction includes a large number of considerations such as student characteristics, teacher characteristics, course goals, etc. However, I will limit my focus in this discussion to three that have direct bearing on each lesson:

1. pre-planning analysis,
2. textbook adaptation, and
3. lesson planning,

and I will treat them in reverse order, proceeding from the most to the least familiar based on the amount of time allocated to each in methods classes, conferences, and journal articles.

Lesson Planning

All of us are aware of lesson plans. We know what they are and why they are important. Although an amazing number of formats exist, they consist basically of goals and sequenced activities to help students achieve those goals.* They are important because they help teachers bring structure and direction to the teaching-learning process. With a properly prepared plan, each part of the class becomes a beneficial activity fitting perfectly into the instructional mosaic preparing the students for each subsequent activity and enabling them to perform it successfully. That is, lesson planning helps teachers make the teaching-learning process efficient and effective.

Textbook Adaptation

Textbook adaptation is a less common topic in second-language learning but certainly one that deserves greater attention. Current materials contain explanations that are clearer and more concise, exercises that are more focused and easier to complete, and larger numbers of more interesting communication activities than previous textbooks. However, no set of materials is perfect for all teachers and all students in all situations. A basic text written for a large number of students is a general purpose tool that teachers must adapt to their own particular situation. Classroom teachers are the ones who are aware of their own preferences and who are familiar with their students' knowledge, interest, and capabilities, and they have the responsibility to make justifiable changes in the   text in order to use it most effectively with their students. They may, and often should, delete from the text, add to the text, or alter explanations, exercises, and activities in the text. As a general rule, they should not require the students to cover all the material in the given order.

Adapting textbooks and preparing lesson plans require innumerable decisions. Planning for instruction is not easy. Plans that are appropriate to the students and that are well organized require considerable forethought, time, and energy. How do teachers select the explanations, the exercises and the activities and put them in the order that will be the most effective? Upon what bases do teachers make these choices?

Pre-planning

If they ask themselves these two fundamental questions, teachers will realize that adapting texts and preparing lesson plans are not the first steps in planning for instruction. The basis for both involves two prerequisite analyses:

1. learning analysis and
2. teaching analysis.

Teachers can best prepare themselves to make rational choices regarding the text and the lesson plans if they first have a clear conception of the learning task facing the students. Therefore, the first step is to consider the answers to three student-related questions.

1. What do the students already know in their native language?

What students already know is the single most influential factor in how they learn most effectively and in what they are able to learn. Therefore, what they know about their native language can be an asset in learning the second *if* teachers base their instruction on students' linguistic knowledge rather than on their knowledge of traditional grammar. (Implied in this cognitive principle is that students by definition know their native language and how it functions in communicative contexts even thought they may not be able to analyze it using traditional grammatical terminology.) Teachers can offer their students clearer explanations of grammatical concepts if they base their presentations on students' native-language knowledge.

2. What have the students already learned in the second language?

Everything that they have learned up to the point at which the present material occurs may provide support for the material to be learned. A brief analysis of what the students have previously learned enables teachers to relate the new material to the old, thus reducing the learning load and increasing the likelihood of comprehension and retention.

3. **What else, other than the related concepts that the students already know in their native language and in the second, do they need to know in order to understand the new material?**

The important concept inherent in this question is that rarely do students need to learn all the material in each chapter or lesson as if it were completely new. Either from their first or second language they already have much knowledge that can be of assistance in completing successfully the learning tasks of the current chapter. One of the teacher's responsibilities is to relate new material to old knowledge, thus reducing the learning load to its absolute minimum.

Teaching Analysis

The first step in teaching analysis is to evaluate the authors' presentation of new material. Normally, each teacher has the insights to incorporate some helpful alterations, and he/she should always proceed on the assumption that he/she can improve the presentation in the text.

The answers to the following questions serve as a guide to appropriate deletions, helpful additions, and/or needed changes.

- What alterations are advisable in the authors' presentation of the new material?
- What is correct, comprehensible, and helpful? What is not?
- What changes might improve the presentation?
- What deletions are advisable?
- What additions would be helpful?

The second step is to assess the strengths and the weaknesses of the drills and exercises in the text. They may be either too difficult or too easy. They may be uninteresting or unrelated to the topic. They may have no useful pedagogical value, or they may be organized in an inappropriate sequence, i.e., they may be arranged in a random fashion rather than in a hierarchy of increasing difficulty leading from knowledge to communication.

The answers to these questions help teachers decide which exercises to use, which to replace, and which to alter.

- What changes are desirable in the authors' practice drills, exercises, and communication activities? Which will stimulate learners and help them improve their ability to communicate in the language? Which will not?
- What improvements should be made?
- Do the exercises and activities progress from easier to more difficult, from less to more communicative?
- Is completion of all the exercises necessary?
- Are there too many exercises? Too few?

The third step is to study the communication activities to determine their interest and their value for the students in the teacher's classes. Can the students do them? Will completing the activity successfully help the students develop their communication skills?

As part of the teaching analysis, teachers evaluate all communication activities, prepared to make needed changes.

Many texts do not provide a sufficient number of communication activities. How many should be added?

Conclusion

Obviously, the answers to these questions serve as guides for adapting the text and for preparing the lesson plans. The resultant adapted course materials will be more attuned to the learning needs of the students if teachers first complete a learning and teaching analysis of the chapter content, while the resultant lesson plans will be better coordinated with the text and more specifically geared toward the students in the class.

My impression is that when teachers consider planning for instruction, they think of lesson plans, which is certainly appropriate. However, my experience has been that planning for instruction is more efficient and more effective if it emerges logically and naturally from a careful and complete analysis of the learning and teaching tasks and if it also includes adapting the materials to the teachers' beliefs and the students' needs.

* Interested readers will find additional information on the preparation and organization of lesson plans in

Chastain, Kenneth. 1988 *Developing Second-Language Skills: Theory and Practice* Third Edition. San Diego: Harcourt Brace Jovanovich, Chapter 12. and

Mollica, Anthony. 1994 "Planning for Successful Teaching: The Lesson Outline ," *Mosaic*, 1: 13-15. See Chapter 5 in this volume.

Reprinted from: Kenneth Chastain, "Planning for Instruction," *Mosaic*, 2, 1(Fall 1994), pp.: 16-17.

12 The Lesson Outline

Anthony Mollica

Effective teaching requires planning and organization. Lesson outlines play a very important role in the planning for successful teaching/learning.

The Oxford dictionary defines a lesson as "a continuous portion of teaching given to a pupil or class at one time; one of the portions into which a course of instruction is divided."

At the elementary and secondary school level, the lesson is based on the school board's curriculum guidelines which, in turn, are based on the provincial or state curriculum in that field. While the following outline focuses on language teaching, there are elements which are also of interest for lectures and seminars.

Successful teaching requires planning and organization. Rare are the teachers who can walk into the classroom with little or no planning. While some experienced teachers may not require lengthy, detailed lesson plans, there is a need even for these teachers to keep materials and methods current and relevant to the needs and the expectations of the students. Teachers must be versatile enough to be able to change plans and outlines (and, in some cases, even activities,) for no two classes are the same, and special attention must be paid to the students' learning styles and interests. As Henson (1993:58) points out,

Often a class will become very interested and enthusiastic about a particular part of the lesson. When this happens, you should be willing to deviate from your plan and let the class explore their interests. On the other hand, when the planned lesson seems boring to a particular class, change your approach drastically.

For young teachers, lesson outlines play a very important role. Classroom routines and discipline problems often tend to disrupt the learning environment and teachers should be well prepared if they do not wish to be affected by such distractions. Henson (1993) stresses the importance of lesson planning by pointing out that

A teacher who attempts to teach without a lesson plan is like a pilot taking off for an unknown destination without a map. Like the map, the lesson plan provides direction toward the lesson objectives. If the lesson begins to stray, the plan brings it back to course. This may be difficult without a plan. (p. 39).

Callahan and Clark (1988:103) identify many uses for the well-written lesson plan:

1. It gives one an agenda or an outline to follow as one teaches the lesson.
2. It gives substitute teachers a basis for presenting real lessons to the class they teach.
3. It is very useful when one is planning to teach the same lesson in the future.
4. It provides one with something to fall back on in case of a memory lapse, an interruption, a distraction such as a call from the office or a fire drill.
5. Above all, it provides beginners security for, with a carefully prepared plan, a beginning teacher can walk into the classroom with the confidence gained from having developed, in an organized form, a sensible framework for that day's instruction.

Borich (1992:140) cautions teachers that before a lesson plan can be prepared, they must decide on

- instructional goals
- learning needs
- contents, and
- methods.

Lesson outlines vary with each individual teacher. Arguing which type of lesson plan is best would be a waste of time and space. Nothing is sacred about any of them. The lesson plan is simply a tool which is as effective as the person using it.

The following is a *proposed* outline. Different teachers may use other headings, but ultimately the end result should be the same: to impart and to acquire knowledge. Along with the outline itself, the teacher should also keep in mind questions and questioning techniques as well as classroom expressions which help the student to participate in the learning process.[1]

What are the divisions of a lesson plan? What should the teacher's lesson plan look like? It is very useful to identify at the beginning of each lesson outline:

1. *the date*

   (This will be useful to compare, the following year, whether the teacher is "ahead" or "behind" in the course of study.)
2. *the Grade*
3. *the title of the textbook used*
4. *the number of students in the class*

   (It is obvious that the same teaching methods cannot be used with a class of thirty and a small class of ten students, or a class of mixed ability.)

The above information should be followed by the following suggested divisions:

1. Theme or topic

2. Aims or Objectives
3. Warm-up period
4. Materials needed by
   a) teacher
   b) students
5. Presentation
6. Application
7. Summary
8. Assignment
9. Evaluation
10. Teacher's references
11. Motivation.

1. Theme or Topic

Unlike the aims or objectives, which are specific, the theme or topic is general. It is something that may take several lessons to complete. For example, a topic might be "The Present Tense." In order to deal completely with this topic, several lessons may be required. Teachers may need to familiarize the students with various conjugations of regular and irregular verbs, with positive, negative and interrogative forms, as well as combinations of the latter: positive-interrogative and negative-interrogative. In other words, the topic/theme is general and will involve many individual lessons.

2. Aims or Objectives

The aims or objectives, on the other hand, are more specific. This section will focus on what the teacher will teach within a time-frame on a given day to a specified class. For example, the aim might be: "To teach the present tense of the first conjugation verbs in the positive form." However, teachers often write this aim in terms of *behavioural objectives*. If this is the case, all statements of performance objectives must meet at least three criteria (Henson, 1993:66):

- Objectives must be stated in terms of expected student behaviour (not teacher behaviour).
- Objectives must specify the conditions under which the students are expected to perform.
- Objectives must specify the minimum acceptable level of performance.

Stating objectives in terms of expected student behaviour is important because all teaching is directed toward the students. The success of the lesson will depend on what happens to the student. In writing performance objectives, Henson suggests that teachers avoid using verbs that cannot be observed or measured, such as *learn, know* and *understand*. Instead the plan should contain specific, action-oriented verbs such as *identify, list, explain, name, describe,* and *compare*. (Henson, 1993:68).

What is to be learned should be made apparent to the students in the title of the lesson. It should be clear to the teachers also when they develop their aim for the lesson.

3. Warm-up period

Before beginning the day's lesson, teachers should involve the students in some "warm-up" activity. This warm-up period may consist of

- *general questions*

  These questions may focus on current events, school activities, news broadcasts, etc. Please avoid asking of every class the day's date and/or inquiring about the weather, unless these questions are used communicatively! (Mollica, 1985.)

- *personal questions*

  These questions may be directed to individual students to show interest on the part of the teacher for an activity in which the student might have been involved:

  "Did you see the hockey game last night?"

  "Who won?"

  etc.)

- *review questions*

  These questions are directed at reviewing the lesson of the day before. They may serve as a basis for introduction to the item(s) about to be presented or may be necessary as a pre-requisite to the new lesson.

- *a combination of the above.*

4. Materials
a. needed by the teacher

Teachers should list the material(s) needed in order to teach a particular lesson. What print, non-print materials, audio and visual equipment are required to teach the lesson effectively? Does the teacher require

- a textbook, notebook,
- illustrations, flashcards,
- coloured chalk,
- an overhead projector (make sure there is a spare bulb!),
- a slide projector,
- an extension cord,
- etc.?

a. needed by the students

What do the students need in order to perform well in class? Have they been told to bring the right textbook and workbook? Do they have extra sheets of paper? Do they have their notebooks? Do they have pencils, ball-point pens to write with? (Keep a few spare ones aside; students have frequent memory lapses...)

5. Presentation

This is the part of the lesson in which the "item" to be learned is presented. The presentation should proceed step-by-step from the simple to the complex. In providing examples in the target language, teachers should use vocabulary which is already known to the student. Every effort should be made to avoid distractions so that students will be able to focus on what is being taught and on what the teacher wants the students to learn. Language should be kept simple and examples meaningful. The language of the teacher should enable the student to follow the teacher and be able to comprehend the presentation of the lesson, and finally to absorb the material with a feeling of understanding and accomplishment. Students should never be left "up-in-the-air" over a lesson.

Teachers should make every effort to *involve* students in the presentation. Where possible, the lesson should be developed by both teachers and students. Teachers may wish to jot down a number of key questions to be asked during the presentation which will help to develop the item to be learned.

Four-by-six index cards are very helpful in providing the teacher with additional examples or vocabulary lists which are useful to keep the lesson moving at an engaging pace.

6. Application

Once the teacher has presented the item to be learned, it is important that students be given an opportunity to *apply* what has been taught/presented. This activity should be done while both the teacher and students are together. While the students are practising (this is often an exercise found in their textbook or workbook), teachers should circulate about the classroom and see that the application is taking place,. They may stop here and there, complimenting a student for his/her good work or assisting students who may have not completely grasped the notion of the item to be learned. Application is doing something about the item taught while the group and teacher are still together.

7. Summary

The summary should terminate the formal instruction and should immediately follow the presentation or follow the application. In the latter case, the summary will serve as a reinforcement of what has been presented. The teacher, by means of the summary, brings together and emphasizes the main points made during the lesson presentation. The summary is meant to crystallize the learning and to highlight the presentation.

8. Assignment

The assignment phase of the lesson may be considered as a continuation of the application. Assignments provide a meaningful extended application of the item just learned. The assignment is an aid to retention. It differs from application, as it may consist of preparation for the next lesson. It may be done at home or in class. Whenever possible, an assignment should be started in class and continued at home. This process will allow the student an opportunity to ask the teacher any questions about the assignment while both teacher and student are present in class. The time spent with a student can never be regained or recaptured. It is time well spent.

9. Evaluation

Teachers should be familiar with the principles and techniques of evaluation in order to discover whether what has been presented/taught has been learned or not. Formative evaluation through observation, check-lists, student self-evaluation, peer evaluation, and comments by the teacher on oral and written work provide concrete information on the day to day learning. For formal evaluation, teachers should perhaps adopt the well-known Holiday Inn slogan "No surprises!" In other words, the method of evaluation should reflect the method of teaching. Simply put, "Test the way you've taught!"

10. Teacher's references

Teachers should identify in their lesson plan other textbooks which have similar explanations or exercises as the lesson just presented. These sources are invaluable for providing additional exercises on the same topic and may show the teacher how the same lesson has been presented by another textbook writer.

11. Motivation

Motivation plays a crucial role in the lesson presentation. In fact, motivation should play a role not only in the presentation, but also should be pervasive throughout the class period. Teachers cannot say to students, "This activity will motivate you for the next five minutes..." (The implication being that teachers will bore the students for the rest of the class...) Motivation means to stimulate something or someone. Motivation is one of the prime tasks of teaching. Motivation should be constant and should not stop at any given point. Motivation is important at the beginning of the lesson as a means of introducing the material, stimulating interest, arousing curiosity and developing the specific aim; but it is equally important for teachers to provide motivational activities which will arouse and retain the interest of the students.

References

Borich, Gary D. 1992. *Effective Teaching Methods.* Second edition.New York: Macmillan.

Callahan, Joseph E. and Leonard H. Clark. 1988. *Teaching in the Middle and Secondary Schools. Planning for Competence.* Third edition. New York: Macmillan.

Henson, Kenneth T. 1993. *Methods and Strategies for the Teaching in Secondary and Middle Schools.* Second edition. New York: Longman.

Mollica, Anthony. 1985. "Communication in the Second-Language Classroom." In Anthony Papalia, ed., *A Communicative Syllabus. Teaching for Proficiency. A Practical Guide.* Schenectady, NY: New York State Association of Foreign Language Teachers.

Reprinted from: Anthony Mollica, "Planning for Successful Teaching: The Lesson Outline," *Mosaic*, 1, 3 (Spring 1994), pp. 13-15.

13 Classroom Expressions

Anthony Mollica

Every effort should be made to conduct the language class using the target language extensively. The following list is by no means exhaustive but permits students to communicate effectively and carry out classroom routines.

In preparing this list of classroom expressions, we have opted to place into groups a number of expressions. Certainly, they do not necessarily fall always in that category. They are so categorized for easier access. The list is by no means exhaustive. It is, nevertheless, a good start. Teachers may wish to illustrate some of these expressions and place the illustrations and the text on the bulletin board as a constant reminder and as an aid to learning .

Greetings
- Good morning.
- Good afternoon.
- Good-bye.
- Hello.
- Until tomorrow.

Formulas of Courtesy
- Please.
- Thank you.
- You're welcome.
- Excuse me.
- I beg your pardon

Warm-up Period
- What is your name?
- My name is…
- Where is (name of student) to-day?
- Present. / Absent.
- He/She is ill.
- Come in!
- Close the door.
- Open the window.

- Turn off the lights.
- Turn the lights on.
- Erase the blackboard.

Inquiry questions

- What is this?
- How do we say (word) in (target language)?
- How do you spell (word)?
- Use the five "W"s: Why? What? Where? Who? When?

Classroom Management

- Are you ready?
- Quiet! / Silence!
- Distribute these sheets.
- Collect the test.
- That's enough!
- Pay attention.
- No talking.
- Listen.
- One at a time, please.
- Stop talking to (name of student), (name of student).
- Faster. / More quickly.
- Stand up.
- Sit down.
- Read quietly.
- Read aloud.
- Louder.
- Come up in front of the class.
- Go back to your seat.
- Line up here.

Praise

- Excellent!
- Very good!
- Bravo!
- Good!
- Well done!
- Correct!
- Perfect!
- Great!
- Terrific!
- Congratulations!

Audio-Visual Equipment

- Blackboard / Chalkboard
- Overhead projector
- Slide projector
- Extension cord
- Cassette taperecorder
- Videocassette recorder
- Tape
- Plug in the overhead projector, please.

Presentation

- Repeat after me.
- All the boys.
- All the girls.
- All together.
- Everybody.
- For example...
- Close your notebooks.
- Close your books.
- Is this clear?
- Do you understand?
- Look at the blackboard.
- Look at the screen.
- Answer the question.
- Look at the bottom of page...
- Look at the top of page...
- Look at the middle of page...
- Once more.

Application

- Copy down the examples in your notebooks.
- Open your notebooks.
- Open your books.
- Open your books on page_
- Turn to page...
- Open your workbooks on page...
- Write. / Do not write.
- Continue...
- Repeat once more.
- It's (name of student's) turn.
- Go to the blackboard.

- Write the answer on the blackboard.
- Go back to your seat.
- Choose a partner.
- Play the role of...
- Look it up in the dictionary.
- For homework, do Exercise...

Students' favourites...

- May I sharpen my pencil?
- I don't have a pencil (pen).
- I forgot...
- I don't remember.
- I don't know.
- I don't understand.
- I left the book in my locker.
- I can't hear.
- May I get a drink of water?
- May I go to the bathroom?

Reprinted from: Anthony Mollica, "Planning for Successful Teaching: Classroom Expressions," *Mosaic*, 2, 1 (Fall 1994): 18.

14 Questioning Strategies

Anthony Mollica

Questioning is an art. Questions can stimulate conversation and discussion. Precise questions will normally elicit precise answers,

As a university student, I worked during the summer months as a Customs officer at the Fort Erie/Buffalo border. I was in the Customs yard one day when a car pulled up. It had a note on the windshield. It read: "Check under front seat." I took the paper and asked the driver:

"Where do you live?"

"Welland," he replied.

"How long have you been away?"

"A couple of hours."

I checked under the seat. There was nothing there. However, on the front seat there were two bottles of liquor, some bedsheets, some pillow covers.

"Do you have anything to declare?" I asked.

"Yes," he replied. "Two bottles of liquor, some bedsheets and some pillow covers."

"Why did you not declare these items to the officer on the line?" I inquired.

"Because he asked me if I had anything special. And this is not special."

I couldn't help smiling. The man was right. My colleague had asked an incorrect question. What the officer should have said was: "Do you have any thing to declare?" (or the equivalent in French, "Avez-vous quelque chose à déclarer?")

At which point the "smuggler" could have (would have?) identified the items. But the officer, obviously bored from asking the same question, tried to change it and thus obtained unacceptable results.

Questions such as: "Did you buy anything today?" are not appropriate. The traveller could easily reply negatively and then be discovered to have his car trunk filled with TV sets. His explanation to the Customs officer could be very simple. "You asked if I *bought* anything. Well, I didn't *buy* these items. My uncle owns a TV store and he *gave* them to me free of charge."

I remember a similar scene from the movie *All the President's Men*. A senior *Washington Post* reporter asked the two investigative reporters, Woodward and Bernstein, why Hugh Sloan had not told the Grand Jury that Haldeman had been involved in the secret slush fund used to re-elect President Nixon. "He was never asked," was the reply.

Questions may be used to solve problems. I recall my practice-teaching days at the Faculty of Education at the University of Toronto. There was a young man in the Latin class by the name of Alvin who was determined to try the patience of even the most courteous student teacher! What seemed to be on the surface the most innocent of questions, turned out to be the most intricate and difficult queries with which he tried to stump enthusiastic future teachers. I was determined to put Alvin in his place, but to do so gently without declaring open warfare.

I had just finished teaching the ablative absolute. I had explained the function of the past participle which, together with the noun in the ablative case, provided a variety of possible translations:

Gallis victis, pacem fecit.

After defeating the Gauls, he made peace.

The Gauls being defeated,…

Having defeated the Gauls,…

After he had defeated the Gauls,…

Since he had defeated the Gauls,…

etc…

Alvin, eager to stump me, asked:

"Can an adverb modify a past participle?"

The eyes of all my colleagues turned on me. I could have simply answered with a "yes/no" answer. I decided instead to use Alvin's question as a springboard for problem solving.

"What is a participle, Alvin?"

Alvin was determined and eager to show off his newly acquired knowledge.

"A participle is part adjective and part verb."

I praised his answer.

"Very good, Alvin," I said. "Can an adverb modify an adjective?"

"Yes," replied Alvin, knowledgeably.

"Can an adverb modify a verb?"

"Of course," said Alvin, annoyed.

"Does that answer your question?" I asked.

Alvin didn't know what had hit him.

"Why… uh… Yes! Thank you, sir," he blurted out.

I had turned Alvin's question to my advantage and he had learned something.

Then there is the classic story of the teacher who, having spent some time trying to obtain class control, noticed that "Johnny" was still continuing to disrupt the class. Being short of patience and wanting to start the lesson, the teacher sarcastically asked:

"Would you like to take over the class, Johnny?"

At this point, Johnny stood up, went to the front of the class and solemnly announced:

"Class dismissed!"

Additional anecdotes and examples abound. The reader has only to watch any TV courtroom drama *(Perry Mason, Matlock, Street Legal)* to see immediately the importance of asking questions which produce the response the lawyer requires. Precise questions will normally elicit precise answers, although this obviously does not apply to members of Parliament who seem to have mastered the art of not answering the question asked by members of the opposition! Teachers should frame their questions in such a manner as to ensure the answer they want, at least within the context of what they are teaching.

Why Ask Questions?

In the classroom, teachers should ask questions:
- to obtain information
- to spark and/or encourage discussion
- to stimulate and encourage participation
- to check facts and to reinforce recently learned material
- to probe more deeply after an answer is given
- to help recall specific information
- to arouse interest
- to gain a student's attention
- to diagnose specific learning difficulties
- to encourage reflection and self-evaluation
- to help determine individual differences
- to focus attention on an issue
- to determine what the students know
- to test learning
- to solve problems
- to teach via students' answers.

During the presentation of the lesson, the teacher may want to ask questions:
- to review content already learned
- for review or for drill
- to bring out or reaffirm the aim of the lesson
- to reinforce recently learned material.

What Types of Questions?

What types of questions should teachers ask? They should ask questions which:

- are brief and clear
- are specific
- are consistent with students' abilities
- call upon the students' past experience
- help develop concepts and thoughts
- are relevant to the lesson
- are suitable for diagnostic purposes
- call for judgement.

Method

Teachers should ask questions

- in a varied rather than a predictable order
- of several students rather than several questions directed to the same student
- in a courteous manner and expect the same courtesy in return
- in a familiar way rather than always formally
- as a teacher, not as a judge in a courtroom
- during class, but enter marks later
- in a sincere manner
- within the scope of students' acquired linguistic skills and using good target language
- according to the students' needs.
- according to the ability of the group.

To Whom Should Questions be Asked?

Teachers should ask questions:

- of the slower as well as the rapid learner
- of the inattentive student

Suggestions and Techniques

- Teachers should keep the following suggestions in mind:
- Ask the question. Pause a little. Only then identify the student who will answer the question.
- Allow a reasonable interval of time before the student answers
- From time to time, ask questions which may require group response.
- Recognize volunteers.
- Praise a good response.
- Praise a good effort even if the answer needs a bit of polishing or correcting.

- Encourage students *to ask* as well as answer questions in the target language.

Key Words in Questions

Practically all questions, whether intended to recall factual information or stimulate discussion, consist of or include one of the following key words:
- What...?
- Who...?
- When...?
- Where...?
- Why...?
- How...?

Questions To Be Avoided

Teachers should avoid asking questions which:
- can be answered with a simple "yes" or "no"
- are vague
- are double-barrelled; i.e. two questions in one
- suggest the answer
- do not have a worthwhile purpose
- can be answered by guessing.

    Following are some examples of questions to be avoided:
1. Can you answer question No. 7?

    (Yes, of course I can, but I don't feel like it...).

    Better:
    Question Number 7, Johnny.
    (An elliptical question in the form of a command.)
2. Has anyone finished the exercise?

    (No, of course no one has finished it!).

    Better:
    Who has finished the exercise?
3. Who killed Julius Caesar and why?

    (One question at a time. First I have to figure out who killed him, let alone try to imagine the reason...).

     Better:
    Who killed Julius Caesar?

    (Teacher first obtains response and then proceeds with:) Why?
4. It was Brutus who stabbed Caesar, was it not?

    (I guess so, if you say so. You're the teacher; I'm not going to disagree with you...).

    Better:
    Who stabbed Caesar?

Level of Behavioral Complexity	Expected Student Behavior	Instructional Processes	Key Words
Knowledge (remembering)	Student is able to remember or recall information and recognize facts, terminology, and rules.	repetition memorization	define describe identify
Comprehension (understanding)	Student is able to change the form of a communication by translating and rephrasing what has been read or spoken.	explanation illustration	summarize paraphrase rephrase
Application (transferring)	Student is able to apply the information learned to a context different than the one in which it was learned.	practice transfer	apply use employ
Analysis (relating)	Student is able to break a problem down into its component parts and to draw relationships among the parts.	induction deduction	relate distinguish differentiate
Synthesis (creating)	Student is able to combine parts to form a unique or novel solution to a problem.	divergence generalization	formulate compose produce
Evaluation (judging)	Student is able to make decisions about the value or worth of methods, ideas, people, or products according to expressed criteria.	discrimination inference	appraise decide justify

Figure 1. A question classification scheme

Reprinted with the permission of Macmillan College Publishing Co. from *Effective Teaching Methods*, 2nd ed., by Gary D. Borich. Copyright © 1992 Macmillan College Publishing Company.

5. Who wants to erase the blackboard?

(Thirty students rush to the front of the classroom...).

Better:

Please erase the blackboard, Mary.

Convergent vs. Divergent Questioning

Questions can be either narrow or broad. A narrow question is often referred to as a memory question, direct question, closed question or convergent question.

A *convergent* question limits the answer, for all the learner has to do is to recall certain facts either read or heard. This type of question generally requires a short answer and little reflection or thought on the part of the respondent. It is based on memory rather than on knowledge and understanding and may even encourage guessing.

The *divergent* question – a broad or open question – encourages an open response. It has no single correct or best answer, but can have wrong answers. Like the convergent question which involves memory, the divergent likewise entails memory, but also requires that the student explain, think about the topic and produce a logical, correct answer. Guessing, therefore, is held to a minimum. Divergent questions challenge the student's efforts and command greater attention and reflection for they stimulate further activity calling for judgment, analysis, organization, comparison, understanding and logical thinking. It follows that the teacher can expect more diverse responses from the divergent question than the convergent one.

Question Classification Scheme

Borich (1992) identifies the types of student behaviours associated with each level in the cognitive-domain taxonomy suggested by Bloom *et al.* (1956)

- Knowledge
- Comprehension
- Application
- Analysis
- Synthesis
- Evaluation

and offers this excellent chart (Figure 1).

There is no doubt in any teacher's mind that the art of questioning is crucial and plays a major role in the process of teaching and learning. Postman (1979) went so far as to urge

> Let us... make the study of the art of question-asking one of the central disciplines in language education (p.140).

and to suggest that

> all our knowledge results from questions, which is another way of saying that question-asking is our most important intellectual tool (p. 140).

References

Bloom, Benjamin, M. Englehart, W. Hill, E. Furst, and D. Krathwohl. 1956. *Taxonomy of Educational Objectives. The Classification of Educational Goals. Cognitive and Affective Domains.* New York: David McKay Company, Inc.

Borich, Gary D. 1992. *Effective Teaching Methods.* Second Edition. New York: Macmillan Company.

Morgan, Norah and Juliana Saxton. 1993. *Teaching Questioning and Learning.* London and New York: Routledge.

Orlich, Donald C., Robert J. Harder, Richard C. Callahan, Constance H. Kravas, Donald P. Kauchak, R. A. Pendergrass and Andrew J. Keogh. 1985. *Teaching Strategies. A Guide to Better Instruction.* Lexington, MA and Toronto, Ontario: D.C. Heath and Company.

Postman, Neil. 1979. *Teaching as a Conservative Activity.* New York: Laurel Press, Dell. Delacorte.

Reprinted from: Anthony Mollica, "Planning for Successful Teaching: Questioning Strategies," *Mosaic*, 1, 4 (Summer 1994), pp. 18-20.

15 Questioning in the Language Classroom

Merle Richards

Most general teaching strategies apply in the language class. If we are to maximize students' language development, we are require us to adapt those strategies Questioning skills represent one such area.

Questioning is often considered the basic skill of teaching. Morgan and Saxton (1991) cite three main functions of questioning: to "tap into what is already known; build a context for shared understanding; and challenge students to think critically and creatively for themselves" (p. x). In the regular first- language class, teachers strive to question and to teach questioning skills that will enable students to reach these goals. Relying on the learners' basic language fluency, they build language and concepts to "stretch" the students' intellectual and emotional capacity, taking for granted that their pupils will attend to the meanings and content of the discussion rather than to the grammar and pronunciation.

But what if that basic fluency is lacking? Language teachers, especially those with adult or adolescent students, know that learners often say, "I could say that in my own language", or "I just can't find the words in English". One student told me that English has no humour, because when she translated jokes from her own language, they just weren't funny anymore! That is, she couldn't show in English the spirit and wit that she could convey in her own language, because she wasn't fluent enough to play with English in the same way. In Smith's (1988) terms, she had the "deep structures" (meanings), with their sources in her life and culture, but not the "surface structures" (forms of expression) in which to clothe her thoughts and feelings in English.

Similar difficulties arise when learners want to address serious topics, such as ethics, social values, and the problems of being not-yet-bilingual - but which, being so, they can't explain. They need support for both the creative and intellectual functioning in the target language, and their teachers can use questions to provide it.

Types of Questions

Several educators have devised ways of classifying teachers' questions (for example, Saxon and Morgan, 1991; Tonjes and Zintz, 1992). Most of them focus on the kind of mental activity the questions are supposed to elicit. In the second language class, this is a special consideration: the learners need variety and complexity to maintain interest, but they also need a lower cognitive level than would be appropriate in their first language. This is because much of their attention is diverted from the meanings to the surface structures. In the weaker language, it takes mental effort to figure out sentence form, word order and pronunciations – effort that in the strong language is directed mainly to meanings and finding the "mot juste".

Even when the forms are familiar, non-fluent learners can seldom express the complex thoughts they can formulate in their first language, although a good language teacher knows that their comprehension is usually greater than their expressive capacity. Therefore, when building listening and reading skills, the teacher pitches questions, statements, and explanations at a cognitive level that is probably below their intellectual capacity but is just above the level of the students' own talk.

Although the Bloom Taxonomy is the best known, the classification system developed by Guilford (1968) to determine levels of thinking is easier to apply in the language class. It has been adapted to help teachers check the levels of their questions and pupil responses, so that a variety of skills can be used (Aschner et al., 1965). This system helps the language teacher to include "thinking questions" at a cognitive level that the students can cope with.

a) *Factual questions* (cognitive-memory) are those used most often. Teachers use them to check that pupils have learned content, understood their reading, acquired vocabulary, etc. Such questions form the basis for most language lessons.

On the other hand, if most questions are merely low-level drills and repetitions, interest soon wanes. "What is this?" questions are excellent for the first few classes, but after that, learners want "real conversation". Factual questions related to interesting content or learners' experience can fill their need.

For example,

Who is the main character in the story?

What does a miller do?

What did the Little Red Hen say when no one would help her?

b) *Convergent questions* require reasoning toward a right answer. Morgan and Saxon (1991) and Mollica (1994) are correct in grouping Convergent with "closed" or ""narrow" questions. However, they can support logical thinking processes, and are used to guide pupils through the steps to a right answer.

For example,

Why did the Little Red Hen take the grain to the miller?

If you wear a snowsuit when it snows, when would you wear a sunsuit? a rainsuit? a swimsuit? a space suit?

Sixteen, seventeen, eighteen…What number do you think would come next?

Could you put your shoes on before your socks?

Compare the way we celebrate weddings today and in the past.

What must you do to subtract 7 from 11?

In the language class, convergent questions also help the teacher understand what idea a student is trying to express and to model an acceptable form.

For example,

Okay, you said that loyalty to friends is important. Does that mean doing what your friends want rather than what you want?

c) **Divergent questions** suggest a more creative response. Any justifiable answer may be accepted.

For example,

What are some other ways this story could have ended?

How may we keep this heritage custom here in Canada?

How else might we say this?

How else might we solve this problem?

What might you do if you see that your friend is headed for trouble?

d) **Evaluative questions** are those which demand a judgement or opinion. They require reasoning about characteristics and values:

For example,

Was the Little Red Hen justified in not sharing?

Which story did you prefer?

What made that story better than the other one?

How did it make you feel about the villain?

Which shows greater loyalty: to report your friend who is selling drugs, or to keep quiet and say nothing?

Scaffolding

The language teacher may have to structure the responses for the students. An easy way to do this is to break the question into parts that the pupils can choose, or to give an answer of your own which they may repeat or modify: "I was really angry with the villain. I wanted to tell her off! How did you feel?" This supplies the words and forms, but allows students to choose their own thoughts and experiences.

Planning Questions

Mollica (1994) and Morgan and Saxon (1991) list types of questions, questions to avoid (stupid questions!), techniques, and reasons for questioning. In the language class, we also plan **key questions** that direct pupils toward the objectives and **backup questions** to assist those who have difficulty with the key questions. For example:

Key Question:

When do we celebrate Thanksgiving?

Backups:

What are we thankful for?

What foods are abundant in the fall?

What do we mean by "harvest"?

Whatever plan or system you use, be flexible. Learners may come up with unexpected answers that are thoughtful and appropriate. Accept them, and when you can, use them to lead to further ideas.

Yet More Tips for Questioning

1. Ask your questions, then remain silent for 3-5 seconds before naming a pupil to respond. (This is hard to do!)
2. Try to call upon all pupils each day. When silence follows your question, don't just ask the pupil who raises a hand first: let the silence continue while the students have time to think. (This is even harder than #1.)
3. When questions require thought or reasoning, the students may not be able to express themselves adequately. Allow them to speak in their first language, then help them to say their idea in the target language.

   You may wish to write the expression on chart paper for future reference, especially if a writing task follows the discussion.
4. With advanced students, encourage use of the target language to develop concepts and understand relationships. When students respond to higher-level questions, withhold judgement. Encourage pupils to elaborate or build upon their own and others' responses.

   Don't say "Good!" or "I agree" in these cases: such statements bring closure to the exchange (you might say, "That's evidence for your opinion. Is there further evidence?").
5. Don't answer your own questions. Provide clues, probe, ask for clarification. In other words, help the pupils find their way to the answer.
6. If children never volunteer to answer, speak to them privately to determine why. If they are shy, you may feed them some answers or call upon them to repeat someone else's answer. (They may be worried about making a mistake in public.)
7. Teach pupils to ask many types of questions, rather than just responding. This both gives them a heuristic device in the target language and provides a different discourse role in the classroom.

References

Aschner, M.J., J.J. Gallagher, J. Perry, S. Afsar, W.C. Jenne, and H. Farr. 1965. *A system for classifying thought processes in the context of classroom verbal interaction.* Urbana: University of Illinois.

Guilford, J.P. 1968. *Intelligence, creativity, and their educational implications.* San Diego: R.R. Knapp.

Mitchell, R. 1988. *Communicative language teaching in practice.* London: CILT.

Mollica, Anthony. 1994. "Planning for Successful Teaching: Questioning Strategies." *Mosaic,* 1: 4, 18-20.

Morgan, Norah and Juliana Saxon. 1991. *Teaching, Questioning and Learning.* London and New York: Routledge.

Smith, Frank. 1988. *Understanding Reading. A psycholinguistic analysis of reading and learning to read*. 4th ed., Hillsdale, NJ: Lawrence Erlbaum.

Tonjes, M.J. and M.V. Zintz. 1992. *Teaching reading, thinking, study skills in content classrooms*. 3rd ed., Dubuque, IA: Wm.C. Brown.

Reprinted from: Merle Richards, "Planning for Successful Teaching: Questioning in the Language Classroom," *Mosaic*, 2, 3 (Spring 1995), pp. 21-22.

16 Classroom Settings

Anthony Papalia

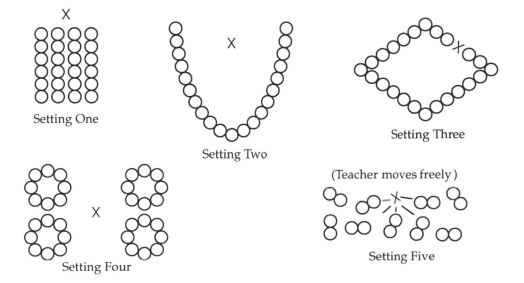

Setting One

Setting Two

Setting Three

Setting Four

(Teacher moves freely)

Setting Five

In his book, *Learner-Centered Language Teaching. Methods and Materials.* (Rowley, MA: Newbury House, 1976), the late Anthony Papalia, identified a variety of learning styles (p. 15) and proposed various classroom settings (pp. 34-35)..

Teachers realize, as Phillips (1976) points out, that

> the neatly wrapped package for uniform distribution to a group of potential language learners has failed to live up to its advertising. There is no one right method for all learners at all stages. Alternatives in pace, content, goals and learning strategies require teachers and students to make choices - choices about *how* they learn and *what* they learn, all within the foreign language context.

Papalia firmly believed that it is necessary to understand and identify the learning styles of the student utilizes in order to enhance motivation and increase learning.

Is the student

- an *incremental learner* who likes to learn step by step?
- an *intuitive learner* who leaps to generalizations?
- a *sensory specialist* who learns better by seeing or hearing?
- An *emotionally involved* learner who depends heavily on interpersonal relationships?

- An *eclectic learner* who is able to adapt to any learning style?

    In seeking answers to these questions, teachers acknowledge that each student is an individual who learns in a unique way and that options in learning should be provided for all students. By seeking these answers, they can better adjust their teaching materials and classroom pacing and grouping, and tailor instruction to the needs of each individual. Individualizing the mode of learning is as essential as individualizing the rate of learning.

    Language teachers interested in individualizing instruction should design learning environments which provide varying degrees of structure, and should use different strategies and materials compatible with the individual differences of the learner.

Setting One:

To facilitate
1. the introduction of new material
2. the use of audio-visual aids
3. testing
4. activities where everyone is doing the same thing
5. independent work and
6. choral work.

Setting One

Setting Two:

To facilitate
1. teacher mobility
2. eye contact
3. pupil attention
4. communication
5. game playing and
6. teacher control.

Setting Two

Setting Three:

To facilitate
1. the introduction of new material
2. participation of the teacher as an equal
3. an informal atmosphere for oral presentations and
4. communication directed to all, not just to t he teacher.

Setting Three

Setting Four:

To facilitate
1. remedial activities

2. tutoring
3. use of tape recorders and media
4. reinforcement of learned material
5. use of self-instructional materials
6. peer teaching
7. skit planning
8. games
9. one-to-one teacher-pupil interaction
10. self-pacing
11. teacher awareness of individual learning problems and
12. grouping according to interests or needs.

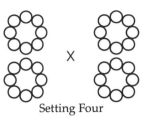

Setting Four

Setting Five:

To enhance

(Teacher moves freely.)

1. peer interaction
2. peer teaching
3. "specific skill" grouping
4. variable pacing
5. tutorial work
6. games, simulations, and role playing in a competitive or noncompetitive setting
7. group projects and
8. oral practice.

Setting Five

References

Papalia, Anthony. 1976. *Learner-Centered Language Teaching. Methods and Materials.* (Rowley, MA: Newbury House.

Phillips, June K. 1976. "Fun! Not for Fridays Only." Paper presented at the Northeast Ohio Teachers' Conference. Cleveland, October. Mimeo.

These pages are reprinted with kind the permission of Judith Papalia.

Reprinted from: Anthony Papalia, "Planning for Effective Teaching: Papalia's Classroom Settings," *Mosaic*, 1, 3 (Spring 1994), p. 165.

17 The Challenge of Multilevel Classes

Jill Bell

Every language class is a multilevel class! How could it be otherwise when language learning is affected by so many personal variables? The author discusses how language teachers can find ways to accommodate and capitalize on this classroom diversity.

One of the most common challenges facing teachers in language classes, particularly in ESL and heritage programs, is the wide variety of language competence which students may have. Even classes which appear relatively homogeneous at the outset soon display varying rates of progress, as factors such as age, levels of prior education, exposure to the target language and so on, all have their effect.

Developing a curriculum which allows each student to make the best possible progress is extremely challenging in such conditions. As well as offering learning opportunities for all students, the teacher must be concerned with the social atmosphere in the classroom so that learners are at ease and comfortable in the group. Splitting students up into permanent groups of advanced, intermediate and basic level learners tends not to promote the kind of group identity which allows learners to feel comfortable. In addition, it prevents the teacher from capitalizing on the various strengths of the students and allowing them to work together and help each other. Ideally then, in each session, the teacher will plan to have the whole group work together for at least part of each lesson.

There are three basic ways in which this can be accomplished:
a) start-up activities suitable for everyone;
b) whole group activities where students perform the task at different levels; and
c) whole group activities which incorporate a variety of different tasks.

a. Start-up activities

By beginning each class with the whole group working together, the tone is set for the rest of the session. Ideally the start-up activity should have a strong visual component, so that even learners with minimal language skills can understand what is going on. It should involve significant oral discussion so that stronger learners get a chance to express their oral competence and beginners hear a variety of spoken language richer than they would encounter in their small group, but with the content knowledge which allows them to comprehend at least some of what is said. Some possible ideas include the following:

- filmstrip
- LEA (Language Experience Approach) story: Students recount a story or an experience. The teacher writes it down on a chart. Once this is done, the students read it back.
- field trip
- demonstration of any subject of interest, maybe jewelry making or car maintenance
- showing of family snapshots, baby photos, etc.
- discussion of strip story, or large poster-type photograph
- photo story where photos carry the dialogue.

A slightly different but highly successful starter is the use of interview questionnaires where students are given a class list and a simple question such as "When is your birthday?" Students must circulate around the room, interviewing each other and recording the results. This activity helps students get to know each other's names and breaks down the barriers between students of different ages or levels. To increase the challenge for the advanced students, a second, more open-ended question can be assigned, to be attempted only when the first set of interviews are successfully completed.

b. Whole group activities where students perform the task at different levels

The level of difficulty of many language tasks is determined less by the complexity of the language being presented than by the complexity of the task which the student is required to perform. A beginner may not be able to totally comprehend the TV Guide for instance, but may still be able to find and circle a favourite program. Meanwhile, a more advanced student might be planning an evening's viewing for a history buff or analyzing the intended audience for different channels. With this principle in mind, many activities can be developed where everyone in the class listens to or looks at the same piece of language but is assigned a task to perform which varies according to interest or ability. Some examples follow:

- Have the students listen to a taped conversation or similar. Develop three or four different sets of follow-up activities. The easiest might be a cloze where students decide which of two words they hear. Slightly more difficult would be simple yes/no questions on factual items. More advanced students might be asked to write a paraphrase.
- Have students read a fairly simple piece, probably a strip or photo story, with different questions to answer. (The task could be copying for literacy students). Advanced students are asked to create the dialogue or continue the story.
- Distribute newspapers or magazine ads. Have students skim or scan to identify different pieces of information. Easy tasks might be to find out whether a certain item is listed for sale. More challenging activities include identifying sources, budgeting, etc.

- Have in-class discussions, choosing topics such as generation problems which all learners will understand, rather than topics such as politics which require reading skill. Allow all students to contribute at their own level.

- Play team games, such as spelling bees, with the teacher choosing words at the appropriate level of difficulty for each student. Another successful game is Who am I, if students take turns to ask questions, and sample questions (such as "Male or Female?") are provided for lower level students.

c. Whole group activities which incorporate different tasks

Major class projects give everyone an opportunity of working towards the same goal and taking pleasure in the joint final product while incorporating a wide enough variety of tasks for everyone to be involved at their own level. One useful idea is to issue regular editions of a class newspaper. This can be mounted on a bulletin board, or printed up for distribution if the class is not always held in the same classroom. The strongest students might interview people and write articles. Others with good literacy skills might work as editors helping reporters to improve their text. Less advanced students might do horoscopes and weather reports, provide captions for photos, or be responsible for lay-out.

Other whole class projects which will involve a wide variety of tasks at different levels of difficulty include organizing, planning and advertising a field trip, making a slide tape show, making a photo story account of a class activity, or planning a bring-a-guest morning.

The activities I have described so far are all designed to help the class develop a sense of being part of a group, and to help them recognize that everyone in the class can contribute. Keeping the whole group working together all the time is not entirely practical, however, and most teachers with multilevel classes find it is fruitful to also have the students work in various patterns of smaller groups.

One general principle to bear in mind when planning small group activities is that the makeup of the small group should be adjusted, depending on whether the focus of the activity is on accuracy or fluency. Accuracy activities will include any work which has as its aim improving the form of what is said. It may focus on learning a new piece of grammar such as a verb tense or the formation of plurals. It may be a pronunciation exercise, or an activity which helps people recognize the most socioculturally appropriate form of an utterance. For activities like these, it makes sense to have students work in groups of more or less equal ability, so that every member of the group is learning a specific item which they do not currently have control of, and which is appropriate for their level of language development. It is also, however, very important that students have the chance to work on their fluency, that is on using language to express oneself, where the task is to get the message over, not to worry about the form by which that is achieved. Such activities are better performed in mixed level groups. The advanced speakers are challenged to find alternate ways of expressing themselves which can be understood by the beginners. The weaker students benefit from hearing a much richer range of language than they would be exposed to in a group composed entirely of beginners.

Equal Ability Groupings

Equal ability small groups will often be doing the same type of tasks as you would assign to a whole class, but this is the teacher's chance to do some accuracy work focusing on a specific language item or function. There are also certain tasks which can be assigned to a small group of five or so which cannot be done with a whole class.

- *problem solving*

  "Who gets thrown out of the life-boat?" type decision making. Suitable problems might include planning the best meal for a particular occasion based on a set of food ads, choosing the best apartment for a specified tenant from the want ads, deciding on the best course of action for an immigrant with aging parents in the native country, and so on.

- *process writing*

  have students read their stories to each other, and edit based on the feedback they receive.

- *group work based on sequencing*

  e.g. deciding on the best sequence for a series of photos which tell a story, cut up comic strip stories, narrative strip stories and so on.

- *planning activities*

  working with a map to plan a route, organizing an end of term party, planning refreshments, etc.

Cross Ability Groups

As with whole group activities described above, this is best for project type tasks where jobs can be assigned based on ability. For example, students might contribute their favourite recipes to make a recipe book, with one responsible for the index, another for sorting, another for the title page, one for proof reading recipes, etc.

Pair Group

Pair work is another useful tool for the teacher of a multilevel class. Asking students to complete even basic seat work in pairs encourages the use of language and makes rather dull exercises into interesting oral interactions. The pairs may be composed of students of roughly equal ability or widely different.

Cross Ability Pairs

Sometimes teachers are reluctant to ask advanced learners to work with beginners as they feel that the stronger students are wasting their time. However, there are quite a few ways in which both students can really benefit from this mix, as many activities put heavier demands on one partner in the pair. The task for the teacher is to ensure that the stronger student does not take over the activity, by making it necessary for the less advanced student to have input. You might try some of the following ideas:

- have one student transcribe the LEA story of the other student and help the writer read it back.
- have the stronger student complete a form on the other student, which will require an interview of the other student.
- assign puzzle type activities where one student has to give instructions to the other. The weaker student is given for instance a set of pictures cut from a catalogue. The stronger student is given a matrix that is a completed grid with the same pictures pasted in a particular order. The task is for the weaker student to duplicate the matrix without looking at the original. The stronger student must give oral instructions as to how to arrange pieces appropriately. (The weaker the lower level student is, the more demanding this is for higher level student.)
- the lower level student selects an object, or famous person. The more advanced student has to find out who or what has been chosen. The beginner student need answer only "Yes/No" or "I don't understand."
- assign a role play such as phoning for information, where one role is dominant or more demanding.

Equal Ability Pairs

Almost any activity which one person can do turns into a more communicative activity if the students work in pairs. Some particularly useful ideas include:

- interviewing each other, perhaps recording responses on some kind of form
- read aloud dialogues, especially those where a choice of answers is provided so that learners must focus on the content of what is said as well as the pronunciation task
- role plays where both parts are equally challenging.

Also useful are information gap activities where both students are given the same text but with different omissions and must question each other to discover the missing information.

Individual Work

A significant problem with multilevel classes is to make the students more responsible for their own learning. Because the class varies so widely in ability it is often difficult for the teacher to be sure that all students are working at their optimum level, and some students will tend to coast along doing easier activities than are really appropriate.

Ideally, students need to be able to select materials which suit not merely their language skill level but also their interests, age, cultural needs, etc. Building up a self access centre in a multilevel classroom is a great help for teacher and student. Some teachers work almost exclusively with self access materials. Others prefer to use it as one component of an overall program. The self access centre should be a large box or cupboard from which students select their own activity. Ideally the materials should provide correct answers for any accuracy based activities so that students can check their own performance and do not have to wait until the teacher is free to discover how well they did.

A self access centre should include materials which address all the skill areas.

Reading Materials

The teacher selects and mounts a variety or reading matter from comic stripsto hydro bills to short stories. A few comprehension questions are provided on each with an answer key on the back. Students select whatever interests them, and check their own work.

Listening

The teacher will need to provide at least one cassette player plus a selection of tapes with accompanying print material. The tapes might include spontaneous native-speaker conversation, recorded simplified language dialogues, radio broadcasts of news, weather or chat shows, songs for use with cloze text, work lists for dictation practice, letter lists for dictation practice.

Writing

A simple way to build up a variety of writing activities is to pull apart your favourite workbooks and laminate the pages. Provide washable felt markers so that the learners can write in their answers and then the sheets can be wiped clean for use by another student. You can also laminate cheques, deposit slips, birthday cards, etc. Pictures, comic strips and photos are also useful to stimulate free writing, with suggestions for vocabulary provided on the back which students can refer to if they wish.

Speaking

Provide puzzles and games calling on speaking skills which students can do in pairs. Provide blank cassettes for students to record whatever they wish, either individual rehearsal or pair role-play or conversation.

Grammar/Vocabulary Development

Again, laminated pages from a favourite text are the easiest way to provide a wide variety of activities.

The Overall Curriculum

As the suggestions above show, there is no shortage of activities for a multilevel class. The problem is not really what to do, but to find a way of organizing these apparently unconnected activities into a well-planned syllabus. Ideally we would consult with each student and with them determine their goals and the time frame in which they hope to achieve them. However, in practice this can mean 25 students all doing different things which require teacher input. For larger classes, therefore, we have to compromise. Although students should still have input into the goal-setting process they will select goals from a curriculum designed by the teacher.

Such a curriculum is normally based on process, where the activities are arranged to ensure that the student is developing all the required skills. This is not just a matter of listening, speaking, reading and writing but also of improving syntax, building vocabulary, inferring meaning from context, watching for nonverbal communication while following a conversation, etc. It also suggests breaking the traditional four skill areas down into the various subskills and ensuring, for example, that reading instruction includes not only detailed comprehension, but quickly grasping the gist of a passage, index skills, familiarity with layout, scanning for specific information, etc. A curriculum which focuses on these sorts of skills should be applicable to all students at all levels.

Editor's Note: A more detailed discussion of ideas and activities for miltilevel classes can be found in Jill Bell's book *Teaching Multilevel Classes* in ESL (Toronto: Pippin Publishing, 1988) from which these ideas are drawn. This material is reproduced by permission of the publisher.

Reprinted from: Jill Bell, "The Challenge of Multilevel Classes." *Mosaic*, 2, 1 (Fall 1994), pp. 1, 3-5.

18 Discipline in the Language Class

Merle Richards

Language teachers need clear routines and practical rules to maintain discipline. The article offers some tips for encouraging good conduct and a positive attitude to language learning.

Second-language teachers often seem to have more than their share of classroom discipline problems. Often, these difficulties appear to be associated with pupils' lack of ability or interest in language learning. However, modifying one's teaching style can improve both discipline and interest, and can even seem to increase the students' language abilities (Gruenewald and Pollak, 1990), thus solving several difficulties at once.

Classroom observation shows that not all language teachers encounter discipline problems. When parents exclaim, "Hey, my kid loves Tamil (Polish, Mohawk, French)!", chances are the language class is not spent in rote repetition, word lists, grammar rules, or uninviting content. More likely, the learners are using language to talk about their lives and interests, building knowledge and skills slowly, but with increasing competence. As their capacity increases, they are encouraged to use the language, however badly, to express their ideas and feelings. Gradually, with feedback and help from the teacher, their form improves and approaches more closely the model of the fluent speaker.

Discipline and Respect

"Discipline" in the language class is the same as in any other. It implies guidance, limits, firmness, and leadership, not harshness, humiliation, or autocratic control.

Good discipline is based on respect: the teacher earns respect by being prepared and knowledgeable, and modelling consideration for self and learners. Children develop respect through example and practice; with it they gain self-control and responsibility.

Since schools have the mandate to teach alternatives to violence, physical punishment is not an acceptable method of discipline. Hence, teachers need to have a system of sanctions, rewards, and penalties to be used as needed. Rewards and incentives are nearly always more effective than punishment, but punishment may be necessary if a serious or harmful behaviour has occurred which must not be repeated. Punishment must work immediately if it is to work at all.

Best of all is to help the student take responsibility for correcting the situation, rather than directing blame or applying punishment. A useful maxim is "When you hurt someone, you have to make them better; when you do damage, you make repairs." Demanding apologies often just teaches children that "you can do whatever you wish if you apologize later".

A Discipline Plan

A discipline plan involves an escalating system leading from unobtrusive signals to outright penalties. Punishments that will cause lasting resentment or defiance should be avoided, but "punishments that fit the crime" or imply a bit of humour can be highly effective.

Step One: Prevention

Misbehaviour is easier to prevent or "nip in the bud" than to change. Observation shows that pupils misbehave when they are bored, confused, uncomprehending, or idle. The teacher who maintains involvement in activities through interest avoids most pupil misconduct. *Prepare thoroughly for each class!*

The same class may behave quite differently with different teachers. Usually the difference lies in the teacher's style and preparation. Active learning methods leave little time for misbehaviour. Using Total Physical Response (TPR) and language experience daily focuses the pupils on the learning task, avoiding "goofing off". Moreover, these approaches ensure that the pupils are comprehending and using the language, so that they do not become frustrated by lack of understanding.

Some kids are rowdy, inattentive, or defiant; a few are difficult under any circumstances. But most pupils' behaviour is guided by the situation - if it is clear. Make your rules simple and explicit: don't expect kids to "just know" what you want. Develop routines to avoid problems, making the rules and limitations clear (Ornstein, 1990). Children will push to try those limits: be cheerfully firm in enforcing them. For example, if pupils wander around during worktime, bring in a few language games. Then state, "When your work is finished, put it in my basket, then you may get a book or a quiet game." Similarly, state, "When I am addressing the whole class, stay in your seat and pay attention. You can sharpen your pencil or get a drink later".

Step Two: Heading Off Problems

1. When small misdemeanours occur just once, you can ignore them. But if they are repeated, you must react: the third time may establish a habit.

   Reaction should be low-key: Say the pupil's name, move to stand nearby, use "the eye". These serve as notice that the misconduct has been noted.

2. For more serious infractions, issue a warning: "We do not like our opening prayer to be interrupted. The next time you are late, please wait at the door until we finish." "If you fight over points, the game will

stop." Then, the next time the same behaviour occurs, carry out your promise. Do not give another warning.

Caution: Don't make threats you won't carry out. Someone will call your bluff, and the kids will think you don't mean what you say.

3. Have some boring jobs to use as punishments. Picking up scraps, straightening the boots, sharpening the pencils, or even writing lines may work.

   For some kids, these may be agreeable tasks; this is okay if they break the pattern of misconduct. In this case, tell the child, "I see you are looking for something useful to do; here's a job for you until you're ready to work properly." Make clear that the academic work still needs to be done; this is not an escape.

4. Realize that many problems are due to attention-seeking (Dreikurs, 1982). Tell the pupil you know this, and give much attention when the child is behaving well. (You have to notice good behaviour too!) Don't be embarrassed to praise when praise is due.

5. Avoid sarcasm or humiliation. They are effective controls, but arouse hostilities that may make the pupil want to get even, thus creating new discipline problems. Worse, the student may simply "opt out", withdrawing from learning or participating, and you will have a hard time recreating a relationship that will involve the student in learning again.

6. Restructure your program. Change the schedule or routines so that pupils have time to finish their tasks and do not have to spend time waiting for your attention or assistance. Use games to provide practice and objects and pictures to ensure that pupils always catch the meaning.

Step Three: Consequences Matter!

1. Serious problems need immediate measures. A "time-out" corner may help some kids to cool off. If you use the hallway, don't leave the pupil alone; try to keep her/him in sight. If you send a student to the office, be sure s/he is expected, or act as escort yourself.

2. Talking with kids about their behaviour helps if you don't nag or blame. "It makes me really mad when I see you marking our books. We all need to use them. How are you going to fix them up?"

3. Discuss consequences of misbehaviour and decide with the class how to deal with repeated problems: "If you can't work with others, you'll have to work alone".

4. Establish incentives and bonuses for good conduct. Privileges can be lost if abused. (But be sure that kids are able to earn the rewards that are promised.)

5. You can use tokens or play money for rewards and for fines for infractions. "You forgot your homework? That will be one dollar. I'll see the homework after school, please". This works well with older children, especially if they can use their "money" for privileges.

6. Discuss problems with the class, and have them suggest solutions they can live with. For example, one group decided they could avoid pro-

voking the class bully and "help him to be good". Some children even said they would allow him one poke, but that if he got really bad, he should be excluded from the room. This tactic was agreed to and acted upon.

7. Don't use tests, homework, or schoolwork as penalties. Learning is not a punishment. But writing "lines" is effective with some pupils.

Step Four: **Crisis Management**

Chronic and serious misconduct usually implies that something is wrong in the child's life. Document all offenses and *get help*! Talk with the principal and the parents to decide on a consistent discipline plan for that child. If behaviour problems are serious enough to threaten others or prevent learning, the miscreant may have to be removed from the class. The parents should be called to pick up the child; until they arrive, an adult should remain with the child. Emotional disorders are beyond most teachers' field of expertise, and the other children have a right to feel - and be - safe at school.

Step four cases are rare; most discipline problems can be dealt with in common-sense ways. The teacher needs to realize that most children want to behave well, and will if they know how. By planning interesting lessons with purposeful learning tasks, the teacher solves most problems before they begin.

These strategies apply to any teaching situations, but especially to the language class, because language learning often seems to be superficial and uninvolving. Switching from drills to practice games, from textbook exercises to language experience, and from recitation to TPR helps to get learners "onside". Then when discipline problems do arise, they are less likely to escalate.

Finally, maintain your sense of humour. Often one can choose to be affronted or to laugh. Ornstein (1990) mentions that choosing humour to defuse a tense situation shows that the teacher is secure and in charge. The students relax and can then return to their real business, learning and using the second language.

References

Dreikurs, Rudolf. 1982. *Maintaining Sanity in the Classroom*. New York: Harper and Row.

Gruenewald, Lee J. and Sara A. Pollak. 1990. *Language Interaction in Curriculum and Instruction: What the Classroom Teacher Needs to Know*. 2nd ed. Austin, Texas: PRO-ED.

McNeil, John D. and Jon Wiles. 1990. *The Essentials of Teaching: Decisions, Plans, Methods.* New York: Macmillan.

Ornstein, Allan C. 1990. *Strategies for Effective Teaching*. New York; Harper and Row.

Reprinted from: Merle Richards, "Discipline in the Language Class," *Mosaic*, 2, 1(Fall 1995): 14-15.

19 Interactive Homework: Creating Connections Between Home and School

Janis L. Antonek, G. Richard Tucker,
and Richard Donato

How can the awareness of foreign language programs in elementary schools be increased among parents? Interactive homework – the involvement of parents and child – may be one solution.

Introduction

Developing, funding, and maintaining elementary foreign language programs are complex tasks which routinely confront educators seeking to broaden the curriculum in the area of world languages and cultures.[1] Once a program of study is established, however, it is important to ensure that support is maintained, interest and enthusiasm are kept alive, and information regarding the contents of the elementary foreign language program is regularly communicated to everyone involved.[2] McLoughlin Carter (1993) states that to ensure future support of foreign language in the elementary school (FLES), teachers must engage in public awareness activities, tasks often deemed by teachers as unrelated to instruction and classroom learning. McLoughlin Carter (1993, p. 389) urges that

> we must force our programs into the awareness of our primary constituents – the students and parents whom we serve.

Rosenbusch (1991) further argues that parental support is crucial for second language programs and suggests that parental involvement can mobilize parents into program advocates.

Evidence of the powerful role that parents play in second language advocacy can be seen in the American organization Advocates for Language Learning (ALL) and the Canadian organization Canadian Parents for French (CPF). ALL was founded in 1983 by Madeline Ehrlich, a Culver City, California parent of three immersion students, because she "began to envision an educational environment where every child would have the opportunity to learn a second language as part of the regular school program" (Erlich, 1987:98-99). CPF, founded in 1977 by parents in Ottawa, has played a significant role in the advancement of French immersion schooling across Canada (Sloan, 1989). Both continue to flourish.

Not all parents are equally convinced of the importance of foreign language education. McLoughlin Carter (1993) outlines four public awareness activities foreign language educators may consider when trying to convince communities that their programs are as important as other more time-honoured subjects. She suggests

- Parent-Teacher Association programs,
- articles in local newspapers,
- vocabulary newsletters, and
- displays of student work.

The purpose of this article is to explore one additional means of increasing parental awareness of FLES programs – the use of interactive homework assignments. We will present a rationale for the use of homework that involves the parent[3] and child, report on an interactive homework project in a Japanese FLES program (Donato, Antonek and Tucker, 1994; Tucker, Donato and Antonek, 1994, Antonek, Donato and Tucker, 1995), discuss parental reactions to these interactive assignments, and provide guidelines for constructing interactive homework assignments for the foreign language class.

Considering the "Home" in Homework

Although a routine practice in school, homework is often assigned with little thought regarding its function, role, or connection with classroom instruction. A brief review of the most commonly used methodology textbooks in foreign language instruction (Curtain and Pesola, 1994; Nunan, 1991; Oller, 1993; Omaggio Hadley, 1993; Richard-Amato, 1988; and Schrum and Glisan 1994) reveals that the issue of homework is never presented or discussed. Why this issue has not been treated more fully in the professional literature is not the purpose of this article. In our investigation of the role and function of homework we question the tacit assumption that homework is exclusively the activity of an individual or merely an opportunity for independent practice. We have been led to explore the role of homework as a powerful and valuable tool and now recommend that systematic guidance be provided to teachers concerning its multiple purposes.

We maintain that the role of homework may be viewed differently from solitary activity of the learner or independent practice opportunities. Assignments a child brings into the home create a vital link between the classroom and outside world and should also be understood for their potential to inform and raise awareness about language instruction in the classroom. We argue that homework implicitly communicates information to parents about two important aspects of the child and the school.

- If attentive to home assignments, parents learn directly about the contents of the curriculum. While observing children completing assignments, the parent can gain access to what the child is being taught, the mode of presentation, and the child's level of mastery with the particular skill or concept. Children who take homework assignments seriously and appear to enjoy and take pride in their work inspire confidence about the school and teacher in parents and demonstrate to them that their children are most likely equally enthusiastic about their classroom learning. Conversely, parents can experience negative feelings or scepticism toward course content and the effectiveness of instruction while observing their children completing assignments that are tedious, needlessly complicated, or for which the child is unprepared.

- Further, assignments communicate directly to parents how the child feels about a particular task. A child's differential enthusiasm, eagerness, or lack of interest across subject areas tells the parent how the child reacts affectively to school activities, in general, and to a specific subject area, in particular.

In short, apart from homework's primary goal as a tool to increase learning opportunities and develop responsible students, it also can have a hidden function – to link the classroom with the home and to communicate implicitly to the parent what children know and can do, their level of mastery and comfort with the information, and their feelings about the subject area.

We suggest, therefore, that homework functions on three interrelated levels:

1. Homework communicates to the parent what and how well the child is learning in the classroom, the child's affective reaction to this learning, and the contents and scope of the curriculum. For this reason, it is curious that no attention whatsoever has been paid to the potential roles of homework in even the most current language teaching methodology textbooks.

2. Second, Homework facilitates classroom learning if it is linked to what the child can realistically carry out in the absence of the teacher and other students, and if the child has been prepared to complete the assignment independent of the myriad forms of assistance a classroom can provide. Homework can also be conceptualized as incorporating other forms of assistance found in the home and community and thus reinforce or extend the child's learning outside the boundaries of the classroom.

3. Homework mediates the relationship of school and home. Homework is an implicit public awareness mechanism which at the same time informs parents of the curriculum and the child's progress and level of engagement. In considering its mediational role, we feel that teachers would be well advised to consider carefully the communicative value of homework and its impact on parents who monitor their children completing assignments in the home. We maintain that well conceived homework has the potential to increase awareness and support for a program through the implicit messages it sends concerning a child's schooling. This message can be either negative or positive and for this reason homework is an important element of schooling and a topic worthy of our attention.

The Concept of Interactive Homework

Homework can build a bridge between the classroom and the home and can serve as an instrument of awareness and ultimately advocacy and support for foreign language programs. If this is so, how can homework be re-conceptualized to benefit both child and parent? Rather than view homework as an independent activity to be completed by the child, assignments can be designed to involve the parent in ways that benefit the child and inform the parent directly about what the child is learning in the classroom. The concept of interactive homework has recently been reported by Epstein (1993) at The Center on Families, Communities, Schools, and Children's Learning at the Johns Hopkins University where interactive homework assignments in math, science, English language arts, and health have been written and piloted. Referred to as "Teachers Involve Parents in Schoolwork" (TIPS), the process includes talking with students about homework in the classroom, asking them to describe the type of homework they like best, and inviting them to tell how their parents help them with their schoolwork at home (Epstein, 1993, p. 73). Central to the TIPS process is the interactive homework assignment which invites parents to work with their child on something they are learning in the classroom. In the discussion that follows, we will extend the concept of interactive homework to the foreign language classroom and present our work on incorporating interactive homework in the context of a Japanese FLES program. Additionally, we believe that interactive homework is well suited to foreign language learning where

- opportunities for functional practice and interaction (Ellis, 1988; Long, 1981; Swain, 1985),

- the need to reflect on language (Brooks and Donato, 1994; Donato, 1994; Swain, 1994), and

- the importance of assessing one's own linguistic achievements (Donato and McCormick, 1994)

are central to the language learning process.

Epstein (1993) states that recent studies indicate that the home directly influences students' skills and achievements but that parents need guidance from schools on how best to assist their children. This assistance is all the more necessary in the case of subject areas where parents do not possess the necessary background or have the requisite knowledge to help their children at home. Foreign language represents a case in point since many parents may have never studied the language or the culture being taught to their children. Foreign language is also set apart from other subjects in that parents may not be able to learn along with their children without sufficient guidance concerning pronunciation, rudimentary knowledge of structure, or cultural information. This need for knowledge of a foreign language is all the more necessary in cases where parents have never studied the language in question. Unlike other subjects where parents may be able to inform themselves on the topic of study, parents have few resources to rely on to help them understand the language their children are acquiring. A further problem is the cumulative nature of language learning. Learning a language requires remembering vocabulary, pronunciation, etc. Parents may find it difficult to retain information from one assignment to the next. If they do remember aspects of the language represented across interactive assignments, this knowledge is, at best, fragmentary. However, given the apparent difficulty of actively incorporating the parent into the foreign language learning activity of their children, we believe that creative planning and thoughtful implementation of interactive assignments can result in the spread of information about foreign language curriculum to parents, parental support for foreign language programs, and the promotion of positive attitudes in children and increased learning.

Interactive Homework and the Japanese FLES Program

After the first year of a three year pilot program (1992-1995) to introduce a Japanese FLES program in grades K-5 at the Falk Laboratory School of the University of Pittsburgh, our team of researchers collected data on the language development of students and the attitudes of parents, teachers, and children concerning this innovative program. Analysis of questionnaires distributed to the parents of the children participating in the program revealed two important findings. First, parents were concerned that they were not well enough informed about what their children were learning and the type of instruction they were receiving. Second, it was apparent that parents had no basis for accurately assessing their children's progress in Japanese. This second finding was manifested when we queried parents regarding how they perceived their children's achievement in Japanese. Comments ranged from extreme satisfaction and enthusiasm for the child's ability to carry out a small but appropriate number of language functions for a 75 minute a week FLES program to scepticism regarding the limited range of topics a child could handle. Curiously, we found that often parents would react differently toward exactly the same behaviours exhibited by the child. For example, one parent expressed satisfaction that her child could count, name colours, and engage in a few greeting protocols. Conversely, another parent citing almost the same language abilities questioned whether this skill was a sufficient return for the time invested in learning Japanese. We concluded that due to their lack of information about the curriculum, parents needed to be directly connected to the activities of the classroom. This conclusion prompted us to explore the use of homework that would involve the parent in observing and assisting the child's use of Japanese. The goal of these assignments was, therefore, to help the child review classwork in the home and to make parents aware of the contents of the Japanese curriculum and the skills their children were developing in the classroom.

Interactive homework assignments were developed by the Japanese teacher, Ms. Mari O'Connell. As previously mentioned, the first task was to address the problem of providing the necessary resources for parents to work with children on a topic about which the vast majority of them had no knowledge. It was decided that vocabulary and culture would be the focus of each interactive assignment and that parents would be supplied with a guide to help them in pronouncing words with their children. Tasks included sharing vocabulary with parents or teaching the parent a few words or expressions in Japanese. Brief cultural information in English, previously discussed in class, was also included. Simple line drawings were used to cue vocabulary practice or to illustrate cultural notes (see Appendix).

After some initial experimentation with format and length during the first semester, we decided upon a one-sided, 8 1/2 x 14" interactive homework sheet presented every other week during the second semester. The interactive homework assignments were generally consistent in format in an effort to minimize time expended on learning how to do each new assignment.

Section 1 of each homework sheet began with a title introducing the topic of the homework such as personal information, courtesy expressions, school subjects, classroom objects and greetings. Following the title was a statement to the family indicating that the homework topic reflected class work and curricular objectives (e.g., "In class we are studying how to greet different people in Japanese. In this homework assignment I will show you how I can say hello and good-bye to different people in Japanese."), a notice of the due date, and a space for the child's signature.

Section 2 featured from one to four language functions thus alerting the parent to what the child should be able to say in Japanese. This section provided all of the phrases necessary for carrying out the language functions in the homework. In this way, parents were provided with a helpful reference tool to use while working with the child. The Japanese examples were written in a modified form of roomaji to assist the parent with pronunciation. We had hoped that this presentation would alleviate pronunciation difficulties. In many ways it proved useful but as one parent noted "Victor (her son) corrects my pronunciation. He speaks so beautifully...but I don't remember the pronunciation from one time to the next." We will return to the problem of pronunciation under guidelines for creating interactive homework.

Section 3, entitled "Let's warm up," asked the students to display their knowledge to their parent by carrying out 3-5 language functions (e.g., "Tell your parents how you would greet them in the morning, in the afternoon, and in the evening. Apologize to your parents.").

In Section 4, the students would teach their parents how to carry out the language functions in the homework. Section 5 provided an opportunity for the parents and children to interact by communicating in Japanese (e.g., "With your parents, exchange greetings and courtesy expressions."). Section 6 presented cultural information relevant to the interactive homework topic.

The last section contained a response form for the parent to sign and provide feedback on the child's performance. Parents were asked to detach

---

Name: _____ Class: _____ Date: _____

Japanese: Greetings

Dear Family,
In Japanese class we have learned how to greet people. This activity will let me show you how I do it. This assignment is due _____

Sincerely, _____
Student's signature

In Japanese I am able to say and respond greetings and courtesy expression properly.

O.high.yo!	"Good morning!"
Cone.knee.chi.wa!	"Hello, Good afternoon!"
Cone.ban.wa!	"Good evening!"
Sa.yo.(o).na.la!	"Good bye!"
Are.lee.ga.toe!	"Thank you!"
Dough.e.ta.she.ma.she.tay.	"You are welcome."
ao.men.na.sigh.	"I am sorry."
Ee.des.yo!	"It's OK!"

To your parent, how do you...
greet him or her in the morning? afternnon? evening?
greet him or her when you go apart?
thank him or her? or respond when he or she says "thank you"?
apologize? or respond when he or she says "I'm sorry"?

Teach your parent how to greet in Japanese!

With your parent, exchange greetings and courtesy expressions.

1. AM	2. early PM	3. Evening	4. Gift	5. Oops!	6. Bye!

The tradition of bowing in Japan is a
common gesture used in introductions,
greetings, partings, apologizing, and thanking.

Student's name _____ Class _____ Date _____
How well do you think your child performed this skill?
1. _____ Child seems to perform this skill well.
2. _____ Please check work. Child needs some help on this.
3. _____ Please note (other comments below):

_____
Parent's signature

---

this last section and return it to the teacher. The response form was kept simple to allow parents simply to check off whether the child performed the task well or still needed additional practice. A space for other comments completed the interactive homework sheet. Students were encouraged to keep the interactive homework sheets to use for future reference.

The interactive homework was short and printed on a single page, followed a regular format, linked to the curriculum, included language resources to help the parent work with the child, included a cultural component, contained simple, direct instructions, provided for practice and interaction, and allowed the parent to respond concerning their child's performance and progress.

Parental Reactions to Interactive FL Homework

Parental reactions to the interactive homework assignments were sought on two different occasions – at the middle and end of the academic year. Mid-year questionnaires revealed that the length of the assignments and the child's level of comfort in completing the homework was problematic. In response to this observation, future assignments were shortened and only material that all children could be expected to complete without the assistance of the teacher was included, i.e., material that was adequately covered in class and was relatively familiar. It was hoped that this familiarity with the material would allow the children to showcase their ability rather than their frustration, which is often the case when assignments are given prematurely or without regard for pre-requisite skills and knowledge needed to work independently or with a parent. To shorten the assignments, language function practice was decreased and there were more activities at the word-level (e.g. "Say the names of the 12 body parts to your parents."). Cultural information was omitted; however, soon after this decision had been made, several parents voiced concerns that the cultural information was one of the most interesting aspects of the interactive homework. For this reason, cultural information was reinstated.

Of the parents who responded to the items regarding the interactive homework on the end-of-year parent survey, 33% stated that both they and their children enjoyed completing the homework together. Forty-two percent of the parents noted, however, that the assignments were frustrating for them and their children. Twenty-five percent of the parents observed that the first round of assignments were too long but since they had been shortened they enjoyed working with their children on Japanese homework. We found these responses encouraging since over half the parents (58%) stated that they and their children enjoyed completing the revised assignments.

We were also interested in determining how consistently parents participated in interactive Japanese homework with their children. Thirty-eight percent of the parents reported having completed all the assignments and 20% estimated that they had completed almost half of the interactive homework. Forty-two percent reported that very few or none of the assignments were undertaken with their children most likely because of the frustrations expressed in the previous question. It is striking that the same percentage of parents who expressed satisfaction with the interactive homework also represents the percentage of parents who report actually "doing homework" with children. That is, these parents' judgments seem to be based on practice and behavioral commitment rather than on merely providing a socially and educationally appropriate answer.

When asked whether interactive homework should continue, a high percentage (76%) of the parents responded affirmatively. The remaining parents (24%) who responded negatively need some qualification however, since this number included several parents of kindergarten students to whom homework is never given in other subject areas. In some cases, parents of kindergarten children felt that homework was not appropriate at all for any subject at this level of schooling. As one parent stated "kindergarten children have too many other things to do after school. They should not be assigned homework." Therefore, the interactive nature of the assignment may not have produced the recommendation to discontinue the project but a belief that kindergarten is not a time for bringing formal academic work into the home.

Anecdotal comments of the parents taken from the end-of-year questionnaires also shed light on the use and function of interactive homework, the characteristics of effective assignments, and their potential to inform and raise awareness about the contents of the curriculum. One parent stated that he liked the interactive assignments because "I'd have an idea of what was going on in class." The majority of the narrative comments centered on the pronunciation issue. Several parents requested that tapes be sent home even at a nominal fee. Another parent observed that her "two children argued over pronunciation and who would teach it." She added "I am bad at languages and found it frustrating to be grilled about it by my children." For this parent, audio tapes keyed to the assignments would have certainly helped to relieve frustration at interactive homework time.

Other comments reflected the need for a consistent format and clear objectives and directions. "Interactive homework should continue if it is made clearer concerning its purpose - to explore? to meet set goals? to assess progress?" All these questions deserve our attention if building interactions between parent and child in the home is to become a reality. Length of assignment also surfaced as a concern –

"Homework should be very short and more frequent (weekly) and they should focus on just one thing a week."

Finally, for a few parents, receiving the assignments was problematic.

"I never received assignments due to my child's not making them available without me asking for them."

Clearly this problem can be solved if parents are informed in advance concerning dates of interactive homework distribution. All the above comments were extremely helpful in refining our homework project. We were also encouraged by the comments of some parents who enthusiastically added

"I learned some Japanese too!"

Recommendations and Guidelines for Creating Interactive Homework Assignments

Based on our experience, we offer the following recommendations and guidelines for the construction of interactive homework assignments for the foreign language class. In this section, we will make recommendations concerning the use of interactive homework and will then conclude with a reference checklist to use in designing interactive homework assignments.

Information

The first step in initiating an interactive homework project is to inform all participants on the nature of the project. Epstein (1993) emphasizes the importance of sending a letter of introduction to the parents describing the frequency, goals, objectives, and procedures of the interactive homework assignments. In turn, parents should be encouraged to provide their observations, comments, or questions to the teacher (Epstein 1993, p. 74). Including a response form at the end of each assignments allows the teacher to monitor the degree of participation in the project and provides the parent with a direct way to communicate with the classroom teacher.

Homework format

As previously discussed consistency is critical. Although covering different material, each assignment should follow a similar format. (e.g., title, note to parent signed by child, objectives, language material used in assignment, child-parent interaction activity, cultural information, response form for parent). This predictable pattern of homework activity will help the parent to focus on the content of the assignments rather than the procedures for its completion. The format should be "user-friendly" by avoiding technical language, complicated or wordy directions, illegible printing and a dense or "busy" layout. In deciding on a format, it is equally important to consider the length of the assignment. It is unrealistic to expect parent and child to spend long periods of time on homework for a single subject. We have found that short 10 minute assignments work best and are viewed by parents as feasible and realistic rather than oppressive and inconvenient. Epstein (1993) also suggests that interactive homework be kept to one-page and be reproduced on coloured paper for easy identification by the parent and child.[4]

Language resources

Make every effort to assist the parent to assist the child. Foreign language represents a subject area different from others whose contents are taught through a language already known to the parent. Provide clear, easy to use pronunciation guides. This year we are sending parents audio tapes of Japanese stories and songs and parents are responding quite favourably to this tool. Additionally, parents can not be expected to learn the language along with their child. Although parents will develop some knowledge of the language through their interactions with their children, an interactive assignment sent home twice a month will simply not provide the necessary input for a parent to make significant language gains. Moreover, parents will not have the continual language exposure and practice necessary for second language acquisition. Therefore, ensure that each assignment is self-contained. Make no assumption that information used in an assignment during the first week of the month will be retained by the parent for use in an assignment during week three of the same month. Each assignment needs to provide the necessary resources to be completed independent of all others.

One way to ensure parent-child interaction at homework time and avoid the problem of the parent who, for whatever reason, believes he or she is incapable of helping in a foreign language is to include activities that can be conducted in the home language of the parent and child. Children can share cultural information with their parents or tell their parents their favourite part of a story they have heard in the foreign language class. This interaction can be conducted in the first language and can serve a useful purpose in introducing the study of the foreign language into the everyday discourse of the family.

Consider the child

Like the parent who requires resources for assisting and interacting with the child, the child also needs to be prepared to enter into the interaction with the parent. Among its multiple purposes, one aim of the interactive homework is its public awareness role to inform, inspire confidence and build enthusiasm for the accomplishments of the child and the foreign language program. The teacher needs, therefore, to consider the level of preparedness of the child for a particular homework assignment. Assignments should be written with the children in mind to allow them to showcase their abilities and developing knowledge. Little positive impact will come from assignments that consistently yield child-parent frustration or leave parents with the impression that their children are confused and learning little from the instruction of the teacher. One innovative aspect of interactive homework is that the children become the spokespersons for the FLES program and have the potential to teach the parents. Therefore, like teachers, they need to have the background knowledge and confidence to instruct. Considering the learners and what they can realistically do on their own without teacher support should motivate and drive the contents of the interactive homework assignment.

In deciding at which grade level foreign language homework should begin, the FLES teacher should consider school policy regarding homework. As found in our program, offering foreign language homework in kindergarten when it was not given in other subjects was a contentious issue.

Consider the contents

What can be included in an interactive assignment? We are still experimenting with the contents of interactive homework but our experience has shown that work on vocabulary and simple language functions works well and directly informs the parent of what the child is learning in the classroom. Children may demonstrate to the parent a language function they have learned and teach the parents a few phrases to allow them to engage in a brief 2-4 line dialogue with them. Pictures on the homework sheet can be used to cue vocabulary. Parents can use these images to help children practice and remember new words and expressions. We have also discovered that cultural information is greatly appreciated by parents. Sample activities might include a discussion about a target culture's holidays, a retelling of a legend or folktale, a discussion around a piece of realia, or information concerning daily cultural practices such as schooling, shopping, meals, and family life. As previously discussed, cultural information can be discussed in the child's home language thus avoiding the problem of the parent's lack of proficiency in the target language.

In the spirit of the TIPS project (Epstein, 1993), the contents of the assignments may also connect directly with the home. That is, rather than try to duplicate the classroom in the home, the home itself may be used as a learning environment. Activities that involve the child and parent in information-gathering or observations of persons, objects, and events in the home are excellent ways to take advantage of the unique contribution the home can make in a child's learning. For example, following a lesson on transportation, children may be asked to interview the parent to gather information on the modes of transportation found in their home or neighbourhood (car, bike, motorcycle, roller-skates, sled, truck, wagon, etc.). After a lesson on rooms of the house, a child may be asked to take a parent on a tour of his own home by identifying as many rooms as possible in the target language. This information can then be used in class for additional projects. Comparisons of a child's home with homes found in the target culture can also be carried out in collaboration with a parent. An illustration of the interior of a house in Japan or Mexico, for example, can be used as a point of departure for a discussion of housing differences. In this case, it will be equally interesting for parents to learn about the dwellings of others in a culture unlike their own. In all the examples above, the important point is that the children make use of their immediate environment by connecting some aspect of the home with school, thus strengthening learning and extending the curriculum beyond the walls of the classroom.

The ideal scenario would be for the FLES teacher to consider grade and language level when developing interactive homework assignments. However, in a program like ours, where the staffing option is the language-specialist model – one FLES teacher for all children K-5, multiple versions of interactive homework may not be logistically realistic. Among our parents and students, there were no complaints regarding all students receiving the same homework. Conversely, parental feedback indicated that siblings, enrolled in the same program, were able to participate on the homework together, an unanticipated interaction.

Consider the parent

In the best case scenario, an interactive homework project will result in unanimous, enthusiastic participation on the part of the parents. But as educators we would be naive to assume that parental support for a child's study exists uniformly in all homes. It is not the intention of the authors to pass judgment on parents who, for whatever reason, do not participate in helping a child with home assignments or monitoring their completion.

Professional obligations, travel, health, educational background of the parent, work schedules, etc. all bear on the parent's ability or willingness to complete assignments with a child. However, we think that two issues are raised by the case of a non-participating parent.

- First, children cannot be held responsible for completion of an interactive assignment in cases where the parent refuses or is unable to participate. Unlike independent homework assignments where the onus is entirely upon the child for their completion, the interactive homework requires the participation of two individuals. Teachers need to be sensitive therefore to the feelings of the child whose parents, for whatever reason, have not participated in the assignment. In discussing interactive homework in class, care needs to be taken not to call attention to or embarrass those children who have nothing to turn in to the teacher due to parental non-involvement. Where parents refuse to interact around homework, the child is truly powerless to fulfill course requirements or to promote positive educational exchanges in the home.

- Second, we believe that the knowledge the teacher has of parental involvement in interactive homework can contribute positively to her better understanding of the child, individual differences in the classroom, and possible reasons for the child's achievement or lack of it. Just as interactive homework has the potential to inform parents about school, it can serve equally as a source of critical information about the support a child receives for schooling in the home. Thus interactive homework creates a bi-directional exchange of information from teacher to parent and from parent to teacher. We believe, however, that information concerning interactive homework shared in newsletters, parent night meetings, and communications from the teacher to the parent can alleviate some of the problems of non-participation by showing parents the importance of home support and the value of the project.

Checklist for Constructing an Interactive Homework Assignment

The following checklist is intended as a reference when writing interactive homework assignments.

Procedural considerations

☐ 1. Has a letter been sent to parents explaining the goals and purposes of the interactive homework?

☐ 2. Are parents aware of the dates of distribution and return of interactive homework?

☐ 3. Are the objectives clearly stated on the interactive homework sheet?

☐ 4. Are directions clear and brief? Have they been piloted on a few individuals before distribution to parents?

☐ 5. Has a brief statement introducing the assignment been written from the point of view of the child and signed by her?

☐ 6. Is a parental response form included at the end of the assignment?

Formatting considerations

☐ 7. Is the physical layout of the homework clear and easy to follow?

☐ 8. Is the interactive homework on a single page?

☐ 9. Is format consistent across assignments?

Content considerations

☐ 10. Have parents been given the necessary background information to help the child (pronunciation guides, glosses, etc.)?

☐ 11. Is the homework self-contained?

☐ 12. Has care been taken to include only that content with which the child is most familiar and capable of completing at home?

☐ 13. Is the assignment representative of what the child can do?

☐ 14. Can the homework be successfully completed in a short time?

☐ 15. Do the activities promote interaction?

☐ 16. Does the assignment include activities involving the home?

☐ 17. Has cultural information been included?

Self-assessment

☐ 18. Do you feel the assignment is a good reflection of your competence as a teacher?

Conclusion

This report focuses on the seldom-explored topic of creating and strengthening connections between home and school through the use of interactive homework assignments in the foreign language program. Three factors triggered our interest in this topic: the complete absence of any discussion of homework in contemporary methodology texts, a desire to provide parents of children in a Japanese FLES program with information about their children's program and with a basis for assessing their children's progress, and a belief that the establishment or strengthening of a home - school partnership would significantly enrich the child's educational experience.

We have adapted, piloted, and revised the TIPS model developed by Epstein (1993) for use in the foreign language classroom. During the 1993-1994 school year, we found that a majority of parents completed and appreciated the interactive homework, but that they had a number of suggestions to offer for improving the form and content of assignments. Based upon our experience last year, and parental, student, and teacher feedback, we have revised the form and content of the assignments for this year, developed some supplementary material for parents, and devised a set guidelines and a checklist for others who may wish to develop their own assignments.

We particularly wish to encourage others who develop similar materials to ensure that the assignments encourage the children to showcase their abilities, and that they establish, extend, and solidify linkages between the home and the school. Some will argue that this is difficult to do when the parent does not speak and has not studied the target language; we disagree. We believe that our data indicate that such parents welcome a teacher's initiatives which help them to understand, to participate in, and to support their children's learning experiences. The use of interactive homework assignments, then, provides a valuable tool for enriching the partnership between home and school that has seemingly been ignored.

References

Antonek, J. L., R. Donato and G.R. Tucker. 1994. "Japanese in the elementary school: Description of an innovative Pittsburgh program." *Mosaic*, 2, 2 5-9.

Brooks, F. B. and R. Donato. 1994. "Vygotskyan approaches to understanding foreign language learner discourse during communicative tasks." *Hispania*, 77, 2, 262-274.

Curtain, H.A. and C. A. Pesola. 1988. *Languages and children – making the match*. Reading, MA: Addison-Wesley.

Donato, R. 1994. "Collective scaffolding in second language learning." In J. P. Lantolf and G. Appel eds., *Vygotskian approaches to second language research*. Norwood, NJ: Ablex. Pp. 33-56.

Donato, R. and D. McCormick. 1994. "A sociocultural perspective on language learning strategies: The role of mediation." *The Modern Language Journal*, 78, 4, 453-464.

Donato, R., J.L. Antonek and G.R. Tucker. 1994. "A multiple perspectives analysis of a Japanese FLES program." *Foreign Language Annals*, 27, 365-378.

Ellis, R. 1988. "The role of practice in classroom language learning," *Teanga*, 8: 1-25.

Epstein, Joyce. 1993. "School and family partnerships." *Instructor*, 74-76.

Ehrlich, Madeline. 1987. "Parents: The Child's Most Important Teachers," in John M. Darcey, ed., *Commitment and Collaboration*. Middlebury, VT: Northeast Conference on the Teaching of Foreign Languages.

Long, M. 1981. "Input, interaction and second language acquisition," in H. Winitz, ed., *Native language and foreign language acquisition*, pp. 259-278. Annals of the New York Academy of Sciences 379.

McLoughlin Carter, Eileen. 1993. "Safeguarding our programs through public awareness." *Hispania*, 76, 388-391.

Nunan, D. 1991. *Language teaching methodology*. New York, NY: Prentice-Hall.

Oller, Jr., J. W., ed. 1993. *Methods that work – ideas for literacy and language teachers*. Boston, MA: Heinle and Heinle.

Omaggio Hadley, A. 1993. *Teaching language in context*. Boston, MA: Heinle & Heinle.

Richard-Amato, P. A. 1988. *Making it happen*. New York, NY: Longman.

Rosenbusch, Marcia H. 1991. "Elementary school foreign language: the establishment and maintenance of strong programs." *Foreign Language Annals*, 24, 297-311.

Shrum, J. L. and E. W. Glisan. 1994. *Teacher's handbook - contextualized language instruction*. Boston, MA: Heinle and Heinle.

Sloan, Tom. 1989. "Canadian Parents for French: Two Provinces," *Language and Society/Langue et société*, 26, spring, 34-36.

Swain, M. 1985. "Communicative competence: Some roles of comprehensible input and comprehensible output in its development." In S. M. Gass and C. G. Madden eds., *Input in second language acquisition*, (pp. 235-253). Rowley, MA: Newbury House.

Swain, M. 1994. "Three functions of output in second language learning." Paper presented at the meeting of the Second Language Research Forum, Montreal, Canada.

Tucker, G. R., R. Donato and J. L. Antonek 1995. "Documenting an exemplary Japanese FLES program: In pursuit of Goals 2000," Unpublished manuscript, Carnegie Mellon University and University of Pittsburgh.

Notes

1. The preparation of this report was supported in part by a grant from the US Department of Education to G. R. Tucker and R. Donato, and in part by the Department of Instruction and Learning at the University of Pittsburgh.
2. Thanks to Claire Donato, age 8, for the child's perspective on the non-participating parent.
3. We will use he word "parent" to include caretakers who play a significant role in the life of children assuming primary responsibility for their upbringing, and emotional, physical, and educational needs. The word "parent" is intended to encompass all individuals present in the home who have the daily responsibility of nurturing and caring for children.
4. For sample interactive homework assignments in mathematics, science, English language arts, and health, see *Instructor* (1993, 1994).

Reprinted from: Janis L. Antonek, G. Richard Tucker, and Richard Donato, "Interactive Homework: Creating Connections Between Home and School," *Mosaic*, 2, 3 (Spring 1995), pp. 1-10.

20 Eight Approaches to Language Teaching

Gina Doggett

What is the "best" method for teaching languages? The article presents a summary of eight language teaching methods in practice today.

Where there was once consensus on the "right" way to teach foreign languages, many teachers now share the belief that a single right way does not exist. It is certainly true that no comparative study has consistently demonstrated the superiority of one method over another for all teachers, all students and all settings.

Presented here is a summary of eight language teaching methods in practice today:

- the Grammar-Translation Method
- the Direct Method
- the Audio-Lingual Method
- the Silent Way
- Suggestopedia
- Community Language Learning
- the Total Physical Response Method, and
- the Communicative Approach.

Of course, what is described here is only an abstraction. How a method is manifest in the classroom will depend heavily on the individual teacher's interpretation of its principles.

Some teachers prefer to practice one of the methods to the exclusion of the others. Other teachers prefer to pick and choose in a principled way among the methodological options that exist, creating their own unique blend.

The summary provides a brief listing of the salient features of the eight methods. For more details, readers should consult *Techniques and Principles in Language Teaching* by Diane Larsen-Freeman, published in 1986 by Oxford University Press in New York, on which this summary was based. Also see references listed at the end of the article.

Grammar-Translation Method

The Grammar-Translation Method focuses on developing students' appreciation of the target language's literature as well as teaching the language. Students are presented with target language reading passages and answer questions that follow. Other activities include translating literary passages from one language into the other, memorizing grammar rules, and memorizing native-language equivalents of target language vocabulary. Class work is highly structured, with the teacher controlling all activities.

Direct Method

The Direct Method allows students to perceive meaning directly through the target language because no translation is allowed. Visual aids and pantomime are used to clarify the meaning of vocabulary items and concepts. Students speak a great deal in the target language and communicate as if in real situations. Reading and writing are taught from the beginning, though speaking and listening skills are emphasized. Grammar is learned inductively.

Audio-Lingual Method

The Audio-Lingual Method is based on the behaviourist belief that language learning is the acquisition of a set of correct language habits. The learner repeats patterns until able to produce them spontaneously. Once a given pattern -for example, subject-verb-prepositional phrase -is learned, the speaker can substitute words to make novel sentences. The teacher directs and controls students' behaviour, provides a model, and reinforces correct responses.

The Silent Way

The theoretical basis of Gattegno's Silent Way is the idea that teaching must be subordinated to learning and thus students must develop their own inner criteria for correctness. All four skills - reading, writing, speaking, and listening – are taught from the beginning. Students' errors are expected as a normal part of learning; the teacher's silence helps foster self-reliance and student initiative. The teacher is active in setting up situations, while the students do most of the talking and interaction.

Suggestopedia

Lozanov's method seeks to help learners eliminate psychological barriers to learning. The learning environment is relaxed and subdued, with low lighting and soft music in the background. Students choose a name and character in the target language and culture, and imagine being that person. Dialogues are presented to the accompaniment of music. Students just relax and listen to them being read and later playfully practice the language during an "activation" phase.

Community Language Learning

In Curran's method, teachers consider students as "whole persons," with intellect, feelings, instincts, physical responses, and desire to learn. Teachers also recognize that learning can be threatening. By understanding and accepting students' fears, teachers help students feel secure and overcome their fears, and thus help them harness positive energy for learning. The syllabus used is learner-generated, in that students choose what they want to learn to say in the target language.

Total Physical Response Method

Asher's approach begins by placing primary importance on listening comprehension, emulating the early stages of mother tongue acquisition, and then moving to speaking, reading, and writing. Students demonstrate their comprehension by acting out commands issued by the teacher; teacher provides novel and often humorous variations of the commands. Activities are designed to be fun and to allow students to assume active learning roles. Activities eventually include games and skits.

The Communicative Approach

The Communicative Approach stresses the need to teach communicative competence as opposed to linguistic competence; thus, functions are emphasized over forms. Students usually work with authentic materials in small groups on communicative activities, during which they receive practice in negotiating meaning.

THE GRAMMAR-TRANSLATION METHOD

Goals

To be able to read literature in target language; learn grammar rules and vocabulary; develop mental acuity.

Roles

Teacher has authority; students follow instructions to learn what teacher knows.

Teaching/Learning Process

Students learn by translating from one language to the other, often translating reading passages in the target language to the native language. Grammar is usually learned deductively on the basis of grammar rules and examples. Students memorize the rules, then apply them to other examples. They learn paradigms such as verb conjugations, and they learn the native language equivalents of vocabulary words.

Interaction: Student-Teacher and Student-Student

Most interaction is teacher-to-student; student-initiated interaction and student-student interaction is minimal.

Dealing with Feelings

n/a

View of Language, Culture

Literary language seen as superior to spoken language; culture equated with literature and fine arts.

Aspects of Language the Approach Emphasizes

Vocabulary, grammar emphasized; reading, writing are primary skills, pronunciation and other speaking/listening skills not emphasized.

Role of Students' Native Language

Native language provides key to meanings in target language; native language is used freely in class.

Means for Evaluation

Tests require translation from native to target and target to native language; applying grammar rules, answering questions about foreign culture.

Response to Students' Errors

Heavy emphasis placed on correct answers; teacher supplies correct answers when students cannot.

THE DIRECT METHOD

Goals

To communicate in target language; to think in target language.

Roles

Teacher directs class activities, but students and teacher are partners in the teaching/learning process.

Teaching/Learning Process

Students are taught to associate meaning and the target language directly. New target language words or phrases are introduced through the use of realia, pictures, or pantomime, never the native language. Students speak in the target language a great deal and communicate as if in real situations. Grammar rules are learned inductively - by generalizing from examples. Students practice new vocabulary using words in sentences.

Interaction: Student-Teacher and Student-Student

Both teacher and students initiate interaction, though student-initiated interaction, with teacher or among themselves, is usually teacher-directed.

Dealing with Feelings

n/a

View of Language, Culture

Language is primarily spoken, not written. Students study common, everyday speech in the target language. Aspects of foreign culture are studied such as history, geography, daily life.

Aspects of Language the Approach Emphasizes

Vocabulary emphasized over grammar; oral communication considered basic, with reading, writing based on oral practice; pronunciation emphasized from outset.

Role of Students' Native Language

Not used in the classroom.

Means for Evaluation

Students tested through actual use, such as in oral interviews and assigned written paragraphs.

Response to Students' Errors

Self-correction encouraged whenever possible.

THE AUDIO-LINGUAL METHOD

Goals

Use the target language communicatively, overlearn it, so as to be able to use it automatically by forming new habits in the target language and overcoming native language habits.

Roles

Teacher directs, controls students' language behaviour, provides good model for imitation; students repeat, respond as quickly and accurately as possible.

Teaching/Learning Process

New vocabulary, structures presented through dialogues, which are learned through imitation, repetition. Drills are based on patterns in dialogue. Students' correct responses are positively reinforced; grammar is induced from models. Cultural information is contextualized in the dialogues or presented by the teacher. Reading, writing tasks are based on oral work.

Interaction: Student-Teacher and Student-Student

Students interact during chain drills or when taking roles in dialogues, all at teacher's direction. Most interaction is between teacher and student, initiated by teacher.

Dealing with Feelings

n/a

View of Language, Culture

Descriptive linguistics influence: every language seen as having its own unique system of phonological, morphological, and syntactic patterns. Method emphasizes everyday speech and uses a graded syllabus from simple to difficult linguistic structures. Culture comprises everyday language and behaviour.

Aspects of Language the Approach Emphasizes

Language structures emphasized; vocabulary contextualized in dialogues but is limited because syntactic patterns are foremost; natural priority of skills -listening, speaking, reading, writing, with emphasis on first two; pronunciation taught from beginning, often with language lab work and minimal pair drills.

Role of Students' Native Language

Students' native language habits are considered as interfering, thus native language is not used in classroom. Contrastive analysis is considered helpful for determining points of interference.

Means for Evaluation

Discrete-point tests in which students distinguish between words or provide an appropriate verb for a sentence, etc.

Response to Students' Errors

Teachers strive to prevent student errors by predicting trouble spots and tightly controlling what they teach students to say.

THE SILENT WAY

Goals

To use language for self-expression; to develop independence from the teacher, to develop inner criteria for correctness.

Roles

Teaching should be subordinated to learning. Teachers should give students only what they absolutely need to promote their learning. Learners are responsible for their own learning.

Teaching/Learning Process

Students begin with sounds, introduced through association of sounds in native language to a sound-colour chart. Teacher then sets up situations, often using Cuisenaire rods, to focus students' attention on structures. Students interact as the situation requires. Teachers see students' errors as clues to where the target language is unclear, and they adjust instruction accordingly. Students are urged to take responsibility for their learning. Additional learning is thought to take place during sleep.

Interaction: Student-Teacher and Student-Student

The teacher is silent much of the time, but very active setting up situations, listening to students, speaking only to give clues, not to model speech. Student-Student interaction is encouraged.

Dealing with Feelings

Teachers monitor students' feelings and actively try to prevent their feelings from interfering with their learning. Students express their feelings during feedback sessions after class.

View of Language, Culture

Language and culture are inseparable, and each language is seen to be unique despite similarities in structure with other languages.

Aspects of Language the Approach Emphasizes

All four skill areas worked on from beginning (reading, writing, speaking, listening); pronunciation especially, because sounds are basic and carry the melody of the language. Structural patterns are practised in meaningful interactions. Syllabus develops according to learning abilities and needs. Reading and writing exercises reinforce oral learning.

Role of Students' Native Language

Although translation is not used at all, the native language is considered a resource because of the overlap that is bound to exist between the two languages. The teacher should take into account what the students already know.

Means for Evaluation

Assessment is continual; but only to determine continually changing learning needs. Teachers observe students' ability to transfer what they have learned to new contexts. To encourage the development of inner criteria, neither praise nor criticism is offered. Students are expected to learn at different rates, and to make progress, not necessarily speak perfectly in the beginning.

Response to Students' Errors

Errors are inevitable, a natural, indispensable part of learning.

SUGGESTOPEDIA

Goals

To learn, at accelerated pace, a foreign language for everyday communication by tapping mental powers, overcoming psychological barriers.

Roles

Teacher has authority, commands trust and respect of students; teacher "desuggests" negative feelings and limits to learning; if teacher succeeds in assuming this role, students assume childlike role, spontaneous and uninhibited.

Teaching/Learning Process

Students learn in a relaxing environment. They choose a new identity (name, occupation) in the target language and culture. They use texts of dialogues accompanied by translations and notes in their native language. Each dialogue is presented during two musical concerts; once with the teacher matching his or her voice to the rhythm and pitch of the music while students follow along. The second time, the teacher reads normally and students relax and listen. At night and on waking, the students read it over. Then students gain facility with the new material through activities such as dramatizations, games, songs, and question- and-answer sessions.

Interaction: Student-Teacher and Student-Student

At first, teacher initiates all interaction and students respond only non-verbally or with a few words in target language that they have practised. Eventually, students initiate interaction. Students interact with each other throughout, as directed by teacher.

Dealing with Feelings

Great importance is placed on students' feelings, in making them feel confident and relaxed, in "desuggesting" their psychological barriers.

View of Language, Culture

Language is one plane; non-verbal parts of messages are another. Culture includes everyday life and fine arts.

Aspects of Language the Approach Emphasizes

Vocabulary emphasized, some explicit grammar. Students focus on communicative use rather than form; reading, writing also have place.

Role of Students' Native Language

Translation clarifies dialogues' meaning; teacher uses native language, more at first than later, when necessary.

Means for Evaluation

Students' normal in-class performance is evaluated. There are no tests, which would threaten relaxed environment.

Response to Students' Errors

Errors are not immediately corrected; teacher models correct form later during class.

COMMUNITY LANGUAGE LEARNING

Goals

To learn language communicatively, to take responsibility for learning, to approach the task non-defensively, never separating intellect from feelings.

Roles

Teacher acts as counsellor, supporting students with understanding of their struggle to master language in often threatening new learning situation. Student is at first a dependent client of the counsellor and becomes increasingly independent through five specified stages.

Teaching/Learning Process

Non-defensive learning requires six elements: security, aggression (students have opportunities to assert, involve themselves), attention, reflection (students think about both the language and their experience learning it), retention, and discrimination (sorting out differences among target language forms).

Interaction: Student-Teacher and Student-Student

Both students and teacher make decisions in the class. Sometimes the teacher directs action, other times the students interact independently. A spirit of cooperation is encouraged.

Dealing with Feelings

Teacher routinely probes for students' feelings about learning and shows understanding, helping them overcome negative feelings.

View of Language, Culture

Language is for communication, a medium of interpersonal sharing and belonging, and creative thinking. Culture is integrated with language.

Aspects of Language the Approach Emphasizes

At first, since students design syllabus, they determine aspects of language studied; later teacher may bring in published texts. Particular grammar, pronunciation points are treated, and particular vocabulary based on students' expressed needs. Understanding and speaking are emphasized, though reading and writing have a place.

Role of Students' Native Language

Use of native language enhances students' security. Students have conversations in their native language; target language translations of these become the text around which subsequent activities revolve. Also, instructions and sessions for expressing feelings are in native language. Target language is used progressively more. Where students do not share the same native language, the target language is used from the outset, though alternatives such as pantomime are also used.

Means for Evaluation

No specific means are recommended, but adherence to principles is urged. Teacher would help students prepare for any test required by school, integrative tests would be preferred over discrete-point tests; self-evaluation would be encouraged, promoting students' awareness of their own progress.

Response to Students' Errors

Non-threatening style is encouraged; modelling of correct forms.

TOTAL PHYSICAL RESPONSE METHOD

Goals

To provide an enjoyable learning experience, having a minimum of the stress that typically accompanies learning a foreign language.

Roles

At first the teacher gives commands and students follow them. Once students are "ready to speak", they take on directing roles.

Teaching/Learning Process

Lessons begin with commands by the teacher; students demonstrate their understanding by acting these out; teachers recombine their instructions in novel and often humorous ways; eventually students follow suit. Activities later include games and skits.

Interaction: Student-Teacher and Student-Student

Teacher interacts with individual students and with the group, starting with the teacher speaking and the students responding non-verbally. Later this is reversed; students issue commands to teacher as well as each other.

Dealing with Feelings

The method was developed principally to reduce the stress associated with language learning; students are not forced to speak before they are ready and learning is made as enjoyable as possible, stimulating feelings of success and low anxiety.

View of Language, Culture

Oral modality is primary; culture is the lifestyle of native speakers of the target language.

Aspects of Language the Approach Emphasizes

Grammatical structures and vocabulary are emphasized, imbedded in imperatives. Understanding precedes production; spoken language precedes the written word.

Role of Students' Native Language

Method is introduced in students' native language, but rarely used later in course. Meaning is made clear through actions.

Means for Evaluation

Teachers can evaluate students through simple observation of their actions. Formal evaluation is achieved by commanding a student to perform a series of actions.

Response to Students' Errors

Students are expected to make errors once they begin speaking. Teachers only correct major errors, and do this unobtrusively. "Fine-tuning" occurs later.

THE COMMUNICATIVE APPROACH

Goals

To become communicatively competent, able to use the language appropriate for a given social context; to manage the process of negotiating meaning with interlocutors.

Roles

Teacher facilitates students' learning by managing classroom activities, setting up communicative situations. Students are communicators, actively engaged in negotiating meaning.

Teaching/Learning Process

Activities are communicative – they represent an information gap that needs to be filled; speakers have a choice of what to say and how to say it; they receive feedback from the listener that will verify that a purpose has been achieved. Authentic materials are used. Students usually work in small groups.

Interaction: Student-Teacher and Student-Student

Teacher initiates interactions between students and participates sometimes. Students interact a great deal with each other in many configurations.

Dealing with Feelings

Emphasis is on developing motivation to learn through establishing meaningful, purposeful things to do with the target language. Individuality is encouraged, as well as cooperation with peers, which both contribute to sense of emotional security with the target language.

View of Language, Culture

Language is for communication. Linguistic competence must be coupled with an ability to convey intended meaning appropriately in different social contexts. Culture is the everyday lifestyle of native speakers of the target language. Non-verbal behaviour is important.

Aspects of Language the Approach Emphasizes

Functions are emphasized over forms, with simple forms learned for each function at first, then more complex forms. Students work at discourse level. They work on speaking, listening, reading, and writing from the beginning. Consistent focus on negotiated meaning.

Role of Students' Native Language

Students' native language usually plays no role.

Means for Evaluation

Informal evaluation takes place when teacher advises or communicates; formal evaluation is by means of an integrative test with a real communicative function.

Response to Students' Errors

Errors of form are considered natural; students with incomplete knowledge of form can still succeed as communicators.

For Further Reading

General

Bowen, D., H. Madsen, and A. Hilferty. 1986. *TESOL techniques and procedures*. Rowley, MA: Newbury House.

Larsen-Freeman, D. 1986. *Techniques and principles in language teaching*. New York: Oxford University Press.

Richards, J. and T. Rodgers. 1986. *Approaches and methods in language teaching*. Cambridge, MA: Cambridge University Press.

On the Grammar-Translation Method

Chastain, K. 1976. *Developing second-language skills* 2nd ed., Chapter 5. Chicago: Rand-McNally.

Kelly, L. G. 1969. *25 centuries of language teaching*. Rowley, MA: Newbury House.

On the Direct Method

Diller, K. C. 1978. *The language teaching controversy*. Rowley, MA: Newbury House.

On the Audio-Lingual Method

Chastain, K. 1976. *Developing second-language skills* 2nd ed., Chapter 5. Chicago: Rand McNally.

Rivers, W. 1968. *Teaching foreign-language skills*, Chapters 2-4. Chicago: University of Chicago Press.

On the Silent Way

Gattegno, C. 1972. *Teaching foreign languages in schools: The silent way* 2nd ed.. New York: Educational Solutions 95 University Place, New York, NY 10003.

Gattegno, C. 1976. *The common sense of teaching foreign languages.* New York: Educational Solutions.

Stevick, E. 1980. *Teaching languages: A way and ways,* Chapters 3-6. Rowley, MA: Newbury House.

On Suggestopedia

Lozanov, G. 1982. Suggestology and suggestopedia. In R.E. Blair Ed., *Innovative approaches to language teaching.* Rowley, MA: Newbury House.

Stevick, E. 1980. *Teaching languages: A way and ways,* Chapters 18-19. Rowley, MA: Newbury House.

On Community Language Learning

Curran, C.A. 1976. *Counselling-learning in second language.* East Dubuque, IL: Counselling-Learning Publications.

Rardin, J. 1976. A counselling-learning model for second language learning. *TESOL Newsletter 10 2.*

Stevick, E. 1980. *Teaching languages: A way and ways.* Chapters 7-17. Rowley, MA: Newbury House.

On the Total Physical Response Method

Asher, J. 1982. *Learning another language through actions. The complete teacher's guidebook* 2nd ed.. Los Gatos, CA: Sky Oaks Productions.

Blair, R.W., ed. 1982. *Innovative approaches to language teaching.* Rowley, MA: Newbury House.

Krashen, S., and T. Terrell. 1983. *The natural approach.* San Francisco, CA: Alemany Press.

On the Communicative Approach

Brumfit, C.J. and K. Johnson, eds. 1979. *The communicative approach to language teaching.* Oxford: Oxford University Press.

Johnson, K.and K. Morrow, eds. 1981. *Communication in the classroom.* Essex, UK: Longman.

Littlewood, W. 1981. *Communicative language teaching.* Cambridge, MA: Cambridge University Press.

Savignon, S. 1983. *Communicative competence: Theory and classroom practice.* Boston: Addison-Wesley.

Widdowson, H.G. 1978. *Teaching language as communication.* Oxford: Oxford University Press.

Wilkins, D.A. 1976. *Notional syllabuses.* Oxford: Oxford University Press.

Editor's Note: The above summary, compiled by Gina Doggett, is based on Diane Larsen-Freeman, *Techniques and Principles in Language Teaching.* New York: Oxford University Press, 1986. The report was prepared with funding from the Office of Educational Research and Improvement, U.S. Department of Education for ERIC Clearing House on Language and Linguistics.It is reproduced here with the permission of ERIC Clearing House on Language and Linguistics.

Reprinted from: Gina Doggett, "Eight Approaches to Language Teaching," *Mosaic,* 1, 3 (Spring 1994), 10-12.

21 The Foray into the Neurosciences: Have We Learned Anything Useful?

Anthony Mollica and Marcel Danesi

An assessment of the impact of neuroscientific interest shown by second language educators during the past thirty years.

Introduction

A perusal of the major journals in second language acquisition published during the last three decades reveals that a growing number of researchers in the field have been looking to the neurosciences for insights and guidance. Between the lines of the published reports there seems to be an implicit belief that knowledge about the brain will provide an empirical basis upon which to construct a truly coherent theory of second language acquisition, or at the very least, a framework for assessing and interpreting theories or models of second language acquisition. The fuss over the brain sciences seems to have started when Eric Lenneberg's widely influential 1967 study put forward convincing evidence to support a "critical period" for the acquisition of language, that is, a biologically-determined timetable for language that starts at birth and is completed at adolescence. Debate on the implications that this finding had for second language acquisition in adolescence and adulthood was ignited almost immediately, and it continues uninterrupted to this day. We mention, as a case-in-point, a recent issue of *Studies in Second Language Acquisition* (vol. 17, 1, 1995) in which the value of studying the brain-language nexus for second language acquisition is argued vigorously (e.g. Eubank and Greggs 1995, Jacobs 1995; see also Schumann 1990, Jacobs and Schumann 1992). In the area of second language teaching (SLT), too, this foray into the neuroscientific domain has been influential in shaping at least three major teaching methods over the last thirty years

- Asher's *Total Physical Response* (e.g. 1977, 1981),
- Lozanov's *Suggestopedia* (e.g. 1979), and
- Krashen's and Terrell's *Natural Approach* (e.g. 1983).

The fundamental feature that differentiates these methods from others is an explicit sequencing and formatting of the material to be learned and practised in ways that are purported to simulate how the brain handles incoming information.

The authors of the present study, too, have not been immune from the "neuroscientific bug" that has been infecting second language acquisition researchers and second language teaching practitioners (e.g. Danesi, 1986, 1988, 1991, 1994; Danesi and Mollica, 1988). Our interest in this line of thinking was triggered in 1986 when one of the authors became involved with neuropsychologists and psychiatrists working with language-handicapped children in Italy (e.g. D'Alfonso, Danesi, De Lellis, and Mastracci, 1986; Danesi and De Lellis, 1994). Collaborative projects on how to design effective teaching materials for such children led to the framing of *bimodality theory*, or the view that the two modes of learning – experiential and analytical – are systematically cooperative in the processing of *verbal input* (language which a learner receives and from which he/she can learn) and in influencing *verbal intake* (input which the learner can actually utilize cognitively). In turn, this has led various second language teaching practitioners (e.g., Lombardo, 1988; Nuessel and Cicogna, 1992; Pallotta, 1993) and second language acquisition doctoral students (e.g. Arnò, 1993; Curro, 1995; Smoor, 1995) to cultivate a more general interest in the implications of *bimodality theory* for the learning and teaching of second languages in all kinds of tutored learning contexts. Incidentally, when the term *bimodality* was proposed in 1986, we were not aware of the fact that it had already been in use among neuroscientists as a synonym for *complementary hemisphericity theory* (e.g. Bogen, DeZure, Tenhouten, and Marsh, 1972; Dunn, 1985). It continues to be used in this way in the relevant literature (e.g. Ressler, 1991). We were also not cognizant of the fact that the term was employed by Laurence Ridge, a professor of mathematical education at the University of Toronto, five years earlier in 1981. Ridge's use of the term in that year was, to the best of our knowledge, the first time it was so employed in the educational literature.

Three decades after Lenneberg's watershed study, the time has come to ask ourselves if the fuss over the neurosciences in second language acquisition and second language teaching has been worthwhile. Can knowledge about the brain truly inform second language acquisition research? And what does it mean to say that a teaching approach is "brain-compatible?" We doubt if these questions can be answered affirmatively, simply because there is no empirical way to demonstrate that a specific teaching procedure, for instance, is capable of activating a certain part of the brain – unless we put our students through a PET (Positron Emission Tomography) scan as we teach them something! And even if it could be shown that certain parts are activated at certain stages or in response to certain instructional stimuli, what does that truly mean? We know so little about the connection between brain activities and learning processes that all it would really show is a "co-occurrence" between an input and a brain activity, not a "correlation" between the two. Nevertheless, it is our cautious opinion that the foray into the neuroscientific domain on the part of second language acquisition researchers and second language teaching practitioners has been anything but fanciful. If nothing else, it has forced us to look more closely at the conditions we create in a classroom and at the theoretical suppositions underlying instructional practices and teaching curricula.

From a biological perspective, language acquisition implies a reorganization of the structure of some, if not most, parts of the brain. Evidence has emerged, for instance, that bilinguals and advanced second language learners are equally lateralized in each of their languages (i.e., they have their two languages distributed equally in the brain) and that there might be a greater right hemisphere involvement in the early stages of second language acquisition. However, we alert the reader to the fact that in their enthusiasm, neuroscientifically-inclined second language educators have perhaps not always been judicious and cautious in applying neuroscientific theories. We cannot but agree with Spolsky (1989: 86) when he remarked a few years ago that

> the body of hard data on the neuroscience of second language learning comes nowhere near matching the enormous amount of speculation or the large number of studies.

The present synopsis, therefore, will highlight only the main ramifications that have ensued from the neuroscientific perspective in second language acquisition research and second language teaching practice. We believe that the use of neuroscientific insights has truly enriched the research agendas, discourses, and practices of our profession.

Some Background Historical Matters

It is now common knowledge that the left hemisphere (LH) is the primary biological locus for language. The apparent superiority of the LH for language was established more than a century ago in 1861 by the French anthropologist and surgeon Pierre Paul Broca, when he published his classic study of a patient who had lost the ability to articulate words during his lifetime, even though he had not suffered any paralysis of his speech organs. Noticing a destructive lesion in the left frontal lobe of the LH at the autopsy of this patient, Broca was thus able to present concrete evidence to link the articulation of speech to a specific cerebral site. Thirteen years later, in 1874, the German neurologist Carl Wernicke brought forward further evidence linking the LH with language. Wernicke documented cases in which damage to another area of the LH consistently produced a recognizable pattern of impairment to the faculty of speech comprehension. Then, in 1892 Jules Déjerine found that reading and writing deficits resulted primarily from damage to the LH alone. So, by the end of the nineteenth century the research evidence was pointing convincingly to the LH as the biological locus for language. This led to "localization theory" – the view that specific mental functions had precise locations in the brain. A corollary to this theory was the notion of "cerebral dominance" – the view that the verbal LH was the dominant one for generating the higher forms of cognition.

With a few notable exceptions (e.g. Lashley, 1929; Vygotsky, 1931; Jakobson, 1942; Luria, 1947), localization theory dictated the research agenda of the neurosciences during the first half of the present century. The dissenters argued that language in a restricted sense – i.e. as sounds, words, and meanings – could indeed have a primary locus in the LH; but as a more encompassing expressive phenomenon it was more likely to involve neural processes that were distributed throughout the brain. Vygotsky (1931) also suggested that the whole brain was endowed at birth with a unique kind of "plasticity" that rendered it highly sensitive and adaptive to environmental stimuli during childhood. Therefore, he put forward the intriguing proposal that the neurological structures associated with the mental functions were constantly subject to modifications from sociocultural influences.

It was, however, during the Fifties and Sixties that the first serious doubts were cast on the theory of dominance by the widely-publicized studies conducted by the American psychologist Roger Sperry and his associates on epilepsy patients who had had their two hemispheres separated by surgical section (see Springer and Deutsch 1993 for a detailed account of the relevant experiments). These studies made three crucial accomplishments possible:

1. they showed that both hemispheres, not just a dominant one, were needed in a neurologically-cooperative way to produce complex thinking;
2. they provided a detailed breakdown of the main psychological functions according to hemisphere;
3. they confirmed that the LH was the primary site for language.

As mentioned, the latter finding was further entrenched in 1967 when Eric Lenneberg published his famous book. On the basis of a large body of clinical studies, Lenneberg noticed that most *aphasias* – the partial or total loss of speech due to a disorder in any one of the brain's language centres – became permanent after the age of puberty. This suggested to Lenneberg that the brain lost its capacity to transfer the language functions from the LH to the nonverbal right hemisphere (RH) after puberty, which it was able to do, to varying degrees, during childhood. Lenneberg concluded that there must be a biologically-fixed timetable for the lateralization of the language functions to the verbal LH and, consequently, that the critical period for the acquisition of language was before adolescence. Although his time frame has been disputed (e.g., Krashen, 1973, 1975; Scovel, 1988), Lenneberg's basic hypothesis that there is a fixed period of time during which the brain organizes its division of labour remains, to this day, a plausible theory and a target for much debate.

By the early Seventies the neurosciences had charted out a flourishing field of inquiry for language scientists to pursue. Neuroscientists were beginning seriously to question the idea that the LH alone was responsible for language, and to entertain the possibility that the functions related to discourse programming – putting a message together to fit a situation, a topic, a need, etc. – were controlled by the RH. If this is indeed the case, then the discussions on comprehensible input (e.g. Krashen, 1985; Gass and

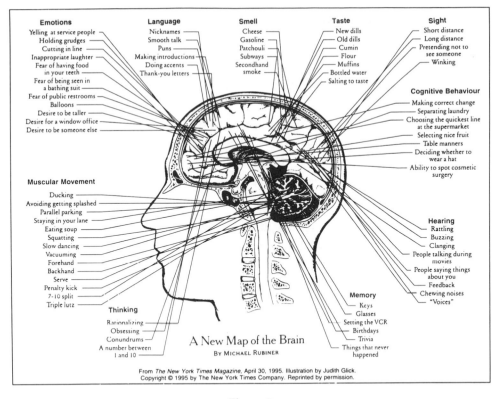

Emotions
Yelling at service people
Holding grudges
Cutting in line
Inappropriate laughter
Fear of having food in your teeth
Fear of being seen in a bathing suit
Fear of public restrooms
Balloons
Desire to be taller
Desire for a window office
Desire to be someone else

Language
Nicknames
Smooth talk
Puns
Making introductions
Doing accents
Thank-you letters

Smell
Cheese
Gasoline
Patchouli
Subways
Secondhand smoke

Taste
New dills
Old dills
Cumin
Flour
Muffins
Bottled water
Salting to taste

Sight
Short distance
Long distance
Pretending not to see someone
Winking

Cognitive Behaviour
Making correct change
Separating laundry
Choosing the quickest line at the supermarket
Selecting nice fruit
Table manners
Deciding whether to wear a hat
Ability to spot cosmetic surgery

Muscular Movement
Ducking
Avoiding getting splashed
Parallel parking
Staying in your lane
Eating soup
Squatting
Slow dancing
Vacuuming
Forehand
Backhand
Serve
Penalty kick
7-10 split
Triple lutz

Thinking
Rationalizing
Obsessing
Conundrums
A number between 1 and 10

Hearing
Rattling
Buzzing
Clanging
People talking during movies
People saying things about you
Feedback
Chewing noises
"Voices"

Memory
Keys
Glasses
Setting the VCR
Birthdays
Trivia
Things that never happened

A New Map of the Brain
By Michael Rubiner

From *The New York Times Magazine*, April 30, 1995. Illustration by Judith Glick. Copyright © 1995 by The New York Times Company. Reprinted by permission.

Figure 1

Madden, 1985) can be seen to have supporting neurological correlates. The brain research suggests, in fact, that for any new input to be comprehensible, it must occur in contexts that allow the synthetic functions of the RH to do their interpretive work. In the case of tutored, or classroom, second language acquisition this has rather far-reaching implications. Above all else, it suggests that the brain is prepared to interpret new information primarily in terms of its contextual characteristics. The whole proficiency movement (e.g. Omaggio, 1986; Pallotta, 1993) will certainly find a highly supportive theoretical framework in such neuroscientific work.

Today, neuroscientists have at their disposal a host of truly remarkable technologies for mapping and collecting data on brain functioning. The use of positron emission tomography (PET brain scanning), for instance, has become a particularly powerful investigative tool for neuroscientists, since it provides images of mental activities such as language (Calvin and Ojemann, 1994). Figure 1 shows the kind of detailed maps of the brain that the new technologies have allowed neuroscientists to draw.

We should mention, for the sake of completeness, that such maps have given us an idea only of how the neocortex is involved in producing various psychological functions, psychomotor movements, etc. However, there are other areas of the brain of which very little is known – such as the areas below the cortex, which are involved in the emotions. In evolutionary terms, these areas are older, tying us to our primate heritage. So, although much has been learned about the neocortex since 1861, the brain in its totality still remains a largely mysterious organ.

Neuroscientifically-Raised Issues for Second Language Acquisition Research

The foray into the neurosciences on the part of second language acquisition researchers and theorists has made it possible to raise several issues that have far-reaching implications for both second language acquisition research and second language teaching practice. These can be summarized as follows:

First, there is the question of a "critical period" (Lenneberg 1967). Krashen (1973, 1975) has argued that the period of lateralization is completed at a much earlier age – by around five or six – than what Lenneberg postulated. This being the case, some other explanatory framework, other than a critical period one, would have to be elaborated to account for the supposed decrease in the capacity of adolescents and adults to acquire native-like competence in another language.

Perhaps the most exhaustive critique of this hypothesis has come from the pen of Thomas Scovel (1988) who, in reviewing the extensive body of research evidence assessing the critical period, has reached the conclusion that there are no clear-cut findings to suggest biological constraints on language acquisition, but rather psychological ones such as motivation, cognitive style, and affective variables. Lenneberg, as Scovel points out, simply assumed that language acquisition was easier for children. Scovel also remarked that the critical period hypothesis applies mainly to the acquisition of pronunciation. This suggests that the hypothesis probably should be recast in order to account for the loss of the ability to acquire native-like pronunciation after puberty. As Seliger (1978) and Walsh and Diller (1981) have suggested, perhaps there are many critical periods corresponding to the various levels, or subsystems, of language.

- The recent work on brain mapping suggests that the two hemispheres differ not so much in the type of stimuli they are designed to process but, rather, in the manner in which they process stimuli. This is why previously (Danesi and Mollica, 1988) we have preferred to adopt the terminology L-Mode and R-Mode, to refer to LH and RH functions respectively (in imitation of Edwards 1979), so as to allow for the fact that the RH may be involved in some contralateral (L-Mode) functions and the LH in R-Mode ones. Moreover, the research now indicates that while each hemisphere is specialized to handle a certain specific function, it does so in tandem with complementary or parallel processing patterns taking place in the other hemisphere – pure analytical thinking simply does not exist in the human brain, nor does pure intuitive thinking!

- Research has shown that the RH has a role to play in semantics and discourse (e.g., Chiarello, 1988; Joanette, Goulet, and Hannequin, 1990).

This has supported theories of second language acquisition and the design of teaching methods and approaches based upon them (e.g., Obler 1980; Galloway and Krashen, 1980; Danesi and Mollica, 1988). These posit that the R-Mode dominates the second language acquisition process during its initial stages, with the L-Mode taking on more of the burden in later stages. Bimodality theory claims, more specifically, that the second language acquisition process will enlist the R-Mode and/or the L-Mode according to the specific nature of the language learning task at hand. It ascribes a crucial role to the R-Mode for discourse and semantic tasks which first language schemata cannot accommodate. But it sees the L-Mode as dominant for other kinds of tasks.

• The neuroscientific focus in second language acquisition research has opened up a meaningful debate on the validity of the notion of Universal Grammar (UG) in linguistics. According to the UG paradigm, there exists a "language organ" in the brain that equips humans by the age of two with the ability to use the rules of a "universal" grammar to develop the specific languages that cultures require of them. The child only has to "set" a few language-specific "parameters" on the basis of parental input, and the full richness of grammar will ensue when those parameterized rules interact with one another and with universal principles. The parameter-setting view has been put forward to explain the universality and rapidity of language acquisition.

Those who disagree with UG theory point out that there is nothing in the neuroscientific research literature, outside of the fact that language acquisition occurs during a critical period, that would support the idea of a "language organ." Some second language acquisition theorists (e.g., White, 1990; Clahsen, 1990; Carroll and Meisel, 1990; Comrie, 1990) have argued that universal principles continue to play an important role in second language acquisition. Whether or not this is the case will have to be seen. At present, the theory of universal grammar excludes the possibility of second language acquisition ever equalling first language acquisition in childhood. To ascribe the inability to master a second language in adulthood to the accessibility of language universals rules out too many other possibilities – life experiences, previous training, etc. – which have nothing to do with biology. As Jacobs (1988: 330) aptly puts it, any theory of second language acquisition "will have to consider what the environment brings to the brain, including both the input itself (e.g., structure, intonation, morphology) and the surrounding situational variables (e.g., gestures, discourse context); and, just as importantly, must also consider what the brain does to this information."

Neuroscientifically-Designed Methods

The foray into the neurosciences has also been a productive one for second language teaching practices. The research on the role of the RH in language, for instance, has led to the design of three major second language teaching methods in the last three decades – Lozanov's (1979) *Suggestopedia*, Asher's

(1977, 1981) *Total Physical Response,* and Krashen's and Terrell's (1983) *Natural Approach.* These can be characterized schematically as follows:

- Lozanov stresses the importance of creating a learning environment that is capable of activating subliminal R-Mode processes. This is why he suggests the technique known as the *séance* a period during which students relax and sit comfortably in reclining chairs listening to background music (usually the slow movements of Baroque composers such as Bach, Handel, Vivaldi, Corelli and Telemann) while new language input is being read in the second language and in translation.

- Asher's *Total Physical Response* method is designed to impart the second language mainly through physical activities. Moreover, he suggests that the criterion for including an item of vocabulary, grammar, or communication at a particular point in the learning sequence should be the ease of assimilation shown by *the students.* If the item is not learned rapidly, then they are obviously not ready for that item. Hence, it should be withdrawn and presented again at some future time. The "flow" of learning which Asher intends to set in motion with *Total Physical Response* goes from concrete actions to linguistic abstractions; i.e., from the R-Mode to the L-Mode. Asher claims that when a sufficient amount of R-Mode learning has taken place, the L-Mode will be triggered naturally to produce the more abstract linguistic notions. So, he views grammatical training as virtually unnecessary.

- Krashen's and Terrell's *Natural Approach* became one of the most discussed teaching proposals in the Eighties, probably because of its intuitive appeal to teachers and learners alike. It too ascribed great salience to the R-Mode during all stages of second language acquisition, but especially during the initial ones. Krashen and Terrell viewed the R-Mode as the natural "acquisitional" mode of the student. They deemed grammar training to be virtually useless, since they claimed that knowledge of structure would emerge inductively through the L-Mode's inbuilt "monitoring" system. However, before his untimely death in the early nineties, Terrell (1991) modified this radical view somewhat.

Suggestopedia, Total Physical Response, and the *Natural Approach* have constituted the first serious attempts to organize classroom second language teaching around the brain's acquisition mode – the R-Mode. In so doing, however, they have downplayed the role of the L-Mode perhaps too drastically. They seem to generate much interest and enthusiasm in teacher and learner alike during the initial stages – the stages during which the R-Mode probably dominates the intake of novel information. But their overemphasis on this mode throughout the course of learning also probably explains why they have not caught on across the entire second language teaching profession. They simply do not place enough importance on the L-Mode and on the analytical learning sub-systems that it encompasses. There really can be no method or approach that is designed in a purely R-Mode or L-Mode fashion. Omaggio (1986: 69) is correct in calling *Total*

Physical Response and the *Natural Approach* modern adaptations of the *Direct Method*, given that they have rehabilitated the second language acquisition = first language acquisition metaphor. Hence, both are really evolutionary second language teaching methods, rather than revolutionary ones.

General Issues and Implications for SLT

In addition to spawning the methods just discussed, the foray into the neurosciences has also raised some important general issues for the entire second language teaching profession. As we have claimed in previous work (Danesi and Mollica, 1988), the neuroscientific evidence suggests at least two "instructional-design principles" for second language teaching generally: the *modal directionality principle* and the *modal focusing principle*.

Modal Directionality

It would appear, before all else, that the teaching of new notions and structures should follow an R-Mode (experiential) to L-Mode (analytical) "flow." This means that during the initial learning stages students need to assimilate new input through observation, induction, role-playing, simulation, oral tasks, and various kinds of interactive activities. But we would quickly add that formal grammatical explanations, drills, and other L-Mode procedures *must* follow these stages, since we have found that control of structure will not emerge spontaneously, as Asher and others claim. Incidentally, identifying a learning task or unit as having an L-Mode or an R-Mode focus implies only indicating which mode is to be emphasized in the overall design of the task, and does not necessarily indicate which specific hemispheric functions will be activated. The *modal directionality principle* thus claims:

1. that experiential forms of tutoring belong to the initial learning stages, and
2. that teaching should move progressively towards a more formal, analytical style in the later stages.

An analogy to music teaching can perhaps be used to illustrate the practical implications of this principle. Learning how to play a new piece on the piano, say, entails the ability to mould the component mechanical skills needed to play the notes, phrases, etc. of the piece successfully into the global skill of "playing the music." So, in order to give the learner's L-Mode a better opportunity to analyze and organize the component skills into automatic psychomotor routines, the teacher normally starts out by playing the piece for the student, making appropriate aesthetic comments here and there. In this way, the student's R-Mode has an opportunity to decipher the new musical input in a global aesthetic way. The component mechanical skills can now be understood separately and practised apart from their expressive modalities.

Needless to say, an advanced music student who is already in firm control of the required L-Mode skills through previous training will not have to spend as much time on this component as would a beginner. When the student has mastered the L-Mode aspects of the piece, then he/she will be in a position to integrate them with the R-Mode ones as he/she performs the piece. A consummate performance of the piece is, from a neurological perspective, a *bimodal* feat, requiring the integrated contribution of both the R-Mode and the L-Mode to the performative task at hand.

The modal directionality principle implies, above all else, that the teacher should leave ample room for student improvisation during the early learning stages. Instructional techniques which focus on discrete categories (words in isolation, sentence structure, rules of formation, etc.) will be of little value, since the students generally have no preexisting L-Mode schemata for accommodating the new input directly. In order to make the new material accessible to the L-Mode (intake), therefore, the early stages should involve teacher and learner alike in activities enlisting exploration, imagination, spontaneity, and induction. Once the initial learning stages have been completed, the teacher can "shift modes" and begin to focus more on formal, mechanical, rule-based instruction.

Modal directionality can be seen to be a different version of the oldest principle in second language teaching – the inductive principle. But unlike its use in strictly inductivist methods (e.g. the *Direct Method*, the *Audiolingual Method*, etc.), it does not require the deployment of induction for *all* learning tasks, only those that involve new input. Thus, if a learning task contains knowledge or input that the learner can already accommodate cognitively, directionality can be efficiently avoided. So, modal directionality is really a common-sensical pedagogical principle that good teachers, and the better second language teaching methods, have always embodied into their *modus operandi*. It is virtually a "law of learning" which claims that teaching should ensure a constant movement from experiential to expository learning conditions, from practical to theoretical content, and from concrete to analytical presentation styles. Indirect evidence in support of modal directionality exists throughout the second language acquisition and second language teaching literature. Jeffries (1985), for example, has shown that the use of grammatical discourse as a presentation technique (an L-Mode practice) poses a serious obstacle to classroom learning.

Modal Focusing

The principle of *modal focusing* claims that at certain points in the tutored learning process the students will need to focus on one mode or the other for various reasons. After the learners have grasped the new concepts in an R-Mode way, for example, their mental systems can be said to be prepared to assign them to appropriate L-Mode categories. At this point, the teacher can step in with suitable L-Mode techniques which focus on pattern practice, grammatical instruction, etc.

Modal focusing might also be required at points in the learning process when, for instance, a learner appears to need help in overcoming some error pattern that has become an obstacle to learning – L-Mode focusing allows the students an opportunity to focus on formal matters for accuracy and control; R-mode focusing on matters of discourse formulation and conceptual meaning. Students themselves use their L-Mode overtly when they search for some ending to a verb, when they try to think of a word they have forgotten, etc. On the other hand, they use their R-Mode when they try to think of what to say. True *acquisition* can be said to occur when the students' attempts at discourse formulation can be seen to enlist both modes in a cooperative way.

It is important to point out that the modal focusing principle in no way implies that mechanical practice be conducted in an uncontextualized way. On the contrary, meaningful contexts should always be provided not only for new input, but also for focusing routines. This allows the R-Mode to complement and strengthen the intake operations of the L-Mode, especially during more mechanically-oriented focusing tasks. Contextualized language instruction enables the learners to relate L-Mode *form* to R-Mode *content*.

To conclude, the general teaching implications that modal directionality and modal focusing call forth can be summarized in point form as follows:

During an R-Mode Stage:
- Classroom activities should be student-centered.
- Novel input should be structured in ways that involve sensory, experiential learning. As in Di Pietro's (1987) *Scenario Approach,* the learners should also be allowed to generate their own strategies for orchestrating role-playing scenarios.
- The students' inductive and exploratory tendencies should be encouraged to operate freely when introducing new grammatical or lexical information.R

During an L-Mode Stage:
- The focus now shifts to the teacher.
- Grammar explanations, drills, etc. should follow the experiential learning phases.
- Focusing on some problematic aspect of grammar, vocabulary, etc. is to be encouraged if a student appears to have difficulty grasping it or using it.

Concluding Reflections

The reader is by now aware that we posed the question in the title of this essay, namely, "Have we learned anything useful from the foray into the neuroscientific domain?", only rhetorically. It has been indeed a fruitful foray. But we also wish to emphasize that it has produced very little in the way of empirical research findings. Most of the current neuroscientifically-shaped theories of second language acquisition, and of the neuroscientifically-designed methods of instruction, have been based primarily on extrapolations from the neuroscientific literature or from the observations of teachers. So, we cannot help but agree with Obler (1983) when she observes that, unless we are very careful, many unnecessary problems are bound to crystallize when extracting too many implications from the work on hemisphericity.

Interpreting the research on the role of the RH for second language acquisition, and then translating it into pedagogical principles, has been particularly instructive (Satz, Strauss and Whitaker 1990). It has now become apparent that the two hemispheres do share some features. The LH has been shown to have the capacity to engage in some holistic and parallel processing, and the RH in some analytic and serial processing. But, for the most part, RH language performance is inferior to that of the LH (see McKeener and Hunt 1989, Segalowitz and Cohen 1989, Cohen and Segalowitz 1990, Richards and Chiarello 1990, Hunter and Liederman 1991, Beeman 1993, Faust, Kravitz and Babkoff 1993a, 1993b for recent work in the field). All attempts to construct models of SLA based on the participation of the RH at various stages, and to translate such models into instructional practices, therefore, must tread very cautiously and judiciously. We are in agreement with Ellis (1986: 273) when he remarks that neuroscientific accounts of second language acquisition are probably more useful in providing "additional understanding about second language acquisition," rather than constituting explanations of it.

In addition to the issues raised above, it should be pointed out that the foray into the neuroscientific domain raises another interesting question, that is rarely addressed. Is it possible or desirable to take account of the likelihood that learners will have different hemispheric learning styles? There exists some evidence in the neuroscientific literature that hemispheric style (a preference for one or the other learning mode) correlates with handedness, gender, and various environmental factors (Geschwind and Galaburda, 1987). From an educational perspective, it is obvious that a student with a dominant L-Mode learning style will gain very little from an abundant use of R-Mode techniques. Similarly, grammar-based instruction for students with an R-Mode learning style would probably prove equally futile. However, much more empirical work would need to be done in this area. Nevertheless, the fact that the above question can be asked in the first place is an outcome of the foray into neuroscientific turf.

As a final word, we would like to remark that the foray should continue in the future, producing interesting hypotheses, constructs, and suggestions for conducting research on second language acquisition and for modelling second language teaching instruction. If second language teachers are truly interested in understanding how their students learn and in responding pedagogically in an appropriate way then, as Spolsky (1985: 279) put it a decade ago, it is "certainly not unreasonable to seek insights from the brain sciences."

References

Arnò, L. 1994. *La bimodalità nell'apprendimento di una lingua straniera*. Thesis. Milan, Italy: Catholic University of Milan.

Asher, J. J. 1977. *Learning Another Language Through Actions: The Complete Teacher's Guidebook.* Los Gatos: Sky Oaks.

Asher, J. J. 1981. "The Total Physical Response: Theory and Practice." In H. Wintz, ed., *Native Language and Foreign Language Acquisition*, pp. 324-331. New York: New York Academy of Sciences.

Beeman, M. 1993. "Semantic processing in the right hemisphere may contribute to drawing inferences from discourse." *Brain and language*, 44, 80-120.

Bogen, J. E., R. DeZure, W. D. Tenhouten, and J. F. Marsh. 1972. "The Other Side of the Brain: The A/P Ratio." *Bulletin of the Los Angeles Neurological Societies*, 37: 49-61.

Broca, P. 1861. "Remarques sur le siège de la faculté du langage articulé suivies d'une observation d'aphémie." *Bulletin de la Société d'Anatomie*, 36: 320-357.

Calvin, W. H. and G.A. Ojemann. 1994. *Conversations with Neil's Brain: The Neural Nature of Thought and Language.* New York: Addison-Wesley.

Carroll, S. and J. M. Meisel. 1990. "Universals and Second Language Acquisition." *Studies in Second Language Acquisition*, 12: 201-208.

Chiarello, C., ed. 1988 *Right Hemisphere Contributions to Lexical Semantics.* Berlin: Springer.

Chiarello, C., L. Richards, and A Pollack. 1992. "Semantic additivity and semantic inhibition: Dissociative processes in the cerebral hemispheres?" *Brain and Language*, 42, 52-76.

Clahsen, H. 1990. "The Comparative Study of First and Second Language Development." *Studies in Second Language Acquisition*, 12: 135-153.

Cohen, H. and S. Segalowitz. 1990. "Cerebral hemispheric involvement in the acquisition of new phonetic categories." *Brain and Language*, 39, 398-409.

Comrie, B. 1990. "Second Language Acquisition and Language Universals Research." *Studies in Second Language Acquisition*, 12: 209-218.

Curro, G. 1995. *A Survey of Neurolinguistic Research and Its Implications for Second Language Teaching.* Thesis, James Cook University of North Queensland.

D'Alfonso, A., M. Danesi, M. De Lellis, and M. Mastracci. 1986. "Problemi di neuropedagogia." *Quaderni L'Ipetro* 29. L'Aquila: Penne.

Danesi, M. 1986. "Research on the Brain's Hemispheric Functions Implications for Second Language Pedagogy." *Lenguas Modernas*, 13: 99-113.

Danesi, M. 1988. "Neurological Bimodality and Theories of Language Teaching." *Studies in Second Language Acquisition*, 10: 13-35.

Danesi, M. 1991. "Neurological Learning Flow and Second Language Teaching: Some Evidence on the Bimodality Construct." *Rassegna Italiana di Linguistica Applicata*, 23: 19-29.

Danesi, M. 1994. "The Neuroscientific Perspective in Second Language Acquisition Research." *International Review of Applied Linguistics*, 22: 201-228.

Danesi, M. and M. De Lellis. 1994. "Apprendimento linguistico bimodale ed educazione emozionale: l'approccio neuropedagogico." In M. De Lellis, ed., *Apnostressterapia: un trattamento preventivo-curativo della patologia psicosomatica dell'infanzia e dell'adolescenza*, pp. 103-113. Roma: Verduci.

Danesi, M. and A. Mollica. 1988. "From Right to Left: A "Bimodal" Perspective of Language Teaching." *The Canadian Modern Language Review*, 45: 76-90.

Déjerine, J. 1892. "Contribution à l'étude anatomo-pathologique et clinique des différents variétés de cécité verbale." *Comptes Rendus des Sciences de la Société de Biologie*, 9, 61-90.

Di Pietro, R. J. 1987. *Strategic Interaction.* Cambridge: Cambridge University Press.

Dunn, B. R. 1985. "Bimodal Processing and Memory from Text." In V. M. Rentel, S. A. Corson, and B. R. Dunn, eds., *Psychophysiological Aspects of Reading and Learning,* pp. 12-29. New York: Gordon and Breach.

Edwards, B. 1979. *Drawing on the Right Side of the Brain.* Los Angeles: J. P. Tarcher.

Ellis, R. 1986. *Understanding second language acquisition.* Oxford: Oxford University Press.

Eubank, L. and K. R. Gregg. 1995. "Et in Amygdala Ego? UG, (S)LA, and Neurobiology." *Studies in Second Language Acquisition,* 17: 35-57.

Faust, M. Kravitz, S. and H. Babkoff. 1993a. "Hemisphericity and top-down processing of language." *Brain and Language,* 44, 1-18.

Faust, M. Kravitz, S. and H. Babkoff. 1993b. "Hemispheric specialization or reading habits: Evidence from lexical decision research with Hebrew words and sentences." *Brain and Language,* 44, 254-263.

Galloway, L. and S. D. Krashen. 1980. "Cerebral Organization in Bilingualism and Second Language." In R. C. Scarcella and S. D. Krashen, eds., *Research in Second Language Acquisition,* pp. 74-80. Rowley, Mass.: Newbury House.

Gass, S. and C. Madden, eds. 1985. *Input in Second Language Acquisition.* Rowley, Mass.: Newbury House.

Genesee, F. 1982. "Experimental neuropsychological research on second language processing." *TESOL Quarterly,* 16, 315-324.

Genesee, F. 1988. "Neuropsychology and second language acquisition." In L. M. Beebe, ed., *Issues in second language acquisition: Multiple perspectives,* 81-112. Rowley, Mass.: Newbury House.

Geschwind, N. and A. Galaburda. 1987. *Cerebral Lateralization: Biological Mechanisms, Associations, and Pathology.* Cambridge, Mass.: MIT Press.

Hunter, N. and J. Liederman. 1991. "Right hemisphere participation in reading." *Brain and Language,* 41, 475-495.

Jacobs, B. 1995. "Dis-Integrating Perspectives of Language Acquisition: A Response to Eubank and Gregg." *Studies in Second Language Acquisition,* 17: 65-72.

Jacobs, B. and J. Schumann. 1992. "Language Acquisition and the Neurosciences: Towards a More Integrative Perspective." *Applied Linguistics,* 13: 282-301.

Jakobson, R. 1942. *Kindersprache, Aphasie und algemeine Lautgesetze.* Uppsala: Almqvist and Wiksell.

Jeffries, S. 1985. "English Grammar Terminology as an Obstacle to Second Language Learning." *Modern Language Journal,* 69: 385-390.

Joanette, Y., P. Goulet,, and D. Hannequin. 1990. *Right Hemisphere and Verbal Communication.* Berlin: Springer.

Krashen, S. D. 1973. "Lateralization, Language Learning and the Critical Period: Some New Evidence." *Language Learning,* 23: 63-74.

Krashen, S. D. 1975. "The Development of Cerebral Dominance and Language Learning: More New Evidence." In D. Dato, ed., *Developmental Psycholinguistics,* pp. 179-192. Washington, D. C.: Georgetown University Press.

Krashen, S. D. 1985. *The Input Hypothesis.* London: Longman.

Krashen, S. D. and Terrell, T. 1983. *The Natural Approach: Language Acquisition in the Classroom.* Oxford: Pergamon.

Lashley, K. S. 1929. *Brain Mechanisms and Intelligence.* Chicago: University of Chicago Press.

Lenneberg, E. 1967. *The Biological Foundations of Language*. New York: Wiley.

Lombardo, L. 1988. "Helping Learners to Establish Criteria in an L2: Promoting Learner Autonomy in the Foreign Language Classroom." In G. Cecioni, ed., *Proceedings of the Symposium on Autonomy in Foreign Language Learning*, pp. 70-79. Firenze: Centro Linguistico di Ateneo.

Lozanov, G. 1979. *Suggestology and Outline of Suggestopedy*. New York: Gordon and Breach.

Luria, A. 1947. *Traumatic Aphasia*. The Hague: Mouton.

McKeener, W. W. and L. J. Hunt. 1989. "Language laterality in Navajo reservation children: Dichotic tests results depend on the language context of the testing." *Brain and Language*, 36, 148-158.

Nuessel, F. and C. Cicogna. 1992. "Pedagogical Applications of the Bimodal Model of Learning through Visual and Auditory Stimuli." *Romance Languages Annual*, 3: 289-292.

Obler, L. 1980. "Right Hemisphere Participation in Second Language Acquisition." In K. Diller, ed., *Individual Differences and Universals in Language Learning Aptitude*, pp. 87-98. Rowley, Mass.: Newbury House.

Obler, L. K. 1983. "Knowledge in neuroscience: The case of bilingualism." *Language Learning*, 33, 15: 9-191.

Omaggio, A. 1986. *Teaching Language in Context*. Boston: Heinle and Heinle.

Pallotta, L. I. 1993. "The "Bimodal" Aspect of Proficiency-Oriented Instruction." *Foreign Language Annals*, 26: 429-434.

Ressler, L. E. 1991. "Improving Elderly Recall with Bimodal Presentation: A Natural Experiment of Discharge Planning." *The Gerontologist*, 31: 364-370.

Richards, L. G. and C. Chiarello. 1989. "Typicality effects in artificial categories: Is there a hemispheric difference?" *Brain and Language*, 37, 90-106..

Ridge, H. L. 1981. "A Two-Way Street: Multiculturalism in Mathematics and Mathematics in Multiculturalism." In K. A. McLeod, ed., *Intercultural Education and Community Development*, pp. 54-62. Toronto: Guidance Centre, Faculty of Education.

Rumelhart, D. E. and J. L. McClelland, eds. 1986. *Parallel distributed processing*. Cambridge, Mass.: MIT Press.

Satz, P., E. Strauss, and H. Whitaker. 1990. "The ontogeny of hemispheric specialization: Some old hypotheses revisited." *Brain and Language*, 38, 596-614.

Schumann, J. H. 1990. "The Role of the Amygdala as a Mediator of Affect and Cognition in Second Language Acquisition." In J. E. Alatis, ed., *Proceedings of the Georgetown University Round Table on Language and Linguistics*, pp. 169-176. Washington, D. C.: Georgetown University Press.

Scovel, T. 1988. *A Time to Speak: A Psycholinguistic Inquiry into the Critical Period for Human Speech*. Rowley, Mass.: Newbury House.

Segalowitz, S. S. and H. Cohen. 1989. "Right hemisphere sensitivity to speech." *Brain and Language*, 37, 220-231.

Seliger, H. 1978. "Implications of a multiple critical periods hypothesis for second language learning." In W. Ritchie, ed., *Second language acquisition research*, pp. 21-35. New York: Academic.

Smoor, E. 1995. *The Role of Cognitive Lateral Eye Movement as an Indicator of Cognitive Activity during Mental Processing in a Structured L1 and L2 Learning Environment*. Thesis. Toronto: Ontario Institute for Studies in Education.

Spolsky, B. 1985. "Formulating a Theory of Second Language Learning." *Studies in Second Language Acquisition,* 7: 269-288.

Spolsky, B. 1989. *Conditions for Second Language Learning.* Oxford: Oxford University Press.

Springer, S. P. and G. Deutsch. 1993. *Left Brain, Right Brain,* 4th ed. New York: W. H. Freeman.

Terrell, T. D. 1991. "The Role of Grammar Instruction in a Communicative Approach." *Modern Language Journal,* 75: 52-63.

Vygotsky, L. S. 1931. *Storia dello sviluppo delle funzioni psichiche superiori.* Firenze: Giunti-Barbèra.

Walsh, T. and K. Diller. 1978. "Neurolinguistic Foundation to Methods of Teaching a Second Language." *International Review of Applied Linguistics,* 16: 1-14.

Walsh, T. and K. Diller. 1981. "Neurolinguistic Considerations on the Optimum Age for Second Language Learning." In K. Diller, ed., *Universals in Language Learning Aptitude,* pp. 34-45. Rowley, Mass.: Newbury House.

Wernicke, C. 1874. *Der aphasische Symptomkomplex.* Breslau: Cohn and Weigart.

White, L. 1990. "Second Language Acquisition and Universal Grammar." *Studies in Second Language Acquisition,* 12: 121-133.

Reprinted from: Anthony Mollica and Marcel Danesi, "The Foray into the Neurosciences: Have We Learned Anything Useful?," *Mosaic,* 2, 4 (Summer 1995), pp, 12-20.

22 Conceptual Fluency Theory and Second-Language Teaching

Marcel Danesi and Anthony Mollica

In order for the student to be able to converse "naturally", in a conceptual accurate manner, the authors propose the application of conceptual metaphor theory to second-language teaching.

Introduction

The second-language classroom today has never before been so sophisticated in terms of instructional methodology and the use of advanced technology. This is because the teaching of second languages has been informed throughout this century by theories and findings coming out of psychology and linguistics, aiming to validate or refute teaching practices. This interplay between the research domain and instructional practices has produced teachers who are among the most informed and pedagogically-knowledgeable teachers of all time. As we approach the end of the twentieth century, it is, in fact, difficult to think of the second-language classroom in high school, college, or university as anything but a highly-advanced learning environment.

So, why is there, despite the apparent sophistication, still so much discussion going on in scholarly journals, and among practitioners, about what to do to make student discourse more native-like? The recent literature has even rekindled an old debate:

- Should we continue to focus on developing in the learner a functional knowledge of the uses of the target language *(communicative competence)*, as we have been doing over the last three decades? Or,
- Should we return to the traditional deployment of techniques that aim to foster control of linguistic structure *(linguistic competence)*?

This debate has been reignited, no doubt, because teachers continue to be frustrated by the inability of their students to speak in ways that go beyond the "textbook literalness" of classroom discourse. The nagging and persistent problem of second-language teaching can be articulated as follows:

> Despite considerable research in second-language learning in classroom environments in this century, and despite the many pedagogical applications that such work has made possible, teachers still complain about the fact that the student's autonomous discourse lacks the conceptual accuracy that characterizes native-speaker discourse.

The manifestations of second-language discourse bear witness to the fact that learners have had little or no opportunity to access directly the conceptual structures inherent in the target language and culture.

The purpose of this article is to present an overview of a paradigm that was put forward a few years ago labeled *conceptual fluency theory* (e.g. Danesi 1993a, 1993b, 1994, 1995, Russo 1997) that aimed to address this very problem. Several practical projects applying conceptual fluency theory have been undertaken recently, leading to the development of various textbooks and related materials (Danesi, Lettieri, and Bancheri 1996, Danesi 1998).

In our view, conceptual fluency theory has important implications for methodology, material development and syllabus design in second-language teaching.

The Primary Claim

The notion of conceptual fluency was derived in large part from the research initiated in 1977 by Howard Pollio and his associates which showed that metaphor is hardly a frill in discourse. The average speaker of English, for instance, invents approximately 3000 metaphors per week and employs over 7000 idiomatic forms (Pollio, Barlow, Fine, and Pollio 1977). This discovery led in the 1980s to the development of two significant trends:

1. *conceptual metaphor theory* (Lakoff and Johnson 1980, Lakoff 1987, Johnson 1987), and

2. a branch of linguistics that now comes under the rubric of *cognitive linguistics* (Langacker 1987, 1990. Taylor 1995).

But conceptual fluency theory was also born of classroom experience with student discourse. Over the last seven years, the authors of this article have undertaken several research projects designed to gear second-language teaching in all its components – methodology, materials development, testing, etc. – towards imparting conceptual fluency to the student, without underplaying the roles of both grammatical and communicative competence. The latter two, in fact, are to be considered constituent aspects of verbal fluency. Using these two notions, the *problem* of second-language teaching enunciated above can now be rephrased as follows:

> While student discourse often manifests a high degree of verbal fluency, it invariably seems to lack the conceptual fluency that characterizes the corresponding discourse of native speakers. To put it another way, students "speak" with the memorized formal and communicative structures of the second language, but they "think" in terms of their native conceptual systems: i.e. students typically use second-language words and communicative protocols as "carriers" of their own native language "concepts." When the native and second-language conceptual systems coincide in an area of discourse, then the student discourse is assessable as "natural"; when they do not, the student discourse manifests an asymmetry between language form and conceptual content. What student discourse often lacks, in other words, is conceptual fluency.

Conceptual Fluency Theory

The research in cognitive linguistics suggests rather strongly that to be conceptually fluent in a language is to know, in large part, how that language "reflects" or encodes concepts on the basis of metaphorical reasoning. This kind of knowledge, like grammatical and communicative (pragmatic) knowledge, is by and large unconscious in native speakers. If one were to speak about "time" in English, our mind would scan conceptual domains that typically reveal metaphorical reasoning. So, if one were to say something like

That job cost me an hour,

the conceptual reasoning enlisted by the speaker can be seen to have the form *time is money*. Of course, the speaker could have enlisted other appropriate metaphorical ideas – e.g.

1. He's wasting my time.
2. That's not worth the time or the effort *(= time is a valuable commodity)*.
3. Build in some time for her too. *(= ideas are buildings)*; etc. –

or combine them in various ways. The grammatical forms and categories that are used in actual discourse are, according to this line of research (e.g. Lakoff and Johnson 1980), consistently linked cohesively to such metaphorical forms.

This kind of conceptual programming is exactly what seems to be lacking in student discourse (Danesi 1993a, 1993b, Russo 1997). This implies that students have had little or no opportunity to access the metaphorically-structured conceptual domains inherent in the second language. *Metaphorical competence* – to coin an analogous term to linguistic and communicative competence – is almost completely lacking from second-language learners.

The work on metaphor in anthropology and linguistics over the past three decades (e.g. Dundes 1972, Beck 1982, Lakoff and Johnson 1980, Kšvecses 1986, 1988, 1990, Lakoff 1987, Johnson 1987) has demonstrated the validity of metaphorical competence and thus can be used to sustain the notion of conceptual fluency in second-language acquisition. The implications of this line of research for second-language teaching are quite clear. The cognitive programming of discourse in metaphorical ways is a basic property of native-speaker competence. As a competence, it can be thought about pedagogically in ways that are parallel to the other competencies on which teaching methodology has traditionally focused (linguistic and communicative).

Particularly influential in getting metaphorical competence onto the agenda of the social and cognitive sciences was George Lakoff and Mark Johnson's 1980 book, *Metaphors We Live By*. The innovative claim of that book was that metaphor is the cornerstone of discourse.

First, Lakoff and Johnson assert what Aristotle claimed two millennia before, namely that there are two types of concepts – *concrete* and *abstract*. But the two scholars add a remarkable twist to this Aristotelian notion –

namely that *abstract concepts* are built up systematically from *concrete* ones through metaphor. They refer to abstract concepts as *conceptual metaphors*. These are generalized metaphorical formulas that define specific abstractions. For example, the expression "John is a gorilla" is really a token of something more general, namely, *people are animals.* This is why we say that *John* or *Mary* or *whoever* is a gorilla, snake, pig, puppy, and so on. Each specific metaphor ("John is a gorilla," "Mary is a snake," etc.) is not an isolated example of poetic fancy. It is really an example of a more general metaphorical idea – *people are animals.* Such formulas are what Lakoff and Johnson call *conceptual metaphors*:

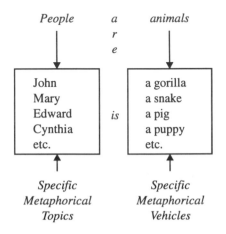

Each of the two parts of the *conceptual metaphor* is called a *domain: people* is called the *target domain* because it is the abstract topic itself (the "target" of the conceptual metaphor); and *animals* is called the *source domain* because it is the class of vehicle that delivers the metaphor (the "source" of the metaphorical concept). An *abstract concept* can now be defined simply as a "mapping" of one domain onto the other. This model suggests that abstract concepts are formed systematically through such mappings and that specific metaphors are traces to the target and source domains. So, when we hear people talking, for instance, of *ideas* in terms of *geometrical figures and relations* –

1. Those ideas are circular.
2. I don't see the point of your idea.
3. Her ideas are central to the discussion.
4. Their ideas are diametrically opposite. etc. –

we can now easily identify the two domains as ideas (= target domain) and geometrical figures / relations (= source domain) and, therefore, the conceptual metaphor as: ideas are geometrical figures and relations.

Conceptual metaphors pervade common discourse. A few examples will suffice to make this evident.

Happiness is up/Sadness is down

1. Today she's feeling *up.*

2. Generally she feels *down*.
3. His comment *boosted* my spirits.
4. My mood *sank* after she told me what happened.
5. His joke gave me a *lift*.

Health and life are up/Sickness and death are down

1. Everyone in my family is at the *peak* of health.
2. Unfortunately, my cousin *fell* ill.
3. My job is an *uphill* struggle.
4. Lazarus *rose* from the dead.
5. They're *sinking* fast.

Light is knowledge/Dark is ignorance

1. The whole class was *illuminated* by that professor.
2. I was left in the *dark* about what happened.
3. Her explanation is very *clear*.
4. Quantum theory is *obscure*.
5. His example *shed light* on several matters.

Theories are buildings

1. Hers is a *well-constructed* theory.
2. His theory too is on solid *ground*.
3. But that theory needs more *support*.
4. Otherwise the theory will *collapse* under criticism.
5. Alexander put together the *framework* of a very interesting theory.

Ideas and theories are plants

1. My professor's ideas have come to *fruition*.
2. That's a *budding* theory.
3. Plato's ideas have contemporary *offshoots*.
4. That idea has become a *branch* of mathematics.

Ideas are commodities

1. My friend certainly knows how to *package* his ideas.
2. However, that idea just won't *sell*.
3. There's no *market* for that idea.
4. That's a *worthless* idea.

As Lakoff and Johnson emphasize, we do not detect the presence of metaphor in such common expressions because of repeated usage. We no longer interpret the word *see* in sentences such as

1. I don't *see* what you mean.
2. Do you *see* what I'm saying?

in metaphorical terms, because its use in such expressions has become so familiar to us. But the association between the biological act of seeing outside the body with the imaginary act of seeing within the mind was originally the source of the conceptual metaphor *seeing is understanding/believing/thinking*, which now permeates com- mon discourse:

1. There is more to this than *meets the eye*.
2. I have a different *point of view*.
3. It all depends on how you *look* at it.
4. I take a dim view of the whole matter.
5. I never *see eye to eye* on things with you.
6. You have a different *worldview* than I do.
7. Your ideas have given me great insight into life.

The next important point made by Lakoff and Johnson is that there are three general kinds of psychological processes involved in conceptualization:

1. Mental orientation
2. Conceptualization process
3. An elaboration of the two above

1. Mental orientation

The first psychological process involves mental orientation. This produces concepts that are derived from our physical experiences of up vs. down, back vs. front, near vs. far, etc. For example, the experience of up vs. down underlies such conceptual metaphors as:

- *Happiness is up* = I'm feeling up.
- *Sadness is down* = She's feeling down today.
- *More is up* = My income rose (went up) last year.
- *Less is down* = Her salary went down when she changed jobs.

In later work, Lakoff and Johnson referred to orientational patterns such as *up vs. down, near vs. far,* etc. as *image schemas* (Lakoff 1987, Johnson 1987). These are defined as largely unconscious mental outlines of recurrent shapes, actions, dimensions, etc. that derive from perception and sensation. Image schemas are so deeply rooted that we are hardly ever aware of their control over conceptualization. But they can always be conjured up easily. If someone were to ask you to explain an idiom such as *spill the beans,* you would not likely have a conscious image schema involving beans and the action of spilling them. However, if that same person were to ask you the following questions

1. Where were the beans before they were spilled?
2. How big was the container?
3. Was the spilling on purpose or accidental? etc.

then you would no doubt start to visualize the appropriate schema; that is, you would see the beans as kept in a container; the container as being about the size of the human head; etc.

2. Conceptualization process

The second type of conceptualization process, according to Lakoff and Johnson, involves *ontological* thinking. This produces conceptual metaphors in which activities, emotions, ideas, etc. are associated with entities and substances:

1. *Time is a valuable commodity* = That is not worth my time.
2. *The mind is a container* = I'm full of memories.
3. *Anger is fluid in a container* = You make my blood boil.

3. An elaboration of the two above

The third type of process is an *elaboration* of the other two. This produces structural metaphors that distend orientational and ontological concepts. A structural metaphor is a conceptual metaphor built from existing conceptual metaphors of an orientational or ontological nature: for example, the structural metaphor *time is a resource* is built from *time is a resource = a quantity:*

- *Argument is war* = I demolished his argument.
- *Labor is a resource* = He was consumed by his job.
- *Time is a resource* = Time is money.

To get a firmer sense of how such abstract concepts shape discourse, consider the *argument is war* metaphor. The target domain of *argument* is conceptualized in terms of *warlike activities* (the source domain), and thus in terms

- of battles that can be won or lost,
- of positions that can be attacked or guarded,
- of ground that can be gained or lost,
- of lines of attack that can be abandoned or defended,
- and so on.

These warlike images are so embedded in our mind that we do not normally realize that they guide our perception of arguments. But they are nonetheless there, surfacing regularly in such common expressions as the following:

1. Your claims are *indefensible.*
2. You *attacked* all my *weak points.*
3. Your criticisms were *right on target.*
4. I *demolished* his argument.
5. I've never *won* an argument.
6. She *shot down* all my points.
7. If you use that *strategy,* I'll *wipe you out.*

The last relevant point made by Lakoff and Johnson in their truly fascinating book is that culture is built on metaphor, since conceptual metaphors coalesce into a system of meaning that holds together the entire network of associated meanings in the culture. This is accomplished by a kind of "higher-order" metaphorizing – that is, as target domains are associated with many kinds of source domains (orientational, ontological, structural), the concepts they underlie become increasingly more complex, leading to what Lakoff and Johnson call *cultural* or *cognitive models*. To see what this means, consider the target domain of *ideas* again.

The following three conceptual metaphors, among many others, deliver the meaning of this concept in three separate ways:

Ideas are food

1. Those ideas left a *sour taste* in my mouth.
2. It's hard to *digest* all those ideas at once.
3. Even though he is a *voracious reader, he can't chew all those ideas.*
4. That teacher is always *spoonfeeding* her students.
5. That idea has *deep roots.*

Ideas are persons

1. Darwin is the *father* of modern biology.
2. Those medieval ideas continue to *live on* even today.
3. Cognitive linguistics is still in its *infancy.*
4. Maybe we should *resurrect* that ancient idea.
5. She *breathed* new life into that idea.

Ideas are fashion

1. That idea went out of *style* several years ago.
2. Those scientists are the *avant garde* of their field.
3. Those revolutionary ideas are no longer in *vogue.*
4. Semiotics has become truly *chic.*
5. That idea is old *hat.*

Recall from examples of everyday discourse cited above that there are many other ways of conceptualizing ideas – for example, in terms of *buildings, plants, commodities, geometry,* and seeing. The constant juxtaposition of such conceptual formulas in common discourse produces, cumulatively, a *cultural model* of ideas (see Figure 1).

The gist of Lakoff and Johnson's 1980 work is that metaphor is at the basis of abstract thought and common discourse, although we are largely unaware of its presence. Everything written in this essay, too, has been structured by metaphorical cultural models. These have served us well in exposing the subject matter of semiotics. So, too, with every verbal text.

There are, of course, other figures of speech that occur in everyday discourse. But following Lakoff and Johnson's discovery of conceptual metaphors, these are now considered subcategories of the general process of metaphorization. Nevertheless, there are two that are regularly studied separately – *metonymy* and *irony* – because of their particular semantic characteristics.

Metonymy is the use of an entity to refer to another that is related to it:

1. She likes to read *Emily Dickinson.* (= *the writings of Emily Dickinson*).
2. He's in *dance.* (= *the dancing profession*).
3. My mom frowns on *blue jeans.* (= *the wearing of blue jeans*).

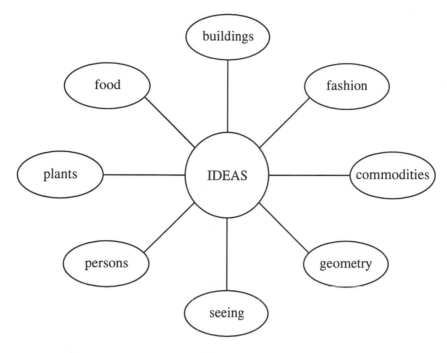

Figure 1

4. New *windshield wipers* will satisfy him. (= *the state of having new wipers*).

Synecdoche is a particular type of metonymy; it is the use of the part to represent the whole:

1. The *automobile* is destroying our health. (= *the collection of automobiles*).
2. We need a couple of *strong bodies* for our teams. (= *strong people*).
3. I've got a new *set of wheels*. (= *car*).
4. We need *new blood* in this organization. (= *new people*).

A conceptual formula of this type that requires special mention is: *the face is the person:*

1. He's just another *pretty face*.
2. There are an awful lot of *faces* in the audience.
3. We need some new *faces* around here.

It is interesting to note that metaphorical and metonymic cultural models permeate other facets of cultural expression and behaviour. The *face is the person* concept, for instance, also crystallizes in the nonverbal domain, especially in the art of portraiture. In other words, conceptual metaphors surface not only in common discourse, but also in nonverbal codes, rituals, and behaviours as well. The metaphorical formula *justice is blind*, for example, crops up not only in conversations, but also in pictorial representations. This is why there are statues of blindfolded women inside courtrooms to symbolize *justice*. The metaphorical expression *the scales of justice*, too, is evident in the sculptures of scales near or inside justice buildings. Similarly, the *love is a sweet taste* concept finds expression not only in discourse

1. She's my *sweetheart*.
2. I love my *honey*. etc.

but in rituals of love-making in Western culture. This is why sweets are given to a loved one on St. Valentine's day, why matrimonial love is symbolized at a wedding ceremony by the eating of a cake, why lovers sweeten their breaths with candy before kissing, and so on. Any ritualistic display of love will depend on what concept people infer to be more representative of a specific situation; for example, at weddings the *sweetness* concept would probably be seen to fit the situation; whereas the *physical attraction* concept would most likely be considered pertinent during other kinds of courtship performances.

Concepts and Grammar

The above discussion lays the basis for an outline of conceptual fluency theory in second-language teaching. But the question that now arises is whether or not conceptual fluency teaching is really no more than a fancy term for the study of idiomatic expressions. First, as the above examples show, the use of metaphor in discourse is not an idiomatic option. It is the basis of abstract conceptualization, forming a system of thought that permeates all of discourse. Second, conceptual fluency teaching has been extended to provide a framework for relating grammatical categories to metaphorical concepts (Langacker 1990, Taylor 1995, Danesi 1998).

As a concrete example of how the two areas are interrelated, consider the use of the prepositions *since* and *for* in sentences such as the following in English:

1. I have been living here *since 1980*.
2. I have known Lucy *since* November.
3. I have not been able to sleep *since* Monday.
1. I have been living here *for* fifteen years.
2. I have known Lucy *for* nine months.
3. I have not been able to sleep *for five days*.

An analysis of the complements that follow since or for reveals that those that follow since are "points in time," i.e. they are complements that reflect a conception of time as a "point" on a "timeline" which shows specific years, months, etc.: "1980," "November," "Monday," etc. Complements that follow *for*, on the other hand, reflect a conception of time as a "quantity": "fifteen years," "nine months," "five days," etc. These two conceptual domains – *time is a point* and *time is a quantity* – have an underlying metaphorical form, reflecting a propensity to imagine an abstract notion like "time" in terms of something concrete. These can now be seen to have a specific effect at the level of syntax by motivating a grammatical dichotomy – complements introduced by *since* are reflexes of the conceptual domain *time is a point*; those introduced by *for* are reflexes of the conceptual domain *time is a (measurable) quantity.* This is, in fact, the kind of *rule of grammar* that conceptual fluency teaching makes possible – it now relates how two specific domains of conceptualization have worked their way into the grammar. In a word, this rule stipulates how a grammatical dichotomy *reflects* a conceptual dichotomy. In French, Italian, and Spanish, on the other hand, this rule does not exist; *depuis, da* and *desde,* respectively, is used in both instances:

French

J'habite ici *depuis* 1980.

J'habite ici *depuis* quinze ans.

Italian

Vivo qui *dal* 1980.

Vivo qui *da* quindici anni.

Spanish

Vivo aquí *desde* 1980.

Vivo aquí *desde* quince años.

and so on. Our claim is that students will be in a better position to avoid making typical "errors" such as

French

*J'habite ici pour quinze ans.

Italian

*Vivo qui per quindici anni.

Spanish

*Vivo aquí por quince años.

only when they learn to conceptualize "time" in French,Italian, or Spanish, appropriately, grasping the conceptual differences between "time in English" and "time in French, Italian, or Spanish". Explaining the phenomenon of depuis, da and desde in such cases in any other way (e.g. in grammatical or lexical terms) will continue, in our view, to prove ineffectual.

Take, as one other example, the selection of certain verbs in particular types of sentences in French, Italian and Spanish. The verb faire, fare and hacer "to make" is used to convey a weather situation

Il fait chaud. Il fait froid.

Fa caldo. Fa freddo

Hace calor. Hace frío.

(literally) "it makes hot","it makes cold." The physical state of "hotness" and "coldness" is conveyed instead by the verb être, essere and estar"to be" when referring to objects

French

L'eau est chaude.

L'eau est froide.

Italian

   L'acqua *è* calda.

   L'acqua *è* fredda.

Spanish

   El agua *está* caliente.

   El agua *está* fría.

by *avoir, avere* and *tener* "to have" when referring to people.

French

   Il a chaud. Il a froid.,

Italian

   Ha caldo. Ha freddo.

Spanish

   Tiene calor. Tiene frío.

The use of one verb or the other

   faire, être, avoir

   fare, essere, avere

   hacer, estar, tener

is motivated by an underlying metaphorical conceptualization of bodies and the environment as containers. So, the "containment context" in which the quality of "coldness" or "hotness" is located determines the verbal category to be employed. If it is in the environment, it is "made" by Nature (*Il fait chaud. Fa freddo. Hace frío*); if it is in a human being, then the body "has" it (*Il a froid. Ha freddo. Tiene frío.*); and if it is in an object, then the object "is" its container (*L'eau est froide. L'acqua è fredda. El agua está fría.*)

The point to be made here is that our unconsciously-embedded concept of "time" as a "point on a line" and as a "quantity," or of "hotness" and "coldness" as being contained in Nature, people, or things, constitute conceptual domains that have reflexes or leave reflexes in the grammars of specific languages. Knowledge of such differentiated reflexive properties is what guides competent translators implicitly when they convert one language text into another successfully. *Grammar* in conceptual fluency teaching is definable, therefore, as a system that reflects the underlying *conceptual* system guiding thought and language.

As a final consideration, any refinement or elaboration of the notion of "reflexive grammatical rule" will have to take into account the presence of different "orders" of metaphor. Take, for instance, the following conceptual models of "ideas." These models are represented by an instance frequently in common discourse by utterances such as the following:

Model 1: ideas/thoughts are food

   1. What he said left a *bitter taste* in my mouth.
   2. I cannot *digest* all that information.
   3. He is a *voracious* reader.

4. We do not need to *spoon feed* our students.

5. That idea has been *fermenting* in me for years.

Model 2: ideas/thoughts are people

1. Darwin is the *father* of modern biology.

2. Medieval ideas are *alive* and *well*.

3. Artificial Intelligence is still in its *infancy*.

4. That idea should be *resurrected*.

5. She *breathed* new life into that idea.

Model 3: ideas/thoughts are clothing/fashion

1. That idea is not *in vogue* any longer.

2. New York has become a center for *avant garde* thinking.

3. Revolution is out of style these days.

4. Studying semiotics has become quite *chic*.

5. That idea is old *hat*.

These sentences suggest that we conceptualize thought processes as extensions or analogues of physical objects and people. Thoughts, like food, can be taken into the mind, like clothing can be in style or not, and so on. Often, however, the conceptual process involves reference to other pre-established conceptual domains, such as, for instance, those based on Euclidean geometry:

Model 4: thoughts are geometrical figures

1. I don't see the *point* of your idea.

2. Your ideas are *tangential* to what I'm thinking.

3. Those ideas are logically *circular*.

These examples show that there are different degrees or "orders" of concepts. The *ideas are food* model, for example, is a lower-order concept because it connects a universal physical process – *eating* – to an abstraction – *thinking* – directly. But, the *thoughts are geometrical figures* model reveals a higher-order conceptualization, since geometrical figures and notions are themselves concepts.

In terms of second-language teaching, the idea would be at first to identify and catalogue the vehicles that underlie specific topics, and then match them to the grammatical categories that reflect them. So, for instance, when analyzing sentences that allude to the "hotness" or "coldness" in French, Italian or Spanish (the topic), it will be necessary to keep in mind how the conceptualization of hotness/coldness as substances that are contained in specific contexts (the vehicles) is codified into a selection rule involving the verbs *faire, avoir,* and *être – fare, avere, essere – hacer, tener. estar* – (including relevant morphological information). It is interesting to note that in French, Italian, and Spanish "being right", "being sleepy", etc. are also conceptualized as "contained" substances. This is why to say "I am right," "I am sleepy," etc. in French, Italian and Spanish one must say

French:

J'ai raison.

J'ai sommeil.

Italian:

Ho ragione.

Ho sonno.

Spanish:

Tengo razón.

Tengo sueño.

Pedagogical Implications

Research conducted previously on university students of Italian (Danesi 1992, 1993a) suggests that typical classroom learners show virtually no traces of metaphorical competence, even after several years of study. The reason for this is not that they are incapable of learning metaphor, but more likely that they have never been exposed in formal ways to the conceptual system of the target language and culture. To be "conceptually fluent" in the second language the student must be able to convert common experiences into conceptually and linguistically appropriate models. At the present time there seems to be very little in second-language methodology that takes this into account.

Metaphorical competence is as teachable as linguistic or communicative competence. It can be claimed, in fact, that this can be done by simply structuring designated units of study around conceptual domains (time, weather, love, etc.), and then by teaching the appropriate grammar and communication patterns of the language as "reflexes" of these domains. If the grammatical system is viewed as a reflexive code of an underlying conceptual system, then a radical rethinking of the second-language classroom will have to be envisaged.

Actually, suggestions exist in the relevant pedagogical literature which we think fit in nicely with the idea of conceptual fluency. Masella and Portner (1981), for instance, show how the term capo for "head" can be taught as the onceptual source for *capostazione, capoluogo and capo d'anno; naso* ("nose") as the source for *ficcanaso, annusare,* etc. Nuessel and Cicogna (1993) suggest simply presenting students with metaphorical statements – e.g. *Lui è una volpe* ("He's a fox") – and then following this up with questions designed to unravel the conceptual structure of the statements:

- What activities are common to both elements in the metaphor? (verbs)
- How are these activities carried out? (adverbs)
- What characteristics do both elements possess? (adjectives)? (Nuessel and Cicogna 1993: 324).

And Maiguashca (1988) shows how contrasting native-language metaphorical vehicles with the target language will prove to be effective in imparting conceptual fluency,

A Practical Example

In preparing instructional methodology or materials focusing on conceptual fluency, teachers should first examine the concepts to be taught. Let us take, as a case in point, the theme of "sports" in Italian. The first step is to identify the main conceptual domains that allow native speakers to deliver this concept in discourse. The following seven examples coincide with English conceptual domains (see Figure 2).

CONCEPTUAL DOMAIN	EXAMPLES IN ACTUAL DISCOURSE
fortuna *(luck)*	Quella squadra è *fortunata.* La loro vincita è *imprevedibile.*
guerra *(war)*	Quella squadra è stata *sconfitta.* Quella squadra ha un buon attacco e una buona *tattica.* Quella partita è stata una *battaglia*
gioco *(game)*	Che bella *mossa!* Quella squadra ha *centrato.*
economia *(economy)*	Quella squadra ha *incassato* dei gol. Quella squadra ha *pagato* il gol.
alimentazione *(food)*	Quella squadra ha una *fame* di vincere. Loro sono *digiuni* di vittorie.
scienza *(science)*	Sono giocatori *sperimentati.*
pensiero *(thought)*	Hanno un'ottima *filosofia* di gioco. Quella squadra ha acquisito una *mentalità* vincente.

Figure 2

This informs the teacher that in order for students to talk or write in a conceptually-natural way about sport in Italian, they will have to be exposed to these domains, which cohere into the following cultural model that the student must acquire (see Figure 3).

After this initial analysis, the rest consists in straightforward traditional pedagogy: i.e. the teacher would want to do such things as:

- prepare dialogues that exemplify this model;
- expose the students to actual sports broadcasts; highlighting how this model is employed;
- prepare exercise and activity material, whereby the students must identify the domains and explain them;
- require the students to write their own sportscast using the above as a framework;
- etc.

Figure 3

So, for instance, when teaching English-speaking students about the weather in Italian (the topic), it will be necessary:

1. to inform them about the conceptualization of hotness/coldness as substances that are contained in specific contexts (the vehicles);

2. to teach them how to use the verbs *fare, avere,* and *essere* as reflexes of the vehicles (including relevant morphosyntactic information);

3. to develop appropriate textual and practice materials based on this explanatory framework.

Considerations

There are many similar ways in which conceptual-fluency teaching can be incorporated into classroom practice. Shibles (1989), too, has shown how easily metaphorical vehicles for emotion in German can be compared to English ones for pedagogical purposes in ways that are very similar to the ones suggested here. But in our view, the most significant implication of conceptual-fluency teaching is in the area of syllabus design. How can a conceptually-based syllabus be organized? In our view, the main idea would be to identify and catalogue the conceptual domains that deliver specific topics in discourse, together with a "reflexive" analysis of the grammatical/communicative categories that encode them. This entails the development of appropriate techniques for identifying grammatical and semantic units in terms of the conceptual domains they reflect. A "conceptual syllabus" would, then, connect the verbal categories to be learned with their related conceptual domains.

Actually, the idea of making concepts the basis for the teaching syllabus was forged by the so-called "notional-functional" theorists of the early '70s (e.g. Van Ek 1975, Wilkins 1976), who deployed speech-act and notional typologies as the organizing frameworks for developing the syllabus (and more recently for developing reading skills [see also Kaplan 1978, Piper 1985, Grabe 1991, Leki 1991 on this point]). Throughout the 1970s, and for most of the 1980s, this new functionalism in language teaching was greeted with widespread enthusiasm throughout Europe and America. Unlike the traditional grammar-based methods, it provided the teacher with greater room for imparting conceptual fluency. But now that the wave of enthusiasm has passed, it has become obvious that notional-functional teaching leaves many gaps to fill and many important questions unanswered. In our view, the main problem with the "notions" delineated by the notional-functional theorists was that they were not conceived in terms of conceptual-fluency teaching. The teacher was simply given a typology of the notions with verbal illustrations. A conceptual-fluency analysis, such as the ones illustrated in this paper, was never envisaged by the functional-notional methodologists. This is not to belittle the excellent work done by those theorists. The research on metaphor that has now become so widely known was really not available to them at the time.

Conceptual-fluency teaching also entails a re-deployment of contrastive analysis as a heuristic pedagogical technique. In its original form, contrastive analysis came to be accepted both as a theory of second-language acquisition and as an organizing principle around which to plan for language teaching. The view was that the native language was a template used by the learner for deciphering and organizing the linguistic and communicative categories of the target language. Perhaps the greatest problem with contrastive analysis is that it portrays the process of second-language acquisition solely in terms of a flow from the native to the target language, assigning no active role to the role of conceptualization in this process.

With or without contrastive analysis, modern instructional techniques have been rather successful in training language learners to gain a firm control over grammar and communication. So, the issue of whether grammatical syllabi and formalistic instructional styles are more or less productive than communicative or functional ones is, in our view, a moot one.

As Savignon (1992) has suggested, it is perhaps more appropriate, and certainly more useful, to think of the two kinds of syllabi as cooperative and complementary contributors to second-language acquisition in the classroom, not as antagonistic or mutually exclusive competitors. Both these kinds of knowledge, as mentioned, are part of verbal fluency. We believe that contrastive analysis will come to have an increasingly larger role to play in the future for studying conceptual systems, not verbal ones. By documenting and analyzing many student discourse errors on the basis of their conceptual appropriateness, we envision the contrastive technique to be used as rather straightforward. Rather than contrasting verbal structures on their own, it will be necessary to contrast them in terms of the conceptual domains they reflect. The errors that result from the unconscious transfer of conceptual formulas can be labeled "conceptual transfers" (Danesi and Di Pietro 1991: 55).

An important question for future research would thus seem to be: To what extent do the conceptual domains of the native and target cultures overlap and contrast? The notion of conceptual fluency, therefore, provides second-language acquisition researchers with a convenient category for viewing certain aspects of interlanguage behaviour that cannot be explained in other ways, such as, for example, the common observation that student-produced discourse texts seem to follow a native-language conceptual flow that is "clothed", so to speak, in target-language grammar and vocabulary. The questions that a conceptually-focused conceptual analysis would ask are therefore:

- What kinds of conceptual interferences come from the student's native conceptual system? (interconceptual interference)

- How much conceptual interference is generated by the target language itself? (intraconceptual interference)?

Concluding Remarks

The second-language teacher wishing to make conceptual fluency the primary focus of teaching should take a number of things into consideration.

1. The materials chosen for a course should reflect a learning flow that starts with experiential learning techniques and ends with more analytical tasks. This sets up a learning flow from conceptualization to verbalization.

2. The teacher will always have to consider which grammatical and semantic categories reflect conceptual structures or domains. The guiding question becomes: What are the verbal clues that reveal conceptual domains? In this paper, the prepositions *since* and *for* were related to the conceptual system as reflexes of differentiated conceptual metaphors: time is a point and *time is a quantity*. The work on cognitive grammar by Langacker (e.g. 1987, 1990) and others is leading the way in showing us how to conduct extensive analyses of this type.

3. To what extent and in what ways, if any, conceptual fluency relates to, or is embedded in, the native speaker's world knowledge? It must always be kept in mind that metaphorically-shaped knowledge is probably just one possible form in which knowledge of the world is encoded and decoded by humans. As Levin (1988: 10) has aptly remarked, there appear to be many modes of knowledge:

   innate knowledge, personal knowledge, tacit knowledge, spiritual knowledge, declarative and procedural knowledge, knowing that and knowing how, certitude (as well as certainty), and many other varieties.

The more appropriate goal for the teacher should be, therefore, to determine to what extent language is based on conceptual knowledge and to what extent it is based on other forms of knowledge.

4. If concepts are to be placed at the core of language courses and curricula, on what basis should they be selected and sequenced? In our view, the conceptual syllabus should be integrated with grammatical and communicative syllabi, since these latter two can be seen to reflect it. As mentioned, units in a textbook, for instance, could be planned around topics such as "time," "love," "health," and then drafted with the "reflexive principle" in mind: i.e. with the idea that language structures (verbal tenses, prepositions, etc.) "reflect" conceptual ones.

The idea of incorporating conceptual-fluency teaching into second-language teaching is meant to be a target for further consideration and research. Not all domains of language and language learning are tied to the conceptual system, as it has been defined here. The interlanguage studies have amply documented error phenomena that are purely grammatical, communicative, etc. We should, of course, continue to assess the role played by such mechanisms in the overall process of classroom language teaching. However, in our view the notion of conceptual fluency can no longer be ignored. The work of Lakoff and Johnson and others has shown that there is a systematicity to metaphorical concepts. The process of learning the conceptual system is, arguably, identical to the one enlisted for learning grammar and communication. To ignore metaphor is to ignore a large segment of the native-speaker's competence.

References

Beck, B. 1982. "Root Metaphor Patterns." *Semiotic Inquiry,* 2: 86-97.

Danesi, M. 1986. "The Role of Metaphor in Second Language Pedagogy." *Rassegna Italiana di Linguistica Applicata,* 18: 1-10.

Danesi, M. 1988. "The Development of Metaphorical Competence: A Neglected Dimension in Second Language Pedagogy." *Italiana,* 1: 1-10.

Danesi, M. 1992. "Metaphor and Classroom Second Language Learning." *Romance Languages Annual,* 3: 189-193.

Danesi, M. 1993a. "Metaphorical Competence in Second Language Acquisition and Second Language Teaching: The Neglected Dimension." In J. E. Alatis, ed., *Language, Communication and Social Meaning.* Washington, D. C.: Georgetown University Press, pp. 489-500.

Danesi, M. 1993b. "Whither Contrastive Analysis." *The Canadian Modern Language Review/La Revue canadienne des langues vivantes,* 50: 47-46.

Danesi, M. 1994. "Recent Research on Metaphor and the Teaching of Italian." *Italica,* 71: 453-464.

Danesi, M. 1995. "Learning and Teaching Languages: The Role of Conceptual Fluency." *International Journal of Applied Linguistics,* 5 (1995), 3-20.

Danesi, M. 1998. *Adesso: A Functional Introduction to Italian.* Boston: Heinle & Heinle.

Danesi, M. 1998. "Conceptual Iconicity and Grammatical Rules: Towards a Reflexive Grammar." In W. Pencak and J. R. Lindgren, eds., *New Approaches to Semiotics and the Human Sciences: Essays in Honor of Roberta Kevelson.* New York: Peter Lang, pp. 241-264

Danesi, M. and R. J. Di Pietro. 1991. *Contrastive Analysis for the Contemporary Second Language Classroom.* Toronto: Ontario Institute for Studies in Education Press.

Danesi, M., M. Lettieri, and S. Bancheri, S. 1996. *Con fantasia: Reviewing and Expanding Italian Language Skills.* Boston: Heinle and Heinle.

Dundes, A. 1972. "Seeing is Believing." *Natural History,* 81: 9-12.

Grabe, W. 1991. "Current Developments in Second Language Reading Research." *TESOL Quarterly,* 25: 375-406.

Johnson, M.1987. *The Body in the Mind: The Bodily Basis of Meaning, Imagination and Reason.* Chicago: University of Chicago Press.

Kaplan, R. D. 1978. "Contrastive Rhetoric: Some Hypotheses." *International Review of Applied Linguistics,* 39-40: 61-72.

Kšvecses, Z. 1986. *Metaphors of Anger, Pride, and Love: A Lexical Approach to the Structure of Concepts.* Amsterdam: John Benjamins.

Kšvecses, Z. 1988. *The Language of Love: The Semantics of Passion in Conversational English.* London: Associated University Presses.

Kšvecses, Z. 1990. *Emotion Concepts.* New York: Springer.

Lakoff, G. 1987. *Women, Fire, and Dangerous Things: What Categories Reveal about the Mind.* Chicago: University of Chicago Press.

Lakoff, G. and L. Johnson. 1980. *Metaphors We Live By.* Chicago: Chicago University Press.

Langacker, R. W. 1987. *Foundations of Cognitive Grammar.* Stanford: Stanford University Press.

Langacker, R. W. 1990. *Concept, Image, and Symbol: The Cognitive Basis of Grammar.* Berlin: Mouton de Gruyter.

Leki, I. 1991. "Twenty-Five Years of Contrastive Rhetoric: Text Analysis and Writing Pedagogies." *TESOL Quarterly,* 25: 123-143.

Levin, S. R. 1988. *Metaphoric Worlds.* New Haven: Yale University Press.

Maiguashca, R. 1988. "Quanto 'valgono' le parole straniere?" *Italiano e oltre,* 3: 136-139.

Masella, A. B. and I.A. Portner. 1981. "'Body Language' in Italian." *Italica,* 58: 205-213.

Nuessel, F. and C. Cicogna. 1993. "Narrative Texts and Images in the Teaching of the Italian language and Italian Culture." *Romance Languages Annual,* 4: 319-324.

Piper, D. 1985. "Contrastive Rhetoric and Reading in Second Language: Theoretical Perspectives on Classroom Practice." *The Canadian Modern Language Review/La revue canadienne des langues vivantes,* 42: 34-43.

Pollio, H. and B. Burns, B. 1977. "The Anomaly of Anomaly." *Journal of Psycholinguistic Research,* 6: 247-260.

Pollio, H. and M. Smith. 1979. "Sense and Nonsense in Thinking about Anomaly and Metaphor." *Bulletin of the Psychonomic Society,* 13: 323-326.

Pollio, H., J. Barlow, H. Fine, and M. Pollio, M. 1977. The Poetics of Growth: Figurative Language in Psychology, *Psychotherapy, and Education.* Hillsdale, N. J.: Lawrence Erlbaum Associates.

Russo, G. A. 1997. *A Conceptual Fluency Framework for the Teaching of Italian as a Second Language.* Toronto: University of Toronto Dissertation.

Savignon, S. J. 1992. "Problem Solving and the Negotiation of Meaning." In C. Cicogna, M. Danesi, and A. Mollica, eds., *Problem Solving in Second Language Teaching*. Welland: éditions Soleil publishing inc., pp. 11-25.

Shibles, W. 1989. "How German Vocabulary Pictures Emotion." *British Journal of Language Teaching*, 27: 141.

Taylor, J. R. 1995. *Linguistic Categorization: Prototypes in Linguistic Theory*. Oxford: Clarendon.

Van Ek, J. A. 1975. *The Threshold Level in a European Unit/Credit System for Modern Language Teaching by Adults*. Strasbourg: Council of Europe.

Wilkins, D. A. 1976. *Notional Syllabuses*. Oxford: Oxford University Press.

Winner, E. 1982. *Invented Worlds: The Psychology of the Arts*. Cambridge: Harvard University Press.

Reprinted from: "Conceptual Fluency and Second-Language Teaching." *Mosaic*, 5, 2 (Winter 1998), pp. 1, 3-12.

23 What Visual Aids Can and Cannot Do in Second Language Teaching

Hector Hammerly

Visual aids are powerfully appealing to both language teachers and students. Such aids have many advantages but also certain limitations. We should be especially leery of attempts to replace competent teachers' presentations with technological visual presentations, no matter how sophisticated the latter may be.

Introduction

Language teachers have used visual aids of some kind or another since ancient times. Since the publication of the first visually oriented second-language textbook, Comenius's *Orbis sensualium pictus* in 1648, visual aids have found a relatively large number of users. Indeed, by the late 1980's it would have been difficult to come across a language teacher who did not use at least one type of visual aid in his courses.

As Brown and Mollica (1988-1989:1) correctly pointed out,

> Visuals have been used as an aid to language and the transmission of information since pre-historic times. From the paintings and drawings found on the walls of cave-dwellers, through Egyptian hieroglyphs and Chinese ideograms to modern visual extravaganzas, man has consistently made visual representations of reality. Throughout history, the world has transformed into an icon, a visual figurativization of internal and external reality. This is not surprising given the fact that sight is the strongest of the five senses.

Curiously, a rigorous definition of visual aids has never been agreed upon. Still, many in our profession consider them simply wonderful, more or less like motherhood, and neither see nor acknowledge their limitations and the practical consequences thereof.

This study attempts to deal with visual aids in language teaching with greater precision and to discuss both their advantages (which are many and have often been described) and limitations (perhaps not so numerous, but very important even though general silence surrounds them).

What Visual Aids Are (and What They Are Not)
What Visual Aids Are Not

Despite various claims and assumptions, visual aids are *not* the following:

1. Written Language

Whatever is a sample of written language, from one grapheme to the complete holdings of our National Library, is not a visual aid but language in its written form. We must be careful, therefore, not to succumb to the temptation certain French audiovisualist scholars have fallen into, of using the same terms *lire, lisibilité,* etc.) for reading a text and viewing images, and thus blurring the distinctions between them.

For the same reason – the need to keep two very different activities carefully apart in our minds – it would be preferable to restrict the word "literacy" to the ability to decode written language (that is, "read" in the established meaning of the term) and to use instead a new term (perhaps "visual competence") for the visual aspects that the linguistic, iconographic and cultural codes have in common.[1]

2. Objects and Animals

Objects, likewise, are not visual aids, although *pictures* or models of objects may be visual aids. Thus, a pencil is not a visual aid. It is an object, specifically a tool used to write with. That it can be used to demonstrate the meaning of the French word *crayon,* for example, doesn't make it any less of an object. Only a picture of a pencil would be a visual aid in this case. The same thing can be said of other objects that are often brought into the classroom, such as realia - whether menus, mantillas or money.

This argument becomes clearer when we consider *animals.* It isn't the fact that an elephant is too large to bring into the classroom that exempts it from the designation "visual aid." However small and portable, an animal is not a visual aid but an animal; only a picture or model of an animal can be considered a visual aid.

3. People

Carried to its illogical extreme, the view that anything visible is a visual aid led certain audiovisualists to consider people "visual aids" and the *teacher* "the most important audio-visual aid" in the classroom (Corder 1966: 33), although with appropriate materials his role was supposed to be "secondary" *(ibid.,* p. 79).

This attitude is similar to views of the teacher as a human tape recorder, a mere coordinator of the learning process, just a conversation stimulator, or a dispensable adjunct ("optional live software"?) to a computer, all teacher-demeaning views held over the years by some of the leaders of, respectively, the audiolingual, individualization, communication, and computerization movements.

Competent language teachers should reject any attempt to reduce their crucial role in the classroom, whatever movement or fad may be the source of such misguided attempts.

4. Activities

Things people do, from presiding over a session of Parliament to acting out a classroom skit, may have visual *impact* but are not visual aids.

5. Media

A consequence of limiting visual aids to nonverbal images and models is that the *means* for presenting them are not themselves visual aids. A projector is a tool that enables us to *show* visual aids. Slides, films, blackboards, flannelgraphs and computer screens are media used to display visual aids; but it is the pictures the students see – whether projected, drawn with chalk, attached, or generated electronically – that may be visual aids.

6. Entertainment

Pictures presented, with or without sound, only or even primarily to entertain, are not visual aids. While audiovisual entertainment may result in incidental learning, its objective is not instructional and thus it often is unsuitable for the classroom.

An *aid is* something used purposefully to facilitate the doing of something, in our case, SL learning. While our visual aids should be interesting and, if possible, entertaining, their entertainment value is clearly a matter of secondary concern.

A Definition of "Visual Aids"

Having freed the overloaded boat from much unnecessary cargo, we can now define "visual aids" more rigorously as "drawings, photos, graphics or models of a nonverbal nature used to facilitate (second language) teaching/learning."

Of course, verbal material often accompanies visual aids, whether in written (cartoons, comic strips, etc.) or spoken (film, television, video, etc.) form. The reverse is also true: visual aids often play a supporting role to verbal material. In audiovisual presentations the primary communicative function almost constantly switches back and forth between the verbal and the visual.

"Authentic" vs. "Contrived" Audiovisuals

The current push to use "authentic" audiovisuals and to minimize the use of "contrived" ones is semantically misleading and misses the point of SL teaching/learning.

It is misleading in its choice of labels: Note how loaded with positive connotations is the word "authentic" and how negative are the connotations of "contrived."

Furthermore, this trend ignores the fact that we can use audiovisuals aimed at two different audiences, native speakers and SL learners. Just labelling them accordingly as "Audiovisuals-for-natives" and "Audiovisuals-for-SL- learners" would clarify matters; of course, only the latter are visual *aids* in our field.

Audiovisuals-for-natives are designed for viewers who are very fluent in the language and command a very large vocabulary. The viewers of audiovisuals-for-SL-learners, on the other hand, are not fluent and have precarious control of a limited vocabulary.

Thus it is hard to see how either type of audiovisual could be used effectively with the other type's audience. Natives would be extremely bored with audiovisuals-for-SL-learners, while SL learners find themselves lost and frustrated with nearly all audiovisuals-for-natives. In terms of the SL classroom, therefore, audiovisuals-for-natives should be called "Unadapted Audiovisuals" (the main connotation being "unsuitable," but there are several others) and audiovisuals-for-SL-learners should be called "Graded Audiovisuals," which could be "Learner-Designed" or "Adapted" (in either case the main connotation being "suitable").

The push for so-called "authentic" (audio) visuals, like the push for "real" communication from Day One of the SL program, is very much part of the current communication movement. Since communicationists believe that all we need to do to ensure good results is to reproduce natural language acquisition conditions in the classroom, it follows that in their view everything, from visuals to classroom activities to the noncorrection of errors, must be "real" and "authentic."[2]

Visual and Verbal Input:
Different, Noncontiguous Stimuli

It is by now well known that verbal and visual data are stored in different brain hemispheres (for about 95 per cent of the human race, verbal data storage and processing occur in the left hemisphere). Evidence of this is the finding that aphasiacs have greater difficulty in distinguishing between word meanings than between their referents (Stachowiak 1982).

Thus, neurally the pathways should be shorter -presumably being close to each other, in the same hemisphere - between a SL word and its closest native language (NL) equivalent than between either of them and their referent.

What this would do to the psychological claims underpinning the Direct Method (Franke 1884, Passy 1899, and many others), on which at least one use of visual aids is based, is not hard to imagine: the claim that the picture-SL word connection is shorter and more "direct" than the SL word-NL word connection is negated.

Their Relative Importance to Communication

It is often said that only a small percentage (between five and 15 per cent) of the meaning of communication acts is verbal and all the rest is nonverbal. While no doubt in some cases the nonverbal element is crucial, the claim seems a gross exaggeration to me.

An empirical game one can play to test the validity of the above assertion is to attend to audiovisual programs with, alternately, the audio and the video off. This "experiment" can easily be completed in one or two evenings of TV watching. See/listen for yourself. What you will notice is that the audio alone generally allows you to understand quite well what is going on, while with only the video on you are very often lost - this in a medium whose visual element is emphasized. The obvious conclusion: Words convey far more information than visuals.

Nearly three decades ago several studies have shown the greater importance of verbal input relative to visual input. While pictures may be more easily remembered than words, by secondary school verbal material is learned faster when presented verbally than pictorially. Two decades ago, Jenkins *et al.* (1967) found that college sophomores tended to encode pictures *verbally*.

Their Effect on the Imagination

Apparently verbal stimuli evoke more "sense-impression" (sensory) associations than pictorial stimuli (Otto and Britton 1965), which perhaps is just another way of saying that sound alone can result in richer mental images (does anyone still remember *The Shadow?)* than sound plus video, or that with adequate verbal stimulation the students' imagination can produce more vivid images and maybe more memorable associations than with the latest, state-of-the-art video display.

To put it another way: Do we, through the too frequent use of visuals, limit the use of our students' imagination and discourage them from the effort of having to elaborate their own mental images? Given that self-generated images and associations may be remembered better than those provided, ready-made, like baby food, we may wonder whether our teaching suffers from an overreliance on visuals.

Their Effect on Comprehension

Pictures assist in the global comprehension of verbal material (Mueller 1980), especially if they are thematic and precede a text (Omaggio 1979). Naturally, the best global comprehension is attained when text *and* pictures are used (Kraif *et al.* 1980), as shown by our little TV "experiment."

That visual support of comprehension is mostly thematic is seen in the fact that illustrations have been found to significantly enhance 11 year-old native English speakers' comprehension of abstract passages but not of concrete ones (Moore and Skinner 1985). This too has important implications for our use of visual aids in SL teaching.

Visual Aids: General Considerations
Types of Visual Aids

As defined above, visual aids include:

1. Drawings

These have the advantage over photographs that one can decide precisely how much detail to show and what to highlight. Drawings include, among other things, cartoons (and comics) and maps.

- *Cartoons and comics* have been thoroughly discussed in terms of SL teaching by Mollica (1976), Brown (1977), and Marsh (1978). "Captionable" cartoons can be varied in successive interpretations. I have found wordless cartoons particularly effective as speech generators. Comics with simple verbal material, such as Snoopy and his friends (available in many languages), and later more challenging ones like Tintin and Astéryx (to mention two in French), stimulate SL practice. Of course, cartoons and comics are subject to misunderstandings arising from cultural differences, so they should be handled judiciously.

- *Maps,* preferably with other aids, can be used effectively to "take a trip" through another region or country, to locate historical or current events, and so forth.

2. Photographs

Scanlan has shown how to use photographs in SL teaching (1976) and how to analyze them in order to, among other things, manipulate linguistic structures and improve language skills (1980). He is aware of the "likelihood" that the students mental verbalizations will be in the NL (1976: 416). One visual medium that combines photographs or drawings with verbal material is the advertisement. Scanlan (1978), Mollica (1979), and Simon (1980) have dealt in detail with the linguistic, communicative and cultural aspects of this.

Carefully chosen photographs, especially those that are a little ambiguous or have emotional appeal, can be excellent conversation stimuli. Mollica (1992a and 1992b) has led the way in the development of this type of SL materials.

3. Graphics

There are at least seven types of graphic visuals aids, as follows:

Text modifiers such as diacritics or the use of one or a few letters with underlining, in a different size, style (bold, italic, etc.) or font have long been used as specific graphic signals.

- *General graphic devices* include lines, colours (a general visual signal used in particular by Gattegno in his *Silent Way* (1972)), and such other devices as circles, boxes (or, for that matter, any shape) and arrows, most of them, again, long part of our arsenal. The best discussion so far of "pedagogical graphics" may be Danesi's (1983).
- *Charts* also have a long history in SL teaching. Recently, the flowcharts used by computer programmers have been adapted for the teaching of SL syntax (Bryant 1983), though one wonders how readable they are for the average SL student.
- *Plans* of cities, streets, stores, houses, and rooms are useful, especially as points of reference to aid comprehension or as conversation stimuli.
- *Articulatory graphics* include face diagrams as well as special symbols that serve as articulatory pointers or reminders (Hammerly 1974-a).
- *Electronically generated non-computer graphics,* using such devices as the oscilloscope, can aid intonation, stress, and rhythm.
- *Computer-generated graphics,* which for some years have shown fine detail, can also help with stress, intonation, and rhythm – and with sound articulation.

4. Models

Two types of three-dimensional representations that are particularly useful in language teaching are models of the speech apparatus and models of places. Tree-dimensional models of the speech apparatus seem to help students visualize more realistically what is involved in the articulation of NL and SL sounds

- *Models of places* like Berlin, the Champs Elysées, a supermarket, or a typical Mexican *casa* can facilitate vocabulary practice and conversation.

  (Although models are normally included loosely under the term "realia," it should be remembered that this Latin word means "real things," which of course models are not. Models are visual aids, real things are not.)

A Few Problems and Possible Solutions

1. Ambiguity

The nature of perceptual ambiguity has been discussed by many, an example being the article by Arndt and Pesch (1984). How to reduce pictorial ambiguity has been dealt with at some length by Corder (1966) and Wright (1976). But most verbal material cannot be represented pictorially, so visual aids are and will remain largely ambiguous and unreliable as conveyors of the meaning of *specific* words or sentences (see below). The hope that visuals capable of conveying all meanings unambiguously would someday be developed must be considered a "pipe dream." The scientifically based "revolutionary visual pedagogies" we were supposed to look forward to in the eighties (Brown 1983:870) did not materialize – except in the sense that the use of video and multimedia has increased. Truly revolutionary successful pedagogies would be primarily a matter of teachers and students interacting in more effective ways, and only secondarily a matter of applications of more sophisticated technology, for we must accept that visuals suffer from inherent limitations.

2. Cultural bias

It has been shown repeatedly and convincingly that people from different cultures interpret visuals differently. Pointing out the culturally relevant features of a visual – relevant from the point of view of both cultures, which calls for contrastive cultural analysis – is clearly the only solution to this problem.

3. Combination of separate visual and verbal material

This is done in various audiovisual media; dubbing is perhaps the best example. In the SL classroom, captions alone, captions plus visuals, or visuals alone can be shown as desired by using two visual sources. As a sort of reading activity, students can match pictures and captions, which could be on cards or, among other possibilities, on dentists' tongue depressors (Flynn and Trott 1972).

4. *Adaptation*

The general unsuitability of audiovisuals-for-native-speakers for the SL classroom has already been briefly discussed. If used, they should first be adapted to the characteristics of the SL learners involved (age in particular) and naturally to their degree of linguistic (grammatical and lexical) and communicative competence, and cultural awareness. For some such visuals systematic advance preparation of the students can compensate for lack of adaptation, but for most "authentic" visuals the amount of advance preparation needed is so great that they become useful only at a higher level of instruction.

5. *Control*

The idea of the student being increasingly self-reliant and primarily responsible for his own learning did not die in the late 70s. In fact, new technologies like the microcomputer, the VCR, and the videodisc player are making it easier, at least in theory, to place control of visuals in the hands of the learner.

However, other student-controlled technologies that have been around for many years, such as the individual 8mm film cartridge viewer, have hardly been exploited in SL teaching. Even student control of *non*-technological devices other than textbooks has been the exception rather than the rule in our profession, so it is difficult to tell, when, if ever, technologically advanced learner control of visuals will become a reality.

Visual Aids: Advantages and Limitations
General Advantages

1. *Atmosphere*

Visuals allow us to bring the SL world into the classroom. Every place frequented by our students should be rich in SL visuals, realia and music so as to create the atmosphere of a "cultural island."

2. *Motivation*

Visuals are an important one among the many factors that contribute to student motivation. Others include

(a) interesting and
(b) relevant content; and
(c) respect for SL learners' rights (Hammerly 1985: 211-20), such as the rights to be taught systematically, step by step; to understand what is going on in class; to be reinforced as needed; to be corrected promptly and appropriately; to have one's individual characteristics and needs taken into account; and to have input into the decision-making process.

Motivation, in short, results primarily from the evident opportunity to succeed in an interesting process of learning in which the learner has considerable input. Visuals can enhance motivation but I doubt very much that they can, by themselves, create it.

3. *Focus of attention*

A visual can draw the students' attention to most things we may want to emphasize. If visuals are simple, rather than cluttered with detail, attention can be focused on what is relevant (Corder 1966: 53). (But see General Limitation 2 below.)

4. Context

Visuals can provide virtually all situations with their most significant non-linguistic contexts.

5. Explanatory support

Visual aids can help explain features of SL structure.

6. General comprehension

Pictures have been shown to aid general comprehension by directing attention towards a theme (Omaggio 1979) or "probable semantic area" (Dethloff 1980).

7. Mnemonic support

Visuals help learners retain and recall

(a) the meaning of words, etc. (Winn 1982) and

(b) the sequences in which they have occurred.

8. Cultural Insights

Picturable cultural features are grasped better when seen than when described; for best results, however, they should be pointed out.

9. Conversation Stimuli

This is one of the most useful functions of visual aids.

General Limitations

1. The "Audiovisual Communication Dilemma"

Although greater redundancy in the text and greater correlation between text and pictures result in greater clarity, less error and less ambiguity, the amount of information transmitted is reduced accordingly (Deichsel 1980). Thus in SL teaching by increasing the amount of information conveyed pictorially we reduce the amount of information conveyed linguistically, and vice versa.

2. Focusing Attention away from Language

This applies to both language forms and comprehension, especially listening comprehension.

- *Forms* or patterns in any component of the language must be attended to first, particulary at the moment of their initial introduction. For example, to the extent that the attention of beginners is on visual aids and their meaning, it won't be on the teacher's articulation of sounds, and as a result the imitation of sounds is bound to suffer.

- *Comprehension of the verbal message* will likewise suffer from the excessive use of visuals and from the use of many specific visuals rather than a few general ones. Specific visuals may make it unnecessary for the students to put in a real effort to understand the *language,* since apparently "to the extent that comprehension of a passage is based on visual aids it is not based on the linguistic message." (Hammerly 1985: 127).

Perhaps we should not be surprised if, at the end of a program in which visual aids are used extensively, graduates cannot follow conversations by natives. What our students need most is training in listening comprehension based on hearing only, not on hearing largely aided by seeing.

3. Unreliability in Conveying Specific Meaning

Research supports the view that visual aids are at their weakest - are, in effect, unreliable – as conveyors and elicitors of the specific meanings of particular words or sentences.

- *Words,* even concrete ones, cannot be conveyed pictorially without ambiguity. An experiment (Hammerly 1974-b) revealed that even when the picture/word pairs were as concrete as *airplane, bird, deer, train,* and *tree,* university students with no knowledge of the words guessed their correct meaning only from 40 to 70 per cent of the time, while they were not sure ten to 40 per cent of the time, and they were wrong 25 to 50 per cent of the time (percentages don't add up to 100 because they varied with each of the five words).

- *Sentences in dialogues* do not fare much better. Dodson (1967: 8-9) found 30 university lecturers unable to guess the meaning of more than ten to 40 per cent of the sentences depicted in audiovisual lessons popular at the time. In research conducted from the mid-70s to the early 80s (Hammerly 1984) it was determined that experienced teachers of French could guess only an average of 54 per cent of the meaning/language conveyed by the ten frames in each of two filmstrips used in a fairly sophisticated French audiovisual textbook (Capelle and Capelle 1970).

   The fact that visuals cannot be relied upon to convey the meaning of SL words or of SL sentences in context has also been noted by several other researchers (e.g., Cole 1967, 1976). Unfortunately, it seems that many SL teachers, who of course know the SL, are so dazzled by ingenious visuals that they fail to realize that the meaning is not clear to their students, who don't know the SL.

   Corder, a strong audiovisualist, saw this problem. As he put it (1966: 50): "...we can never take it for granted that what we present is immediately recognized." A few pages later (58) he added: "...our pupils must never be put in the position of needing to ask: 'What is going on here?' " Yet this is precisely what happens, much of the time, when meaning is "conveyed" monolingually, with or without visual aids, at the beginning level: learning under such conditions becomes an ongoing, frustrating guessing game.

- *Problems with the monolingual approach* to conveying meaning have already been discussed in detail elsewhere (Hammerly 1982). Suffice it to say here that monolingual methods are inefficient ("very slow" (Corder 1966: 27)); often result in vague semantization; and do not prevent the formation of SL/NL associations anyway, even when not a single word in the NL is heard in class (Sweet (1899) already observed this, and Dodson (1967: 51) called it "the eureka experience"). Too, monolingual methods are *less* direct than bilingual ones.

While it is understandable that the lack of multilingual materials makes a monolingual approach (usually with heavy use of visuals) necessary with linguistically heterogeneous classes such as those in ESL, even there such an approach is neither desirable nor unavoidable. When all the students in a SL class speak the same NL, a monolingual approach is no longer justifiable, either on theoretical or practical grounds; even when the teacher cannot speak the NL of the students, it is possible to arrange to convey meaning in it initially.

It is not the initial monolingual SL presentation of meaning with the aid of visuals that prevents the establishment of incorrect SL/NL associations; this can be accomplished best, instead, by actively and *overtly* discouraging one-to-one word "translation" (which is often mistranslation) and by relying instead on contextual equivalents, with pointers as needed. Only this -not pictures - will ensure the prompt and precise conveyance of SL meaning.

How meaning is initially introduced seems to have little to do with its subsequent internalization (Preibusch and Zander 1971). Internalization, consolidation, and expansion of meaning are a function of meaningful practice in the second language. A monolingual guessing game aided by visuals is still a guessing game, not, as some assert, communication.

The weight of available empirical evidence and of reason support the hypothesis that meaning is best conveyed by means of triads composed of

(a) contextualized SL words and sentences plus

(b) visual aids plus

(c) contextualized NL equivalents.

Using visuals enhances retention and recall, and using the NL ensures comprehension.

Principled bilingual teaching in the SL classroom, which is another way of putting it, should yield the best results. This means using the NL as little as possible (certainly not to generate SL sentences) and as much as necessary (e.g., for the initial conveyance of meaning). I realize that this recommendation, which contradicts what many SL teachers believe, runs against the long-standing Direct Method tradition of Europe, and especially of France.

But principled bilingual SL teaching also has long roots, going at least as far back as the late nineteenth century. Few today seem aware that the precursor of the much-distorted and now largely rejected Audiolingual Method was bilingual, not monolingual. It followed the Sweet (1899)-Palmer (1917, 1922) - structural linguists' (1940s) route, and by the late 50s its results (which I was able to observe) were very good indeed. Even in Europe, bilingual SL teaching has made some headway, especially in Great Britain, with the work of Dodson (1967), and in Germany, taking the lead form Butzkamm (1973).

Principled bilingual SL teaching may use visual aids in many ways but it is not a reincarnation of the Grammar-Translation Method: it is also the very opposite of the "trial and error" approach to SL learning.

4. *Unreliability in eliciting specific meaning*

The predictability of language, even given a list of specific situations (which in itself is very arbitrary) and specific pictures, is low. The expectation of certain members of our profession, such as Corder and Wright, that some-day the language which goes with specific visuals could be predicted "with a high degree of certainty" (Corder 1966: 46) will not be realized.

The best proof of this comes from SL testing. After much research, Pimsleur concluded that "even the clearest pictures tend to elicit a variety of utterances, rather than only the one we want." (1966: 198).

5. *Cost*

Although there has been a substantial reduction in cost over the years, most visuals and audiovisuals are still fairly expensive, some extremely so. The cost-effectiveness factor cannot be ignored.

Visual or Teacher Presentations

In recent years, video presentations are being promoted as being more effective than teacher presentations (e.g. Hanley *et al.*, 1995; Herron *et al.*, 1995). This reminds me of the audiovisual practice, many years ago, of having the teacher present a filmstrip accompanied by an audiocassette rather than say anything herself. Furthermore, because these audiovisual presentations – whether via video or filmstrip/audiocassette – are Direct Method monolingual presentations done strictly in the SL, they become a very difficult and, for many students, a frustrating guessing game.

This promotion of presentations via video seems to be another attempt – there have been several – to replace the teacher, or at least some of her important functions, with technology. However, there will always be many things a competent teacher can do that technology, visual or otherwise, cannot.

Although this article is not meant to discuss in detail how to use visual aids, the strong trend to use videos for presentations calls for the following practical suggestions:

- While the best initial step in presenting new material might well be the viewing of a very short video, this should be immediately followed by a much slower review of the video, with the teacher observing, the class carefully and stopping the tape after every sentence or two for random individual repetition and occasional choral echoing, accompanied as needed by deep correction, by any bilingual clarification of sounds, structures or meaning the students may request or require , and by interaction through questions and answers, role playing, retelling, and so forth.
- Visual or multimedia technology will never be able to do well any of the things just listed, for they all require the use of an intelligent,

competent and *adaptable* mind – which machines do not and *cannot* have. While technologically aided self-instruction supplemented with graded conversation with a native speaker may be the best way to proceed when a competent teacher is not available, best results in the SL classroom will always be obtained by a competent, caring teacher *aided* – and at no time replaced – by visual technologies.

Conclusion

More could be written about, among other things, specific applications of visual aids to the teaching of SL components, skills, cultural awareness, and literary appreciation, what the various (audio) visual media are, their relative advantages and disadvantages and how to use them in the SL program. But time and space are always in short supply. My hope is that through these pages the reader has become more aware of what, precisely, "visual aids" are and what they can and cannot do, and that he or she will have the opportunity (or the courage, if need be) to put this extended awareness into practice.

References

Arndt, Horst and Helmut W. Pesch. 1984. "Non-verbal Communication and Visual Teaching Aids: A Perceptual Approach." *The Modern Language Journal*, 68: 28-36.

Brown, James W. 1977. "Comics in the Foreign Language Classroom: Pedagogical Perspectives." *Foreign Language Annals*, 10: 18-25.

Brown, James W. and Anthony Mollica, eds. 1980-1981. *Essays in Visual Semiotics*. Toronto: Toronto Semiotic Circle.

Brown, James W. 1983. "Trends in Pictorial Pedagogics: Adding to the Ads." *The Canadian Modern Language Review/La Revue canadienne des langues vivantes*, 39: 858-888.

Bryant, William H. 1983. "Syntax Flowcharts For Advanced French Courses." *Foreign Language Annals*, 6: 469-476.

Butzkamm, Wolfgang. 1973. *Aufgeklärte Einsprachigkeit: zur Entdogmatisierung der Methode im Fremdsprachenunterricht*. Heidelberg: Quelle und Meyer.

Capelle, Janine and Guy Capelle. 1970. *La France en direct*. Waltham, MA: Ginn.

Cole, Leo R. 1967. "The Visual Element and the Problem of Meaning in Language Learning," *Audio-Visual Language Journal*, 4: 84-87.

Cole, Leo R. 1976. "Relationships Between Visual Presentations and Linguistic Items in Second-Language Teaching." *International Review of Applied Linguistics*, 14: 339-350.

Comenius, Johann A. 1648. *Orbis sensualium pictus*. Reprinted, Sidney: Sidney University Press, 1967.

Corder, S. Pit. 1966. *The Visual Element in Language Teaching*. London: Longman.

Danesi, Marcel. 1983. "Pedagogical Graphics in Second-Language Teaching." *The Canadian Modern Language Review/La Revue canadienne des langues vivantes*, 40: 73-81.

Deichsel, Ingo. 1980. "Quelques conséquences de la cognition audio-visuelle en vue d'une méthodologie des media." *Études de linguistique appliquée*, 38: 52-64.

Dethloff, Uwe. 1980. "La réception des textes télévisuels en langue étrangère." *Études de linguistique appliquée*, 38: 106-118.

Dodson, Carl J. 1967. *Language Teaching and the Bilingual Method*. London: Pitman.

Flynn, Mary and Nora Trott. 1972. "300 Tongue Depressors." *The French Review*, 45: 6 54-656.

Franke, Felix. 1884. *Die praktische Spracherlernung auf Grund der Psychologie und der Physiologie der Sprache dargestellt von Felix Franke*. Heilbronn, Germany .

Gattegno, Caleb. 1972. *Teaching Foreign Languages in Schools: The Silent Way*. Second edition. New York: Educational Solutions.

Hammerly, Hector. 1974a. *The Articulatory Pictorial Transcriptions: New Aids to Second Language Pronunciation*. N. Burnaby, B.C.: Second Language Publications.

Hammerly, Hector. 1974b. "Primary and Secondary Associations with Visual Aids as Semantic Conveyors." *International Review of Applied Linguistics*, 12: 119-125.

Hammerly, Hector. 1982. *Synthesis in Second Language Teaching. An Introduction to Languistics*. N. Burnaby, B.C.: Second Language Publications.

Hammerly, Hector. 1984. "Contextualized Visual Aids (Filmstrips) as Conveyors of Sentence Meaning." *International Review of Applied Linguistics*, 22: 87-94.

Hammerly, Hector. 1985. *An Integrated Theory of Language Teaching and Its Practical Consequences*. N. Burnaby, B.C.: Second Language Publications.

Hammerly, Hector. 1994. "A Picture is Worth 1000 Words and a Word is Worth 1000 Pictures.," *Mosaic*, 1, 4: 13-19.

Hammerly, Hector. 1995a. "Annotated Publication Abstracts on the (French) Immersion Approach;" unpublished research paper. P.O. Box 64522, Como Lake Postal Outlet, Coquitlam, BC V3J 7V7: Lexcel Enterprises Inc.

Hammerly, Hector. 1995b. "Preliminary Results of the French Immersion Test – Home Version (FIT-HV)." Unpublished research report. Coquitlam, BC: Lexcel Enterprises Inc.

Hammerly, Hector, Monique McDonald, Trude Heift and Siok Lee. 1994. "Some Observations About the Grammaticality of French Immersion and Core French Graduates," unpublished research paper. Coquitlam, BC: Lexcel Enterprises, Inc.

Hanley, Julia E.B., Carol A. Herron and Steven P. Cole. 1995. "Using Video as an Advance Organizer to a Written Passage in the FLES Classroom." *The Modern Language Journal*, 79: 57-66.

Herron, Carol, Matthew Morris, Teresa Secules and Lisa Curtis. 1995. "A Comparison Study of the Effects of Video-Based versus Text-Based Instruction in the Foreign Language Classroom." *The French Review*, 68: 775-795.

Jenkins, Joseph R., Daniel C. Neale and Stanley L. Deno. 1967. "Differential Memory for Picture and Word Stimuli." *Journal of Educational Psychology*, 58: 303-307.

Kraif, André *et al*. 1980. "Compréhension de documents publicitaires TV: une approche empirique." *Études de linguistique appliquée*, 38: 82-105.

Marsh, Rufus K. 1978. "Teaching French with the Comics." *The French Review*,   51: 777-785.

Mollica, Anthony. 1976. "Cartoons in the Language Classroom." *The Canadian Modern Language Review/La Revue canadienne des langues vivantes*, 32: 424-444.

Mollica, Anthony. 1978. "The Film Advertisement: A Source for Language Activities." *The Canadian Modern Language Review/La Revue canadienne des langues vivantes*, 34,2:221-243

Mollica, Anthony. 1979. "*A Tiger in Your Tank:* Advertisements in the Language Classroom." *The Canadian Modern Language Review/La Revue canadienne des langues vivantes,* 35: 691-743.

Mollica, Anthony. 1992a. *A Picture is worth...1000 words...*Book 1. Welland, Ontario: éditions Soleil publishing inc.

Mollica, Anthony. 1992b. *A Picture is worth...1000 words...*Book 2. Welland, Ontario: éditions Soleil publishing inc.

Moore, Phillip J. and Michael J. Skinner. 1985. "The Effects of Illustrations on Children's Comprehension of Abstract and Concrete Passages," *Journal of Research in Reading,* 8: 45-56.

Mueller, Gunther A. 1980. "Visual Contextual Cues and Listening Comprehension: An Experiment." *The Modern Language Journal,* 64: 335-340.

Omaggio, Alice C. 1979. "Pictures and Second Language Comprehension: Do They Help?" *Foreign Language Annals,* 12: 107-116.

Otto, Wayne and Gwenyth Britton. 1965. "Sense-Impression Responses to Verbal and Pictorial Stimuli." *International Review of Applied Linguistics,* 3: 51-56.

Palmer, Harold E. 1917. *The Scientific Study and Teaching of Languages. London: Harrap.* Reprinted in 1968 by Oxford University Press.

Palmer, Harold E. 1922. *Principles of Language-Study.* London: Harrap. Reprinted in 1964 by Oxford University Press.

Passy, Paul. 1899. *De la méthode directe dans l'enseignement des langues vivantes.* Cambridge, England: Association Phonétique Internationale.

Pellerin, Micheline and Hector Hammerly. 1986. "L'expression orale après treize ans d'immersion française." *The Canadian Modern Language Review/La Revue canadienne des langues vivantes,* 42: 592606.

Pimsleur, Paul. 1966. "Testing Foreign Language Learning." In Albert Valdman, ed., *Trends in Language Teaching.* New York: McGraw-Hill, pp. 175-214.

Preibusch, Wolfgang and Heidrun Zander. 1971. "Wortschatzvermittlung: auf der Suche nach einem analytischen Modell." *International Review of Applied Linguistics,* 9: 131-145.

Scanlan, Timothy. 1976. "A Picture's Worth a Thousand Words? Then Let's Hear Them!" *The Canadian Modern Language Review/La Revue canadienne des langues vivantes,* 32: 415-21.

Scanlan, Timothy M. 1978. "French Mail-order Catalogues as Teaching Tools: Vocabulary, Culture and Conversation." *The French Review,* 52: 217-241.

Scanlan Timothy M. 1980. "Another Foreign Language Skill: Analyzing Photographs." *Foreign Language Annals,* 13: 209-13.

Simon, Ronald H. 1980. "Images publicitaires: Images culturelles." *The French Review,* 54: 1-27.

Stachowiak, Franz-Josef. 1982. "Haben Wortbedeutungen eine gesonderte mentale Repräsentation gegenüber dem Weltwissen? Neurolinguistische Überlegungen," *Linguistische Berichte,* 79: 12-29.

Sweet, Henry. 1899. *The Practical Study of Languages.* London: J.M. Dent and Sons. Reprinted in 1964 by Oxford University Press.

Winn, William. 1982. "Visualization in Learning and Instruction: A Cognitive Approach." *Educational Communication and Technology,* 30: 3-25.

Wright, Andrew. 1976. *Visual Materials for the Language Teacher.* New York: Longman.

Notes

1. Brown [1983: 873-7] has proposed a semiotically structured model of "visual literacy" in terms of these three codes; my point is that the term "literacy" should be reserved for the written linguistic code. (An ever stronger argument can be made against the use of terms such as "computer literacy.")

2. Natural language acquisition conditions *cannot* be reproduced in the classroom, as both the learners and the environment differ in major unavoidable ways. The linguistic results of communicative/acquisitionist/ naturalistic language "teaching" are poor. After 13 years (about 7000 hours) of French "immersion" (it isn't) graduates make very frequent errors of the most basic nature [Pellerin and Hammerly, 1986; Hammerly *et al.*, 1994; Hammerly 1995a and 1995b]. Will communicative language "teaching" ever get a better chance to show what it can do? Does it deserve it?

Reprinted from: Hector Hammerly, "What Visual Aids Can and Cannot Do In Second Language Teaching," *Mosaic*, 2, 3 (Spring 1995), pp. 11-18.

24 A Picture is Worth... 1000 Words... Creative Activities for the Language Classroom

Anthony Mollica

Language teachers have always made use of pictorial material either to associate word and image or to have the image serve as a stimulus for conversation and discussion. The article identifies several activities whose aim is to encourage the use of pictures in the classroom.

Introduction

As James W. Brown and Anthony Mollica point out in their "Introduction" to *Essays in Applied Visual Semiotics* (1988-89:1),

> Visuals have been used as an aid to language and the transmission of information since pre-historic times. From the paintings and drawings found on the walls of the cave-dwellers, through Egyptian hieroglyphs and Chinese ideograms to modern visual extravaganzas, man has consistently made visual representation of reality. This is not at all surprising, given the fact that sight is the strongest of the five senses. Most of the information we have about the world derives from the condition of seeing.

It is precisely because the sense of sight is the strongest of all senses that we have decided to capitalize on this element and to suggest the introduction of images in the language classroom. Moreover, as Clifford T. Morgan and Richard A. King (1966:197) have concisely stated,

> Most, if not all, people experience images and images often help thinking. Some individuals have such a vivid imagination that they can recall things almost perfectly; this is called eidetic imagery.

The use of visual imagery in learning, as psycholinguists often point out, is crucial to recall mechanisms and the development of eidetic memory, and this, of course, is beneficial to language learning.

Students are frequently reluctant or even unwilling to speak in the language classroom for, quite often, the stimulus is too difficult and requires considerable research and linguistic knowledge. As we have stated elsewhere (Mollica, 1985b),

> Exchanging views on such diverse topics as "abortion", "capital punishment", "the role of women", and the like will not produce in the learner the mechanical ability to apply the target language in a communicatively-appropriate way to the various situations which make up verbal interaction. Moreover, the nature of these topics

is such that it requires a sophisticated command of the structural and lexical modalities of the target language. It comes as no surprise, therefore, to find beginning students unwilling and unable to speak about these topics.

Granted, our ultimate aim should be to prepare students to speak about these and other topics of interest to them. And, in fact, these, and other "hot" topics of current interest, should be introduced and discussed at an advanced stage once the students have mastered an appropriate or comfortable command of the language, have read widely on these subjects and/or have such an intense personal interest that they willingly share it with their peers and perhaps even try to impose their views on them.

The increasing research over the last decade on the development of communicative competence has made it abundantly clear that the spontaneous use of the target language will have to be guided and will have to be taught systematically in ways that grammatical structures are taught. To relegate the development of audio-oral writing skills to the "Friday afternoon conversation class" has proven continually and consistently to be a fruitless exercise (Mollica, 1985a).

There has, however, been an ever increasing amount of literature on the development of appropriate pedagogical strategies for the teaching and encouragement of authentic and autonomous communication in a classroom setting.

Our purpose in this paper is, in fact, to describe one of several communication-focused strategies that we have been developing and experimenting with over a number of years. We will refer to them as "visual stimuli" because their psychopedagogical focus is the elicitation of target language words, phrases, sentences and entire discourse units. This discussion summarizes and refines the points made in previous studies (Mollica 1985a, 1985b, 1981, 1979a, 1979b, 1978, 1976).

The Stimulus

Psycholinguistically, a stimulus can be defined to be any physiological or sensorial phenomenon to which an organism will respond according to some predictable pattern of behaviour. The "visual stimulus" has been deliberately chosen to elicit either oral or written responses, depending on the language skill teachers will wish to focus on.

It is important to note that some stimuli are better suited for oral interaction, while others are better suited for written ones; there are, obviously, still many others which are equally well suited for both oral and written activities.

The visual stimulus consists of a series of photographs which may be grouped into the following categories:
- humorous
- descriptive
- dramatic
- tragic

- cultural

Each photograph can serve as a stimulus for discussions and compositions at various linguistic levels:

- beginning
- intermediate
- advanced.

This means that if the teacher chooses judiciously a classroom assignment based on the students' linguistic background, the same photo may be used at different levels of language instruction and will be quite appropriate in multi-level classes.

The three linguistic levels suggested above coincide with the following suggested hierarchical stages of the photograph:

- Visual Comprehension
- Personal Interpretation
- Creativity.

These three stages may be illustrated using *Photo 1* as an example. At the *visual comprehension* stage, students may be asked questions directly related to what is seen in the photograph. The lexical items to be elicited will be simple and the structures required to "converse" will be quite basic.

1. How many people do you see in the picture?

2. What are they doing?

3. Name some of the items which are being used to plant a tree.

and so on.

At the *personal interpretation* stage, students may be asked to express their own opinion about the actions/scenes depicted in the photograph.

1. Why, do you think, these are people planting a tree?

2. Who, in your opinion, should be involved in these ceremonies?

and so on.

At the *creativity* stage, students may be asked questions focusing on their imagination and inventiveness. In some cases, teachers will want to guide the creativity process by suggesting some possible topics for consideration. At this level, some visual stimuli may be well suited to lead to further research.

1. *Write a short paragraph giving necessary information relating to the photograph. Identify*

   a. *the man and the young people,*

   b. *the occasion for planting a tree,*

   c. *the location where the scene is taking place, etc.*

2. *Using your research skills, find as much information as possible about tree-planting ceremonies.*

3. *Imagine that you are the anchor person for a local TV station. Give an oral account of what is portrayed by the photograph as it is being flashed on the screen.*

4. *Imagine that you are the man at the left. Write a brief speech which you would give preceding or following the ceremony,* etc.

The point to be made here is that a visual stimulus can be utilized to generate spontaneous conversation in the target language without recourse to some previously-prepared dialogue on a specific theme. Since teachers are obviously aware of the linguistic background of their students, they may wish to fuse all three stages and ask questions or suggest assignments which involve visual comprehension, interpretation and creativity.

Photo 1

   The activities we suggest below for using photographs are not meant to be exhaustive, but rather are intended to aid the teacher to provide contextualized, meaningful oral exchanges or written assignments in the language classroom. They constitute a type of triggering device which should start conversation on a specific theme in an autonomous way.

General Pedagogical Applications

The following are some general pedagogical applications which may be used by the teacher whenever s/he feels them appropriate. They are not being presented in a pre-established hierarchical structure, but we are confident that teachers will first emphasize the speaking skill and then reinforce it with writing activities. Talking about the visual stimulus before the written assignment allows students to gather the necessary vocabulary they need as well as to help organize their thoughts in a logical sequence and thus enrich the writing activity.

Vocabulary Brainstorming

Students may be asked to do some brainstorming. For this task, students maybe divided into pairs or into a small group and asked to jot down on paper as much vocabulary as possible elicited by the visual representation in the photograph. It is obvious that each student will contribute according to his/her linguistic background and the end-result will be a comprehensive, if not exhaustive, list of varied and interesting lexical items. If the exercise is being done in a language other than English, students should be encouraged to consult a dictionary, a native speaker who may be in the classroom, or even the teacher, in order to provide as many words as possible which will enrich the speaking or writing experience.

Questions/Answers

Students may be asked to speak solely about the photograph. Teachers may decide to select only those questions based on the photo, the answers to which can be given by looking at the image. Since the teacher is aware of the linguistic background the student has, s/he will be able to choose questions which will elicit the correct response and involve the student at a certain level.

Questions/Answers activities, if logically and sequentially planned, may lead to a short written paragraph.

The Five "W"s

Teachers should constantly remind their students to attempt to answer the questions

- Who...?
- What...?
- Where...?
- When...?
- Why...?

Photo 2

Photo 3

The answers to these and other similar questions are very suitable at the "visual comprehension" stage and, if asked often, will instill a sense of inquisitiveness in the learners and sharpen their visual acuity.

Word/Line/Paragraph Captions

Students may be asked to write a caption for the photograph. Here the students will examine the photograph and come up with an appropriate caption. This will be an excellent exercise since the students will have to compress in a short phrase or in two or three words the spirit of the scene. For example, the original photograph showing a set of twins in a fountain (*Photo 2* was labelled "Two hot", focusing on an English pun; the original caption of the three youths sitting on a bench (*Photo 3*) was identified as "A situation well in hand". Students should be encouraged to think of both serious and humorous captions. These can come from everyday language or crystallized language (namely, proverbs, maxims, etc.)

Public Speaking

The visual stimulus is also suitable for "public speaking" presentations. Students are asked to speak about the photo or use the photo as a point of departure. A discussion of ethics could be done for *Photo 3* ("A situation well in hand").

Photo 4

Cause/Effect

Some photographs will show an effect to a given cause; others may show a cause which may produce varied effects. Students may be asked to identify either one or the other or both. See *Photo 4*.

Kim's Game

This is the popular memory game in which students are shown the photograph for a pre-determined number of seconds and then asked questions on what they saw. For this activity a copy of the photograph should be given to the students who are asked to look at it for a pre-determined number of seconds. They will then be required to turn it over and then the teacher asks a series of questions. This activity works best with photographs showing people demonstrating or protesting, with photos depicting accident scenes or with photographs which are full of details. Depending on the depth and the number of questions the teacher may wish to ask, this game can be played with practically all photos. All questions will focus on visual recall. (*Photo 5*).

Newspaper Articles

Teachers may ask students to write an article for a local or school newspaper (or for a year book) based on the activities seen in the photograph. To assist each other students may be grouped together and brainstorm the lexical items and ideas or descriptions they would like to see included. Teachers

Photo 5

items and ideas or descriptions they would like to see included. Teachers may help by answering vocabulary questions or the students may seek the answers in a dictionary.

Before and After Sequence

In a discussion on cartoons, Roger Tremblay (1987) pointed out that vignettes are often pictures in a "state of imbalance"; that is, there is

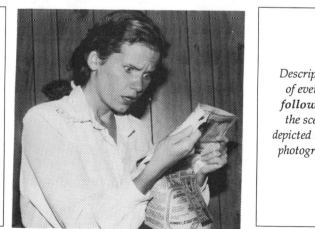

*Description of events **preceding** the scene depicted in the photograph.*		*Description of events **following** the scene depicted in the photograph.*

Before **Photo in the "state of imbalance"** **After**

something which has taken place before the photo was taken and something which will follow.

Since students are provided with the "middle" photo, they should be encouraged to imagine the events which happened before and after. They will, as a result of this activity, invent or create a story with a beginning, middle and an end.

Radio/TV Announcements

Teachers may ask students to assume the role of a newscaster and to describe verbally the activities portrayed in the photograph. In this case, obviously, the emphasis will be on the speaking.

Problem-Solving

Since photographs are in a "state of imbalance", the teacher may want to elicit from students the problem since the solution has already been shown by the photograph. *Photo 6* is a good example. Here, obviously, the little girl could not reach the fountain and enlisted the help of her sister.

Writing Poetry

The photograph is also an effective stimulus for poetry writing. Many colleagues are reluctant to introduce or indeed teach poetry in the classroom and yet many students are «closet poets». They tend to be so because poetry is personal and they may be unwilling to reveal their personal feelings. If the stimulus is visual, students will focus on it rather on their personal experiences which they may not want to share and will produce very good results. Why poetry? Poetic writing demands preciseness. The word precise embodies the ideas of delineation and limit. Writing poetically helps children develop this language skill. The suggestions we are putting forth for consideration are «recipes» which students can follow with little or no difficulty. To assist them at the early stages of poetry writing, we recommend that they be asked to co-author their poetry by working in pairs or in groups. The following are some suitable examples but the choices are certainly not exhaustive:

a) *The Cinquain*

After learning the present tense and the agreement of adjectives, students may be asked to become "instant" poets by following these rules:

1. On the first line, write down a noun: a person, a place or thing.
2. On the line below that, write two adjectives (or two present participles, or two past participles). Separate the adjectives by a comma.
3. On the third line, write three verbs that tell what the noun on the first line does. Separate the verbs by commas.
4. On the fourth line, write a thought about the noun. A short sentence will be quite acceptable.
5. On the fifth line, repeat the word you wrote on the first line or write down a synonym or some other related word.

Photo 6

The best way of approaching this task is to do a brainstorming of vocabulary with the entire class while the teacher or a student records on the blackboard the lexical items suggested by the class. Once the topic or title has been selected, the brainstorming begins. For example, the topic may be "Love".

- Teachers should ask students to suggest adjectives which, in their opinion, describe the title or the topic. The answers will obviously vary; the vocabulary suggested will be drawn from each student's own linguistic background which may vary. This variation of vocabulary may very well bring to light new words; hence the activity will not only be a review of vocabulary already known to most students but also an introduction to new lexical items. Suggestions received during the brainstorming session may be:

  tender, passionate, kind, faithful, painful, friendly, confusing, hot, everlasting, fickle, romantic, exciting, emotional, sensitive, erotic, platonic, comforting, physical, sensual, wild, selfish, selfless, primal, paradoxical, fragile.

- Ask students to suggest verbs - action words – that come to mind when they think of "Love". Lexical suggestions may be:

  protects, destroys, unites, separates, exhilarates, excites, protects, grows, changes, endures, hurts, heals, gives, shares, stimulates, burgeons, blossoms.

- Ask students to provide a thought about the topic.

  Love makes the world go round.

  Love is unconditional.

  Love is everything.

  Love is companionship.

The thought may be from a proverbial or Biblical phrase:

  Love is blind.

  Love is patient, love is kind.

from a maxim or saying:

  Lucky at cards, unlucky in love.

  Love is a double-edged sword.

  It's better to have loved and lost than not to have loved at all.

from a movie title or movie dialogue:

  Love is a many splendoured thing.

  Love means never having to say "You're sorry."

from a song:

  Love me tender, love me true.

  I love the way you love me.

or from other poems:

  My love is like a red red rose.

  How do I love thee? Let me count the ways.

Ask students to provide a synonym for the topic:

  passion, affection, friendship, adoration

or an antonym:

  hate.

Some students, instead of selecting a synonym or antonym for the topic, decide to insert the name of the boyfriend or girlfriend! This is bound to create some humour in the classroom and this emphasizes the "fun" element of the activity.

Once teachers feel that they have "exhausted" the various possibilities, they should then ask students to create their own poem by following the instructions suggested above. Teachers should then ask all students to jot down the title of the poem, "Love".

Next, teachers should ask a student to read slowly from the blackboard all the adjectives which describe the topic. Students are asked to select three adjectives from the list. It is obvious that different students will select different adjectives.

The same process – namely, asking a student to read the suggested answers written on the blackboard – is followed for the verbs (third line), the thought (fourth line) and the repetition of the topic/title or antonym for the fifth line. The reading of the lexical items on the blackboard will provide repetition to the activity.

When students have completed the task, no poem contains exactly the same vocabulary because each student has selected the lexical items of his/her choice. The poem, although done with the assistance of the entire class, becomes *personal* since it is the poem of the student who has selected the words.

Students who generally would be reluctant to share their feelings will probably do so willingly for they attribute the vocabulary as not being theirs but selected from the lists given by the class.

Since the poem deals with "love", students may decide to insert their poem in a suitable illustration, such as a heart.

Students may be asked to find suitable illustrations from magazines or newspapers to embellish their written task.

Once teachers have established this as a "fun" activity, they may be encouraged to work on other types of poetry such as the following.

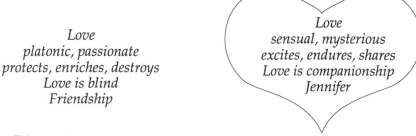

Love
platonic, passionate
protects, enriches, destroys
Love is blind
Friendship

Love
sensual, mysterious
excites, endures, shares
Love is companionship
Jennifer

b) *The Diamante*

Students should be asked to follow these suggestions:

1. On the first line, write down a noun.

2. On the second line, write down two adjectives describing the noun. Separate the adjectives by a comma.

3. On the third line write three participles.

4. On the fourth line, write down four nouns related to the subject. (The second two nouns may have opposite meanings from the subject.)

5. On the fifth line, write three participles indicating change or development of the subject.

6. On the sixth line, write two adjectives carrying on the idea of change or development.

7. On the seventh line, write a noun that is the opposite of the subject.

c) *The Haiku*

The haiku is a Japanese unrhymed poem about nature and the seasons of the year. Several questions contained in the Teacher's Guide which accompanies the book A picture is worth...1000 words...refer to seasons. It may be appropriate for students to write a haiku poem for those photographs. The haiku has three lines and totals seventeen syllables. Students do not have to follow the syllabic count exactly but they should use a word that hints of the season of the year as they write these nature poems. The simplicity of the form of this type of poetry centers in its syllable count. The Haiku has seventeen syllables divided into lines of five, seven and five syllables. Students should keep in mind that the seventeen syllable count serves as a guide for writing a haiku; it is not a stringent, inflexible rule.

Editorials

Some photographs lend themselves quite well as a stimulus for Editorials. For example, a photo showing a child drinking from a public fountain (*Photo 7*) may lead to the importance of water in various cultures. North Americans use it to cultivate their lawns, wash their cars, etc. In many parts of the world there is a shortage of water, people drink bottled water, etc.

Bulletin Board Displays

The photographs are published in such a way so that the first large photo will serve as a basis for individual or group work. The second photo, in reduced size, with a lot of space around it, has been so designed to allow students to write/type their assignment on the page. This can then be posted on the bulletin board for display. Since the photos and the assignments will vary, this activity will provide reading material for the entire class.

Sequencing

Teachers may wish to leaf through the book and find photos which, if placed one after another, will constitute a sequence. While each photograph may be discussed on its own merit, several photos may be grouped together to form a story. For example,

    Photo 8: Drugs seized...

Photo 7

Conclusion

The visual element, then, is an effective stimulus to trigger conversation in the classroom. It is by no means the only solution but it will certainly contribute to meaningful verbal and written activities. If used at different levels, it will answer the learner's linguistic needs and will provide hours of enjoyment and learning.

Photo 8

Photo 9

Photo 10

Photo 11

Photo 12   Photo 13

References

Brown, James W. and Anthony Mollica. 1988-1989. *Essays on Visual Semiotics.* Toronto: University of Victoria Semiotic Circle.

Mollica, Anthony. 1988. "Verbal Duelling in the Classroom: Audio and Visual Stimuli for Creative Communicative Activities." In Valeria Sestieri Lee, ed., *Language Teaching and Learning: Canada and Italy/Insegnare ed imparare lingue: Canada e Italia.* Ottawa: Canadian Mediterranean Institute / Roma: Centro Accademico canadese in Italia, 1988. Pp. 101- 122.

Mollica, Anthony. 1985a. "Not for Friday Afternoons Only!: The Calendar of Memorable Events as a Stimulus for Communicative Activities." *The Canadian Modern Language Review/La Revue canadienne des langues vivantes,* 42, 2 (November): 487-511.

Mollica, Anthony, 1985b. "Oral Stimuli for the Language Classroom." In Pia Kieber and Marcel Danesi, eds., *Language Teaching Strategies,* Vol. 1. Toronto: The Faculty of Arts and Science, 1985. Pp. 39-53.

Mollica, Anthony. 1981. "Visual Puzzles in the Second-Language Classroom." *The Canadian Modern Language Review/La Revue canadienne des langues vivantes,* 37, 3 (March): 583-628.

Mollica, Anthony. 1979a. "*A Tiger in Your Tank*" Advertisements in the Language Classroom." *The Canadian Modern Language Review/La Revue canadienne des langues vivantes,* 35, 4(May): 697-743.

Mollica, Anthony. 1979b. "Print and Non-Print Materials: Adapting for Classroom Use." In June K. Phillips, ed., *Building on Experience Building for Success.* ACTFL Foreign Language Education Series, Volume 10.Skokie, IL: National Textbook Company, 1979. Pp.157-198.

Mollica, Anthony 1978. "The Film Advertisement: A Source for Language Activities." *The Canadian Modern Language Review/La Revue canadienne des langues vivantes,* 34, 2 (January): 221-243.

Mollica, Anthony. 1976. "Cartoons in the Language Classroom." *The Canadian Modern Language Review/La Revue canadienne des langues vivantes,* 32, 4 (March): 424-444.

Morgan, Clifford T. and Richard A. King. 1966. *Introduction to Psychology.* 3rd edition. New York MacGraw-Hill.

Tremblay, Roger. 1980. "La bande dessinée: Une typologie." *The Canadian Modern Language Review/La Revue canadienne des langues vivantes,* 36, 3 (March): 504-513.

Acknowledgements

For their kind permission to publish the photographs which appear in this article, I should like to thank:

Photo 1: Cec Mitchell, *The Welland Evening Tribune*

Photo 2: Zoran Milic, *The Toronto Star*

Photo 3: Anthony Bruculere

Photo 4: Carl Turton, *The Guardian Express*é

Photo 5: John Hryniuk, *The Toronto Star*

Photo 6: Staff, *The Kitchener-Waterloo Record*

Photo 7: Ken Kerr, *Canada Wide*

Photo 8: Chuck Stoody, *CanaPress*

Photo 9: Stan Behal, Canada Wide

Photo 10: J. Wilkes, *The Toronto Star*

Photo 11: Rick Madonik, *The Globe and Mail*

Photo 12: Staff, *The Welland Evening Tribune.* Actor-Director Blake Heathcote in the 1991 Showboat Festival Theatre's production of *Harvey.*

Photo 13: Staff, *The Welland Evening Tribune.* Actress Teresa Kolysnyk in a scene from *The Mousetrap.*

This revised, expanded, and up-dated version contains sections from: Anthony Mollica, "Creative Writing: Poetry in the Language Classroom," *Mosaic,* 3, 1, (Fall 1995), pp. 18-20.

Reprinted from: Anthony Mollica, "A Picture is worth... 1000 words... Creative Activities for the language classroom." In *A Picture is worth...1000 words...*Books 1 and 2. Welland, Ontario: éditions Soleil publishing, 1992. Pp. vii-xii

25 A Picture is Worth 1,000 Words and A Word is Worth 1,000 Pictures

Hector Hammerly

Visual aids are very helpful in performing many pedagogical functions in the second-language classroom. There are, however, two such functions they cannot perform well. In some contexts, their use may even be cognitively disadvantageous. Much further research is needed on visual aids and their effects.

Pictures and *visuals* are not synonymous. *Visuals* is the cover term that refers to anything visible – other than writing systems, which are part of *language*. Visuals include

- *pictures* (realistic representations of objects, people, etc.);
- *graphics* (charts, diagrams, and so on); and
- *symbols* (arrows, ideographs, and so forth).

Recent books about the use of visuals in second-language teaching (Wright, 1989; Hill, 1990; Wright and Haleem, 1991) seem to accept without qualification the idea that "visuals are good for you" and simply go on to explain how to develop and use visuals. These authors do not acknowledge any limitations on the use of visuals as second language instructional aids.

There can be no question that visuals, whether still, serial, or moving, can enhance several aspects of second-language teaching. Among their positive contributions are their ability to

- represent sounds or structures,
- portray cultural features,
- provide situational awareness, and
- elicit verbal output - both controlled and free.

Sound and Structure Representation

The pronunciation of certain second-language sounds, especially those whose articulation is not directly observable, can be made clearer through the use of sagittal sections or pictorial articulatory symbols (Hammerly, 1974a). Of course, only a few sounds require and benefit from such a visual approach. Using it with all sounds would be inefficient and would probably confuse the students.

(The use of a complete phonetic alphabet – a linguistic rather than a visual aid – seems unnecessary in second-language teaching. Besides, the

International Phonetic Alphabet [IPA], for example, has many strange-looking symbols. Most IPA symbols are not effective reminders of the articulations they represent. The IPA is not, of course, based on the particular needs of speakers of language X trying to learn language Y and it does not provide a gradual shift from pronunciation symbols to spellings. These are all features that a good pedagogical transcription should have.)

Second-language stress and intonation can be shown visually in many ways – the best one perhaps being a scale graphic resembling a musical scale. As well, the potential of video technology to help teach pronunciation and intonation has hardly begun to be exploited. Think, for example, how useful it would be to have prerecorded videos using half the frame, then have students record the audio and video for the other half and compare the two halves.

Grammatical structures can be represented with diagrams using lines, shapes and colours, with arrows, and with other graphic devices (Danesi, 1990; Brown, 1990). It seems clear that, when properly designed and used, the various visual devices that may represent second-language sounds and structures can be very helpful. What is puzzling is that, so far, there has been very little research, that I am aware of, on their relative effectiveness in the classroom.

Culture Depiction

The use of visuals is an excellent way to convey information about all four aspects of a second culture - informational (geography, demography, institutions, and so on), behavioral (customs and everyday behaviour), achievement (heroes, artists, writers, *et al.*), and attitudinal (work ethic, ethnocentrism, xenophobia, etc.). Of course, only the visible manifestations of the second-language culture can be portrayed. With some ingenuity much can be done, whether through the use of cartoons, photographs, videos or other visual media. (In many cases, colour is essential. How would one otherwise teach that to find a mailbox one has to look for something red in Canada and something blue in the U.S.? And how about taxis in different countries? Not all are yellow.) Video can enhance the presentation of cultural information to children (Herron and Hanley, 1992). But, note that students from a different cultural background may not understand visuals very well. Tuffs and Tudor (1990) found that non-native speakers of English from Asian cultural backgrounds understood an ESL video played silently significantly less than native English speakers. There is no need to compare such radically different cultures to see certain cross-cultural difficulties. As Mollica (1994) notes, a *coffeepot* looks very different in Italy and in North America, and pictures of a Canadian university campus may be difficult to understand for Europeans, for whom a university is just buildings.

Situational Awareness

Good thematic pictures can provide awareness of important elements of a situation in which language activity occurs. They can offer the nonverbal setting or context to spoken or written language. When they perform this function, pictures provide general support to listening or reading comprehension (Mueller, 1980; Snyder and Colón, 1988), in the form of global comprehension support that is especially useful if it precedes a text (Omaggio, 1979; Dethloff, 1980) or presentation. Here the picture helps play the role of "advance organizer" (Ausbel, 1960). During the presentation of a second-language story, however, video enhances comprehension in general, but does not necessarily   help understand the text itself (Baltova, 1994). I emphasize that in this function pictures provide *general* comprehension support for, as we shall see, pictures are far from adequate at conveying the meanings of *specific* words or phrases in context (Cole 1967, 1976).

Verbal Output Elicitation

The ability of pictures and other visuals to elicit verbal output has long been known. In recent years, Anthony Mollica has amply demonstrated this fact with his 1992 series of books of unusual photographs, *A picture is worth...1000 words*. These photos either tell a story or entice the imagination to invent one. They have been carefully selected for their ability to elicit conversation.Guides with questions and exercises to accompany these books are available in eleven languages.

Another visual aid I have found effective in eliciting verbal output is the "wordless" – captionless – cartoon strip that tells a story. For years I collected them and used them particularly in my intermediate and advanced classes. First, I would teach any essential new vocabulary and tell the story. Then I would ask the students questions about the story. I usually followed these first two steps twice. After that, I would ask them to tell the story themselves. Finally, they would ask each other questions about it. The same "wordless strip" could be used to tell a story in the present tense first, in the past tense later in the program, in the future tense still later, and finally as contrary to fact or from a particular point of view. This activity was very effective.

Pictures for verbal output elicitation should be chosen very carefully and used at appropriate times within a definite structural/lexical program progression. Asking students to describe scenes or tell stories for which they lack the necessary language is inviting them to make numerous errors, far more than can be corrected effectively. The result of speaking in the classroom beyond one's second-language competence is the early habituation of a very faulty inter-language, as has happened in French immersion programs (Hammerly, 1989). Careful gradation in language teaching is essential – even when using pictures.

In the four aspects discussed above – sound and structure representation, cultural depiction, situational awareness, and especially verbal output elicitation – there is little doubt that a good picture (or other visual) is worth many words, perhaps even 1,000 or more. But there are two other aspects of language teaching in which the opposite happens, that is, where a word is worth 1,000 pictures. Indeed, in those two aspects of language teaching pictures are not only unnecessary but may be harmful in a variety of ways. Moreover, a third concern is that some uses of pictures may curtail cognitive activity.

I am referring to

- the conveyance of the *specific meaning(s)* of new words and phrases,
- the elicitation of *specific* words and phrases, and
- the likelihood that providing a given picture may restrict or even eliminate, in certain activities, the generation of mental imagery.

Conveyance of the Meaning(s) of New Words and Phrases

When we know the native language of the students or have appropriate materials that allow us to address each student in his or her native language (in the case of multilingual classes), then we can use the native language to convey meaning. The use of the native language instead of pictures is much more precise and much faster. Also, it saves the students from the frustration of having to play an ongoing guessing game - a game they often lose.

To clarify what I mean by a word being worth 1,000 pictures in conveying specific word or phrase meanings, consider the following example. Suppose we want to teach the French word *voiture* ("car") to an English speaker. A picture of a car would necessarily have to show a particular kind of car, which is, of course, misleading, for *une voiture* can be any kind of car. But the *word* "car" would transmit precisely the meaning we want to convey. And it is literally worth thousands of pictures as all the stored images of cars the student has ever seen contribute to the concept of both *car* and *voiture* – a concept the student *already* carries in his or her mind. This is certainly not a new concept that needs to be experienced physically or pictorially in order to be learned.

In attempting to convey meaning through pictures, we risk several problems. The likelihood of a narrower interpretation has already been mentioned. The opposite is also possible, though probably less likely: the learner may think of a hyponym, such as the word *vehicle* instead of *car* in our example. Or the learner may think we are trying to teach him something else, such as a colour, size, or shape. In fact, we can never be sure that the learner will interpret the picture the way we hope he or she will (Hammerly, 1974b).

Incidentally, when analyzed logically, the monolingual demonstration procedure seems downright silly: here is a grown-up teacher of English showing a book or a picture of a book and saying the inanity "This is a book" to, e.g., French-speaking students *who know perfectly well what a book looks like!* You may say the students are thereby learning the English word for "livre," but clearly all they need to readily accomplish that is for the equation book = "livre" to be made in some meaningful, informative context. Constantly trying to guess what "new" words mean in inane little sentences can hardly be a defensible activity for intelligent second-language students.

In the case of phrases and sentences that form part of an audiovisually presented dialogue, the learner may fail to understand many of the sentences. This has happened in empirical studies involving the monolingual presentation of filmstrips, even when the subjects were experienced second-language teachers (Dodson, 1967; Hammerly, 1984). The same thing no doubt happens with video presentations, although they should help make action verbs a little clearer. In fact, it has been found that the most beneficial input, as far as understanding videos is concerned, is bilingual bimodal - in the two languages and both audio and written -rather than monolingual audio (Danan, 1992).

By making overt but very brief use of the students' native language to convey specific meanings, we can ensure that the interlingual equations the students make are correct. For even if not a single word of the first language is used in class, the students *will* make mental interlingual equations: relating the unknown to the known is an inevitable psychological process. The problem with allowing these equations to be formed covertly is that they are often incorrect – and unavailable for correction. If this matter is not dealt with openly, incorrect interlingual equations may be reinforced over a long period of time and be difficult to eradicate when the teacher finally becomes aware of them. For example, Direct Method students of French who have never heard a word of English in class say things like **fenêtre de magasin* for *vitrine* ("store window"), which proves that in their minds they have made the imperfect equation *fenêtre* = "window." This common phenomenon was noted by Sweet nearly a century ago (1899).

When specific meanings are conveyed in the native language, the problem just alluded to can be prevented. Oral presentations can include a clarification or warning about the limitations of the equation, as follows: *fenêtre* = "window – but a regular window, *not*, for example, a store window." Another advantage of conveying specific meanings clearly and quickly in the first language is that much time is saved by not having to spend it on slow, inefficient attempts to guess the meanings of words. Even Corder, a committed audio-visualist, admitted that monolingual methods are "very slow" (Corder, 1966:27). The time saved by conveying meanings briefly in the native language can then be spent, much more effectively, on using the words or phrases meaningfully in the second language. Of course, once new words or phrases and their meanings have been learned bilingually, pictures can be used effectively, in either a general or directed way, to help practice their communicative use.

Elicitation of Specific Words and Phrases

The second difficulty with pictures in language teaching is that they are also unreliable in *eliciting* specific words and phrases. Language test developers, to their disappointment, discovered that long ago (Pimsleur, 1966). A picture of a dog could be shown, for example, to English-speaking students of Spanish in the expectation that they would say *perro* and thereby show whether or not they controlled the sound [rr], but often some examinees would say other things, such as *animal* or *mascota* ("pet"), thus frustrating the whole purpose of the test item. This unreliability of pictures in eliciting specific words and phrases often extends, of course, to conversational output activities that may be thus attempted.

Curtailed Imagery Generation?

We should research the possibility that by providing our students with a given picture or pictures we may be asking them to be cognitively passive rather than participate actively in the process of mental imagery generation. It may be, for example, that far more images are activated or generated in reading a story than in seeing it acted out. It also seems that images one generates oneself are remembered better than those one is given. Since, more generally, ability to recall depends largely on the number and the vividness of associations, this whole question deserves study.
Conclusion

Pictures and other visuals offer numerous advantages. It has been shown that videos can profitably be used in numerous ways (Cummins, 1989; Liebelt, 1989; March, 1989; Seidler, 1989; Orban and McLean, 1990). New technologies such as the VCR and interactive video (Schmidt, 1989; Forrest, 1993) and satellite television (Oxford *et al.*, 1993; Yi and Majima, 1993) allow us to bring moving pictures into our classrooms from anywhere in the world. The integration of video (Reese *et al.*, 1988; McCoy, 1989-90) with the other elements of language programs is also beginning to be considered.

But the advantages visuals offer and the fact that for certain functions a picture is worth 1,000 words should not distract us from the empirical and logical evidence that in at least two aspects of language teaching -the conveyance of specific meanings and the eliciting of specific words and phrases – pictures are imprecise, slow and unreliable. For those pedagogical functions, just one or two words in the first language are usually worth 1,000 pictures.

Far more research is needed on visual aids, their various classroom uses, and their effects on comprehension, recall and other cognitive activities. The author hopes that this article may further encourage such research.

References

Ausubel, D.P. 1960. "The use of advance organizers in the learning and retention of meaningful verbal material." *Journal of Educational Psychology*, 51: 267-72.

Baltova, I. 1994. "The impact of video on the comprehension skills of core French students." *The Canadian Modern Language Review/La Revue canadienne des langues vivantes*, 50:507-31.

Brown, James W. 1990. "Visual materials in contemporary French textbooks: A critique." In James W. Brown and Anthony Mollica, 1990, pp. 43-56.

Brown, James W. and Anthony Mollica, eds. 1990. *Essays in applied visual semiotics.* Toronto: Monograph Series of the Toronto Semiotic Circle, No. 3, Victoria College of the University of Toronto.

Cole, L.R. 1967. "The visual element and the problem of meaning in language learning." *Audio-Visual Language Journal*, 4: 84-7.

Cole, L.R. 1976. "Relationships between visual presentations and linguistic items in second-language teaching." *International Review of Applied Linguistics*, 14: 339-50.

Corder, S.P. 1966. *The visual element in language teaching.* London: Longman.

Cummins, P.W. 1989. "Video and the French teacher." *French Review*, 62: 411-26.

Danan, M. 1992. "Reversed subtitling and dual coding theory: New directions for foreign language instruction." *Language Learning*, 42: 497-527.

Danesi, M. 1990. "The visual display of grammatical information in L2 methodology." In Brown and Mollica 1990, pp. 57-64.

Dethloff, U. 1980. "La réception des textes télévisuels en langue étrangère." *Études de linguistique appliquée*, 38:106-18.

Dodson, C.J. 1967. *Language teaching and the bilingual method.* London: Pitman.

Forrest, T. 1993. "Technology and the language classroom: Available technology." *TESOL Quarterly*, 27: 316-8.

Hammerly, H. 1974a. *The articulatory pictorial transcriptions: New aids to second-language pronunciation.* Blaine, W.A.: Second-language Publications.

Hammerly, H. 1974b. "Primary and secondary associations with visual aids as semantic conveyors." *International Review of Applied Linguistics*, 12:119-25.

Hammerly, H. 1984. "Contextualized visual aids (filmstrips) as conveyors of sentence meaning." *International Review of Applied Linguistics*, 22: 87-94.

Hammerly, H. 1989. *French immersion: Myths and reality -Toward a better classroom road to bilingualism.* Calgary, Alberta: Detselig Enterprises.

Hammerly, H. 1990. "Advantages and limitations of visual aids in second-language teaching." In Brown and Mollica 1990, pp. 11-26.

Herron, C.A. and J. Hanley. 1992. "Using video to introduce children to a foreign culture." *Foreign Language Annals*, 25:419-26.

Hill, A.A. 1990. *Visual impact: Creative language learning through pictures.* Essex, England: Longman.

Liebelt, W. 1989. "Anregungen für den Umgang mit Video im Fremdsprachenunterricht." *Praxis des neusprachlichen Unterrichts*, 3:250-61.

March, C. 1989. "Some observations on the use of video in teaching of modern languages." *British Journal of Language Teaching*, 27:13-7.

McCoy, E.L. 1989-90. "From *French in Action* to *Travessia*: The integral video curriculum in interactive language classrooms" *Journal of Educational Techniques and Technologies*, Winter, pp. 30-4.

Mollica, Anthony. 1992. *A picture is worth... 1000 words... Creative activities for the language classroom.* Welland, Ont: éditions Soleil publishing inc.

Mollica, Anthony. 1994. Personal communication.

Mueller, G.A. 1980. "Visual contextual cues and listening comprehension: An experiment." *The Modern Language Journal*, 64:335-40.

Omaggio, A.C. 1979. "Pictures and second-language comprehension: Do they help?" *Foreign Language Annals*, 12:107-16.

Orban, C. and A.M. McLean. 1990. "A working model for videocamera use in the foreign language classroom." *French Review*, 63:652-63.

Oxford, R. *et al.* 1993. "Learning a language by satellite television: What influences student achievement?" *System*, 21:31-48.

Pimsleur, P. 1966. "Testing foreign language learning." In A. Valdman, ed., *Trends in language teaching*. New York: McGraw-Hill, pp. 175-214.

Reese, L.G. *et al.* 1988. "Integrated use of videodisc for intensive Spanish language learning." *CALICO Journal*, September, pp. 69-81.

Schmidt, H. 1989. "Real conversation as a motivational factor through inter-active video." *The Canadian Modern Language Review/La Revue canadienne des langues vivantes*, 45: 329- 38.

Seidler, K. W. 1989. "Old wine in new bottles? A video-letter exchange project as a means of organising cross-cultural learning." *British Journal of Language Teaching*, 27: 30-5.

Snyder, H.R. and I. Colón. 1988. "Foreign language acquisition and audio-visual aids." *Foreign Language Annals*, 21: 343-48.

Sweet, H. 1899. *The practical study of languages*. London: J.M. Dent and Sons. [Reprinted in 1964 by Oxford University Press.]

Tuffs, R. and I. Tudor. 1990. "What the eye doesn't see: Cross-cultural problems in the comprehension of video material." *RELC Journal*, 21, 2: 29-44.

Wright, A. 1989. *Pictures for language learning*. Cambridge, England: Cambridge University Press.

Wright, A. and S. Haleem. 1991. *Visuals for the language classroom*. Essex, England: Longman.

Yi, H. and J. Majima. 1993. "The teacher-learner relationship and classroom interaction in distance learning: A case study of the Japanese language classes at an American high school." *Foreign Language Annals*, 26: 21-30.

Reprinted from: Hector Hammerly, "A Picture is Worth 1000 Words and a Word is Worth 1000 Pictures" *Mosaic*, 1, 4 (Summer 1994), pp. 14-17.

26 Reducing Stress in the Foreign Language Classroom: Teaching Descriptive Adjectives Through Humour

Domenico Maceri

In teaching descriptive adjectives one can use humorous associations to lower the affective filter and make students feel comfortable and eager to participate.

Although many instructors have been emphasizing the oral aspect of the language for quite a while, the publication of the ACTFL (American Council on the Teaching of Foreign Languages) proficiency guidelines created a greater awareness of the importance of this facet of language learning. Recently-published textbooks reflect this trend and more of them continue to expand the oral communication activities.

This stress on oral communication with its inevitable goals on student performance brings about many positive changes since it puts more into focus the linguistic objectives inherent in language learning. At the same time, however, it increases a problem students have in our classes – their anxiety in having to perform orally in class. As we all know, the biggest fear people have is public speaking. In surveys, in fact, it rates highest, surpassing even the fear people have of death. The ACTFL guidelines added to this fear.

In our foreign language classes this fear is apparent on a daily basis. Not simply are students called upon to speak in front of teachers and classmates, but they have to do it in a language that they are struggling to learn. Their fear is caused by the perceived notion of vulnerability to the teacher's and classmates' "assaults." Students' fear may be irrational as many phobias are, yet it is nevertheless true that students feel anxiety in a foreign language classroom because of the emphasis on performance.

Although studies indicate that anxiety has only a modest relationship to actual performance in achievement (Phillips, 1991) students do feel that apprehension and that is all that really matters. Their anxiety will affect their performance and their feelings will affect their decision as to whether to continue their study of the language or drop it.

There are a number of ways to combat this fear. Humour is certainly one of them. As Powell and Andresen point out, a hearty laugh wipes out, if only momentarily, differences in status and viewpoint (p. 80).

In teaching descriptive adjectives one can use humorous associations to lower the affective filter and make students feel comfortable and eager to participate. The lesson is conducted entirely in Spanish. The teacher begins by drawing a short and a long line on the board and identifies them with numbers 1 and 2, respectively. Students repeat after the instructor.

– *La línea número uno es corta.* (*corta* is stressed).

– *La línea número dos es larga.* (*larga* is stressed).

Students have no trouble understanding everything. Questions can then be put to the entire class.

– *¿Cómo es la línea número uno?*

– *¿Cómo es la línea número dos?*

After a few chorus responses, the teacher should ask a few individual questions and then ask for negative and affirmative answers:

– *¿Es corta la línea número uno?*

– *¿Es corta la linea número dos?*

Finally, one can ask,

– *¿Cómo es la línea número 1?*

– *¿Cómo es la línea número 2?*

to several students individually. The purpose of beginning with *corto, -a* and *largo, -a* is twofold:

• it serves as a prelude to the teaching of other adjectives and

• at the same time it reviews the interrogative *¿Cómo?* which is essential in the lesson.

I am using Spanish examples. However, the same lesson works well with other Romance languages and quite likely with additional ones.

Once this has been done, one can proceed with other descriptive adjectives.

– *Brasil es grande.*

– *Rhode Island es pequeño.*

Students have no problem understanding these two adjectives. To make them absolutely clear, one can open the arms very wide and close them to show big and small. A few examples about a very small local city and asking them

– *¿Es grande Harmony?*

bring smiles to students. (Harmony is a very small city on the central coast of California). They understand that you are asking for a negative answer and will gladly give it. The opposite also works very well.

– *¿Texas es pequeño?*

By this time students are beginning to feel very comfortable and are warming up to the "game" of learning descriptive adjectives.

At this point one can go on with adjectives to describe people, which is really the most enjoyable part. It's a good idea to use the names of famous people. Teaching *alto, -a* and *bajo -a* is very easy especially if the instructor happens to be *bajo*D or *baja*. Have students repeat:

– *Michael Jordan es alto.*

– *El profesor no es alto.*

– *El profesor es bajo.*

Then ask them:

– *¿Cómo es Michael Jordan?*

– *¿Cómo es el profesor?*

Continue with the negative.

– *¿Es alto el profesor?*

– *¿Es bajo Michael Jordan?*

If the instructor is *bajo, -a,* students will find humour in the contrast and will feel more comfortable about answering the teacher's questions orally. Afterwards, use some of the students in the class. Choose a tall student and ask the class if s/he is *bajo -a.* Students will begin to chuckle and give you the correct response. You may want to begin to point out the masculine and feminine forms especially if you have picked a young lady as your model. *Bonita* and *guapo* follow. The names of famous men and women are again very useful. Kevin Costner, Julio Iglesias, Brooke Shields, Sharon Stone, may do the trick.

– *Kevin Costner es guapo.*

– *Brooke Shields es bonita.*

Students will repeat and understand. You may want to teach the opposite right away. Ask the class,

– *¿Quién es feo?*

explaining that "feo es el contrario de *bonita* o *guapo.*"

Then ask individually about some famous names and whether they are *guapo, bonita, feo, -a.* You may want to begin to pick up *alto* and *bajo* as review. Cognates that students might have already learned can be easily integrated into these questions.

Casado, -a, soltero, -a, delgado, -a and *gordo, -a, inteligente, tonto-a* (Gilligan?) *rico, -a* and *pobre, viejo, -a* and *joven* can be taught using similar approaches and other famous names. It's a good idea to occasionally ask

– *¿Quién es guapo?*

– *¿Quién es rico?*

– *¿Quién es alto?* *joven, viejo,* etc.

It's also a good idea to bring it all back to the class. Have a few students stand up and ask the class,

– ¿Cómo es...?

Students are very good about saying positive things about their class-mates. Some students may show particular interest in a certain classmate. Asking them,

– ¿Ud. quiere el número de teléfono de...?

will surely bring out laughter. Questions can be asked such as

– ¿Es alto, -a...? rico, -a?

(They aren't; all of them are poor). Eventually you may want to ask several individual students to describe themselves using the adjectives they have just learned and other cognates.

At this point one may want to explain that gordo, -a and viejo, -a:

– En español no son negativos; en español y en otras culturas – orientales, por ejemplo – gordo y viejo son positivos. Gordo indica rico. Viejo indica inteligente, tiene experiencia, etc.

Students understand these simple sentences in Spanish, and in addition to learning the adjectives, they are also learning culture.

Humour in a second language differs considerably from that of a first language. What would most certainly be a cliché in the first language: "Gilligan is silly," "Sharon Stone is pretty," "Michael Jordan is not short" may gain life in a foreign language. The cliché of the first language becomes fresh and humorous in a language students do not know very well.

Humour is something that instructors need to use in the foreign lan-guage classroom. It does not substitute for quality teaching, yet it is a key ingredient in any learning situation. The integration of humour in the foreign language classroom can make the lessons enjoyable for students as well as instructors. If the material studied is interesting, students' achieve-ment will increase, fulfilling in this way Horace's maxim Omne tulit punc-tum, qui miscuit utile dulci.(He who manages to blend the useful and pleasurable has achieved perfection.)

References

Phillips, Elaine M. 1991. "Anxiety and Oral Competence: Classroom Dilemma." The French Review, 65: 1-14.

Powell, J. P., and L. W. Andersen. 1995. "Humor and Teaching in Higher Education." Studies in Higher Education, 10: 79-80.

Reprinted from: Domenico Maceri, "Reducing Stress in the Foreign Language Classroom: Teaching Descriptive Adjectives Through Humour," Mosaic, 2, 4 (Summer 1994), pp. 21-22.

27 Focus on Descriptive Adjectives: Creative Activities for the Language Classroom

Anthony Mollica, Herbert Schutz,
and Karen Tessar

Using examples in English, French, German, Italian, and Spanish, the authors suggest a variety of activities to teach/learn/review descriptive adjectives and expand the student's active vocabulary.

Teachers are constantly searching for ways of changing formal exercises (i.e., exercises focusing on *form* into activities which focus on *communication*. One such activity which may be used to teach/drill/review descriptive adjectives is the association of an adjective with the student's name. At the same time, this is a good source for conversational exchanges. This activity has often been used as an "ice-breaker" in many initial classes at the intermediate level and has proven to be both interesting and humorous.

The activity involves the teacher's providing students with a list of adjectives listed alphabetically in the target language. The activity has worked well in both English-as-a-second-language classes and other second-language classes.

Describing Self

In this first activity, students are asked to describe themselves by associating the first letter of their name with the first letter of an adjective suggested on the list. The Teacher/Student exchange, in the target language, may resemble the following:

Teacher: What is your name?
Student: My name is Anthony and I am *attentive.*
Teacher: How do you show your *attention*?
Anthony: I always pay attention to what the teacher says…

The teacher, in asking how the student displays a particular characteristic, will change the *adjective* into a *noun*, thus expanding the vocabulary. It may be that students in providing an explanation about the characteristic with which they identify themselves may make a statement which causes laughter in the classroom. Humour should not be discounted from this activity; quite often, in fact, it is the vocabulary found in the humorous explanations which will be remembered…

Describing a Friend

A variation of the above activity may focus on a description of a student's friend.

> *Student:* My friend's name is Ann and she is *affluent.*
>
> My friend's name is Tom and he is *talkative.*
>
> *Teacher:* How does Ann show her *affluence*?
>
> How does Tom show his *talkativeness?*
>
> *Student:* [Replies…]

Both the above and the previous activity may focus on the negative:

> *Student:* My friend's name is *Ann* but she is not *affluent.*
>
> My friend's name is *Tom* but he is not *talkative.*

Describing Classmates

In this activity, students may be asked to name their classmates. This is particularly appropriate during the first class when students try to learn each other's names. A suitable activity is a variation of the classic *I pack my suitcase…* game. In this game, the player must identify the student's name and the adjective associated with his/her name. Each subsequent player must repeat the names previously identified and add one more to the list. For example:

> *Student 1:* My name is Joe and I am *jovial.*
>
> *Student 2:* His name is Joe and he is *jovial.* My name is Mary and I am *morose.*
>
> *Student 3:* His name is Joe and he is *jovial.* Her name is Mary and she is *morose.* My name is Irene and I am *intuitive.*
>
> *Student 4:* His name is Joe and he is *jovial.* Her name is Mary and she is *morose.* Her name is Irene and she is *intuitive.* My name is Paul and I am *popular.* etc.

The activity may move faster by having the player simply repeat the name of the student and the descriptive adjective. For example,

> Joe is *jovial*; Mary is *morose*; Irene is *intuitive*; Paul is *popular*; etc.

Finding a Person Who Is…

In this activity, students are given a list of characteristics for which they must find suitable students. If the teacher wishes to introduce the competitive element, the player who completes the list first is declared the winner. This activity is suitable for practising questions/answer.
The student's activity sheet may look something like this:

Find a student who is…

1. … *intelligent.*   *Pamela*
2. … *outspoken.*   *Hans*
3. … *apprehensive.*   *Fidel*

4. ... *creative.*
5. ... *helpful.*
6. ... *brilliant.*
7. ... *optimistic.*
8. ... *courageous.*
9. ... *famous.*
10. ... *talented.*

Helen
Sophia
Jennifer
Karen
Mohamed
Paul
David

Once a name has been associated with the characteristic and the game is over, the teacher may ask the student how he or she displays that characteristic. Suppose, for example, that the answer for the first adjective is:

Mario is intelligent.

The teacher or a student may question Mario's quality by asking:

Teacher: How do you show your intelligence, Mario?

The Ideal Companion...

In this activity, the teacher may wish to divide the blackboard or blank overhead transparency into two sections and write "The Ideal Boy" on one section and "The Ideal Girl" on the other section. Students are then urged to identify the characteristics for each. This activity is useful for a review of the formation of masculine and feminine adjectives in languages with differing adjectival forms since some qualities attributed to boys may be suitable for girls.

Le garçon "idéal"	*La fille "idéale"*
riche	riche
jeune	jeune
intelligent	intelligente
gentil	gentille
curieux	curieuse
actif	active
fier	fière
doux	douce
beau	belle

The activity summarizes the formation of French adjectives in the feminine form:

- To form the feminine of an adjective, add *e* to the masculine form *(petit, petite).*

- An adjective ending in *e* remain the same in the feminine form *(riche, jeune).*

- Some masculine adjectives ending in a consonant, double the final consonant and add *e (gentil → gentille).*

- Masculine adjectives ending in *er* change *er* to *ère (cher → chère).*

- Masculine adjectives ending in *if* change *if* to *ive* (*actif* → *active*).
- Masculine adjectives ending in *eux* change *eux* to *euse* (*curieux* → *curieuse*).
- Some masculine adjectives do not follow the above rules when forming the feminine: (*sec* → *sèche, public* → *publique, grec* → *grecque, long* → *longue,* etc.)
- Some masculine adjective have a double form in the singular. Note should be made of the feminine form (*beau, bel* → *belle*).

My Attributes

The student may be given a list of the adjectives and be asked to check his or her attributes, positive or negative:

☐ active / activity
☐ affectionate / affection
☐ affluent / affluence
☐ aggressive / aggression
☐ agile / agility
☐ agitated / agitation
☐ altruistic / altruism
☐ ambitious / ambition

☐ anxious / anxiety
☐ apprehensive / apprehension
☐ arrogant / arrogance
☐ astute / astuteness
☐ attentive / attention
☐ autocratic / autocracy
☐ avaricious / avarice

It is obvious that some lists are not long or varied enough to be suitable for this activity. In this case, the student may choose from the entire list (i.e. all letters of the alphabet).

Qualities I Would Like to See in...

In this activity, students identify the positive characteristics that a person of their choice should have. To provide a model, the teacher may begin the activity with any one of the following examples:

Teacher: What characteristics should the Prime Minister of Canada (the President of the United States) have?

Student: He or She should be decisive, incorruptible, eloquent, etc.

Teacher: What qualities should your teacher have?

Student:

Teacher: What qualities do you look for in a political candidate?(This question may stress the positive.)

Student:

Teacher: What qualities do you think political candidates *actually* have? (The answers may stress the negative!)

Student:

Teacher: What qualities would you like to see in your future husband/wife?
(A "personalized" answer, similar to the "Ideal Boy/Girl" activity.)

Written or Oral Compositions

Of course many, if not all, of these activities can be turned into oral and/or written composition depending on the particular linguistic skill(s) the teacher wishes to emphasize.

Suggested Vocabulary

The following lists in English, French, German, Italian and Spanish are by no means exhaustive. They are presented here to save teachers hours of research time. Teachers may decide to select only items from these lists or edit these lists according to their needs.

English

A
active / activity
affectionate / affection
affluent / affluence
aggressive / aggression
agile / agility
agitated / agitation
allergic / allergy
altruistic / altruism
ambitious / ambition
anxious / anxiety
apprehensive / apprehension
arrogant / arrogance
astute / astuteness
attentive / attention
autocratic / autocracy
avaricious / avarice

B
bashful / bashfulness
beautiful / beauty
bilingual / bilingualism
bold / boldness
boring / boredom
brilliant / brilliance

C
calm / calmness
cold / coldness
composed / composure
cooperative / cooperation
corrupt / corruption
crazy / craziness
creative / creativity

credible / credibility
cruel / cruelty
curious / curiosity

D
dainty / daintiness
dangerous / danger
daring / daring
decisive / decisiveness
delinquent / delinquency
desperate / desperation
destructive / destructiveness
disgusted / disgust
distant / distance
dynamic / dynamism

E
eager / eagerness
efficient / efficiency
egoist / egoism
elegant / elegance
eloquent / eloquence
energetic / energy
enthusiastic / enthusiasm
envious / envy
exasperated / exasperation

F
fair / fairness
famous / fame
free / freedom
friendly / friendliness
frivolous / frivolity
frustrated / frustration
furious / fury

G
gaudy / gaudiness

good / goodness
graceful / gracefulness
grateful / gratitude
gregarious / gregariousness

H

handsome / handsomeness
happy / happiness
healthy / healthiness
helpful / helpfulness
hot-headed / hot-headednes
humanitarian/ humanitarianism
hypocrite / hypocrisy

I

idealist / idealism
idle / idleness
imaginative / imagination
immoral / immorality
impetuous / impetuosity
implacable / implacability
inattentive / inattention
incorrigible / incorrigibility
incorruptible / incorruptibility
independent / independence
indifferent / indifference
infallible / infallibility
insensitive / insensitivity
insolent / insolence
intuitive / intuition
ironic / irony
irrational / irrationality

J

jealous / jealousy
ocular / jocularity
jovial / joviality
joyful / joyfulness
judicious / judiciousness

K

kind / kindness
kleptomaniac / kleptomania

L

lavish / lavishness
light-hearted / light-heartedness
lively / liveliness
loquacious / loquacity

M

macho / machismo
magnetic / magnetism
maniac / mania
mean / meanness
misanthropist / misanthropy
mischievous / mischievousness

morose /moroseness
mysterious / mystery

N

naïve / naïveté
neat / neatness
negative / negativitism
negligent / negligence
noble / nobility
nonchalant / nonchalance

O

obese / obesity
obnoxious / obnoxiousness
odd / oddness
optimistic / optimism
outspoken / outspokenness

P

passive / passivity
patient / patience
pensive / pensiveness
perfectionist / perfection
perspicacious / perspicacity
pessimistic / pessimism
philanthropic / philanthropy
pompous / pomposity
popular / popularity
proud / pride

R

rational / rationality
reasonable / reasonableness
rebellious / rebellion
reflective / reflection
relieved / relievement
reserved / reservation
rich / wealth, richness

S

sarcastic / sarcasm
sceptical / scepticism
scrupulous / scrupulousness
sentimental / sentimentality
sincere / sincerity
sober / sobriety
sociable / sociableness
stubborn / stubbornness

T

tactful / tact
talented / talent
talkative / talkativeness
tall / height
thorough / thoroughness
tired / tiredness
tolerant / tolerance

U

underestimated/under-
estimation
understanding/under-
standing
up-to-date / up-to-dateness

V

vain / vanity
valuable / value
vengeful / vengefulness
vibrant / vibrancy
vulnerable / vulnerability

W

warm / warmth
wary / wariness
weird / weirdness
wicked / wickedness
wild / wildness
willy / witticism, wit

Y

young / youth
youthful / youthfulness

Z

zealous / zeal
zestful / zest

French

Nouns in the following list are feminine, except where otherwise noted.

A

actif, -ive / activité
adorable / adoration
affable / affabilité
affectueux, -euse / affectuosité
agile / agilité
agité, -e / agitation
agressif, -ive / agression
aimable / amabilité
ambitieux, -euse / ambition
amnésique / amnésie
amoureux, -euse / amour *nm*
animateur, -trice / animation
anxieux, -euse / anxiété
apathique / apathie
appliqué, -e / application
appréhensif, -ive / appréhension
arrogant, -e / arrogance
attentif, -ive / attention
audacieux, -euse / audace

autocratique / autocratie
avare / avarice

B

bagarreur, -euse / bagarre
barbare / barbarisme *nm*
batailleur, -euse / bataille
beau, bel, belle / beauté
belliqueux, -euse / belligérance
besogneux, -euse / besogne
bienfaisant, -e / bienfaisance
bienveillant, -e / bienveillance
bilingue / bilinguisme *nm*
bizarre / bizarrerie
blagueur, -euse / blague
brillant, -e / brillance
bruyant, -e / bruit *nm*
buveur, -euse / boire *nm*

C

calme / calme *nm*
chaleureux, -euse / chaleur
champion, -onne / championnat *nm*
charmant, -e / charme *nm*
charmeur, -euse / charme *nm*
constant, -e / constance
craintif, -ive / crainte
cruel, -elle / cruauté
curieux, -euse / curiosité

D

délicat, -e / délicatesse
délicieux, -euse / délice
despotique / despotisme *nm*
destructeur, -trice / destruction
diligent, -e / diligence
diplomate / diplomatie
doux, douce / douceur

E

effervescent, -e / effervescence
effronté, -e / effronterie
énergique / énergie
ensorceleur, -euse/
ensorcellement *nm*
enthousiaste / enthousiasme *nm*
envieux, -euse / envie
exceptionnel, -lle / exception
extravagant, -e / extravagance

F

fameux, -euse / renommée
fervent, -e / ferveur
fidèle / fidélité
fier, -ère / fierté
fou, fol, folle / folie

frivole / frivolité
frugal, -e / frugalité
furieux, -euse / fureur

G

généreux, -euse / générosité
gentil, -le / gentillesse
gourmand, -e / gourmandise
gracieux, -euse / gracieuseté
grossier, -ière / grossièreté

H

habile / habilité
hardi, -e / hardiesse
hésitant, -e / hésitation
honnête / honnêteté
hostile / hostilité
hypocrite / hypocrisie

I

idéalisateur, -trice / idéalisation
imaginatif, -ive / imagination
immoral, -e / immoralité
impartial, -e / impartialité
impassible / impassibilité
impertinent, -e / impertinence
imperturbable / imperturbabilité
impétueux, -euse / impétuosité
impressionnable /
    impressionnabilité
impudent, -e / impudence
impulsif, -ive / impulsivité n
incompatible / incompatibilité
inconscient, -e / inconscience
inconsistant, -e / inconsistance
incorrigible / incorrigibilité
indépendant, -e / indépendance
indulgent, -e / indulgence
indolent, -e / indolence
infaillible / infaillibilité
infatigable / infatigabilité
ingénieux, -euse / ingéniosité
inquiet, -ète / inquiétude
insensible / insensibilité
insolent, -e / insolence
insomniaque / insomnie
insoucieux, -euse / insouciance
instable / instabilité
instruit, -e / instruction
intelligent, -e / intelligence
intolérable / intolérance
irresponsable / irresponsabilité
irritant, -e / irritation

J

jaloux, -ouse / jalousie
jaseur, -euse / jasement nm
jeune / jeunesse
jobard, -e / jobarderie, jobardise
jovial, -e / jovialité
juste / justesse

K

kleptomane / kleptomanie

L

lent, -e / lenteur
libertin, -e / libertinage nm
libre / liberté
logique / logique
loyal, -e / loyauté

M

maigre / maigreur
malade / maladie
malheureux, -euse / malheur
manipulateur,-trice/
manipulation
mélancolique / mélancolie
méticuleux, -euse / méticulosité
militant, -e / militantisme nm
misanthrope / misanthropie
misérable / misère

N

naïf, -ïve / naïveté
négligent, -e / négligence
nerveux, -euse / nervosité n
nonchalant, -e / nonchalance

O

opiniâtre / opinion
oppressif, -ive / oppression
opulent, -e / opulence
original, -e / originalité

P

paresseux, -euse / paresse
passionné, -e / passion
patient, -e / patience
perspicace / perspicacité
prévenant, -e / prévenance
prudent, -e / prudence
pudique / pudeur

Q

querelleur, -euse / querelle

R

radical, -e / radicalisme nm
raffiné, -e / raffinement nm
railleur, -euse / railleusement nm
raisonnable / raisonnement nm

rancunier, -ière / rancoeur
réactionnaire / réaction
renommé, -e / renommée
réticent, -e / réticence
riche / richesse
rude / rudesse

S

sage / sagesse
sarcastique / sarcasme *nm*
sauvage / sauvagerie
sensible / sensibilité
serein, -e / sérénité
sérieux, -euse / sérieux *nm*
sociable / socialité
somnolent, -e / somnolence
sophistiqué, -e / sophistication
soupçonneux, -euse / soupçon
sournois, -e / sournoiserie
sportif, -ive / sportivité
subtil, -e / subtilité
surexcitable / surexcitation
susceptible / susceptibilité
sympathique / sympathie

T

taciturne / taciturnité
télépathe / télépathie
tendre / tendresse
théoricien, -enne / théorie
timide / timidité
tolérant, -e / tolérance
tranquille / tranquillité
travailleur, -euse / travail *nm*
triste / tristesse
tyrannique / tyrannie

U

ulcéré, -e / ulcération
urbain, -e / urbanité
usurier, -ière / usure
usurpatoire, -trice / usurpation

V

vacillant, -e / vacillation
vaniteux, -euse / vanité
vengeur, vengeresse / vengeance
vertueux, -euse / vertu
vexé, -e / vexation
vieux, vieille / vieillesse
violent, -e / violence
voluptueux, -euse / voluptuosité
vorace / voracité
vulnérable / vulnérabilité

Z

zélé, -e / zèle *nm*

German

Since only adjective forms are provided here, for space reasons, they are simply grouped alphabetic-ally under each letter heading.

To use the German list for the activities described above, students may have first to consult a dictionary to obtain the correct form of a suitable noun.

A

abgehetzt, abwesend, aktiv,
allein,alleinstehend, allergisch,
allsehend, allwissend, alt,
altmodisch, amüsant, angenehm,
angeschnallt, anonym,
anständig, anwesend, ärgerlich,
arm, arrogant, artig, atemlos,
aufgeklärt, aufgeknöpft, aufgeregt,
aufmerksam, ausgebildet,
ausgelassen, ausgeruht,
ausgeschlafen

B

bankerott, bärtig, bedächtig,
bedrohlich, bedroht, bedrückt,
beeindruckt, beeinflußt, befangen,
befriedigt, begabt, begeistert,
behilflich, behindert, bekannt,
beleidigt, belesen, berechnet, bereit,
berühmt, beschäftigt, besonnen,
beständig, blank, blau, bleich,
blind, blond, borniert, bösartig,
boshaft

D

dankbar, dekadent, diabolisch,
dick, dickköpfig, diskret,
dramatisch, draufgängerisch,
dreist, dunkel, dunkelblond, dünn,
durstig

E

eifrig, eigen, eingebildet, einfach,
einsam, einseitig, eisern, eitel,
elegant, empfindsam, energisch,
enttäuscht, erwachsen, exotisch,
exzentrisch

F

fähig, falsch, faszinierend, faul, feig(e), fein, feindlich, feindselig, fertig, fest, feurig, fieberfrei, fieberkrank, finster, fleißig, flink, flott, frech, frei, friedfertig, froh, fröhlich, fromm, frostig, furchtbar, furchtlos, furchtsam,

G

ganz, garstig, gehorsam, geistesabwesend, gelehrig, genial, gerecht, gesellschaftlich, gesichert, gespannt, gesund, gewiß, gewitzt, giftig, glaubhalft, gläubig, glücklich, golden, gräßlich, grau, grell, grob, groß, grotesk, gründlich, gut

H.

hager, hart, häßlich, häuslich, heiser, heiß, heiter, hellblond, herrisch, herrlich, herzlich, hilflos, hilfreich, himmlish, inderlich, hoch, hübsch, humorlos, humorvoll, hungrig

I

impertinent, imponierend, imposant, impulsiv, indifferent, interessant, intolerant, intrigant, irrational, irr(e), irritiert, isoliert

J

jämmerlich, jovial, jubelnd, jung

K

kahl, kahlgeschoren, kahlköpfig, kalt, kapriziös, kaputt, kariert, keck, kennbar, kess, klar, klebrig, klein, kleptoman, klug, kokett, komisch, kompetent, konservativ, konventionell, kräftig, krank, kränklich, kriminell, kritisch, krumm, künstlerisch, künstlich, kurios, kurz.

L

labil, lahm, lang, langsam, lästig, laut, ledig, leer, leicht, leichtfertig, leichtgläubig, leichtherzig, leichtsinnig, liberal, lieb, liebenswert, liebenswürdig, liederlich, locker, logisch, loyal, luftig, lumpig, lustig, luxuriös

M

mächtig, magnetisch, männlich, mäßig, matt, meschugge, mobil, modern, müde, mündig, munter, musikalisch, müßig, mutig, mystisch

N

nachdenklich, nachgiebig, nachhaltig, nachlässig, nachsichtig, nackt, nah, naiv, namhaft, naß, natürlich, nett, neugierig, neutral, niedergeschlagen, niederträchtig, niedlich, niedrig, nobel, notorisch, nutzlos, nützlich

O

offen, ordentlich, ordinär, originell

P

passiv, pathetisch, patzig, pausbackig, persönlich, pfiffig, platt, plattfüßig, plump, populär, prächtig, prähistorisch, präzis, primitiv, privat, privilegiert, profan, prominent, prompt, prüde, pünktlich

Q

qualifiziert

R

rabiat, radikal, raffiniert, rar, rasch, rasiert, rational, ratlos, ratsam, rätselhaft, rauh, redlich, redselig, reel, rege, reich, reichhaltig, reif, rein, reizbar, reizend, reizlos, religiös, renommiert, reserviert, richtig, rigoros, rosig, ruhig, ruhelos, rund, ruppig

S

salopp, sanft, sanftmütig, satt, sauber, säuberlich, sauer, säuerlich, saumselig, schal, schamlos, scharfsinnig, scharmant, schauderhaft, schaurig, scherzhaft, scheu, scheußlich, schief, schläfrig, schlaff, schlank, schlapp, schlau, schlecht, schleunig, schlicht, schlimm, schmächtig, schmackhaft, schmal, schnell, schrecklich, schrill, schroff, schrullig, schüchtern, schwach, schwanger, schwierig, selbständig, selig, sensibel, sentimental, seriös, sicher, sichtbar, solidarisch, sorgfältig, sorglos,

sorgsam, sozial, spaßhaft, spaßig,
spät, spießig, sportlich,
sprachgewandt, stabil, städtisch,
stark, starr, steif, still, strittig,
stumm, subtil, süchtig, süß

T

tapfer, taub, teuer, tief, tiefsinnig,
tödlich, tolerant, toll, träge, traurig,
treu, trocken, trostlos, trübe, tüchtig

U

übergeschnappt, überstürzt,
umständlich, unabhängig,
unachtsam, unauffällig, unbegabt,
unbeholfen, unbekannt,
unbelehrbar, unbeliebt,
unbescheiden, unbesorgt,
undiszipliniert, unehrlich,
unempfindlich, unentschieden,
unentschlossen, unerkannt,
unermüdlich, unerschschrocken,
unfähig, unfreundlich, unfrisiert,
ungebildet, ungeduldig,
ungefährlich, ungefällig,
ungehorsam, ungeniert,
ungeschickt, ungeschminkt,
ungläubig, unglaubwürdig,
unglücklich, unheilbar, unheimlich,
unhöflich, uninteressant, unklar,
unklug, unleserlich, unmodern,
unmöglich, unmoralisch,
unmündig, unmusikalisch,
unnatürlich, unordentlich,
unpersönlich, unpolitisch,
unpraktisch, unpünktlich,
unqualifiziert, unrasiert,
unregelmäßig, unsauber,
unscheinbar, unschuldig,
unselbständig, unsicher,
unterentwickelt, unterernährt,
untreu, untröstlich, unüberlegt,
unveränderlich, unverantwortlich,
unverbesserlich, unverh eiratet,
unverständig, unvollendet,
unvollständig, unwissend,
unwürdig, unzivilisiert,
unzufrieden, unzuverlässig

V

väterlich, veraltet, verängstigt,
verantwortlich, verbissen,
verbittert, verdächtig, verehrt,
verfolgt, verführt, vergeßlich,
vergnügt, verhaßt, verheiratet,

verlobt, vernünftig,
verständig, verträglich, verwaist,
verwundbar, volljährig, vorlaut,
vornehm, vorsichtig, vulgär

W

wacker, wählerisch, wahnsinnig,
weich, weltlich, widerlich,
willenlos, willig, willkommen,
winzig, wirr, witzig, wund, würdig,
wütend

Z

zackig, zaghaft, zanksüchtig,
zappelig, zart, zartfühlend, zärtlich,
zauberhaft, zerstreut, zimlich

Italian

All nouns listed are feminine, except where otherwise noted

A

affabile / affabilità
affettuoso, -a / affettuosità
affluente / affluenza
aggiornato, -a / aggiornamento *nm*
agitato, -a / agitazione
allegro, -a / allegria
allergico, -a / allergia
altruista / altruismo *nm*
ambizioso, -a / ambizione
amnesico, -a / amnesia
amoroso, -a / amore *nm*
analfabeta / analfabetismo *nm*
ansioso, -a / ansia
antipatico, -a / antipatia
apatico, -a / apatia
applicato, -a / applicazione
apprensivo, -a / apprensione
ardito, -a / arditezza
arrogante / arroganza
astuto, -a / astuzia
attento, -a / attenzione
attivo, -a / attività
audace / audacia
autocratico, -a / autocrazia
avaro, -a / avarizia
avvilito, -a / avvilimento *nm*

B

balbuziente / balbuzie
bello, -a / bellezza
bigotto, -a / bigottismo *nm*
bilingue / bilinguismo *nm*

bisognoso, -a / bisogno *nm*
briccone / bricconeria
bugiardo, -a / bugia

C

calmo, -a / calma
cattivo, -a / cattiveria
celebre / celebrità
cleptomane / cleptomania
cocciuto, -a / cocciutaggine
crudele / crudeltà
curioso, -a / curiosità

D

degenerato, -a / degenerazione
delicato, -a / delicatezza
diplomatico, -a / diplomazia
disamorato, -a / disamore *nm*
disgustato, -a / disgusto *nm*
disinteressato, -a / disinteresse *nm*
disperato/ disperazione

E

efficiente / efficienza
elegante / eleganza
energico, -a / energia
entusiastico, -a / entusiasmo *nm*
esagerato, -a / esagerazione
esasperante / esasperazione

F

facilone / faciloneria
famoso, -a / fama
fastidioso, -a / fastidio *nm*
fedele / fedeltà
felice / felicità
fiero, -a / fierezza
frivolo, -a / frivolezza
furioso, -a / furia

G

geloso, -a / gelosia
generoso, -a / generosità
gentile / gentilezza
giovane / gioventù
gioviale / giovialità
grasso, -a / grassezza

I

infallibile / infallibilità
immorale / immoralità
imparziale / imparzialità
impressionabile / impressionabilità
imprudente / imprudenza
indifferente / indifferenza
indipendente / indipendenza

innamorato, -a / innamoramento
   nm
inquieto, -a / inquietudine
insensibile / insensibilità
insincero, -a / insincerità
insistente / insistenza
insolente / insolenza
insopportabile / insopportabilità
intelligente / intelligenza
intollerabile / intolleranza
intrepido, -a / intrepidezza
invidioso, -a / invia
ipocrita / ipocrisia
impassibile / impassibilità
irrazionale / irrazionalità
irresponsabile / irrespon- sabilità
irritante / irritazione
irriverente / irriverenza

L

laborioso, -a / laboriosità
leggiadro, -a / leggiadria
libero, -a / libertà
logico, -a / logicità

M

magro, -a / magrezza
malinconico, -a / malinconia
malizioso, -a / malizia
maniaco, -a / mania

N

nervoso, -a / nervosismo *nm*
noioso, -a / noiosità

O

obeso, -a / obesità
onesto, -a / onestà
orgoglioso, -a / orgoglio *nm*

P

paziente / pazienza
perspicace / perspicacia
pettegolo, -a / pettegolio *nm*
pomposo, -a / pomposità
povero, -a / povertà
pudico, -a / pudore *nm*

Q

quieto, -a / quietismo *nm*

R

ragionevole / ragionevolezza
ribelle / ribellione
ricco, -a / ricchezza
risentito, -a / risentimento *nm*

S

sarcastico, -a / sarcasmo *nm*

sazio, -a / sazietà
sciocco, -a / sciocchezza
sensibile / sensibilità
sentimentale / sentimentalità
sereno, -a / serenità
sfrenato, -a / sfrenatezza
sfrontato, -a / sfrontatezza
simpatico, -a / simpatia
spietato, -a / spietatezza
stanco, -a / stanchezza
superbo, -a / superbia

T

taciturno, -a / taciturnità
telepatico, -a / telepatia
tenero, -a / tenerezza
timoroso, -a / timore *nm*
tiranno, -a / tirannia
triste / tristezza

U

ubbidiente / ubbidienza
ubriaco, -a / ubriachezza
umano, -a / umanità
usurpatore / usurpazione

V

vanitoso, -a / vanità
vendicativo, -a / vendetta
veridico, -a / veridicità
vittorioso, -a / vittoria
volubile / volubilità
vulnerabile / vulnerabilità

Z

zelante / zelo *nm*

Spanish

A

afable / la afabilidad
afectuoso, -a / la afectuosidad
alegre / la alegría
alérgico, -a / la alergia
altruista / el altruismo
ambicioso, -a / la ambición
amoroso, -a / el amor
analfabeto, -a / el analfabetismo
ansiosa, -a / el ansia
antipático, -a / la antipatía
aprensivo, -a / la aprensión
ardido, -a / el ardimiento
arrogante / la arrogancia
audaz / la audacia
autocrático, -a / la autocracia
avaro, -a / la avaricia

B

balbuciente / la balbucencia
belicoso, -a / la belicosidad
bello, -a / la belleza
bilingüe / el bilingüismo
brillante / la brillantez
bueno, -a / la bondad

C

calmo, -a / la calma
cariñoso, -a / cariño
célebre / la celebridad
cleptomaníaco, -a / la cleptomanía
conmovido, -a / la conmoción
cruel / la crueldad
curioso, -a / la curiosidad

D

delicado, -a / la delicadeza
desesperado, -a / la desesperación
despótico, -a / el despotismo
diplomático, -a / la diplomacia

E

económico, -a/ la economía
eficiente / la eficiencia
elegante / la elegancia
emocionado, -a / la emoción
encantador, -a / el encanto
enérgico, -a / la energía
enfadado, -a / el enfado
entusiástico, -a / el entusiasmo
espontáneo, -a / la espontaneidad
exagerado, -a / la exageración

F

falso, -a / la falsedad
famoso, -a / la fama
fanático, -a / el fanatismo
feliz / la felicidad
feminista / el feminismo
fiel / la fidelidad
fuerte / la fuerza
furioso, -a /la furia, el furor

G

gallardo, -a / la gallardía
garboso, -a / el garbo
generoso, -a / la generosidad
genial / la genialidad
gentil / la gentileza
goloso, -a /a la golosina
gordo, -a / las gordura
grosero, -a / la grosería
guapo, -a / la guapura

H

herido, -a / la herida
hermoso, -a / la hermosura
hipócrita / la hipocresía

I

ignorante / la ignorancia
imaginativo, -a / la imaginación
imbécil / la imbecilidad
impulsivo, -a / la impulsividad
incompetente / la incompetencia
incorruptible / la incorruptibilidad
incrédulo, -a / la incredulidad
indignado, -a / la indignación
individualista / el individualismo
inepto, -a /la ineptitud
infeliz / la infelicidad
inquieto, -a / la inquietud
insolente / la insolencia
inteligente / la inteligencia
intrépido, -a / la intrepidez

J

joven / la juventud
juicioso, -a / el juicio

L

laborioso, -a /la laboriosidad
lascivo, -a / la lascivia
libre / la libertad
lindo, -a / la lindeza
loco, -a / la locura

M

magnánimo, -a / la magnanimidad
majestuoso, -a / la majestuosidad
malicioso, -a / la malicia
misantrópico, -a / la misantropía
monógamo, -a / la monogamia
mundano, -a / la mundanería

N

negligente / la negligencia
nervioso, -a / la nerviosidad
noble / la nobleza
nostálgico, -a / la nostalgia

O

odioso, -a / la odiosidad
opulento, -a / la opulencia

orgulloso, -a / el orgullo
osado, -a / la osadía

P

paciente / la paciencia
parsimonioso, -a / la parsimonia
pasivo, -a / la pasividad
pedante / la pedantería
pérfido, -a / la perfidia
perspicaz / la perspicacia
persuasivo, -a / la persuasiva
pesimista / el pesimismo
polémico, -a / la polémica

Q

quejoso, -a / la queja
quieto, -a / la quietud
quijotesco, -a /el quijotismo

R

razonable / el razonamiento
radical / el radicalismo
recto, -a / la rectitud
rencoroso, -a / el rencor
rico, -a / la riqueza
rústico, -a / la rusticidad

S

sarcástico, -a / el sarcasmo
seductor, -ora / la seducción
seguro, -a / la seguridad
sensual / la sensualidad
simpático, -a / la simpatía
soberbio, -a / la soberbia
soñador, -a / el sueño

T

tacaño, -a / la tacañería
taciturno, -a / la taciturnidad
temeroso, -a / el temor
tímido, -a / la timidez
tiránico, -a / la tiranía
tolerante / la tolerancia
triste / la tristeza

V

valiente / el valor
vanidoso, -a / la vanidad
vicioso, -a / la viciosidad
visionario, -a / la visión

Reprinted from: Anthony Mollica, Herbert Schutz, and Karen Tessar, "Focus on Descriptive Adjectives: Creative Activities for the Language Classroom," *Mosaic*, 3, 2 (Winter 1996): pp. 18-23.

28 French in Disguise

Fred Howlett and Alain Péchon

Students can use their knowledge of English to expand their French vocabulary quickly. In the process, they learn more than words: they discover the interrelationship of languages, a powerful motivating force.

English is a gold mine for any student wishing to learn French words. If students were taught to use this resource, they might find the process exciting. It might just dawn on them that French and English have a lot in common. A long shared history, as well as a common vocabulary.

This article provides just a few of the ways a student can use English to help learn what at first appear to be unfamiliar French words. The following is a vastly abbreviated outline of the riches available to French students in the gold mine of the English language.
Identical Words

In a gold mine, some ore is actually found on the surface and is obvious. On the surface we will find plenty of gold that others have never seen because they aren't looking for it. This gold on the surface is the thousands of words in English and French that are identical in spelling and meaning. Here are just a few examples:

absent, accident, accuse, admire, alibi, amuse, animal, argument, assume, bandit, bar, basket-ball, biscuit, brutal, budget, building, camp, cause, certain, cognac, compose, constant, courage, danger, direction, discussion, distance, divorce, dose, dynamite, effort, encourage, expert, explosion, stop, etc.

There are over 3,000 such words with identical spelling in English and French.

Slightly Disguised Words

Now let us enter the gold mine. Not far within, we find ore that is really rich. If beginning students saw these French sentences, could they understand them without the instructor's help? *Paul signe le chèque* or *Ce boxeur est le champion du Canada.* If the beginners succeed, they are ready to guess the meaning of thousands of French words that look almost like English but are slightly disguised in their spelling. Here are a few:

1. Accent in French:

   une nièce, une scène, une atmosphère, un câble, un âge
2. *-e* at the end of French words:

   la soupe, la liste, la princesse, la tente

3. Accent + *e* in French:

   une comète, un hélicoptère, l'hydrogène, l'oxygène, la planète

4. Accent + one *s* in French:

   l'accès, le succès, l'excès, le progrès, l'abcès

5. *-r* at end of French verb = *-e* in English:

   changer, préparer, arriver, recycler, comparer

6. -er in French = *-ate* in English:

   participer, décorer, créer, imiter

7. *-eur* = *-er/or*:

   un boxeur, un skieur, un danseur, un acteur, un docteur

8. *-aire* = *-ar*:

   populaire, cellulaire, spectaculaire, circulaire, triangulaire

9. *-oire* = *-ory*:

   l'histoire, la gloire, l'ivoire, la victoire, le territoire

10. *-té* = *-ty*:

    l'université, l'électricité, la qualité, la quantité, la beauté

11. *-ien* = *-ian*:

    l'électricien, le végétarien, le musicien, le magicien, le Canadien

12. final *-e* = *-a*:

    la Floride, la Russie, l'idée, la banane, l'Afrique

13. *-ai* = *-ea/-ee*:

    une saison, un traitement, un aigle, une raison, faible

14. *-e* = *-ea*:

    elle répète, la crème, les perles, il cesse, il révèle

More-difficult spelling disguises

Now it is time to get serious about goldmining. Deep down in the mine there are familiar English words that will help you recognize countless more French words without the aid of a dictionary. But you must unmask the spelling disguise. Here are nine important spelling disguises.

1. French words beginning with *esc* or *éc, esp,* or *ép* and *est* or *ét* often begin in English with *sc, sp,* and *st*.

   espace = space

   éponge = sponge

   Some easy examples:

   espèce, esprit, esturgeon, estomac

   More difficult examples:

   épars, école, éperon, échafaud, étalon, épelle, écluse, écran, épagneul, écossais, épine, écume, écope, écureuil, équarrir, échauder, écaille, état, écarlate, épargne, épier, écharpe, écolier, épineux

2. The circumflex accent (^) in many French words is represented in English by *s*.

   Example: *mât* = mast

   forêt, hâte, hôtesse, île, crête, côte, coût, croûte, quête, plâtre, château, pâte, rôti, maître

   Some difficult examples:

   bête, prêtre, dégoût, tâche, guêpe

3. The *dé* or *dés* at the beginning of French words is often spelled *dis* in English.

   Example:

   déguise = disguise

   désarme = disarm

   décourage, dégoûte, désarme, désobéit, déshonore, désastre, découvre, déloge, dédaigne, détresse, déplaît, désaccord, déloyal, défigure, décolore

4. Some French words have a *u* where English uses an *l*.

   Example: *paume* = palm

   Also: *saumon, échafaud, feutre, peau, fausse*

5. In a few words French has -*prime* where English has -*press*.

   Example: *réprime* = repress

   Also: *exprime, opprime, supprime, déprime, comprime*

6. Sometimes French words have an *i* whereas English has a *c*. Example: *instruit* = instruct (s). English uses both *uce* and *uct* as endings: *réduit, produit, déduit, construit*

7. French almost never uses the letter *k*. The *k* sound is spelled *c* or *qu* in French. Similarly, the *w*-sound is written *ou* in French.

   Example: *banque* = bank

   Also: *lac, parc, masque, ouest*

   Many verbs ending in -*que* in French end in -*cate* in English:

   complique, communique, indique, abdique, éduque

8. French frequently uses -*x* at the end of a word, where English prefers -*ce* or sometimes -*ze*.

   Example: *voix* = voice

   Also: *paix, choix, prix*

9. Some French verbs ending in -*ir* correspond to English verbs ending in -*ish*.

   Example: *polir* = polish

   Also: *accomplir, chérir, établir, fleurir, nourrir, périr, ravir, ternir*

10. French frequently uses *g/gu* where English prefers *w*.

    For example:

    guerre = war

Guillaume = William

guichet = wicket

guerrier = warrior

gages = wages

guêpe = wasp

Gauthier = Walter

gaufre = wafer

(le pays de) *Galles* = Wales

gallois = Welsh

garantie = warranty

garde-robe = wardrobe

Disguises and Associations

We are now deep within the English language gold mine. Down here the French words are even more disguised. But with a little help, even a beginner can recognize them. Here the problem is that the French words have two possible roots, one of which is familiar to English-speakers, the other not.

The Indo-European connection

The Latin (French, etc.) and Germanic (English, etc.) languages have a common origin. But when these related peoples were separated for thousands of years, the spelling of many common words changed radically. There is, however, a pattern to the spelling changes. As a matter of fact, we can illustrate the pattern of these changes even within English. Here is a short summary of the spelling disguises that make it difficult for us to recognize Germanic and Latin words that have the same origin:

1. *g,b,d* in a word of Latin origin could be represented by *c* or *k, p, t* in a word of Germanic origin.

   Latin Word in English and Related Germanic in English

   grain = kernel

   labial = lip

   denture = (false) teeth

2. *f* and *h* in a word of Latin origin are sometimes represented by *b* and *gh* (*gu*) in a word of Germanic origin.

   fragile = breakable

   host = guest*

   *Note: In spite of their common origin, a *host* now provides hospitality whereas a *guest* receives it.

3. *p,t,c* in a word of Latin origin are sometimes represented by *f, th, h, sh* in a word of Germanic origin.

paternal = fatherly

Pisces (the) = Fish (constellation)

triple = threefold

maternal = motherly

cordial = hearty

curt = short

Now apply the above patterns to French words (i.e., Latin) and English words (i.e., Germanic).

1. French *g,r,d* English *c* (or *k*) *p,t*

    grain = kernel

    genou = knee

    agri(culture) = acre*

    bourse = purse

    labial = lip**

    denl = tooth

    Note: *Although "agri-" is not a translation for "acre" these words do have a common origin. "agri-" means "field" and "acre" is now a measurement for a "field".

    *La *lecture labiale* is "lip reading". The latin word *labrum* (sometimes *labia* or *labium*), meaning *lip* evolved into the French word *lèvre*. Since *labial* in French shows no evolution in spelling, it was introduced at a later period in the history of the language, about 1600 AD.

2. French *f* and *h* = English *b* and *g* or *gu*:

    perfore (Latin *for*) = bore through

    fève (Latin *fab*) = bean

    aurifère (Latin *fer*) = gold-bearing*

    hôte (Latin *host*) = guest**

    Note: *The *fer* in such French words as *préfère* (prefer), *confère* (confer), *conifère* (coniferous), etc., corresponds to "bear", meaning "carry", in English. Therefore, *coniferous* not only has the same meaning as *cone-bearing* but also has the same origin.

    **The French word *hôte* usually means *host* in English, but oddly enough it also means *guest*.

3. French *c,p,t* = English *f,t* (or *th*), *sh*

    *poisson** (Latin *pisc*) = fish

    paternal (Latin *pater*) = fatherly

    trois (Latin *tres*) = three

    maternal (Latin *mater*) = motherly

    coeur (Latin *cord*) = heart

    court (Latin *curt*) = short

    *Yes, the word *poisson* in French has the same origin as *fish* in English. The ancestor of both the French and the English is the root *pisc*.

Use the above patterns to find the English words which have the same Indo-European root as these French words:

connais (Latin *cognosc* or simply *gnosc*)

cor (Latin *corn*)

neveu (Latin *nepos*)

dis (Latin *dic*)

deux (Latin *duo*)

pied (Latin *ped*)

colline (Latin *coll*)

tonnerre (Latin *ton*)

fleur (Latin *flor*)

larme (Latin *lacrim*)

genre (Latin *gener*)

fracture (Latin *frag* or *fract*)

nuit 1 (Latin *noct*)

sue 1 (Latin *sud*)

Answers: know, horn, nephew, teach 2, two, foot, hill, thunder, bloom, tear, kind, break, night, sweat.

1 *nuit* and *sue* have the same original root as *night* and *sweat*, but don't follow the patterns.

2 *dis* and *teach* share the same original root but *teach* is no longer the modern translation for *dis* (say).

French words with an unfamiliar form of the root	Related French with root like that of English	Related English that provides the meaning (Not a translation!)
bois, boit, boivent	buvons	beverage (what you drink)
croyable, le crois	crédule	credible (believable)
connais, connaît	connaissons	connoisseur (one who knows)
devons, dois, doivent	débit	debit (what is owing)
dites, disons, dis, dit	dicton	diction
écrivons, écris, écrit	scribe	scribe
envoie, envoient	envoyons	envoy
un fait, fais, fait, faisons, faites, font	facteur	fact, factor, feat
meurs, meurt, mourons, mourez, meurent	mortel, mort	mortal
peux, peut, peuvent	pouvons, pouvoir	power

The English connection

So far we have dealt with words that are 100 percent parallel in English and French such as

bleu/blue,

chat/cat,

guerre/war,

détruire/destroy,

fragile/breakable.

Perhaps more important are the French words we can know by association. For example, *bien, chutes,* and *fer* can be recognized by English-speakers who know *benevolent, parachute* or *ferric*.

French word	English word with same root as French	Meaning of French word
chaud	cauldron, scald (pot for heating food)	hot
contre	counter (against) contradict	against
ciel	celestial (of the heavens, sky)	sky, heavens
marin	mariner (seaman)	sailor
an/année	annual (yearly)	year
fil	filament (slender thread)	thread
incendie	incendiary (causing fire)	fire
lieu	in lieu of (in place of)	place
faim	famine, famished (hungry)	hunger
soleil	solar (of the sun)	sun
maison	mansion (large house)	house
malade	malady (sickness)	sick
pensée	pansy, pensive	thought
poulet	pullet (young chicken)	chicken
bec	beak	bill
enterrer	inter	bury
fatigué	fatigued	tired
bouche	embouchure, buccal	mouth
colère	choler	anger

If the French teacher constantly encourages students to go from the known to the unknown, to use English language resources to decipher what seem to be unfamiliar French words, students will acquire a large reading vocabulary quickly. But more important, they will begin to see the interrelationship of language, acquire a favourable attitude to language learning... and improve their English!

References

Bodmer, Frederick. 1955. *The Loom Of Language*, edited and arranged by Lancelot Hogben. London: George Allen & Unwin Ltd.

Clairborne, R. 1983. *Our Marvelous Native Tongue*. Toronto: Fitzhenry and Whiteside Ltd.

Clairborne, R. 1989. *The Roots of English*. Toronto: Doubleday.

Davies, P. 1981. *Roots*. New York: McGraw-Hill.

Greimas, A.J. 1968. *Dictionnaire de l'ancien français*. Paris: Librairie Larousse.

Johnson, E.L. 1931. *Latin Words of Commom English*. Boston: D.C. Heath and Company.

Morris, Wm. 1981. *The American Heritage Dictionary*. Boston: Houghton Mifflin.

Pope, M.K. 1973. *From Latin To Modern French*. Manchester: Manchester University Press.

Simpson, J.A. and E.F.C. Weiner, 1989. *Oxford English Dictionary*, complete edition. Oxford: Clarendon Press.

Reprinted from: Fred Howlett and Alain Péchon, "French in Disguise." Mosaic, 3, 3 (Spring 1996), pp. 20-23.

29 Mnemonics for Mastering the Imperfect and Irregular Future in French, Italian and Spanish

Keith Mason

Mnemonic devices serve to summarize and simplify grammar rules, especially when applied to the many verb tenses and forms found in the Romance languages. This article presents two mnemonic devices helpful in summarizing the uses of the imperfect and the irregular future tense forms, respectively.

Students of French, Italian, and Spanish are challenged by the abundance of verb forms in the Romance languages and their uses. Teachers of Romance languages are equally challenged to come up with methods that simplify the mastery of verbs for their students. Two areas particularly troublesome for students are the imperfect/preterite distinction and the irregular future verb forms. In order to simplify these two points of grammar, the author developed two mnemonic devices, outlined in the following sections.

Imperfect: C-H-E-A-T-E-D

Dialects of French, Italian, and Spanish use either a simple verb tense (the preterite) or a compound tense (the present perfect) for those actions in the past showing a definite beginning or end. However, the distinction between the imperfect and preterite/present perfect is problematic for English-speaking students acquiring the Romance languages.

Castilian speakers of Spanish, much like the French and the Italians, tend to use the present perfect tense in cases when New World speakers of Spanish would use the preterite. For example, consider the phrase "I read the book." A New World speaker of Spanish would express that phrase as "Leí el libro." However, a Castilian speaker of Spanish would likely express the same phrase as "He leído el libro."

Students have difficulty identifying which form corresponds to a particular aspect of the past action. This difficulty in selection is mainly attributable to the fact that both the imperfect and preterite/present perfect of the target language may be translated with the English preterite (e.g. Spanish *hablé* and *hablaba* = "I spoke.") Furthermore, teachers and textbooks often confuse students by claiming that a clearcut distinction exists between the two forms; in reality, some cases allow for either, depending upon how the speaker wishes to represent the past action. Nevertheless, those unambiguous usages of the imperfect aspect may be conveniently summarized using the mnemonic device C-H-E-A-T-E-D. The letters stand for the following uses of the imperfect when narrating in the past:

Continuous Actions
Habitual Actions
Emotions
Age
Time
Endless Actions
Descriptions

Examples of each use are illustrated below:

Continuous Actions

English:
Mary *was singing* while Charles was reading the newspaper.

French:
Marie *chantait* pendant que Charles lisait le journal.

Italian:
Maria *cantava* mentre Carlo leggeva il giornale.

Spanish:
María *cantaba* mientras Carlos leía el periódico.

Habitual Actions

English:
We always *used to go* to the movies on Fridays.

French:
Nous *allions* toujours au cinéma le vendredi.

Italian:
Venerdì *andavamo* sempre al cinema.

Spanish:
Siempre *íbamos* al cine los viernes.

Emotions

English:
He *was* very happy because he had received a present for his birthday.

French:
Il *était* très content parce qu'il avait reçu un cadeau pour son anniversaire.

Italian:
Era molto contento perché aveva ricevuto un regalo per il suo compleanno.

Spanish:
Él *estaba* muy contento porque había recibido un regalo para su cumpleaños.

Age

English:

The man *was* 34 years old.

French:

L'homme *avait* 34 ans.

Italian:

L'uomo *aveva* 34 anni.

Spanish:

El hombre *tenía* 34 años.

Time

English:

It *was* 3 o'clock.

French:

Il *était* trois heures.

Italian:

Erano le tre.

Spanish:

Eran las tres.

Endless Actions

English:

Thomas *was walking* in the park when I saw him.

French:

Thomas *marchait* dans le parc quand je l'ai vu.

Italian:

Tommaso *passeggiava* nel parco quando l'ho visto.

Spanish:

Tomás *caminaba* en el parque cuando lo vi.

Descriptions

English:

It *was* a lovely spring day.

French:

Il *faisait* très beau.

Italian:

Era una bella giornata di primavera.

Spanish:

Era un hermoso día de primavera.

C-H-E-A-T-E-D neatly summarizes the uses of the imperfect for both students and teachers. One may deduce that the preterite (or present perfect) should be used when the past action is not among the seven categories covered in C-H-E-A-T-E-D. See Miller (1956) for the ideal number of items the brain can process.

The Irregular Future: The Mexican Hat Dance

Romance languages are indeed rich in verb forms and tenses. It is a challenge for our students to memorize all the verb forms, especially the irregular ones. For this reason, I devised a mnemonic device to aid students with the irregular future tense verb forms. Twelve frequently occurring irregular future verbs exist in Spanish and many of these same verbs share irregularities in French and Italian: *caber, decir, haber, poder, poner, querer, saber, salir, tener, valer,* and *venir*. The irregularity lies in the verbal stem: students generally have less trouble with the future endings (e.g. Spanish *-é, -ás, -á, - emos, -éis, -án*) since they are the same for both regular and irregular verbs and for verbs of all three conjugations (*-ar, -er, -ir*). One commonality of the Spanish irregular future forms is that the singular forms and third person plural have one less syllable that the regular verbs (except for monosyllabic verb stems such as Spanish *ser* or *ir*). To represent the two syllables for these forms in a rhythmic, singable way, one may use the tune "El jarabe tapatío" also known as "The Mexican Hat Dance" (Use the part that goes duh dúh duh dúh duh dúh duh dúh duh duh dúh duh dúh). Match the future forms with the tune as shown:

For Spanish,

diré dirás dirá diremos diréis dirán.

For French,

dirai diras dira dirons direz diront.

The Italian forms fit the rhythm similarly to French and Spanish except for the *loro* form in which you must add an additional beat:

dirò dirai dirà diremo direte diranno.

I usually project on a transparency a *sombrero* with the irregular future forms of the irregular verbs or draw one on the chalkboard as shown above Another idea especially for younger learners is to bring in an actual "sombrero" and have students pull out slips of paper with one of each of the infinitives written on them. Students would then conjugate the correct future forms. Incidentally, many students enjoy singing the forms instead of just repeating them.

Conclusion

Two previous articles (Mason 1990, 1992) outlined mnemonic devices to help students with *ser/estar*, *por/para*, and affirmative commands with clitic pronouns in Spanish. Tuttle (1981) also presented several mnemonic devices in his article, including the shoe verb diagram for stem-changing verbs and a time line for pictorially expressing different verb tenses. The two mnemonic devices described in this article have been used successfully in basic level courses. Properly integrated into the grammar curriculum, these new mnemonics should greatly facilitate your students' mastery of the imperfect versus preterite/present perfect distinction and the irregular future verb forms in the Romance languages.*

*I would like to thank Wayne Shackelford and William S. Wheatley, III for their comments on this article.

References

Mason, Keith, 1990. "*Ser* vs. *estar*: A Mnemonic Device That Puts *estar* in Its P.L.A.C.E." *Hispania*, 73: 506-507.

Mason, Keith, 1992. "Successful Mnemonics for *por/para* and Affirmative Commands with Pronouns." *Hispania*, 75: 197-98.

Miller, G.A., 1956. "The Magical Number Seven, Plus or Minus Two: Some Limits on Our Capacity for Processing Information." *Psychological Review*, 63: 81-97.

Tuttle, Harry Grover, 1981. "Mnemonics in Spanish Classes." *Hispania*, 64: 582-584.

Reprinted from: Keith Mason, "Mnemonics for Mastering the Imperfect and Irregular Future in French, Italian and Spanish." *Mosaic*. 3, 4 (Summer 1996), pp. 16-17.

30 Games and Puzzles in the Second-Language Classroom: A Second Look

Marcel Danesi and Anthony Mollica

Introduction

The posing and solving of puzzles, conundrums, rebuses, riddles, and the like is as old as history itself. The first surviving "think-of-a-number" puzzle dates back to an Egyptian papyrus written around 1650 BC (Wells 1992: 1). The oldest book of games in existence, known as the *Libro de juegos*, was commissioned more than 700 years ago by King Alfonso X of Castile and Leon (Mohr 1993: 11). It contains clear descriptions of how to play chess, checkers, and various card and board games. The antiquity of the puzzling instinct in human beings shows that it is a fundamental feature of the human mind. And the widespread popularity of puzzle magazines, puzzle sections in newspapers, puzzle books, TV quiz shows, game tournaments in chess, checkers, cards, etc., reveals that puzzles and games are alive and well in the contemporary human mind.

Puzzleology, to coin a term for the field that deals with the study of puzzles and games in human cultures, has enjoyed a long-standing role in the educational domain, where games, problem-solving tasks, and puzzle techniques have been the standard fare in the curricula of many school subjects for a long time. As puzzleologist James Fixx (1978: 18) once wrote, the reason for this is, no doubt, because "puzzles not only bring us pleasure but also help us to work and learn more effectively." In the area of second-language teaching, puzzleological techniques such as crosswords, word searches, scrambled words, simulations, interactive games, board games, etc. have now become intrinsic components of many approaches, and the choice of many teachers, as formats for students to review and reinforce grammar, vocabulary, and communication skills. Puzzleological activities have become such common features of commercially-available textual materials, and the topic of discussion of virtually every teacher-training seminar, that it would be impossible today to think of second-language teaching without them. They are now seen to be highly versatile techniques that serve both specific discrete-point learning tasks (*reinforcing structural and lexical knowledge*) and more interactive ones (*communication and functionality*). But it was not that long ago that the injection of this fun element in second-language teaching would have been considered a frivolous waste of time by the teaching profession. And even in today's more accepting climate, puzzleological techniques are viewed as tangential, or at best supplementary, to more mainstream techniques.

The most memory-enhancing way in which humans develop concepts, from infancy to adolescence, is through some form of recreational mental play. While the specific characteristics of such mental gymnastics might vary somewhat from culture to culture, the need to solve problems constitutes a cognitive, cross-cultural universal.

Our purpose in this essay is to revisit puzzleology in second-language teaching, in order to give the teacher an overview of what the most relevant facts on file are *vis-à-vis* their incorporation into classroom instruction and to provide an elementary typology of puzzleological techniques for the teacher interested in incorporating them in his/her language classes.

Puzzleological Techniques and Second-Language Learning

The experimental literature dealing with the learning-efficacy of puzzleological techniques is not extensive. Outside of a few scattered attempts to assess their validity and to develop a psychologically- appropriate typology for their instructional utilization, very little has been done in the way of giving this topic a thorough empirical treatment (e.g., Omaggio 1978, 1982, Mollica 1979, 1981, Wright, Betteridge and Buckby 1979, Danesi 1979, Webster and Castonon 1980, 1985a, 1987, 1981, Rixon 1981, Rodgers 1981, Jones 1982, 1986, Palmer and Rodgers 1983, Crookall 1985, Crookall, Greenblat, Cooke, Klabbers, and Watsin 1987, Crookall and Oxford 1988, Crookall and Saunders 1989, Cicogna, Danesi, and Mollica 1992). Two clear facts have emerged from the literature.

The sketchy experimental evidence that does exist has generally shown such techniques to be supportive of language learning processes.

For such techniques to be effective, they must be designed with specific instructional/learning objectives in mind.

The empirical work of Rodgers (1981), Palmer and Rodgers (1983), and a few others (see the studies in Crookall 1985, Crookall, Greenblat, Coote, Klabbers, and Watson 1987, Crookall and Oxford 1988, and Crookall and Saunders 1989) has shown, by and large, that games are effective learning-enhancers, but that they raise several critical questions which, to the best of our knowledge, have not as yet been addressed. So, from a purely research and learning theory perspective, the general indication would seem to be that the basis for using puzzleological techniques to complement, supplement, or even completely shape the second-language teaching process is psychologically sound. Recently, Sandra Savignon (1992) has observed that such techniques have become favourites of communicative methodologists precisely because they serve the elusive goal of meaning negotiation.

But perhaps the greatest support for puzzleological techniques in second-language teaching is anecdotal evidence and common sense. The general research in educational psychology, the corpus of case studies of learners, the everyday observations of school teachers, and the common perceptions of anyone in daily contact with children and adolescents point collectively to what appears to be a fundamental requirement of learning:

namely that the most memory-enhancing way in which humans develop concepts, from infancy to adolescence, is through some form of recreational mental play. While the specific characteristics of such mental gymnastics might vary somewhat from culture to culture, the need to solve problems constitutes a cognitive, cross-cultural universal. It would seem, therefore, that the logical question for second-language teaching is not whether or not to include puzzleological techniques into its repertory of instructional options, but rather how best to tap the natural tendency to solve problems in an instructionally-meaningful way. Rodgers (1981) has shown how this can be done by highlighting five properties of puzzleological techniques that are reflective of current-day practices in second-language teaching. In our view, these properties explain why they are easily insertable into the frameworks of most contemporary proficiency-oriented approaches to second-language teaching:

1. *They are competitive.*
2. *They are rule-governed* (i.e. they have a limited numbers of specific and clearly-defined rules).
3. *They are goal-defined.*
4. *They have closure* (i.e. there is a specific point at which a puzzle is solved or a game is finished).
5. *They are engaging*, in that they constantly seem to challenge the participants.

So, it would seem that puzzleological techniques are ancillary activities that can be easily used in combination with other kinds of instructional activities in. the framework of some broader methodological blueprint for second-language teaching. Rarely has anyone ventured to design a syllabus, or teaching system, aimed at making the whole second-language teaching process puzzleological in orientation. One of the few to have done so, as reported in his Ph.D. dissertation of 1992, is Mark Miller of the University of Delaware. Miller designed an entire syllabus and instructional system based on interactive game-playing. Adopting the usual experimental-statistical approach of a controlled study, he found his game-playing design to be an effective means of imparting both linguistic and communicative competence to university language students, while at the same time allowing for the maintenance of a high level of interest and motivation in the course. While this was designed only as a pilot study, it nonetheless endorses what the previous literature has been documenting in bits and pieces.

From a purely research and learning theory perspective, the general indication would seem to be that the basis for using puzzleological techniques to complement, supplement, or even completely shape the second-language teaching process is psychologically sound.

Play vs. Game

Given the paucity of so-called hard evidence in favour of the learning-efficacy of puzzleological techniques in second-language teaching, it is perhaps useful to cast a quick glance at what psychologists have to say about the use of play, problem-solving, and games in education generally. While the meaning of the word play is certainly intuitively obvious, it turns out to be a rather difficult one to define formally. It is perhaps most useful to think of play as a kind of innate and unreflective form of psycho-motor behaviour that allows children to interact in a meaningful way both with their environment and with others. It manifests itself across cultures primarily as a form of physical involvement with people and things, invariably stimulating affective and experiential responses that lead progressively to the build-up and coding of knowledge. As Munzert (1991: 37) point out:

> Infants learn through exploration of the physical world by random movement, crawling, touching, and coming into direct contact with people and objects in the environment.

Culturally-structured or routinized forms of play are the games that children learn from their peers, older children, or adults in a participatory way. Spontaneous playing behaviours can occur within or outside of games. But a game always enlists some form of the play instinct. The essential requirement of a game is that it have a structure or a clearly-predictable format within which the play instinct can operate. For educational purposes one can refer to game-playing in classroom settings as a pedagogically-designed system for imparting knowledge or skill based on playing. (For a comprehensive treatment of the positive effect of games on cognitive development see, for example, Loftus and Loftus 1983).

Cognitively, game-playing invariably involves the deployment of problem-solving strategies. The goal, or end-state, of any game constitutes a problem that the child/adolescent must attempt to solve within the format of the game. This forces the learner to go from a random, experiential form of thinking to a more organized and representational one shaped by the structural elements of the game format. As Lesgold (1988: 190) observes, in order to solve a problem, the person must know what steps are possible and "how to represent the problem."

The solution path that the student discovers can be said to result from a creative strategy because the learner must use the given elements of the game to locate the path. Creativity can thus be constrained for the present purposes to mean the ability to arrange the given elements of a game or a puzzle in ways that bring about a solution to the problem posed by a game or puzzle. The arrangements will vary from individual to individual; but they will do so within the limits defined by the structural elements of the game or puzzle. Thus, unlike most popular notions of the term, creativity in game-playing or puzzle-solving involves   the utilization of structures within a pre-established format. It is in coming up with the solution path that the learner is forced to explore alternative and innovative ways to use the structures to access the end-state. In this sense, therefore, it can be argued that puzzle-solving and game-playing are effective means for channelling the student's innate tendency to be creative towards some specific learning goal. As Munzert (1991: 63) has aptly remarked, creativity is an educationally-meaningful notion only if it "involves a sense of purpose coupled with action." This means that the creative act "requires that emerging ideas and thoughts be organized into new or different patterns from their previous organization" (see also Perkins 1988 for empirical studies on problem-solving creativity as purposeful behaviour; and Gowan, Khatena and Torrance 1981 for a comprehensive treatment of the associated educational implications).

Puzzle-solving and game-playing are effective means for channelling the student's innate tendency to be creative towards some specific learning goal.

Arguing from this general research base, it can be hypothesized that puzzleological techniques are effective insofar as they allow the students to come up creatively with solutions to a specific problem posed. It is in formalizing each solution through the medium of language that the students come to acquire the conceptual domains underlying the puzzle or game in terms of the language structures that express them.

It is clearly beyond the scope of the present review essay to go any further into the details of the psychology of problem-solving and game-playing and of its supporting empirical base. Suffice it to say here that it can be used to understand why puzzleological techniques constantly manifest themselves as learning-enhancing activities in second-language teaching. Extrapolating from all the discussions, anecdotal experiences, and the studies that do exist on puzzleological and game-playing techniques, the following general findings, terminological clarifications, and *caveats* can now be brought to the reader's attention:

It has been found necessary to distinguish between language teaching puzzles and language teaching games, since the former are problem-solving texts that require the individual learner to come up with a solution within the framework of the text, while the latter involve problem-solving activities involving group interaction, and therefore are more focused on contextual parameters.

The effectiveness of language-teaching puzzles has, to the best of our knowledge, rarely, if ever, been studied experimentally. The anecdotal evidence, however, portrays them as useful primarily as control, reinforcement, and review techniques (e.g. Mollica 1981, 1992b, Danesi 1985a, Nuessel 1994).

The research on language-teaching games (e.g. Palmer and Rodgers 1983, Crookall 1985, Crookall, Greenblat, Coote, Klabbers, and Watson 1987, Crookall and Oxford 1988, and Crookall and Saunders 1989, Miller 1992, Musumeci 1992) raises several questions that still require an answer.

1. Are they usable with all groups of students, especially since different groups and individuals respond differently to kinds and degrees of competition?

2. Do the same kinds of benefits that have been documented in other areas of education and development over the last two decades with the use

of problem-solving and game-playing techniques (e.g. Edwards, Devries, and Snyder 1972, Livingston and Kidder 1973, Devries and Slavin 1978, Loftus and Loftus 1983, Sawyers and Rogers 1994, Berk 1994) accrue in similar ways with the use of language-teaching games in second-language teaching?

3. Do language-teaching games encourage interaction or can they inhibit classroom participatory behaviours?

Despite such *caveats* and questions, there seems to be a general feeling among users of language-teaching puzzles and language-teaching games that they foster learning, if in no other way than through the inducement of recreational states of mind.

Language-teaching puzzles and language-teaching games should be used judiciously. They should be used to motivate students and to challenge them. They should never be used as time-fillers.

A Typology of Puzzleological Techniques

Before selecting or preparing the specific language-teaching puzzles or language-teaching games for his/her course, the teacher should always keep in mind that the age, learning styles, and previous training of the students must be taken into consideration. Children can handle language-teaching puzzles that are cast in reduced and simplified form (e.g. elementary crosswords, word searches, etc.). But very young children have great difficulty in handling such language-teaching puzzles as logic puzzles, rebuses, etc. Therefore, bearing in mind that language-teaching puzzles and language-teaching games must be synchronized to the learner's age and level of competence, teachers can generally rest assured that the use of these techniques will produce favourable results:

Language-teaching puzzles are usable primarily for form-based and meaning-based language tasks, and language-teaching games for more communication-based and group interaction tasks.

Both language-teaching puzzles and language-teaching games can be easily constructed and keyed to specific and general instructional objectives. Once the learning task has been determined, the teacher can select or construct the appropriate language-teaching puzzle or language-teaching game to accomplish it.

Language-teaching puzzles and language-teaching games are useful primarily as review, recall, reinforcement,   control, and occasionally as expansion techniques.

Language-teaching puzzles and language-teaching games should be used judiciously. They should be used to motivate students and to challenge them. They should never be used as time-fillers. So, the learners should be made to understand that they are just as much a part of the course as are other kinds of exercises, drills, activities, etc. The teacher should also keep in mind that the over-use of language-teaching puzzles and language-teaching games is not desirable. To maintain interest, the teacher should always diversify the types of language-teaching puzzles and language-teaching games used together with other kinds of techniques.

Pedagogical writing in the area of language-teaching puzzles and language-teaching games within the last three decades has been rather extensive (e.g. Lee 1965, Bressan 1970, Crawshaw 1972, Wolfe 1972, Hupb 1974, Latorre and Baeza 1975, Schmidt 1977, Schloss 1977, Caré and Debyser 1978, Omaggio 1978, 1982, Wright, Betteridge and Buckby 1979, Mollica 1979, 1981, 1992, Danesi 1979, 1985a, 1985b, 1987, Hendrickson 1980, 1983, Maley and Grellet 1981, Ervin 1982, Irwing 1982, McKay 1985, Schultz and Fisher 1988, Steinberg 1991, Cicogna, Danesi, and Mollica 1992, Dickson 1992, Nuessel 1994). In general, methodologists suggest that at least three categories of these techniques can be employed in second-language teaching. These can be called as follows:

1. *form-based* language-teaching puzzles,
2. *meaning-based* language-teaching puzzles, and
3. *communication-based* language-teaching games.

This terminology attempts to synthesize into a few manageable categories the many and diverse kinds of instructional objectives suggested in the literature vis-a-vis the utilization of language-teaching puzzles and language-teaching games.

Form-Based Language-Teaching Puzzles

A form-based language-teaching puzzle focuses the individual learner's attention on language form. It is one of the most popular types of puzzeological techniques that has been in use as a regular feature in most textbooks and ancillary materials for at least three decades. Scrambled letters, crosswords, word searches, tic-tac-toe, word mazes, cryptograms, and the like make up a truly rich and broad repertory of language-teaching puzzles that can be tailored to fit specific form-based learning tasks. They are popular with both teachers and learners because they cast the reinforcement and control of spelling, grammar, and vocabulary into a challenging and recreational problem-solving format.

The following examples are suggestions that we have extracted from the literature, which we reproduce here simply to demonstrate how versatile form-based language-teaching puzzles can be. Some recent collections and discussions of such language-teaching puzzles can be found in Steinberg 1991, Mollica 1992b, and Nuessel 1994.
Word search

Danesi (1985a) created a word-search language-teaching puzzle in which he hid the French colour adjectives *rouge, noir, blanc, vert,* and *jaune.* The words can be read from left-to-right, right-to-left, up-down, and down-up. He suggests that this puzzle can be used for different objectives by simply changing the instructions for solving it. It is up to the teacher to decide which level of reading difficulty to employ. The teacher can use this puzzle for a variety of review, control and reinforcement tasks. The following are some suggested activities:

En la escuela

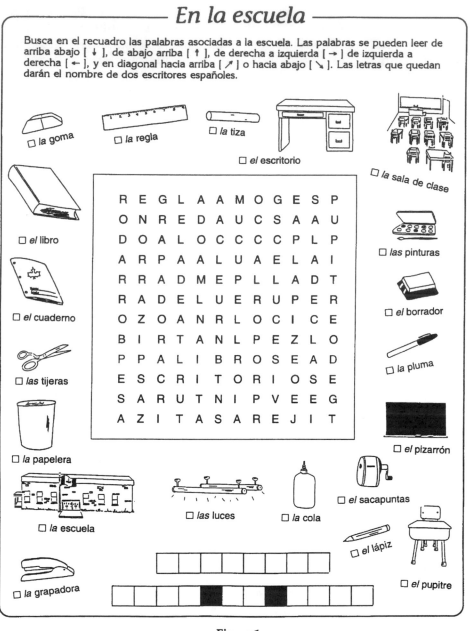

Busca en el recuadro las palabras asociadas a la escuela. Las palabras se pueden leer de arriba abajo [↓], de abajo arriba [↑], de derecha a izquierda [→] de izquierda a derecha [←], y en diagonal hacia arriba [↗] o hacia abajo [↘]. Las letras que quedan darán el nombre de dos escritores españoles.

☐ *la* goma   ☐ *la* regla   ☐ *la* tiza   ☐ *el* escritorio   ☐ *la* sala de clase

☐ *el* libro   ☐ *las* pinturas

☐ *el* cuaderno   ☐ *el* borrador

☐ *las* tijeras   ☐ *la* pluma

```
R E G L A A M O G E S P
O N R E D A U C S A A U
D O A L O C C C C P L P
A R P A A L U A E L A I
R R A D M E P L L A D T
R A D E L U E R U P E R
O Z O A N R L O C I C E
B I R T A N L P E Z L O
P P A L I B R O S E A D
E S C R I T O R I O S E
S A R U T N I P V E E G
A Z I T A S A R E J I T
```

☐ *la* papelera   ☐ *el* pizarrón

☐ *las* luces   ☐ *la* cola   ☐ *el* sacapuntas

☐ *la* escuela   ☐ *el* lápiz

☐ *la* grapadora   ☐ *el* pupitre

Figure 1

- The students can be asked simply to locate the colour adjectives in the puzzle, after having given them the words (= *simple recognition task/orthographic task*).
- The students can be asked to locate five colour adjectives in the puzzle, without telling them which ones (= *vocabulary task*).

- The students can be given definitions or incomplete sentences for each word and then asked to find the words in the puzzle (= *vocabulary review/cloze task*).

- The students can be given the feminine forms of the adjectives and then asked to locate their corresponding masculine forms in the puzzle (= *morphological task*).

The number and diversity of the instructions is limited only by the imagination and specific requirements of the teacher. All form-based language-teaching puzzles have this feature.

Mollica (in preparation) is in the process of developing for various languages a series of word-searches in which the stimulus for the hidden word is either *print* (i.e., a word), or *non-print* (i.e., an illustration) or both *print* and *non-print* (i.e., word associated with the illustration.) He arbitrarily chooses 20 words on a given topic or theme and creates the first three puzzles using both print and non-print as stimuli, followed by two puzzles in which only the visual stimulus is given (Figure 1). In this way, he is encouraging the student to learn new vocabulary or review it by going from print (word), to non-print *(illustration associated with word)* to print *(word to be found in the puzzle.)* This repetition is designed to help the student to learn or recall vocabulary. (Figure 2).

Mollica (1981b, 1982) has also created word-search puzzles in which the form reflects the theme or topic. Moreover, he suggests on "hiding" a message closely related to the theme or topic. The student solving the puzzle, therefore, cannot help but feel a sense of accomplishment in solving the puzzle but also in feeling satisfied in "finding" the related hidden message. Once all the words *(ange, berger, boules, cadeau, cheminée, crèche, décorations, étable, étoile, gui, renne, sac, sapin, voeux)* have been circled on the "Christmas tree", the hidden message revealed will spell out "Joyeux Noël. Bonne et heureuse année." (Figure 3).

A similar word-search puzzle can be created in the shape of a heart for St. Valentine's Day (Figure 4). Again, once all the words directly related with the theme are found *(aimer, amis, amitié, amour, baisers, cadeau, cartes, chocolats, coeur, embrasser, fête, fêter, filles, fleurs, garçons, gentil, joli, lettre, rose, sourire, Valentin),* a hidden proverb related to "love" will appear: "On peut tout cacher sauf l'ivresse et l'amour." *Everything can be hidden except drunkenness and love* (Mollica 1981-1982).

Hidden messages may also be used to provide cultural, linguistic, historical or geographical information (Mollica 1992c). Teachers may decide to "hide" some of the *chefs-lieux* of France *(Ajaccio, Amie, Châolon-sur-Marne, Clermont-Ferrand, Dijon, Lille, Limoges, Lyon, Marseilles, Metz, Montpellier, Nantes, Orléans, Paris, Poitiers, Rennes, Rouen, Strasbourg, Toulouse)* in the shape of the country itself (Figure 5).

But the hidden words may not necessarily always be thematic in nature. Teachers might wish to select words which are merely *associated* with the topic or theme. In the following word-search puzzle, (Figure 6), Mollica

En route!

Trouve dans la grille les mots associés à l'auto. Les mots peuvent se lire horizontalement, verticalment, en diagonale, de droite à gauche, de gauche à droite, de haut en bas, ou de bas en haut. Transpose ensuite les lettres qui te restent pour finir la phrase ci-dessous.

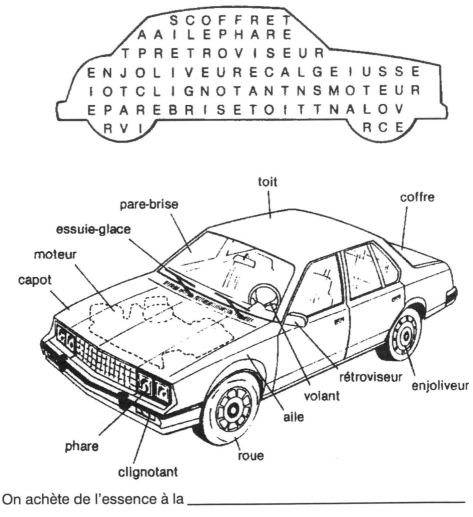

On achète de l'essence à la _____

Figure 2

(1992c) includes names of rivers, mountains, cities, composers, writers, wines, as well as lexical items relating to capital "C" culture and lower case "c" culture. (*Adige, Alitalia, Alpi, Arno, arte, Bari, Barolo, Capri, Dante, Elba, esploratori, espresso, Etna, Fiat, Ionio, musicista, Papa, pecorino, Pisa. Po, poeta,*

```
                    J
                    O
                Y   S   E
                C   N   S
            U   R   O   E   X
            N   E   I   L   O
        B   U   C   T   U   E   L
        E   A   H   A   O   B   O
    N   R   E   E   R   B   I   U   G
    I   G   D   N   O   N   E   L   E
T   P   E   A   H   C   A   S   E   E   U
R   A   R   C   H   E   M   I   N   E   E
E   U   S   S   E   A   D   A   N   G   E   N   N
E   L   B   A   T   E   E   E   V   O   E   U   X
                    R
                    E
```

Figure 3

```
        D   C   E                   U   R   X
    N   C   A   O   H             O   C   E   O   S
E   S   I   R   N   E   E     I   S   H   R   E   S   S
B   P   E   T   S   R   U   E   L   F   O   T   U   V   E
E   A   E   E   N   N   T   R   O   C   C   T   R   A   L
A   M   I   S   F   E   T   E   J   C   O   E   E   H   L
E   M   B   S   O   R   L   L   I   V   L   L   M   R   I
G   L   I   R   E   U   C   A   D   E   A   U   I   E   F
    A   I   T   A   R   R   S   V   S   T   E   A   E
    R   T   I   S   S   I   T   L   S   A   A
        C   N   E   S   F   R   M   O   M
        O   E   U   E   R   E   O
        N   G   T   R   U
        S   E   R
                R
```

Figure 4

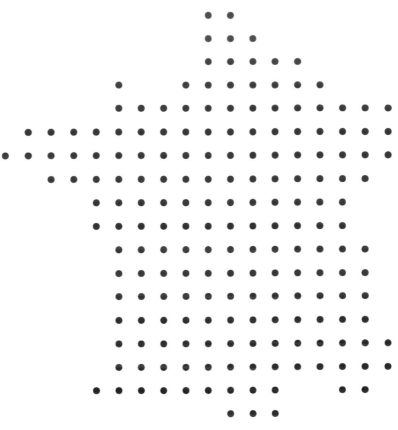

Figure 5

repubblica, Roma, scrittori, stivale, tenori, Tevere, Torino, Verdi). Once all the words have been found, students will realize that the hidden message will inform them that "Dante è il padre della lingua italiana."

Crossword Puzzles

When Arthur Wynne published the first crossword puzzle in the puzzle pages of Sunday's New York *World* on December 21, 1913, he probably did not realize the instant success the puzzle was to enjoy. The biggest puzzle craze that America had ever set in motion. Roger Millington 1977: 24,25) describes the situation anecdotally. The following are some examples:

> Engaged couples announced their good news by composing appropriate crosswords and sticking them in the local paper. The Rev. George McElveen, a Baptist pastor of Pittsburgh, was the first of many preachers to use the crossword puzzle to attract bigger congregations. He announced that a large blackboard would be placed in front of his pulpit. On it was an original puzzle and the audience was required to solve it before he would begin his sermon. The solved puzzle, needless to say, proved to be the text for his sermon. In Atlantic City, crosswords were distributed in church to stir interest in a current missionary campaign in China and Persia. Churchgoers were requested, however, not to solve the puzzles during the service [...]

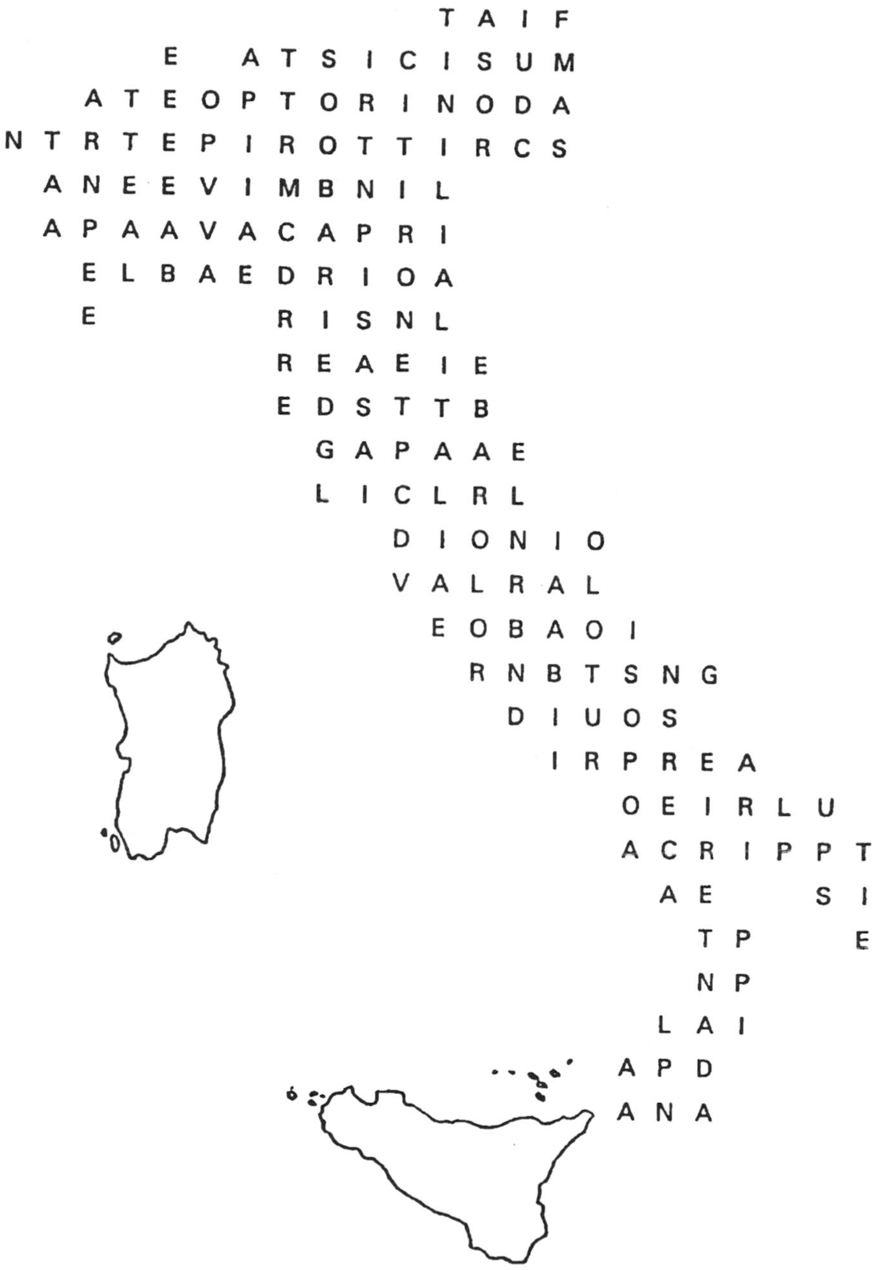

```
                        T  A  I  F
            E     A  T  S  I  C  I  S  U  M
      A  T  E  O  P  T  O  R  I  N  O  D  A
N  T  R  T  E  P  I  R  O  T  T  I  R  C  S
   A  N  E  E  V  I  M  B  N  I  L
   A  P  A  A  V  A  C  A  P  R  I
      E  L  B  A  E  D  R  I  O  A
      E           R  I  S  N  L
                  R  E  A  E  I  E
                  E  D  S  T  T  B
                  G  A  P  A  A  E
                  L  I  C  L  R  L
                  D  I  O  N  I  O
                  V  A  L  R  A  L
                  E  O  B  A  O  I
                  R  N  B  T  S  N  G
                  D  I  U  O  S
                  I  R  P  R  E  A
                  O  E  I  R  L  U
                  A  C  R  I  P  P  T
                  A  E        S  I
                  T  P        E
                  N  P
                  L  A  I
                  A  P  D
                  A  N  A
```

Figure 6

In December 1924, unaware the craze was shortly to achieve similar magnitudes in Britain, *The Times* took pity on America. In an articles headed AN ENSLAVED AMERICA, it noted that "All America has succumbed to the crossword puzzle." Guessing inaccurately, it continued: "The cross-word puzzle is by no means a new

Articles of Clothing

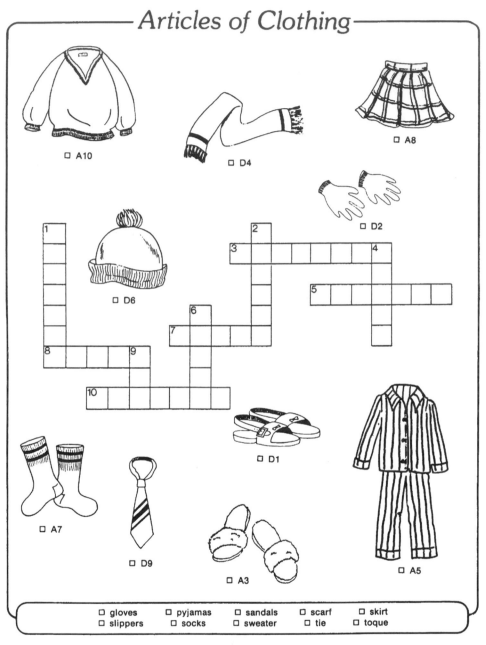

| □ gloves | □ pyjamas | □ sandals | □ scarf | □ skirt |
| □ slippers | □ socks | □ sweater | □ tie | □ toque |

Figure 7

thing; in all likelihood it was known as long as the Civil War." *The Times* felt that the crossword was "a menace because it is making devastating inroads on working hours of every rank of society." How devastating? Well, according to their New York correspondent, five million hours daily of American people's time - most of them nominally working hours -were used in unprofitable trifling.

A great deal has been written on the crossword puzzle in the language class using the printed word as a stimulus. In his classic study of this puzzeological technique, Dino Bressan (1970), for example, likes the crossword puzzle for the obvious contribution it can make from a linguistic point of view. "A carefully graded selection of crosswords in order of complexity," maintains Bressan, "will contribute to the acquisition of new words and phrases as well as the consolidation of previous knowledge through repetition." Bressan classifies direct-definition clues into nine different headings:

1. *Generic.* Clue: Prénom. Answer: *Ils*

2. *Synonymic.* Clue: Tout naturel. Answer: Inné

3. *Antonymic.* Clue: Pas fictif. Answer: Réel

4. *Allusive.* Clue: Échappe au rêveur. Answer: Réalité.

5. *Allusive-negatory.* Clue: Bien de gens ne connaissent que sa marge. Answer: Loi.

6. *Definitory.* Clue: Dont rien ne vient troubler la quiétude. Answer: Sereine.

7. *Descriptive.* Clue: Recueillent des malheureux. Answer: Asiles.

8. *Punny.* Clue: Il avait vraiment la bosse du théâtre! Answer: Polichinelle.

9. *"In" clue.* Clue: Lettres d'amour. Answer: Am.

David E. Wolfe (1972) acknowledges Bressan's worthwhile contribution and offers a number of examples "as perhaps more realizable in the language class, assuming that the crossword puzzle is teacher- prepared and is based on material previously studied by the student." One of the examples Wolfe suggests is the picture clue. "Any concrete noun which the teacher can draw, " declares Wolfe, "is appropriate as a clue, assuming the noun has been taught."

Mollica (1987, 1988a,1988b, 1991a, 1991b, 1992a), for example, has published in various languages a series of line master puzzles based on everyday vocabulary themes. These puzzles are designed to test students have mastered the vocabulary and, at the same time, provide hours of fun in or outside the classroom scene. He presents four sets of puzzles, A,B,C,D, for each theme and arbitrarily chooses twenty words for each one. Each set builds upon the previous one, reviewing the words studied and then by adding new related vocabulary words to each puzzle. The final set, D, contains all 20 illustrated words without the printed words. The following is an example for the reinforcement and control of clothing vocabulary in English (Figure 7).

As it stands this language- teaching puzzle constitutes an elementary type of exercise, whereby the beginning student will simply associate each word with its visualizable referent and then write it into the crossword arrangement. More difficult uses of this puzzle can be envisioned as follows:

1. the words can be removed from the puzzle;

2. the visual referents can be replaced by definitions, synonyms, antonyms, etc.;

3. a story containing the vocabulary can be written and the student asked to select the items that fit into the crossword arrangement; and so on.

More recently, Phillips, Brown, Bannister and MacRae (1995: 9) have proposed "cooperative crossword puzzles," whereby four different clues are given and four students must work together. They suggest that

> Students work in groups of four. Each group is given one crossword puzzle grid and each member of the group is given a different set of clues (A,B,C,D). While the clues are different, they all relate to the same answer. Students take turns reading their clues and decide together on the answers. Generally all four clues are needed to determine the answer.

It is obvious that in constructing the various clues, the "key clue" not appear always on the same set. Such a practice would give one player always the upper hand for he/she would hold the clue to the answer.

For Phillips *et al.* cooperative crosswords provide students not only an opportunity to communicate but also a forum to develop further their social skills, such as valuing the opinions of others.

Anagrams

The followings anagram that can be used for word recognition and spelling in Italian (Danesi 1988: 152). In this case the words to be unscrambled give common first-conjugation verbs in Italian:

Anagrammando le lettere seguenti, trovare dieci verbi.

1. *GERLEGE (leggere)*

2. *ALPRARE (parlare)*

3. *ARMIPRAR (imparare)*

4. *GARANIME (mangiare)*

5. *ecc.*

Cryptograms

A cryptogram, such as the following, can be used for obvious word-recognition, syntactic, morphological, and discourse expectancy reinforcement and control in French (Danesi 1985a: 27). The hidden message, "L'amour est une grande illusion" translates, *Love is a great illusion.*

```
 _ '  M _ U _ _     _ _ _     _ _ _     _ _ _ _ _ _     _ _ _ _ _ _ _ _
 1  2 3 4 5 6      7 8 9     5 10 7    11 6 2 10 12 7   13 1  1  5  8 13 4 10
```

Tic-tac-toe

A tic-tac-toe puzzle in German that has an obvious lexico-semantic focus, by which the student is expected to find three words in a line that have something in common, is the following one (Danesi 1985a: 23). The answer is three types of fruits: *Apfel, Brine* and *Pfirsich.*

Apfel	Brine	Pfirsich
Blume	Land	Baum
Hand	Kopf	Buch

Word Circle

A word-circle puzzle in Spanish, can be used to test the plural formation of nouns (Danesi 1985a: 25).

Mazes

Mazes are also useful for both oral or writing (i.e., copying) activities. The task in Figure 11 is to visit all the French relatives only once, using the arrows as point of departure and point of return. As the student "visits" the relatives, each name can be either spoken or written out depending on the skill the teacher wishes to emphasize. Several answers are possible, thus providing variety to the activity.

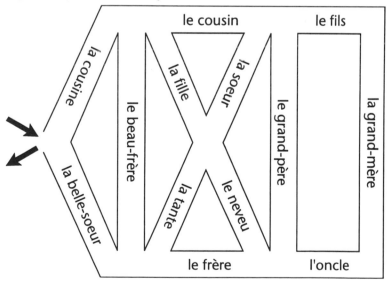

Meaning-Based Language-Teaching Puzzles

Language-teaching puzzles which focus the learner's attention on meaning are especially useful at intermediate and advanced levels. Riddles, sequences, logical deductions, and the like all allow the learner to employ the abstract language schemas of the target language fruitfully within the specific meaning domains outlined by the solution path of the puzzle.

Logical Puzzles

This type of puzzle provides factual infromation from which students draw a solution by logical thinking. These puzzles demand no technical mathematical knowledge, but "call for clear thinking and an ability to establish the logical relationships which the data presented imply." (Phillips, 1961: 2). Wylie best describes the method of obtaining a solution for such puzzles:

> By drawing clonclusions from it, and examining their consistency within the total framework of the problem, the answer is ultimately wrested from the seemingly incoherent information initially provided.

Consider as one example the following puzzle. Teachers may want to adapt this according to their teaching topics. The "professions" may be changed into "nationalities", into "food preferences," and so on.

MM. Martin, Blanchet et LeBlanc travaillent dans le même édifice. Ils sont banquier, avocat et bijoutier mais pas nécessairement dans cet ordre. Le bijoutier qui est l'ami de M. Blanchet est le plus jeune des trois. M. LeBlanc est plus âgé que l'avocat. Essayez ed deviner leur métier ou profession. (Mollica, 1976: 26)

In solving this problem, Danesi (1985) suggests a table in order to keep track of the possibilities. He suggests that an X be placed in the box of the item to be eliminated; if we conclude the opposite, he suggests an O. The table for the above puzzle will be as follows:

	banquier	avocat	bijoutier
M. Martin			
M. Blanchet			
M. LeBlanc			

The third sentence leads us to conclude that M. Blanchet is not the jeweller. We can, therefore, put an X in the appropriate cell in the array to eliminate M. Blanchet:

	banquier	avocat	bijoutier
M. Martin			
M. Blanchet			X
M. LeBlanc			

The fourth sentence allows us to conclude that M. LeBlanc is not the lawyer:

	banquier	avocat	bijoutier
M. Martin			
M. Blanchet			X
M. LeBlanc		X	

Sentence three and four also allow us to deduce that M. LeBlanc is not the ajeweller. This is because the jeweller is the youngest of the three, while M. LeBlanc is at least older than the lawyer:

	banquier	avocat	bijoutier
M. Martin			
M. Blanchet			X
M. LeBlanc		X	X

A look at the table makes it clear that M. LeBlanc is the banker. We note this by putting an O in the appropriate cell and eliminating the banker possibility for the other two:

	banquier	avocat	bijoutier
M. Martin	X		
M. Blanchet	X		X
M. LeBlanc	O	X	X

We now see that M. Blanchet is the lawyer and M. Martin is the jeweller. As a result of our careful reading the final table will look like this:

	banquier	avocat	bijoutier
M. Martin	X	X	O
M. Blanchet	X	O	X
M. LeBlanc	O	X	X

Tables may become more complex with some more difficult problems involving more than three items or people.

Consider, as an example, the following logical deduction puzzle in Italian (Mollica 1992: 110).

Il giovane Marco Ferrara ha chiesto una raccomandazione a Carlo Rossi, Mario Bruni, Paolo Moretti e Gianni Martino. Purtroppo non ricorda quale professione esercitano (avvocato, architetto, chirurgo, ingegnere). Sa che...

1. *Mario Bruni è più anziano dell'avvocato e dell'ingegnere.*
2. *Il chirurgo cena sempre da solo.*
3. *Mario Moretti cena spesso con Gianni Martino.*

4. *Il più anziano è anche il più ricco.*
5. *Carlo Rossi cena spesso in compagnia dell'avvocato e dell'ingegnere.*
6. *Gianni Martino è più anziano dell'avvocato e dell'ingegnere.*
7. *A Mario Bruni non piacciono le attività sportive.*
   Sapresti dirgli quale professione esercitano questi quattro signori?

The following table will be very useful in solving the problem.

	avvocato	ingegnere	chirurgo	architetto
Mario				
Paolo				
Gianni				
Carlo				

A table (similar to the one for the previous puzzle) can be set up to help the student keep track of the possibilities, alternatives, etc. An X in a cell indicates an elimination, and an O a finding.

It is not necessary to go into the details of the simple solution to this puzzle here. The reader will be able to figure out the answer with little difficulty. The important features to note here about the solution can be summarized in point form as follows:

These language-teaching puzzles allow the learner to become cognitively involved in the problem space created by the puzzle.

The learner must decipher the meaning of the language-teaching puzzle, making limited changes but creative ones to the components of its problem space.

By reflecting on the whole problem-solving event in conceptual and verbal ways, the learner assimilates the meaning-to-form relations that are inherent in the puzzle.

A few more examples will suffice to show the features that such puzzles embody.

Legal Cases

In a legal case such as the following French one (Mollica 1992b: 124-125), the student has to verbalize a plausible solution:

Si vous étiez le juge...

En écoutant le testament de feu M. Henri Marchand, Georges est très content d'apprendre qu'il va hériter du portefueill de son oncle. En recevant et en examinant le porte-feuille, il y trouve dix billets de cent dollars. Son cousin, jaloux, exige qu'il partage la somme avec lui. Georges soutient que son oncle lui a laissé à lui le portefeuille et, par conséquent, tout ce qu'il contient. Ce cas finit au tribunal.

Si vous étiez le juge, diviseriez-vous l'argent parmi le deux cousins ou donneriez-vous la somme entière à Georges?

(Choisissez parmi vous deux avocats: un qui plaidera la cause de Georges, l'autre qui représentera son cousin.

Sequencing

In the following sequencing problem in French (Mollica 1992b: 126), students are told that two anecdotes are out of sequence:

Un mauvais écrivain et un agent de police.

1. *Arrivé à "Conclusion du test d'haleine", il inscrit consciencieusement:*
2. *Un mauvais écrivain confie à un ami:*
3. *Puis l'agent rédige son rapport.*
4. *– Tiens! Il sait déjà lire!*
5. *Un agent de police arrête un automobiliste en état d'ébriété et le conduit au poste de police.*
6. *– Quelle catastrophe! Mon fils de quatre ans a jeté au feu mon manuscrit.*
7. *"Saint Émilion 1953."*
8. *On lui fait passer tous les tests, y inclus un examen à l'alcotest.*

(Answers: *Anecdote 1:* 5,8,3,1,7; *Anecdote 2:* 2,6,4.)

More examples and discussions of meaning-based language-teaching puzzles can be found in Wright, Betteridge, and Buckby 1979, Maley and Grellet 1981, McKay 1985, Danesi 1985a, and Mollica 1992b.

Communication-Based Language-Teaching Games

The literature on this type of language-teaching game is quite extensive, but the reader can consult Schultz and Fisher (1988) for a good comprehensive typology. The general definition of a language- teaching game is a problem-solving game that involves more than one learner. So, it unfolds in terms of a group-based, interactive format that focuses on language use and meaning negotiation. Games like *Charades, What's My Line?* and others (including board and card games), that create contexts in which the language is used in discourse-appropriate ways, constitute communication-based language-teaching games. Here are some examples that are self-explanatory.

Charades

Danesi (1985a: 45) proposes the following activity for charades:

Rules/Procedures:

> The class can be divided into two teams once again, and the object is to guess a word or expression that a member of each team must act out in pantomime. Team members are allowed to ask questions and make statements in the target language. The words or expressions are prepared in advance by the teacher and put into a box from which each team draws. The team taking the least time overall to guess the answer wins.

Instructional Objectives/Types of Communication Skills:

By tying the words and expressions to some theme or unit, the primary objective of this game is to review vocabulary. However, since it requires the students to participate verbally in finding a solution, it also encourages the use of the language in an autonomous and meaningful way.

Family Feud

Danesi (1985a: 48) suggests that even the ever popular TV show "Family Feud" can be a source for communication-based language-teaching games.

Rules/Procedures:

The teacher should survey a group of students on a series of general questions (your favourite colour, make of car, type of food, and so on). The frequency of each response is then tabulated. The class is divided into two teams. Ten questions are asked by the teacher in the target language and a student delegated by each team must attempt to respond to all questions within a specified time frame (for example, one minute). The answers of the two students must be different. The more popular the answer according to the survey, the higher the score. Each team then chooses a different player for the next ten questions, and the game continues as before. At the end, the scores are added up, and the team with the highest score is declared the winner.

Instructional Objectives/Types of Communicative Skills:

This game is clearly useful in building up the ability to understand and respond to target language messages. This type of activity con- sequently develops fluency. Vocabulary is also practised.

Biographical Bingo

Dickson 1992: 231-232) suggests Biographical Bingo For the achievement of similar objectives.

Played in the same way as "Find Someone who...," but uses a Bingo grid for the actions. As in Bingo, the winner is the student who finds people for 5 spaces in a row.

Questions and Answers

For a questions-and-answer activity, designed to stimulate oral participation in the classroom, Dickson (1992: 237) proposes the following:

Form two teams. Using a large picture or map on the wall, the teacher calls out a word indicating an object or a place. One team must form a question about that object or place and the other team must answer the question. Each team wins points for correct questions or answers.

Purpose: Students get practice in both asking and answering questions. If a picture is used, the game can review certain vocabulary. If a map is used, it could review geography.

Predicaments

For this interactive activity, Dickson (1992: 236) suggest that:

One student leaves the room while the other students think of a predicament such as running out of gas, the school burning down, losing their money, getting home long after their curfew, etc. The student who went out returns and asks the others in turn: "Qu'est-ce tu ferais si ceci t'arivais?" Each person must give a reasonable answer based on the predicament agreed on. The student whose answer finally reveals the predicament is "It" next.

Concluding Remarks

It is perhaps useful to conclude this essays by reviewing some of the main aspects of puzzleological techniques in second-language teaching in point form:

- These techniques have an important role to play in second-language teaching as versatile exercises, drills, etc. alongside other kinds of practice and reinforcement techniques.
- Although there is no experimental literature on the learning- efficacy of language-teaching puzzles, and only a handful of studies on the psychological effectiveness of language-teaching games, there are no indications or evidence to the contrary, namely data showing that puzzleological techniques are ineffectual or detrimental. More research is obviously required in this domain.
- Language-teaching puzzles are useful as form-based and meaning-based reinforcement and control activities.
- Language-teaching games are useful as communication-based activities.
- Although there exists some evidence that entire courses or curricula can be based on a language-teaching game approach (e.g. Palmer and Rodgers 1983, Miller 1991), by and large puzzleological techniques are useful primarily as supplementary or complementary activities that can be used in tandem with other techniques within broader methodological and curricular frameworks.
- These techniques should be given the same treatment and weight as other exercises, drills, and activities; otherwise the student will tend not to take them seriously.
- Both teacher and students must find puzzleological technique enjoyable; otherwise they will become counterproductive.
- Given all these provisions, we are convinced, as have been many teachers over the last three decades, that puzzleological techniques have as much a role to play in second-language teaching as they have been shown to have in many other areas of education.

Our purpose in this revisitation was not to be exhaustive, nor to be innovative in showing how language-teaching puzzles and language-teaching games can be incorporated into second-language teaching. Our goal was simply to highlight the diversity and versatility of these recreational forms of language and communication exercise and practice. We conclude by emphasizing one more time to the reader that puzzleological techniques do not constitute a method or an educational paradigm. They are enjoyable activities that can be used together with other kinds of practice devices for reinforcement, review, thinking, control, and communication in the classroom. All these techniques really aim to do is to achieve the same kinds of exercise and practice goals that more traditional drills and activities do. But, they inject so much fun into the process that they end up invariably fostering a positive attitude in teacher and students alike to the learning tasks at hand. And this is the primary condition for learning to occur.

References

Berk, L.E. 1994. "Vygotsky's Theory: The Importance of Make-Believe Play." *Young Children*, 50, 1: 30-39.

Bressan, D. 1970. "Crossword Puzzles in Modern Language Teaching." *Audio-Visual Language Journal*, 8: 93-95.

Caré, J.M. and F. Debyser. 1978. *Jeu, langage et creativité*. Paris: Hachette.

Cicogna, Caterina, Marcel Danesi, and Anthony Mollica, eds. 1992. *Problem-Solving in Second-Language Teaching*. Welland, Ontario: éditions Soleil publishing inc.

Crawshaw, B.E. 1972. *Let's Play Games in French*. Skokie: National Textbook Co.

Crookall, D., ed. 1985. *Simulation Applications in L2 Education and Research*. Special Issue. *System*, 13, 3.

Crookall, D. and R. Oxford, eds. 1988. *Language Learning Through Simulation/Gaming*. New York: New-bury House-Harper and Row.

Crookall, D. and D. Saunders, eds. 1989. *Communication and Simulation: From Two Fields to One Theme*. Clevedon: Multilingual Matters.

Crookall, D., C. Greenblat, A. Coote, J. Klabbers, and D.R. Watson, eds. 1987. *Simulation-Gaming in the Late 1980's*. New York: Pergamon.

Danesi, Marcel. 1979. "Puzzles in Language Teaching." *The Canadian Modern Language Review/La Revue canadienne des langues vivantes*, 35: 269-277.

Danesi, Marcel. 1985a. *A Guide to Puzzles and Games in Second Language Pedagogy*. Toronto: Ontario Institute for Studies in Education Press.

Danesi, Marcel. 1985b. *Language Games in Italian*. Toronto: University of Toronto Press.

Danesi, Marcel. 1987. "The Psychology and Methodology of Puzzles and Games in L2 Teaching." In: J. Lantolf and A. Labarca, eds., *Research in Second Language Learning: Focus on the Classroom*, pp. 107-116. Norwood, N.J.: Ablex.

Danesi, Marcel. 1988. *Manuale di tecniche per la didattica delle lingue moderne*. Roma: Armando.

De Vries, D.L. and R.E. Slavin. 1978. "Teams Games Tournaments: Review of Ten Classroom Experiments." *Journal of Research and Development in Education*. 12: 23-38.

Dickson, P. S. 1992. "Quick and Easy Games for Language Learning." In Caterina Cicogna, Marcel Danesi, and Anthony Mollica, eds. *Problem-Solving in Second-Language Teaching*, pp. 223-241. Welland, Ont.: éditions Soleil publishing inc.

Edwards, K., D.L. De Vries, and J.P. Snyder. 1972. "Games and Teams: A Winning Combination." *Simulation and Games*. 3: 247-269.

Ervin, G. L. 1982. "Using Warm-Ups, Wind-Ups, and Fillers: All of Your Class Time is Valuable." *Foreign Language Annals*, 15: 95-99.

Fixx, J. F. 1983. *Solve It!* London: Muller.

Gowan, J.C., J. Khatena, and E.P. Torrance, eds. 1981. *Creativity: Its Educational Implications.* Dubuque: Kendall-Hunt.

Hendrickson, J. M. 1980. "Listening and Speaking Activities for Foreign Language Learners." *The Canadian Modern Language Review/La Revue canadienne des langues vivantes,* 36: 735-748.

Hendrickson, J.M. 1983. "Listening and Speaking Activities for Foreign Language Learners: Second Collection." *The Canadian Modern Language Review/La Revue canadienne des langues vivantes,* 39: 267-284.

Hupb, L.B. 1974. *Let's Play Games in Spanish.* Skokie, Illinois: National Textbook Co.

Irwing, P. 1982. "Games for Use at the Intermediate Level." *The Canadian Modern Language Review/La Revue canadienne des langues vivantes,* 38: 726-727.

Jones, K. 1982. *Simulations in Language Teaching.* Cambridge: Cambridge University Press.

Jones, K. 1986. *Designing Your Own Simulations.* New York: Methuen.

Latorre, G. and G. Baeza. 1975. "The Construction and Use of EFL Crossword Puzzles." *English Language Teaching Journal,* 30:45-55.

Lee, W.R. 1965. *Language Teaching Games and Contests.* Oxford: Oxford University Press.

Lesgold, A. 1988. "Problem Solving." In R. J. Sternberg and E.E. Smith, eds., *The Psychology of Human Thought,* pp. 188-213. Cambridge: Cambridge University Press.

Livingston, S.A. and S.J. Kidder. 1973. "Role Identification and Game Structure: Effects on Political Attitudes." *Simulation and Games,* 4: 131-144.

Loftus, G.R. and E.F. Loftus. 1983. *Mind at Play.* New York: Basic Books.

Maley, A. and F. Grellet. 1981. *Mind Matters.* Cambridge: Cambridge University Press.

McKay, S. L. 1985. *Teaching Grammar.* Oxford: Pergamon Press.

Millington,Roger. 1977. *Crossword Puzzles. Their History and Their Cult.* New York: Pocket Books.

Miller, M.C. 1992. *Two Experimental Studies of the Effectiveness of Interactive Game-Playing in the Acquisition of Japanese by American Students.* Ph.D. Dissertation, University of Delaware.

Mohr, M.S. 1993. *The Games Treasury.* Shelburne: Chapters.

Mollica, Anthony. 1979. "Games and Activities in the Italian High School Classroom." *Foreign Language Annals,* 12: 347-354.

Mollica, Anthony, ed. 1980-1981. *Les Gamins.* Toronto: Grolier.

Mollica, Anthony. 1981. "Visual Puzzles in the Second Language Classroom." *The Canadian Modern Language Review/La Revue canadienne des langues vivantes,* 37: 583-622.

Mollica, Anthony. 1987 *Mots croisés pour les débutants.* Welland, Ontario: éditions Soleil publishing inc.

Mollica, Anthony. 1988a. *Crossword Puzzles for Beginners.* Welland, Ontario: éditions Soleil publishing inc.

Mollica, Anthony. 1988b. *Crucigramas para principiantes.* Welland, Ontario: éditions Soleil publishing inc.

Mollica, Anthony. 1991a. *Parole crociate per principianti.* Welland, Ontario: éditions Soleil publishing inc.

Mollica, Anthony. 1991b *Latin Crossword Puzzles for Beginners.* Welland, Ontario: éditions Soleil publishing inc.

Mollica, Anthony. 1992a *Palavras cruzadas para principiantes.* Welland, Ontario: éditions Soleil publishing inc.

Mollica, Anthony. 1992b. "Reinforcing Language Skills through Problem-Solving and Pencil and Paper Activities." In Caterina Cicogna, Marcel Danesi, and Anthony Mollica, eds. *Problem-Solving in Second-Language Teaching,* pp. 102-129. Welland, Ontario: éditions Soleil publishing inc.

Mollica, Anthony. 1992c. *A te la scelta! Libro primo.* Welland, Ontario: éditions Soleil publishing inc.

Mollica, Anthony. (in preparation). *Buscapalabras.* Welland, Ontario: éditions Soleil publishing inc.

Munzert, A.W. 1991. *Test Your I.Q.* New York: Prentice-Hall.

Musumeci, D. 1992. "Selecting Games for the Second-Language Classroom: Criteria for Multiple Functions." In Caterina Cicogna, Marcel Danesi, and Anthony Mollica, eds., *Problem-Solving in Second-Language Teaching,* pp. 242-253. Welland, Ontario: éditions Soleil publishing inc.

Nuessel, F. 1994. "Recreational Problem-Solving Activities for Teaching Vocabulary and Intermediate Spanish." *Hispania,* 77: 118-124.

Omaggio, A. 1978. *Games and Simulations in the Foreign Language Classroom.* Washington, D. C.: Center for Applied Linguistics.

Omaggio, A. 1982. "Using Games and Interactional Activities for the Development of Functional Proficiency in a Second Language." *The Canadian Modern Language Review/La Revue canadienne des langues vivantes,* 38: 515-546.

Palmer, A. and T.S. Rodgers. 1983. "Games in Language Teaching." *Language Teaching,* 16:2-21.

Perkins, D.N. 1988. "Creativity and the Quest for Mechanism." In R.J. Sternberg and E.E. Smith, eds., *The Psychology of Human Thought,* pp. 309-336. Cambridge: Cambridge University Press.

Phillips, Gail, Doreen Brown, Sheila Bannister, and Lori MacRae. 1995 "Cooperative Crosswords." *Communication. Newsletter of The Ontario Modern Language Teachers' Association.* Winter, 9-10.

Phillips, Hubert. 1961. *My Best Puzzles in Logic and Reasoning.* New York: Dover.

Rixon, S. 1981. *How to Use Games in Language Teaching.* London: Macmillan.

Rodgers, T.S. 1981. "A Framework for Making and Using Language Teaching Games." In *Guidelines for Language Games,* pp. 1-7. Singapore: RELC.

Savignon, S. 1992. "Problem-Solving and the Negotiation of Meaning in Second-Language Theory and Practice." In Caterina Cicogna, Marcel Danesi, and Anthony Mollica, eds., *Problem-Solving in Second-Language Teaching,* pp. 11-25. Welland, Ontario: éditions Soleil publishing inc..

Sawyers, J.K. and C.S. Rogers. 1994. *Helping Children Develop through Play.* Washington: National Association for the Education of Young Children.

Schloss, B. 1977. *Jeux linguistiques.* Toronto: OISE Press.

Schmidt, E. 1977. *Let's Play Games in German.* Skokie: National Textbook Co.

Schultz, M. and A. Fisher. 1988. *Games for All Reasons: Interacting in the Language Classroom.* Reading: Addison-Wesley.

Steinberg, J. 1991. *Games Language People Play.* Markham, Ontario: Dominie Press.

Webster, M. and E. Castonon. 1980. *Crosstalk: Communication Tasks and Games at the Elementary, Preintermediate and Intermediate Levels.* Oxford: Oxford University Press.

Wells, D. 1992. *The Penguin Book of Curious and Interesting Puzzles.* Harmondsworth: Penguin.

Wolfe, D. E. 1972. "Teacher-Made Crossword Puzzles." *Audio-Visual Language Journal.* 10:177-181.

Wylie, C.R. 1957. *101 Puzzles in Logic and Reasoning.* New Tork Dover.

Wright, A., D. Betteridge, and M. Buckby. 1979. *Games for Language Learning.* Cambridge: Cambridge University Press.

Reprinted from: Marcel Danesi and Anthony Mollica, "Games and Puzzles in the Second-Language Classroom: A Second Look," *Mosaic,* 2, 2 (Winter 1994), pp. 14-22.

31 Postage Stamps: A Pedagogical Tool in the Language Classroom

Frank Nuessel

Postage stamps provide second-language instructors with colourful and appealing materials to emphasize the four language skills and to introduce cultural topics.

Introduction

Postage stamps are fascinating official public documents. The hobby of philately, in fact, is one of the most popular avocations in the world. The variety of postage stamps created annually by each nation provides a rich resource for second-language (henceforth, L2) instructors who wish to introduce these colourful cultural artifacts in their curriculum.

Jung (1981) cites four essential functions attributed to the postage stamp:
- They are official documents that constitute receipts for revenues collected by a sovereign stage
- Stamps serve as collectors' items for a variety of people (amateur hobbyists, investors, professional philatelists, people with an interest in popular culture, and so forth.)
- These cultural documents have propaganda value frequently exploited by different nations (Stoetzer 1953).
- They constitute an official vehicle to commemorate persons, places, events, and objects highly valued by specific nations at different points in time.

To Jung's (1981) four functions of the postage stamp, one can add a fifth, i.e., a didactic or instructional purpose (Nuessel 1984c). Several factors make the postage stamp an appealing pedagogical resource. Issuance of these paper documents provides an annual thematic diversity at a relatively low cost. Moreover, many countries exert a high degree of quality control over their production to ensure that these popular icons have a great deal of visual appeal. Furthermore, postage stamps offer important insights into the cultural and political values of other nations.

Rationale for Visual Materials in the Second-Language Classroom

Postage stamps are outstanding visual aids for use in the L2 classroom because they are colourful and may be displayed in a variety of formats

(Overhead projector, slide projector, photocopy, and display of the specimens themselves).

Recognition of the significance of the visual dimension in pedagogy has received much attention (Mollica 1976, 1978, 1979, 1981; Danesi 1983, 1990; Hammerly 1995). Wright (1989), for example, notes three reasons for the inclusion of visuals in the L2 classroom; namely,

- interest and motivation
- a sense of the context of the language
- a specific reference point of stimulus.

Moreover, Stevick (1986) has long argued persuasively for the use of images and imagery to enhance language instruction. Recent work on brain research and its application to L2 education points out that a visual component improves learner retention of materials introduced in this way (Danesi, 1987, 1988a,b,c; Danesi and Mollica 1988; Brown and Mollica 1988-1989; Mollica and Danesi 1995). This claim is, in fact, borne out by psychological research in the psychological subdiscipline of mental imagery (Finke 1989). Danesi's (1988a,c) findings show that in order to be effective, i.e., to assist in recall, the second-language teacher must tap into both hemispheres of the brain. Nevertheless, Hammerly (1995) points out that visual aids must be used properly to be effective. According to Hammerly (1995), appropriate introduction of visuals requires a suitable atmosphere, motivation, focus of attention, a context, explanatory support, general comprehension, mnemonic support, cultural insights, and conversational stimuli if the visuals are to be pedagogically effective. We believe that postage stamps fulfill all these requirements.

Pedagogical Activities for the L2 Classroom

Strategies for incorporating postage stamps into second-language curriculum may focus on the four skills (listening comprehension, speaking, reading and writing) and cultural awareness.

Listening Comprehension

Exercises designed to enhance students' listening comprehension are very important in L2 acquisition. One strategy once again involves the projection of the images of postage stamps on a screen with an overhead projector or slide projector. In this activity, the teacher asks specific questions based on the content represented on the projected icon, as well as any ancillary presented in previous class sessions. Students then write a brief response during a timed pause. Another technique would involve oral questions with a set of multiple-choice responses on a sheet of paper provided to students.

A specific example of listening comprehension exercise might involve Figure 1. The students would view the document and then m\be asked specific questions to which they would respond on a sheet of paper. Since Figure 1 is a map, the teacher might provide a limited series of questions based on the map itself. Thus the following questions might be used for Figure 1:

Figure 2

← Figure 1

- *In what part of South America is Columbia located?*
- *What countries are contiguous with Colombia?*
- *What is the capital of Colombia?*
- *What South American countries are not depicted on the postage stamp?*
- *What ocean borders Colombia?*

The teacher might also construct a multiple-choice test with questions related to the content of the postage stamp.

Speaking

Many L2 scholars, as noted above, are vigorous advocates of pedagogical graphics in the L2 classroom. Because of the wide variety of images depicted on postage stamps, these official documents can provide a visual stimulus to engage students in meaningful communicative activities. The projection of a postage stamp on an overhead projector or on a slide is an excellent way to evoke response from students.

The art of creative questioning is an important technique in its own right as Mollica (1994) and Richards (1995) have noted. In virtually all the exercises that we discuss, appropriate questioning strategies are important for eliciting student responses. Questioning as a means of eliciting verbal responses from students may involve the following behaviours (Mollica 1994):

- knowledge (remembering)
- comprehension (understanding)

- application (transferring)
- analysis (relating)
- synthesis (creating)
- evaluation (judging).

We would suggest that the five questions that might be asked in relation to the following stamp (Figure 2) which depicts bicyclists pedalling up mountainous terrain.

- *What are these people doing?*
- *Where are they?*
- *What time is it?*
- *Where are they?*
- *What season is it?*

Figure 3

Figure 4

Reading

Various nations occasionally issue postage stamps that feature a well-known quotation from a literary work to commemorate a prestigious author or famous literary work. Such citations, of course, constitute the briefest of all possible texts. Nevertheless, these key passages can form a point of departure for the discussion of various authors and their literary works. The instructor can ask students if they can locate these important excerpts in the original work. When students engage in this activity, they will read significant portions of the original text itself. The example in Figure 3 is a page from the illuminated edition of Dante's *Divine Comedy*.

Writing

Development of writing skills is another dimension of acquiring a L2. Students frequently state that they are unable to think of a suitable theme for a writing assignment (see Nuessel and Cicogna 1993, 1994). For this reason, it is necessary to provide the members of the language class with an explicit set of questions to facilitate what some students consider to be the awesome task of writing in another language.

One strategy again involves the projection of a postage stamp image on a screen in the classroom. In this approach, the students would receive a previously prepared paper with a set of questions to be answered. In responding to these questions, the students would, in effect, have written a mini-composition. In the case of Figure 4 which depicts Christopher Columbus soliciting funds from Queen Isabella for his proposed new route to Asia, the following questions might be used.

- *Who are these people?*
- *Where are they?*
- *What are they doing?*
- *What is the significance of this historical event?*
- *What other nations of the world were involved in this event?*
- *How is this event commemorated today?*

The following strategy may be more exciting, and more challenging to students. In this type of exercise, students view a postage stamp, and the instructor asks students to suggest an appropriate caption to describe the graphic scene illustrated. The purpose of this activity is to summarize the action depicted (Figure 5). In this instance, the postage stamp depicts a figure of a hockey player, and was issued in anticipation of the Winter Olympics held in Calgary, Alberta, in 1988.

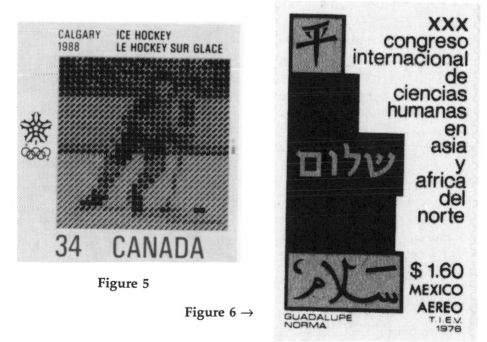

Figure 5

Figure 6 →

Cultural Comprehension

One of the goals of a second-language course is to enhance the understanding of another culture. Kroeber and Kluckhohn (1960) have provided the following useful definition of culture:

Culture consists of patterns of and for behaviour and transmitted by symbols, constituting the distinctive achievements of human groups, including their embodiments in artifacts; the essential core of culture consists of traditional [= historically derived and selected] ideas and especially their attached values.

That culture has many distinct manifestations becomes obvious when viewing postage stamps which feature virtually every possible example of a nation's culture (literature, music, sculpture, painting, monuments, historic figures, and so forth).

Ian Finlay was one of the first language instructors to recognize the potential value of postage stamps as pedagogical instruments in an article published in 1968. His suggestions for the use of postage stamps in the classroom (linguistic history, alphabets, orthography, bilingualism, isolated vocabulary, texts and quotations, history of literature) deal with various manifestations of culture.

It is wise to present the students with an example of the type of finished product that a cultural investigation should involve. For this reason, we advocate that the teacher provide a model for the students to follow. The instructor may wish to provide an in-depth discussion of a single theme exemplified by a series of postage stamp images on a screen in the classroom. An evaluation of this lesson might involve short-answer questions, a multiple-choice quiz, or even a true-false format.

Another strategy involves the assignment of a single postage stamp to students in the class, together with a set of generic questions related to its content. When the students have completed research on the answers to the questions,they will then present a brief in-class oral presentation of their findings. Exemplary questions for this type of research activity include the following:

- *What does the person (event, musical piece, painting, sculpture) on the postage stamp represent?*
- *To what historical period does the person/work of art belong?*
- *Who is this person (date and place of birth, date and place of death)?*
- *In the case of a work of art, have you seen/read/heard the piece? Where? Did you like it? Why? Why not?*

Yet another activity involves small groups of students engaged in the creation of a thematic project on well-known people who speak the second-language of the classroom. Each group of students would be charged with gathering appropriate postage stamps, and carrying out research on this theme. Such a project might involve a competition. The completed projects then could be displayed in the school, public library, or local business. A side benefit of this kind of project is provide positive publicity for your second-language program.

The following topics, derived in part from Finlay (1968), demonstrate some of the interesting themes for students to explore and for which existing research is already available.

World Writing Systems

Contemporary world writing systems vary widely. DeFrancis (1989), an authoritative scholar in writing systems, categorizes the world's systems in the following way:

- The "pure" alphabetic systems (Greek, Latin)
- The meaning-plus-sound systems (English, Korean)
- The "pure" consonantal systems (Hebrew, Arabic)
- The "pure" syllabic systems (Japanese, Yi).

Many of these systems appear regularly on postage stamps (Nuessel 1984a,c). One Mexican postage stamp (Figure 6) exemplifies the word for "peace" in Chinese, Japanese, Hindi, and Arabic scripts.

Another interesting example relates to the fact that the nations of North Korea and South Korea have set aside October 9 *(Han'Gul Day)* as a national holiday to celebrate the promulgation of the Korean writing system in 1456 by royal decree during the reign of King Sejong (1418-1450). The writing system and King Sejong are depicted on Figure 7. (See Nuessel 1984a,e for further discussion.)

Bilingualism and Multilingualism

Switzerland, with its three official languages (French, German, Italian) and one national language, the Romance language known as *Romansch* provides multilingual lexical examples (Figure 8). This stamp features the phrase *Eliminate obstacles* in the three official languages of Switzerland.

Canada, an officially bilingual nation, provides vocabulary items and phrases in English and French (Figures 9 and 10). (See also Wood 1979, 1980). These postage stamps feature handicrafts created by Canada's Inuit population. Such specimen demonstrate Canada's commitment to the notion of being a nation where the "cultural mosaic", i.e., the maintenance of its multicultural foundations is fundamentally important.

Walker (1969) studied the variety of languages found on postage stamps and found that approximately 100 of an estimated 2,800 (his figures) world languages appear on various postage stamps. According to his calculations,the most frequently used are English, French, German, latin, Spanish, Arabic, and Italian. Nearly all the languages found on postage stamps are currently spoken vernacular. Nevertheless, some "dead" languages such as Greek, Punic, Old Egyptian, Old Norse, and Latin are printed on these official documents. The created, or planned language, Esperanto has appeared on numerous postage stamps (Nuessel 1984b). See Figure 11.

Famous Historical Personages

Another activity is to carry out a detailed study of a well-known historical person such as Andrés Bello (1781-1865). Though born in Caracas, Venezuela, he spent most of his life in Chile where his achievements were extraordinary. Figure 12 (See Nuessel 1985a).

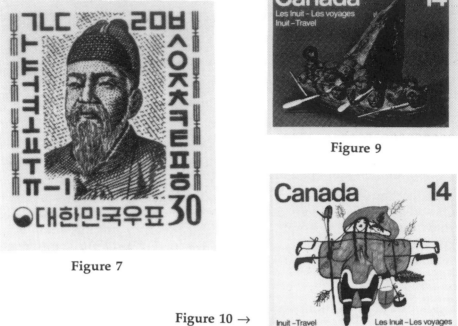

Figure 9

Figure 7

Figure 10 →

Figure 8

Likewise, the system of raised dots developed by France's Louis Braille's (1809-1852) (see Nuessel 1985b) allowed blind people to "read" with their hands (Figure 13).

Territorial Boundaries

Many nations have utilized postage stamps as a means of asserting territorial claims or boundary disputes in a public way (Nuessel 1992). The publication of maps which depict a particular are within the territorial domain of a given nation provides that nation with a means of affirming

Figure 12

← Figure 11

Figure 14

← Figure 13

the right to a given geographical area. One example of this is seen in Figure 14. On this postage stamp, issued prior to the initiation of hostilities with England, the sentence, *Las Malvinas son argentinas* ("The Malvinas Islands are Argentine") has been inscribed. The British, of course, call this very same territory the Falkland Islands.

Recommendations for the Use of Postage Stamps in the L2 Classroom

Nuessel and Cicogna (1992) provide a series of recommendations to the L2 teacher for the incorporation of postage stamps into the curriculum which we reproduce here, in part and with some modifications.

- Accumulate a sufficient number of inexpensive postage stamps to permit a variety of activities in a given class. Such a collection ought to include cultural themes (fine arts, literature, science, historical and political events). See for example,

  Linn's Stamp News, P. O. Box 29, Sidney, OH 45365; and

  The American Philatelist, P. O. Box 8000, State College, PA 16803; or

  Topical Time, P. O. Box 630, Johnstown, PA 15907

  for sources of materials as well as local philatelic shops in your yellow pages.
- Acquire the modest amount of paraphernalia necessary to handle and display postage stamps properly (tongs, protective cellophane containers, and display mounts).
- Consult a current, basic reference catalogue to determine prices and kinds of postage stamps available. (Consult the *1996 Standard Postage Stamp Catalogue*, 6 vols. Sidney, OH: Scott Publishing Company, 1995). This important basic reference is available in most public libraries.
- Refer to previous research on the incorporation of postage stamps into the second-langauge classroom (Di Napoli, 1980; Elton 1979; Finlay 1968, Jung 1981, Nuessel 1984a,b,c,d,e, 1985, 1992; Nuessel and Cicogna 1992; Stoetzer 1953; Walker 1969; Wood 1979, 1980).
- Prepare colour slides of stamps on specific themes (literature, painting, music) to be presented periodically to the L2 class. An alternate method of display is the use of transparencies on the overhead projector. McKay (1981), for example, discusses inexpensive procedures for achieving this objective.
- Prepare a separate file folder for each type of activity to allow the recycling of successful techniques and the elimination of ineffective strategies.
- Present various activities to ensure that everyone is familiar with the regulations and procedures. The time spent initially in establishing a routine will facilitate future reintroduction of the activities.
- Evaluate the activities so that students know that these form an integral part of the L2 curriculum and are not "frills". In most instances, the formats on the classroom exercises can be used as a means of assessment. (See Nuessel 1991 for assessment strategies).

Concluding Remarks

The above suggestions are only small sample of the incorporation of postage stamps into L2 curriculum,m for pedagogical purposes. The instructional possibilities for these documents are virtually limitless. Creative teachers and students alike will be able to utilize postage stamps for a wide variety of learning situations. We believe that teachers will find them as stimulating for L2 curriculum as we do.

References

Brown James W. and Anthony Mollica, eds. 1988-1989. *Essays in Applied Visual Semiotics.* Monograph Series of the Toronto Semiotic Circle, 3. Toronto: Toronto Semiotic Circle.

Danesi, Marcel. 1983. "Pedagogical graphics in Second-Language Teaching." *The Canadian Modern Language Review/La Revue canadienne des langues vivantes,* 40, 1: 73-81.

Danesi, Marcel. 1987. "Practical Applications of Current Brain Research to the Teaching of Italian." *Italica,* 64:377-392.

Danesi, Marcel. 1988a. *Cervello, linguaggio ed educazione.* Roma: Bulzoni Editore.

Danesi, Marcel. 1988b. *Neurolinguistica e glottodidattica.* Padova: Liviana Editrice.

Danesi, Marcel. 1988c. "Neurolinguistic Bimodality and Theories of Language Teaching." *Studies in Second Language Acquisition,* 10:13-31.

Danesi, Marcel. 1990. "Thinking is Seeing: Visual Metaphors and the Nature of Abstract Thought." *Semiotica,* 80, 3-4:221-237.

Danesi, Marcel and Anthony Mollica. 1988. "From Right to Left: A "Bimodal" Perspective of Language Learning." *The Canadian Modern language Review/La Revue canadienne des langues vivantes,* 45:76-90.

DeFrancis, John. 1989. *Visible Speech: The Diverse Openness of Writing Systems.* Honolulu: University of Hawaii Press.

Di Napoli, Thomas. 1980 "Postage Stamps and the Teaching of GDR Culture and Civilization." *Unterrichtspraxis,* 13, 2: 193-205.

Elton, Maurice G. 1979. "Culture Via Airmail." *Foreign Language Annals,* 12, 2: 117-120.

Finke, Ronald A. 1989. *Principles of Mental Imagery.* Cambridge, MA: Michigan Institute of Technology Press.

Finlay, Ian F. 1968. "Postage Stamps in Modern Language Teaching." *Modern Languages,* 48: 119-121.

Hammerly, Hector. 1995. "What Visual Aids Can and Cannot Do in Second-Language Teaching." *Mosaic,* 2, 3:11-18.

Jung, Udo H. 1981. "Germany through Stamps." *Unterrichtspraxis,* 14, 2: 246-259.

Kroeber, A.L. and Clyde Kluckhon. 1960 *Culture: A Critical Review of Concepts and Definitions.* New York: Vintage Books.

McKay, Douglas R. 1981. "The In-House Approach to Visual Aids." *Hispania,* 54:494-495.

Mollica, Anthony. 1978. "The Film Advertisement: A Source for Language Activities." *The Canadian Modern Language Review/La Revue canadienne des langues vivantes,* 34: 221-243.

Mollica, Anthony. 1979. "*A Tiger in Your Tank:* Advertisement in the Language Classroom." *The Canadian Modern Language Review/la Revue canadienne des langues vivantes,* 35: 691-743.

Mollica, Anthony. 1981. "Visual Puzzles in the Second Language Classroom." *The Canadian Modern Language Review/La Revue canadienne des langues vivantes,* 37: 583-622.

Mollica,Anthony. 1994. "Planning for Successful Teaching: Questioning Strategies." *Mosaic*, 2, 4: 18-20.

Mollica, Anthony and Marcel Danesi. 1995. "The Foray into the Neurosciences: Have We Learned Anything Useful?" *Mosaic*, 2, 4: 12-20.

Nuessel, Frank. 1984a. "The Commemoration of the Korean Alphabet on Postage Stamps." *The American Philatelist*, 98, 11: 1100-1101, 1145.

Nuessel, Frank. 1984b. "Esperanto on Postage Stamps." *The American Philatelist*, 98, 5:453-456.

Nuessel, Frank. 1984c. "Postage Stamps as Instructional Aids in the Foreign Language Classroom." *The American Philatelist*, 98, 1: 46-48.

Nuessel, Frank. 1984d. "Teaching Hispanic Culture with Postage Stamps." *The Canadian Modern Language Review/La Revue canadienne des langues vivantes*, 40:429-439.

Nuessel, Frank. 1984e. "World Writing Systems on Postage Stamps." *Topical Time*, 35, 6: 14-15.

Nuessel, Frank. 1985a. "André Bello: Hispanic Renaissance Figure." *The American Philatelist*, 99, 7:643-644.

Nuessel, Frank. 1985b, "Louis Braille Helped the Sightless to See." *The American Philatelist*, 99, 11: 1005- 1007.

Nuessel, Frank. 1991 "Foreign Language Testing Today." In Richard V. Teschner, ed., *Assessing Foreign Language Proficiency of Undergraduates*. Boston: Heinle and Heinle, pp. 1-20.

Nuessel, Frank. 1992. "Territorial and Boundary Disputes Depicted on Postage Stamps." *Studies in Latin American Popular Culture*, 11: 123-141.

Nuessel, Frank and Caterina Cicogna. 1992. "Postage Stamps as Pedagogical Instruments in the Italian Curriculum." *Italica*, 69: 210-227.

Nuessel, Frank and Caterina Cicogna. 1993. "Teaching Writing in Elementary and Intermediate Classes: Suggestions and Activities." *Mosaic*, 1, 2: 6-8.

Nuessel, Frank and Caterina Cicogna. 1994. "Writing in the Elementary and Intermediate Italian Class: Theory, Practice and Assessment." *Romance Languages Annual*, 5: 265-271.

Richards, Merle. 1995. "Planning for Successful Teaching: Questioning in the Language Classroom." *Mosaic*, 2, 3: 21-22.

Stevick, Earl W. 1986. *Images and Options in the Language Classroom*. Cambridge: Cambridge University Press.

Stoetzer, Carlos. 1953. *Postage Stamps as Propaganda*. Washington, DC: Public Affairs Press.

Walker, Ralph. 1969. "Languages on Stamps." *Scott's Monthly Stamp Journal*, 50, 9: 289, 292-293, 301. [Reprinted in *Topical Digest*, 1972, 7: 23-25.]

Wood, Richard E. 1979. "Teaching *Francophonie* with Postage Stamps." *The Canadian Modern Language Review/La Revue canadienne des langues vivantes*, 36, 1: 105-124.

Wood, Richard E. 1980. "Visible Language Policy - Bilingualism and Multiculturalism on Postage Stamps." *Visible Language*, 14, 1: 30-51.

Wright, Andrew. 1989. *Pictures for Language Learning*. Cambridge: Cambridge University Press.

Reprinted from: Frank Nuessel, "Postage Stamps: A Pedagogical Tool in the Language Classroom," *Mosaic*, 3, 2: (Winter 1996), pp. 12-17.

32 The Five-Step Performance-Based Model of Oral Proficiency

Rebecca M. Valette

What can language teachers learn from the football coach? The author presents a five-step model which can be used to organize instruction so that the focus is on performance, that is, on using the second language for real-life communication.

Although we second language teachers have been unanimous in proclaiming "oral proficiency" as one of our major goals of instruction, there has been much debate as to how this goal is best achieved. For instance, how important is it to provide "comprehensible input" in the classroom? What is the role of grammar and/or linguistic analysis? Are drill and practice activities useful? How much time should be spent on simulated oral communication activities: role play, information gap activities, conversational exchanges? How and when should teachers engage in error correction? The current interest in "authentic assessment" is forcing all of us to focus on evaluating the outcomes of our second language courses. In doing so, we will need to adopt a "performance-based curriculum" in which our success and that of our students will be measured in terms of how well they can use the second language for communication in real-life situations.

The term "performance-based instruction" evokes, and perhaps appropriately so, the image of a sporting event, such as a football game. Indeed, at the secondary school level, the one faculty member who is the most rigorously evaluated in terms of student performance or student outcomes is usually the football coach. Almost every weekend during the fall season, coach and players focus their attention on outcomes, or performance, namely on how well they will play in the "real" game against another school in their league. During the week, however, there is training and practice of various sorts.

In order to elaborate a second-language model for performance-based instruction based on the football analogy, we must closely observe how young people learn to play football. At first, a child is happy to zigzag down the lawn carrying the ball. But soon the young player needs to learn what real football is by:

- watching actual football games,
- learning the rules of the game, and
- drilling the skills, such as throwing, receiving, blocking and running.

Furthermore, the young player needs to gain experience in: scrimmage practice, and

• participating in actual games.

Clearly a young player who cannot understand the game on television, who cannot catch a pass, and who does not know what is meant by "offside", may have fun "playing football" with friends, but certainly is not "proficient" at the game.

Of course, there are levels of performance in football, each with its corresponding levels of proficiency. In the United States, young players participate in the Pop Warner League. Then they may play junior high varsity and senior high varsity, before moving to university varsity, and perhaps even professional football. Each level becomes more complex and more challenging.

Common to all levels of football, however, is the emphasis on performance. The focus is on playing the game well, that is, responding creatively and effectively to situations as they develop on the field and initiating new moves and strategies as needed. Then, during the following week, the performance in the previous game is closely studied and criticized. There is training and practice, with much of the practice time spent on drills, building strength, and developing accuracy of execution of plays and routines. Daily workouts are not simply scrimmages followed by congratulations. Even the scrimmage sessions are followed by close critiques, in an effort to improve performance the next time.

Building oral proficiency in a foreign language is very similar to building proficiency in football. In the Five-Step Performance-Based Model outlined on the next page, the first four steps each contribute to preparing students for the last step which is using the language for actual communication with native speakers.

Step 1. Guided Observation:
Listening to the Spoken Language

In Step 1, the students come into contact with the second language as it is spoken in authentic situations. At its most difficult, this means listening to conversations between native speakers, watching television, listening to the radio, etc. Listening to the second language in its most authentic manifestation is like going to a professional football game: people unfamiliar with the game have no idea what is going on, people with some notions of football follow the main movements of the game, avid fans know the players, the plays, the signals, and can analyze not only what did happen but what might have happened. At the highest level of comprehension, listening to authentic speech, like attending professional football games, requires an awareness and a sensitivity to cultural connotations and allusions.

The learner needs guidance in developing this initial skill of comprehension.

Steps	Oral proficiency	Football
1. Guided Observation	Listening to the spoken language	Watching actual football games
2. Guided Analysis	Learning how the language works	Learning the rules of the game
3. Guided Practice	Building the skills	Training: drill and practice
4. Simulated Performance	Participating in guided conservations and role play	Scrimmage practice
5. Performance	Speaking in real-life situations	Participating in actual games

- At a beginning level, Step 1 consists of listening to the simplified but none the less real language of contrived and/or scripted spoken materials. This type of activity might include TPR (Total Physical Response) activities, listening to simplified narrations, watching videos scripted for language learners but filmed on location by native speakers. This activity is like attending a Pop Warner league game, where one can observe the main features of football in a less complex environment.
- At a more advanced level, this step will include listening to authentic material that has been specifically selected or edited so as to be more comprehensible. Usually this means listening to authentic material with the opportunity of stopping and replaying parts of a recording, perhaps even using captioned versions of a video to enhance comprehension. This is like watching a football game on television where instant replays and charts help clarify the action.

What the students understand from the material they are watching and/or listening to is often termed *comprehensible input*. With language learning as with football, the focus must be on moving from a general notion of what is going on to increasingly more accurate levels of comprehension and more precise appreciation of the complexities of the language.

The better a student understands a second language, the more effectively that student will eventually be able to participate in a conversation, just as the more a young player understands the game of football, the better that player will eventually be able to perform on the field.

Step 2. Guided Analysis:
Learning How the Language Works
In Step 2, students learn how the second language is put together, how it works.

- At first, attention is focused on isolated, individual elements, such as the sound system, syntax patterns, grammatical structures, and vocabulary. This is like learning the rules of football, such as what type of movements are considered "clipping" or "holding" and what penalty such calls carry.

- Then students are expected to recognize and understand the elements in the context of a spoken message: can they make phonemic distinctions, can they hear a gender marker and tell whether a noun is feminine or masculine, can they notice whether a verb is in the preterite or the imperfect, are they aware of the use of a subjunctive or the choice of a particular adjective and do they know how this affects the meaning of what is said. This linguistic analysis is similar to the football player or spectator recognizing an offside movement when it occurs during a game without waiting for the referee to make the call.

Study of the language itself has traditionally been the focal point for second language instruction. Many types of techniques have been developed: inductive and deductive presentations, charts and paradigms, grammars of various sorts (e.g., classical, structural, transformational), mnemonic devices, illustrated vocabularies, flash cards, etc. In the context of the Five-Step Performance-Based Model, these activities constitute one of the five essential steps, but they must be viewed in the context reaching Step 5, which is the ability to use the second language in authentic oral communication situations.

Step 3. Guided Practice:
Building the Skills

In Step 3, the students move from understanding and learning to actually manipulating elements of the spoken language.

- At first, students learn to handle short meaningful phrases, for example, giving their names, exchanging greetings, describing the time and weather. Practising these brief contextualized and meaningful phrases is like tossing the football and encouraging a young player to catch it and run.
- Then, students begin to drill and practice the second language more intensively, often by concentrating on specific elements in isolation. They may repeat verb forms, or practice difficult sounds like the French /y/, or mimic sentence intonations. They may identify colours, recite numbers, name objects on a transparency. These non-contextualized, word-level activities may be compared to the football team's push-ups, blocking practice, and running drills.
- Finally there are the meaningful, contextualized activities where students respond to guided questions and various oral and printed cues to produce correct sentences. This is similar to drills where the football team runs through plays, with a focus on careful, accurate performance.

The above types of guided language-learning activities are not goals in themselves, but enabling outcomes. Their mastery enables learners to speak the language more effectively, just as precise drill and practice helps football players to perform more effectively during the game.

Step 4. Simulated Performance:
Participating in Guided Conversations and Role Play

In Step 4, students have the opportunity to use, in simulated conversational exchanges and role play situations, the new words, phrases and patterns they have learned. The emphasis is on self-expression and conveying information fluently in a meaningful context. Much as one might try to have these exchanges resemble real-life conversations, for example by using props to establish a café scene or a TV game show, teachers and students both recognize that the context is artificial. This type of language practice is similar to football scrimmage practice. In scrimmage, the players divide into two teams and play against one another: it may look like a real game from a distance, but everyone knows that it is not. Scrimmage gives the players the opportunity of running their plays in a game-like context where the focus is on performing effectively.

An important aspect of scrimmage practice is that although the coach allows the game to go on uninterrupted, he/she afterwards brings the team together to analyze weaknesses, criticize poor moves, and outline further drill and practice activities. The scrimmage practices may even be videotaped to allow the players themselves the opportunity of seeing how they performed and where they need to improve. Similarly, Step 4 activities in language classes can be rendered much more effective if they are followed up by analysis and individualized suggestions for additional practice.

Step 5. Performance:
Speaking in Real-Life Situations

Step 5 represents the ultimate desired outcome of the Performance-Based Model of Oral Proficiency. This is the point where students have the opportunity to use the second language for real communication in an authentic situation. The type of situation may vary: e.g., the student is abroad or in an area where the language is spoken and uses the language to order food or ask for a service; the student has a casual conversation with an exchange student or with members of a host family abroad; the student makes a telephone call to request information. At this step, as one becomes increasingly proficient, one needs to be aware of the more complex aspects of communication, including cultural values and expectations, linguistic registers, and conversational characteristics such as turn-taking.

In real communication, as in the real football game, the "clock is running." One cannot start over, one must continue playing. The aim is to communicate as effectively as possible within existing constraints.

After the communication event, like after the game, the student can try to recall what went well and what caused comprehension to break down. Often the teacher is not available, and the "performance" was not recorded, unless the communication event was videotaped or recorded. In the latter case, there may be the opportunity for teacher and student to review the performance and use this diagnostic information to plan for other learning activities.

Conclusion

The five steps described above are not simply moved through once in sequential order. In second-language acquisition as in learning to play football, there is a continuous upward spiralling as students improve their skills. As students move from elementary to more advanced levels, they grow to understand more complex speech, to learn about more difficult structures, to acquire a more extensive vocabulary, to practice these new linguistic aspects in more challenging activities and more complex simulated conversational exchanges. Each of the steps, however, continues to play an important role and none should be omitted.

It is particularly important to recognize that scrimmage practice is meaningless unless the players demonstrate during practice that the running backs know how to hold the ball, that the quarterback can pass the ball with some degree of accuracy, and that the pass receivers know how to catch it. Similarly, it is the role of the language teacher not to engage students in Step 4 (Simulated Performance) activities until they demonstrate at Step 3 (Guided Practice) that they can pronounce the language so as to be understood by native speakers, and that they have a reasonable control of the vocabulary and structures with the role-play activity will require.

In conclusion, one might reflect on the respective roles of the teacher and the coach. The good coach is constantly asking for more demanding and more precise effort from the players, but both coach and players know that they are working together to perform well in the next game. The coach is task-master, judge and trainer, as well as facilitator and provider of encouragement and praise. The coach knows that player self-esteem is linked to a job well done, a game well played. Similarly, the effective teacher in a performance-based language program must maintain high expectations, provide appropriate practice activities, and also motivate students to want to express themselves well so that they, too, begin to view themselves as effective second-language speakers.

Editor's Note: This text has been abridged and adapted from the opening chapter of the 1994 Northeast Conference Reports. Cf. Rebecca M. Valette, "Teaching, Testing, and Assessment: Conceptualizing the Relationship," in Charles Hancock, ed., *Teaching, Testing, and Assessment: Making the Connection* (Lincolnwood Illinois: National Textbook Co., 1994), pp. 1-42.

Reprinted from: Rebecca M. Valette, "The Five-Step Performance-Based Model of Oral Proficiency," *Mosaic*, 2, 2 (Winter 1995, pp. 1-5.

33 Immersion: Why Not Try Free Voluntary Reading?

Stephen Krashen

Immersion programs have not given comprehensible input a real chance. The author suggests reading as one of the solutions.

In recent years, observers of immersion programs have been very concerned about the finding that immersion students do not speak the second language perfectly, even after years of participation.[1] There is the widespread conviction that the solution lies in focusing more on form and using more direct teaching of grammar. I maintain that this conclusion is premature and that immersion programs have not yet given comprehensible input a real chance.

We can explain the "imperfection" of immersion easily without abandoning the Input Hypothesis. As others have pointed out, immersion students are exposed to a limited range of input and have no peer interaction. In addition, immersion has never attempted to exploit one of the best sources of comprehensible input: free voluntary reading. There is an enormous amount of research that confirms that free voluntary reading is the source of a great deal of our reading ability, our writing style, our ability to use complex grammatical constructions, our vocabulary, and much of our spelling ability (Krashen, 1993). Students who participate in free voluntary reading programs in school, such as sustained silent reading, typically outperform traditionally taught comparison students on a variety of measures of literacy competence (second language studies of in-school free reading include Elley and Mangubhai, 1983; Elley, 1991; Pilgreen and Krashen, 1993), and that more reading outside of school is associated with more literacy development (second language studies include Tudor and Hafiz, 1989; Cho and Krashen, 1994; Constantino, 1994).

Immersion children do not read for pleasure in their second language. Romney, Romney and Menzies (1995) reported no relationship between the amount grade 6 immersion students said they spent reading in French, and their scores on a test of reading comprehension. The reason for this result is that the children hardly read at all in French: "They spent an average of 3 1/2 minutes a day reading French books and one minute reading French comics, magazines, and newspapers..." (p. 485). In comparison, they averaged 26 minutes per day reading English books and seven minutes reading English language comics, magazines and newspapers. When asked to name their favourite French authors, only 3% of the students could name an author; in contrast, 81% were able to name their favourite English author.

There is, in addition, no clear evidence that focusing on form is effective. I have argued that focusing on form leads typically to short-term gains for limited aspects of language, and these gains are apparent only on   form-based measures; the knowledge gained in this way does not become part of true linguistic competence (Krashen, 1992, 1994a, 1994b).[2]

In light of the overwhelming evidence that free reading is a powerful source of language competence, the finding that immersion children do not do free reading, and the lack of clear evidence for focusing on form, one is led to the conclusion that free reading should at least be considered as an option. Students interviewed by Romney et al. explained why they didn't do much reading in French: there was little for them to read in French that was both interesting and comprehensible. The solution to this problem means assembling collections of interesting (and comprehensible) books in the second language, providing some sustained silent reading time, reading good stories to students in class, and discussing good books in class. This is certainly an easier, more pleasant, and more promising route than doing more activities that focus on the conditional and Imperfect.[3]

Notes:

I should like to thank Jeff McQuillan for helpful comments on an earlier draft of this paper.

1.   One often reads that immersion students have "fossilized." Harley and Swain (1984), however, conclude that for the early French total immersion students they studied, "there is currently no evidence that immersion students' interlanguage stops developing... while growth towards target language norms in productive language may seem remarkably gradual, we find at any grade level...that there is new development relative to earlier grades" (p. 300). Duchesne (1995) arrives at a similar conclusion. In a study of errors of French immersion students from grades 1 to 6, he found that while some errors did remain, "les erreurs, en général, diminuent en fréquence d'année en année... on obtient une image beaucoup plus dynamique et optimiste de la situation que celle que dessine la fossilisation." (p. 527). Improvement slows down after grade three, but continues to take place.

2.   Studies specifically done with immersion students have not made the case for focusing on form: Harley (1989) provided grade six French immersion students with eight weeks of special instruction on the *imparfait/passé composé* distinction. Her experimental groups averaged 11.9 hours of work on this comparison, while control groups did less than half that amount. Experimental students scored significantly better on two out of three (form-based) measures, but differences on one measure (the cloze test), while significant, were small (less than 3%), and delayed post-testing done three months later revealed no significant differences among the groups.

In Day and Shapson (1991), seventh graders focused on the conditional for six weeks and showed better gains than a comparison group on two out of three measures, but tests were form-based, and delayed post-testing was done 11 weeks after the treatment ended. This interval may have been too short: As noted above, Harley's subjects' gains disappeared after three months. Using adult subjects,

White (1991) reported that gains from conscious learning were lost when subjects were tested one year later. Scott and Randell (1992)'s adult subjects showed clear declines in performance on consciously learned aspects of French grammar four weeks after post-testing. Their subjects studied each grammar rule for only four minutes while Day and Shapson's subjects had three periods per week of instruction for six weeks. Working much harder, however, may only delay the inevitable).

In Lyster (1994), grade 8 French immersion students showed some gains in the use of *tu/vous* after 12 hours of instruction over five weeks, and held these gains at delayed post-testing one month later; as in Day and Shapson, this interval may have been too short. Improvement in another feature of politeness and polite closings in letters did not endure to the post-testing. One post-test, a multiple-choice test, clearly focused students on form, and the others, involving written and oral production, had elements of form-focus as well, as students taking these tests had just experienced a great deal of instruction on just those forms required on the tests (e.g. the written task required students to write an informal letter and a formal letter).

Salomone and Palma (1995), in a study of French immersion in the United States, assert that "increased attention to students' grammatical competence…has made this particular immersion school even more successful" (p. 232), but provide no data. In their thorough analysis of six teachers' implicit theories and classroom behaviour, there is no mention of free voluntary reading in French. Duchesne (1995) suggests that immersion students' improvement in certain structures (e.g. agreement of possessive adjectives) was due to an increased emphasis by teachers on these structures, but without a comparison group that did not receive instruction, there is no evidence this is so.

In at least one instance in Salomone and Palma's report, "grammar instruction" was really "language appreciation." Mr. Loffland, the principal, explained: "We're teaching a lot more grammar now. I was observing in an upper-grade classroom, and the children were conjugating 12 verbs. They loved it. One boy couldn't do the *passé composé* of *lire* so I said: 'Jason, j'ai…' and he said, 'lu.' They know it intuitively." (Salomone and Palma, p. 230). What Mr. Loffland observed was language performance, not language acquisition or language learning: Jason had already acquired the correct form, and Mr. Loffland elicited it.

I find it very hard to believe that the children love grammar instruction. McQuillan (1994) asked 49 adult second language students who had participated in extensive reading about their preferences: 84% said that reading was more pleasurable than grammar, and 78% felt reading was more beneficial than grammar, suggesting that once students do it, they like it and understand its benefits. In addition, there is a great deal of evidence that children enjoy hearing stories and reading books that they select on their own (Krashen, 1994b).

3. It has been pointed out, most recently by Tarone and Swain (1995), that immersion children lack competence in the nonacademic, conversational style of the second language. Light reading might be of help, because it contains a great deal of everyday language. For some evidence, see Cho and Krashen (1994).

References

Cho, K.S. and Krashen, S. 1994. "Acquisition of vocabulary from the Sweet Valley Kids series: Adult ESL acquisition." *The Journal of Reading*, 37: 662-7.

Constantino, R. 1994. "Pleasure reading helps, even if students don't believe it." *The Journal of Reading*, 37: 504-5.

Day, E. and Shapson, S. 1991. "Integrating formal and functional approaches to language teaching in French immersion: An experimental study." *Language Learning* ,41: 25-58.

Duchesne, H. 1995. "Évolution de d'interlangage chez les élèves de la 1re à la 6e année en immersion française." *The Canadian Modern Language Review/La Revue canadienne des langues vivantes*, 51: 512-536.

Elley, W. and Mangubhal, F. 1983. "The impact of reading on second language learning." *Reading Research Quarterly*, 19: 53-67.

Elley, W. 1991. "Acquiring literacy in a second language: The effect of book-based programs." *Language Learning*, 41: 375-411.

Harley, B. 1989. "Functional grammar in French immersion: A classroom experiment." *Applied linguistics* 10: 331-359.

Harley B. and M. Swain. 1984. "The interlanguage of immersion students and its implications for second language teaching." In A. Davies, ed., *Interlanguage. Edinburgh*: Edinburgh University Press. pp. 291-311.

Krashen, S. 1992. "Under what circumstances, if any, should formal grammar instruction take place?" *TESOL Quarterly*, 26: 409-411.

Krashen, S. 1993. *The Power of Reading*. Englewood, Colorado: Libraries Unlimited.

Krashen, S. 1994a. "The input hypothesis and its rivals." In N. Ellis, ed., *Implicit and Explicit Learning of Languages*. London: Academic Press. pp. 45-77.

Krashen, S. 1994b. "The pleasure hypothesis." In J. Alatis, ed., *Georgetown Round Table on Languages and Linguistics*. Washington, DC: Georgetown University Press. pp. 299-322

Lyster, R. 1994. "The effect of functional-analytic teaching on aspects of French immersion students' sociolinguistic competence." *Applied Linguistics*, 15: 263-287.

McQuillan, J. 1994. "Reading versus grammar: What students think is pleasurable and beneficial for language acquisition." *Applied Language Learning*, 5: 95-100.

Pilgreen, J. and Krashen, S. 1993. "Sustained silent reading with English as a second language high school students: Impact on reading comprehension, reading frequency, and reading enjoyment." *School Library Media Quarterly*, 22: 21-23.

Romney, J.C., D. Romney, and H. Menzies. 1995. "Reading for pleasure in French: A study of the reading habits and interests of French immersion children." *The Canadian Modern Language Review/La Revue canadienne des langues vivantes*, 51: 474-511.

Salomone, A. and E. Palma 1995. "Immersion grammar: A changing portrait of Glenwood School." *Foreign Language Annals*, 28: 223-234.

Scott V. and S. Randell. 1992. "Can students apply grammar rules for reading textbook explanations?" *Foreign Language Annals*, 25: 357-367.

Tarone, E. and M. Swain. 1995. "A sociolinguistic perspective on second language use in immersion classrooms." *The Modern Language Journal*, 79: 166-178.

Tudor, I. and Hafiz, F. 1989. "Extensive reading as a means of input to L2 learning." *Journal of Research in Reading*, 12: 164-178.

White, L. 1991. "Adverb placement in second language acquisition: Some effects of positive and negative evidence in the classroom." *Second Language Research*, 7: 133-161.

Reprinted from: Stephen Krashen, "Immersion: Why Not Try Free Voluntary Reading?," *Mosaic*, 3, 1 (Fall 1995), pp. 1,3-4.

34 The Effects of Pleasure Reading

Rebecca Constantino

Constantino's research supports Krashen's theory on the benefits of free voluntary reading. She identifies the impact it makes on the TOEFL test.

Evidence strongly supports that free voluntary or pleasure reading makes an impact on language acquisition in terms of vocabulary improvement and writing ability, as well as oral/aural development (Elley, 1991; Elley & Mangubhai, 1983; Krashen, 1993; Cho & Krashen, 1994). This evidence is also substantial in terms of second language acquisition and literacy (Krashen, 1993; Constantino, 1994). However, for varying reasons, many second language learners do not do much pleasure reading in the target language.

Many second language learners hold the notion that reading is a task-laden, rule-oriented skill that requires close attention to detail and meaning (Constantino, 1994). They claim that good reading involves decoding and searching for meaning. A good reader is loyal to the dictionary and pays close attention to ensure every word is understood. This often results in discouraging and unrewarding experiences with reading in a second language. Quite often, these notions stem from the type of instruction received in home countries as well as in the U.S. system. Instead of receiving ample opportunity and encouragement to simply read for pleasure, second language learners are given timed reading practice that entails vocabulary tests and grammar knowledge.

There is a large population of non-native speakers of English who are living in the United States for various reasons but who are unable to study at the university or graduate level because of poor TOEFL (Teaching of English as a Foreign Language) scores. Since free reading is beneficial in various aspects of language acquisition, it is logical that it would be beneficial for those hoping to improve TOEFL scores. My hypothesis was that if students were provided an array of interesting and understandable texts (following the comprehensible input hypothesis set out by Krashen, 1985), they would engage in pleasure reading that would result in progress in language development. This language development would be evidenced in several ways, but for the purpose of the study, in improved TOEFL scores.

Defining Free Voluntary or Pleasure Reading

It is necessary that students, as well as teachers, have a clear understanding of pleasure reading. There are a few key points as to what free voluntary reading involves:

1. Students choose the reading material.
2. There is no book report.
3. There is no work sheet.
4. There is no journal or log about the reading material.
5. There is no pre-reading exercise.
6. If a student does not like the reading material, he/she does not need to finish it; he/she just chooses another.
7. There is no set amount of time for reading; students read when they want to.

The Subjects

Four English-as-a-Second-Language speakers participated in the study. All had previously taken the TOEFL and received disappointing scores (400-450). Like many immigrants and foreign students in the U.S., they had little, if any contact, with native speakers of English. They each had a television, but they did not watch it, because as Julia said, "It is difficult for me to understand because there is so much of slang and things I don't understand. Also, a lot of the things on TV are areas I don't understand."

Julia is a Russian immigrant who has lived in the United States for six months. As a geologist, she has a good chance of receiving several scholarships for graduate study. Maybe because of the scientist in her, Julia pays close attention to all her work in English and always strives for the perfect answer and pronunciation. Several times Julia was encouraged to throw out her grammar book and dictionary and read for pleasure. She refused and set out to study for the TOEFL with a list of vocabulary words and a handbook on sentence structure. Julia never reads for pleasure in English stating, "I need to do well on my test and I have no time for reading – I don't see how it will help." The only book Julia was interested in reading was one related to TOEFL preparation.

Lus, who is staying in the U.S. with her husband who is a visiting journalist from Mexico, wants to study psychology in the United States. With some time to spare she is more interested in seeing Los Angeles and raising her sons than sitting at a desk studying. She immediately took to the idea of reading for pleasure. Lus' main worry was finding books or other reading material she could understand and enjoy.

An artist and musician from Thailand, **Prinda** hopes to study one of her subjects in the U.S. In preparation for her previous TOEFL test, she had studied with grammar books and vocabulary builders, but she was unsuccessful in receiving a high enough score for university admission (450). In the hope of improving her TOEFL score, as well as filling hours of loneliness, Prinda was interested in reading for pleasure in English.

With an exuberant and inquisitive personality, **Ilmi,** like Lus, did not want to spend hours studying and was interested in doing well on the TOEFL. She was also worried about finding interesting materials to read, but with little encouragement she agreed to read for pleasure instead of spending time with grammar-based materials.

The Study

While a great attempt was made to get all four students to read for pleasure, Julia opted to continue her preparation with TOEFL books, grammar drills and vocabulary lists. The other three agreed to merely read for pleasure. Since one issue in free reading is access to an array of reading materials (Elley, 1992), great effort was taken to ensure that students had a great variety and number of books, magazines, and newspapers to read. Students were invited and encouraged to join "the literacy club" of English readers (Smith, 1988). I brought in several magazines and books such as romance novels and other paperbacks. Since a previous study showed that immigrants and foreign visitors may not be aware of the availability of pleasure reading materials in the public library (Constantino, 1992; Constantino, 1993), we, as a group, visited the local library where the students obtained library cards and toured the library so they became aware of the abundance of pleasure reading materials.

Students were told to read whatever interested them, whenever they felt like it. In other words, to imitate good native language reading practices. If they chose a book that they later did not enjoy, they were instructed to choose another. Also, they were discouraged from decoding practices and searching for the meaning of unknown words. If the material seemed too difficult, they were to choose another book, again, as they would do in their native language. A brief explanation was given concerning the "input hypothesis" introduced by Krashen (1985) that states that for language acquisition to occur, input must be comprehensible yet somewhat beyond the learner's ability. They understood this concept and agreed to discard materials that were too difficult while keeping with material that provided some challenge, as long as it interested them. Lastly, the students were told to read when they wanted to and had time. They did not need to keep a log or journal of time they spent reading nor did they need to be sure to read a certain amount of time each day. (This they found hard to believe since all other reading assignments required these types of activities).

For three months, Julia passed her time with gruelling pre-TOEFL tests, vocabulary drills and extensive writing exercises. Lus, Prinda and Ilmi read what they wanted, when they wanted and for any amount of time they chose. They did not do any exercises or TOEFL pre-tests.

They started out by reading current magazines such as *People*, *The Star*, and *Newsweek*. Within about six weeks, they were reading popular romances by Danielle Steele and Judith Krantz. They became bored with the romance novels and so, eight weeks into the study, were reading popular best sellers such as those by John Grisham or Richard Creighton. Lus even tackled a biography of Fidel Castro.

Results:

Attitudinal Changes Toward Reading

While the ultimate goal was a passing score on the TOEFL score, in the three months the three readers had attitudinal changes about reading in English. They realized that they did not have to spend hours looking up words and focusing on minute details about the text. Rather, they could relax and enjoy reading as they do in the native language. Not only were they thoroughly enjoying reading in English, they were extolling its praises to others. They began to exchange books and magazines, and they tried to recruit others as well.

Moreover, they insisted that they were not only becoming more confident readers and speakers but also very knowledgeable about American culture. As Ilmi said, "I feel that I can really read in English now. Since there was no stress for tests or homework, I could just read. That made it fun. I feel now more comfortable to talk and speak. Another thing, I now know more about American things like the law and relationships."

Changes Toward Writing

Also, students who engaged in free voluntary reading were very eager to do more language activities. For example, all became more comfortable writing in English – something they previously had tried to avoid. As we had discussed the psychological benefits of writing about their experiences as visitors or immigrants in the U.S., they were all keeping diaries or journals in their native language. After reading for several weeks, they decided to write their experiences in English. As Lus said, "Now that I am reading and reading well in English, I think it is better to record my feelings in English; that way they are more authentic and true to my thoughts." Ilmi responded, "I feel that I want to practice more since it feels more natural. Now I am not so scared."

Comprehension

All three pleasure readers felt that their comprehension ability had increased. They attributed it to the new vocabulary words they had acquired. Prinda said, "I was watching TV and I understood a lot. I think a lot of the words were ones I had read and I knew what they meant from the books I have been reading." Lus added, "Since I have been reading, I feel I understand so much more of what is around me. Also, I am not so scared to try to understand. I know so many words now."

TOEFL

The reason that Prinda, Lus and Ilmi had decided to read for pleasure was to improve TOEFL scores. The day before the test, we discussed tactics they should use in preparing for the test. For instance, I advised them to get a good night's sleep, to eat a big breakfast, and to tell themselves that this is only one test in their life and that they could take it again. The main thing was to relax and to do their best. During this discussion, Julia was quite worried about the pleasure readers and tried to coax them to take her TOEFL preparation materials home for an all-night cram session. I convinced them that they would not learn anything in one night and to just relax.

I called all the students the day after the test. The three pleasure readers felt that they had done well, but more importantly, their best. They were confident that they had passed. Julia was certain she had done well on the written sections but had "so much trouble with the listening that it seems no good."

We waited several weeks and were quite pleased with the scores. Prinda, Lus and Ilmi received scores of 550, 590 and 600 respectively. Julia received a score of 450 [out of 900] – not high enough for graduate school admission or the much needed scholarships. However, she will take the test again.

Conclusion

There are several factors involved in TOEFL scores such as test anxiety, exposure to the English speaking environment, and personality. However, these students show the strong effect that reading for pleasure had, not only on the TOEFL scores but also on their general attitudes toward reading and their own comprehension. The improved TOEFL scores are a measurable and viable result of reading for pleasure. However, the attitudinal changes that the students had are not as easily measured but no less significant. With pleasure reading came increased confidence to use the language for other purposes such as watching TV, writing, and interacting with native speakers. These notions are perhaps more valuable than increased TOEFL scores. As Ilmi said, "I feel that I am now and forever a reader of English. I feel comfortable and even happy now when I am reading English."

References

Cho, S.K. and S. Krashen. 1994. "Acquisition of vocabulary from the Sweet Valley Kids Series: Adult ESL acquisition." *Journal of Reading*, 37 (8): 662-667.

Constantino, R., Y. Tai, and S. Fang Lu. 1992. "Minority use of the library." *California Association of Bilingual Education*, 15 (3): 6.

Constantino, R. 1994. "It's like a lot of things in America: Linguistic minority parents' use of libraries." *School Library and Media Quarterly*, Winter. 87-89.

Constantino, R. 1994. "Pleasure reading helps, even if readers don't believe it," *Journal of Reading*. 37 (6): 504-505.

Elley, W. 1992. *How in the world do students read?* Hamburg, Germany: The International Association for the Evaluation of Educational Achievement.

Elley, W. 1991. "Acquiring literacy in a second language: The effect of book-based programs." *Language Learning*, 41, 375-411.

Elley W and F. Mangubhai. 1983. "The impact of reading on second language learning." *Reading Research Quarterly*, 19, 53-67.

Krashen, S. 1985. *The input hypothesis: Issues and implications.* Torrance, CA: Laredo.

Krashen, S. 1993. *The power of reading.* Englewood, CO: Libraries Unlimited.

Smith, F. 1988. *Joining the literacy club.* Portsmouth: Heinemann.

Reprinted from: Rebecca Constantino, "The Effects of Pleasure Reading," *Mosaic,* 3 ,1 (Fall 1995), pp. 15- 17.

35 Four Approaches to "Authentic" Reading

Rebecca M. Valette

Currently, schools and colleges are witnessing a renewed interest in the teaching of reading within the foreign language curriculum. However, there is a lack of consensus as to what reading is and how reading comprehension skills are best taught (by the teacher) and acquired (by the student). Given the present increasing concern for "authentic assessment", it is incumbent upon us to look at the types of readings our students are likely to encounter in the "real" world and how they will interact with them.

In their daily life, people encounter wide varieties of reading texts which vary from one-word signs and short ads to lengthy informational articles, from the entertaining features found in illustrated magazines to several hundred pages of straight text in a novel or biography. Not only do these texts look different from each other, but, as people read them, they do so for different purposes and use different reading strategies.

In order to prepare students for reading second language materials once they leave our classrooms, we not only need to select "authentic materials", we need also to try to replicate "authentic conditions". We should ask ourselves:

- When would people normally read this type of text?
- Why would they normally read it?
- What reading techniques would they probably use as they read it?
- What would they do after they have read it?

An analysis of common reading texts in the light of the above considerations would indicate that there are four main approaches to real-life reading comprehension, each of which activates different pre-reading, while-reading and post-reading activities:

Four Approaches to "Authentic" Reading

Approach 1: Reading in a Daily-Life Context

- realia
- advertisements
- instructions
- notes
- forms
- e-mail, etc.

Approach 2: Reading for Information

- newspaper articles
- reference works
- internet, etc.

Approach 3: Reading for Pleasure

- "light" reading:
  - magazine features and articles.

Approach 4: Participatory Reading

- "serious" reading:
  - short stories
  - novels
  - plays
  - poetry.

Note that not all four approaches must be taught in a given course, nor are all students interested in all approaches. (For example, a person who is not planning to go abroad may be less interested in Approach 1. A student of international law would be more interested in Approach 2.)

Approach 1: Reading in a Daily-Life Context

In our modern world, people use their reading skills constantly as they go about their daily activities. Our contemporary civilization requires that people be "functionally literate", that is, that they be able to read and interpret a wide variety of printed messages, ranging from signs and product names to menus, from bus schedules to movie announcements, from help-wanted ads to headlines, from printed instructions to notes or e-mail from colleagues or friends.

Foreign language learners who intend to visit or reside in a community where that second language is spoken need to acquire similar functional reading skills. In addition to being able to read the texts aloud (a necessary factor, for example, in ordering food from a printed menu), and to understand the relevant vocabulary, students need to know how the culture works so that they interpret the texts correctly. For example, in consulting a railroad schedule, readers must understand how times are expressed, what different types of trains appear on the listing, which days each train runs, which services are offered, etc. In addition, many types of print materials, such as classified ads and movie schedules, also require that the reader be familiar with frequently used abbreviations.

In a daily-life context, reading is done for a purpose: one is making one's way around a city, one is looking for a specific type of restaurant, one is trying to decide which movie to see. The aim is to find and focus on the relevant information, and to interpret it accurately. (It is not common practice to waste one's time reading the irrelevant sections.)

Pre-reading activities

Within the classroom, activities based on realia and similar documents should duplicate authentic reading tasks. Functional reading is almost always purposeful, rather than random. This focus should be reflected in the pre-reading activities. (Teachers will want to avoid artificial questions, such as "What information do these realia contain?")

Prompt students by setting the scene. For example: "Here is a movie listing from a French newspaper. You and your friends want to see *Cyrano*255 tonight. Find out where the movie is playing and when the last show starts."

Encourage students to create their own scenarios. For instance, have pairs of students decide what type of food they would like to eat for supper, and then distribute a listing of restaurants so that they can decide where to go.

While-reading activities

In functional daily-life reading, students need to skim and scan in order to find the information they need. It is just as important that they know which things to skip, so that they economize their efforts.

- As students read a listing with several options, have them check off those which they want to consider and cross out those which are inappropriate. For example, have them look for vegetarian dishes on a menu, trains that run on Sundays, hotels that accept pets.
- Have students write down the information they are looking for. For instance, if they are planning to see *Jean de Florette*, they can list the movie theatres where the film is playing and note the times of the showings.
- Prepare and distribute a chart or grid on which students will note specific information. For example, they could take a page of rental ads from a newspaper and classify each of the listings by number of rooms, size, availability of an elevator, etc.

Post-reading activities

In a daily-life context, reading activities are typically followed by some sort of action: one reserves a hotel room, one buys a train ticket, one decides which movie to see or which apartment to visit. In the classroom, post-reading activities most frequently take the form of a conversation or a rôle-play, although in some situations written responses are also appropriate.

- Have students discuss with one another which apartment they would like to rent and why, basing their conversation on the real estate listings they have been consulting.
- Have students prepare an appropriate rôle-play, based on the documents they have read. For instance, after reading a newspaper schedule of concerts, students can phone the hall to reserve seats for the performance they have selected.
- Have students fill in a visa form or a job application form that they have been studying.

Approach 2: Reading for Information

The purpose of this type of reading is to expand one's knowledge. The reader is motivated to get more information on a certain topic and thus searches out appropriate sources. In the area of current events, people reading for information usually turn to newspapers. For example, they may have heard about a robbery and want more details, or they would like to get the full report on a sports event or an international confrontation. For less current topics, people in need of information turn to reference works (almanacs, encyclopedias, now often via internet), professional journals, and non-fiction books of all sorts.

Whereas functional literacy is activated only within the setting of the culture of the second language, the students' ability to read for information can also be put into practice in an Anglo context. Students in immersion courses and in programs fostering "languages across the curriculum" are often asked to refer to second-language materials. At the university level, students may consult texts in a second language as part of their coursework in a variety of fields such as business, international law, history or journalism (cf. Lange 1994).

In reading for information, the readers select what they are going to read on the basis of the specific questions they would like to have answered. Their purpose is to expand their knowledge. If one text does not contain all the information they are looking for, they search out and read additional sources. Sometimes their reading opens up new areas of exploration or new fields of investigation.

Pre-reading activities

Clearly the preparatory step in reading for information is to formulate the appropriate questions. What information do the students expect to find in the text?

- Show the reading to the class (for example, a newspaper article about a plane accident), and have the students work together in small groups to draw up a list of related questions, such as: When did the accident occur? How many casualties? How many people were saved? Why did the accident happen?
- Present the class with the topic of the reading (for example, bull-fighting), and have the students first generate a list of related questions, and then rank these questions in order of importance.
- Prepare a list of statements, some accurate and some not, concerning the topic of the reading (for example, French Impressionism, or the voyages of Jacques Cartier). As a pre-reading activity, have students indicate which of the statements they think are true and which are false.

While-reading activities

As the students read for information, they are actively looking for answers to previously established questions. Because the focus is on content, and not skill-building, it is important that the reading material be accessible to the students. Depending on the level of the class and the difficulty of the text, it may be necessary to provide reading helps: glosses, a bilingual dictionary, etc. If reading is done in class, the teacher can move around the room acting as a resource person, explaining what certain words and phrases mean.

- If students have prepared a list of questions, have them fill in the answers that they find while reading the text. Then have them place a large question mark next to those questions which the text did not address.

- Have the students refer to a list of true/false statements as they read the text. For each true statement, they are instructed to underline the corroborating sentences in the selection. For each false statement, they are to underline the contradictory information.

- Have students surf the internet to find answers to a series of questions. For each site where they find an appropriate answer, they write down the internet address and (if possible) print out the information they have found.

Post-reading activities

Since the goal of reading for information is to expand one's knowledge, one generally learns new things. In addition, it is not unusual to find that the reading has inspired some additional questions.

- Have students each list the most interesting fact that they learned from the reading, together with one follow-up question they would like to explore.

- If the text did not answer all the pre-reading questions the students had prepared, encourage them (if appropriate) to do further research on the topic.

- Have students list other things they would like to find out about as a result of having read the text. These may turn out to be somewhat tangential topics. (For example, an article on Lafayette's rôle in the American Revolution might spark an interest in locating on a map all the cities in the United States named in Lafayette's honour.)

Approach 3: Reading for pleasure

Reading for pleasure, or "light" reading, is what people do while waiting at the doctor's office or before falling asleep at night or at other leisure moments. They flip through a magazine, and look at the various articles and features: some are informative, some give advice, some take the form of self-tests or letters to a confidential advisor who offers professional help, some treat more serious topics such as environmental concerns or archaeological findings, others reveal incidents in the lives of celebrities or offer uplifting tales of heroism. An average reader often has many magazines to choose from: news magazines, detective magazines, sports magazines, fashion magazines, science magazines, etc.

The style in these articles and features is typically straightforward and does not require reader interpretation. Any background information the reader might need is made explicit within the article itself.

When flipping through a magazine, second-language readers, like first-language readers, read those articles and features that have attracted their attention. If a person is struck by some interesting points, he or she might decide to discuss these with a friend, either by describing the content of the article or by reading salient passages aloud.

Pre-reading activities

In the "real" world, it is the reader who decides what magazine to look at and which articles to choose. Illustrations and typography play an important role in the selection process. In order to make pre-reading activities as "authentic" as possible, it is important that readings be presented with their original art and layout.

- Typically readers select an article because they have some notion as to its content. Similarly, students who are "reading for pleasure" should be encouraged to try to discover the content of an article before they read it.
- Have students look at title and illustrations and try to guess or brainstorm what the article is about.
- Have students look at the format of a magazine selection and try to guess what type of article or feature it most likely is (story? biography? self-test? advice column?).

While-reading activities

Very quickly students will discover whether their guesses about the theme and the format of the article are correct. Magazine pieces are meant to be transparent. More importantly, the actual reading of the article is meant to be relaxing, and so it is essential that students understand what the text is saying. (Students do not need to understand every word, but they should have a fairly accurate notion of the basic content.) In the "real" world, people do not usually have a dictionary available while reading a magazine: if a text is too hard, they simply stop reading it. In "light" readings prepared for classroom use, unfamiliar terms and expressions should be glossed or footnoted so that students find the reading experience to be a pleasurable one.

- As students read, encourage them to find and note down one or two interesting things they would like to discuss or share with others.
- If the reading is a self-test, have students actually take the test and then analyze their scores.
- Since articles are often written in a casual or colloquial style, encourage students to note down new words or expressions that they would like to incorporate into their active vocabulary.

Post-reading activities

Reading for pleasure is largely a private experience. Sometimes, however, one is eager to share with others the main points of what one has read, or some interesting trivia one has picked up. In this sense, magazine articles often act as a catalyst for conversation.

- Have students in pairs or small groups engage in conversation about an article they have just read.

  ("Did you see that article on...?

  It says that...

  What do you think?")

- Have students select a sentence or short passage they find interesting and read it aloud to their partner.

- If the magazine article consists of a set of interviews, the students can compare the various views presented and indicate which of the interviewees they tend to agree with, or which of the people they would like to spend an evening with, etc.

Approach 4. Participatory reading

Participatory reading, or "serious" reading, goes beyond the acquisition of information or new knowledge. The texts, whether fiction (such as short stories, plays, novels, poetry), or non-fiction (such as essays and critical pieces), have been written so as to require the reader's personal involvement. Frequently these readings assume a certain background knowledge on the part of the readers, and then provide a new interpretation or an original view. More often than not, they function as a springboard for deeper reflection about some aspect of the human condition.

Literary texts are meant not only to be read, but also to be re-read. Of course, on the first reading, the readers need to discover WHAT is being narrated or expressed. Then, on a second reading, they may wish to explore HOW the author creates an effect or portrays a character or develops a theme.

Frequently literary readings elicit a personal response on the part of the reader. Some students may even be inspired to create related texts of their own.

Pre-reading activities

In the "real" world, one rarely reads a book or a story without some sort of background knowledge about the work; either one has seen the corresponding movie, or one has read a review, or a friend has recommended a book because of its humour or its surprise ending. In addition, when American readers read works by contemporary American writers (especially writers of the same socio-economic milieu), they have a common bond: they share a similar cultural background and are sensitive to the same cultural referents. In order to appreciate a work written at a different historical period or for a different ethnic group, and especially a work written in a second and as yet somewhat unfamiliar language, most readers require additional background information in order to approach the reading task in a natural way.

- Have students look at the illustrations and read a blurb on the author (and the work) to get a general idea of the theme, the locale and the time period. Book jackets are excellent for this activity.
- Use posters, maps, pictures, documentary films, etc., to familiarize the students with the background information that the author expects them to possess. (For example, students would more readily relate to Camara Laye's *L'enfant noir* if they could see pictures of village life in West Africa in the 1930s. Similarly, before presenting Ronsard's *Ode à Cassandre*, the teacher could show a poster of a Renaissance castle like Chenonceau, and have students see how the flower gardens are at a certain distance from the castle itself; this allows them to realize that the poet, by inviting Cassandre to come admire a rosebush, is in reality enticing the young woman to go with him to a fairly secluded area where the two can be together without being disturbed.)

If appropriate, help students anticipate what the crux of the reading will be so as to involve them from the outset with the development of the plot. (For example, in introducing Diop's *L'Os*, you could have students imagine a more contemporary scene. "You are living in a remote country and your family in the States has just sent you a package of brownies. You are about to enjoy this unexpected treat when a friend arrives. Since you do not want to share the brownies – after all, they were sent to you!, – you try to get your friend to leave. What approach would you take?")

Together with the students, read the opening paragraphs (or scenes or lines) and help them determine the general tone or mood of the work. If the opening is particularly descriptive (as in Mérimée's *Mateo Falcone*), focus briefly on the essential elements (e.g., the fact that the Corsican *maquis* offers an excellent hiding place for outlaws). Then encourage the students to move on to the actual story.

While-reading activities

The most important consideration as students are reading a work of fiction is that they all understand what is happening. Vaguely getting the "gist" is not enough. Nor is it helpful for students to approach such a reading in a dogged linear fashion word by word, for the author's meaning almost always goes far beyond the actual sentences. At the most basic level, students need to know who is where and how the plot is developing. (In the real world of "authentic reading", if one does not understand what is going on in a novel or a play or a story or a poem, one simply puts the book down.)

Since the goal of participatory reading activities is to simulate a positive reading experience, we might do well to let students determine what formats make the story the most accessible for them. A few might be challenged by guessing meanings and reading an unglossed text. Some might prefer glosses in the second language, while others might opt for glosses in English. Some might like to have an end vocabulary for quick reference, while others would be happier consulting their own dictionary. Still others would be most comfortable reading with a bilingual text. When using a bilingual text in class, students should be encouraged to discuss the reading in the second language. The presence of a facing-page English equivalent means that the teacher no longer needs to check whether certain words and phrases have been understood, and is free to focus on the story itself, the themes, the plot development, the author's style. (In the "real world" there is no such thing as "cheating" while reading – either one is reading or one is not. For many second-language learners, a bilingual text is an excellent way of approaching a text that would otherwise be above their heads.)

- Divide a longer text into scenes or meaningful segments. In some anthologies, the editors introduce each scene of a story with a brief title which functions as an advance organizer, cuing a key element or theme. (Cf. Valette and Renjilian-Burgy, 1993.) If you wish, you might give a short title to each scene. At the end of each segment, ask a few questions to check general comprehension, and then have students in small groups try to anticipate what will happen next. This can be done as a game, with groups writing out their guesses and placing them in an envelope. After the class has read the next segment, the guesses are taken from the envelope and read aloud. How many groups guessed correctly what would happen?

- For each segment of the reading, prepare a résumé of the action in which you insert four or five errors. As students in pairs read the summary, they are instructed to underline and correct the errors. (This error-correction technique can also be used as an oral activity. One student begins to summarize what happened, but inserts an error. The classmate who first hears the error interrupts to correct the inaccurate sentence, and then continues the summary, eventually inserting a new error, which in turn is corrected by another alert classmate, and so forth.)

- To check whether students understand descriptive passages, have them work in small groups to sketch out the scene as if they were going to film it. This type of activity leads to lively discussion and a close reading of the text. When all the groups are finished, have them compare their sketches. (For example, in reading Camus' *L'Hôte*, you might have students draw the floor plan of the school teacher's living quarters.)

- For certain types of readings, it is valuable for students to hear the text as they are reading it. By giving a dramatic reading of the selection the teacher can significantly enhance the students' comprehension. Poetry, especially, comes to life when read aloud, as do prose texts written in dialect or with idiosyncratic phonetic spelling (for example, Queneau's *Zazie dans le métro*.)

Post-reading activities

- Since participatory reading by its very nature requires student involvement, literary texts are an excellent springboard for the development of writing activities. In addition, with certain genres such as plays and song lyrics, it is not only appropriate but almost essential that students hear the texts performed.

- Have students present the story they have read from a different angle. (For example, after reading Maupassant's *En voyage*, students could imagine they were the Countess and write diary entries describing her trip from Russia to Menton, or they could imagine themselves as her admirer and narrate the story of her death from his point of view.)

- Have students extend the story, imagining a follow-up scene which they act out as a dialogue. (For example, after reading Michelle Maurois' *Le Bracelet*, students can invent a conversation between the young girl and the shopkeeper's mysterious fiancé.)

- If your language laboratory has a collection of literary recordings, make a tape of two or three different actors interpreting the same text (for example, a poem of Prévert). Have students determine which interpretation they prefer and why.

- If a poem that the students have read in class has been put to music, or if the poem consists of the lyrics of a song, play the corresponding piece in class. Ask students how the music influences or changes their interpretation of the text. (For example, after listening to Zachary Richard's stirring rendition of *Réveille*, students become emotionally drawn to the tragic history of the Acadians.)

- As a class project, take students to see the actual performance of a play or the movie version of a novel they have read.

- Give students the opportunity to develop their own artistic interpretation of a work they have particularly enjoyed. These projects may take many forms: for instance, a poster depicting the mood of a play, a series of photos to accompany a poem, an original poem inspired by one read in class, a montage of musical selections to accompany a scene from a play, a video version of a dramatic episode, a dancer's interpretation of the protagonist's emotions, etc.

Readings of the types described in these four approaches have been used by teachers for decades, as have many of the suggested techniques. What characterizes these four approaches, however, is that the emphasis throughout the corresponding activities is not on what Rivers (1975, p.4) calls "skill-getting" (that is, the "learning-to-read" component of the second-language class), but rather on the "skill-using" (the often neglected "real reading" component). Their aim is to simulate the "authentic" reading experiences that second-language learners will engage in when one day they have the opportunity to interact with real texts in the real world. Some of these reading approaches and their corresponding techniques are being tried in current textbooks. See for example Freed and Knutson (1989) for Approach 1; Davies et al. (1990) for Approaches 1 and 3; Valette and Valette (1995a, 1995b) for Approaches 2, 3 and 4.

References

Barnett, Marva A. 1988. *Lire avec plaisir: Stratégies de lecture*. New York, NY: Harper & Row.

Been, Sheila. 1975. *"Reading in a Foreign Language Teaching Program."* TESOL Quarterly 9,3: 233-242.

Bernhardt, Elizabeth B. 1986. *"Reading in the Foreign Language,"* pp. 93-115, in Barbara H. Wing, ed. *Listening, Reading, and Writing: Analysis and Application* [1986 Northeast Conference Reports]. Middlebury, VT: Northeast Conference.

Davies, Evelyn, Norman Whitney, Meredith Pike-Baky, and Laurie Blass. 1990. *Task Reading.* Cambridge, Eng.: Cambridge Univ. Press.

Freed, Barbara and Elizabeth Knutson. 1989. *Contextes: French for Communication.* Cambridge, MA: Newbury House.

Grellet, Françoise. 1981. *Developing Reading Skills: A Practical Guide to Reading Comprehension Exercises.* Cambridge, Eng.: Cambridge Univ. Press.

Lange, Dale L. 1994. *"The Curricular Crisis in Foreign Language Learning."* ADFL Bulletin, 25, 2: 12-16.

Mackay, Ronald, Bruce Barkman and R.R. Jordan, eds. 1979. *Reading in a Second Language: Hypotheses, Organization and Practice.* Rowley, MA: Newbury House.

Nance, Kimberly A. 1994. *"Developing Students' Sense of Literature in the Introductory Foreign Language Literature Course."* ADFL Bulletin, 25, 2: 23-29.

Omaggio Hadley, Alice. 1993. *Teaching Language in Context.* 2nd edition. Boston, MA: Heinle & Heinle.

Papalia, Anthony. 1987. *"Interaction of reader and text",* pp. 70-82, in Wilga M. Rivers, ed., *Interactive Language Teaching.* Cambridge, Eng.: Cambridge Univ. Press.

Rivers, Wilga M. 1975. *A Practical Guide to the Teaching of French.* New York: Oxford Univ. Press.

Rivers, Wilga M. 1981. *Teaching Foreign-Language Skills,* 2nd ed. Chicago: Univ. of Chicago Press.

Rivers, Wilga M. 1987. *"Interaction as the Key to Teaching for Communication,* pp. 1-16, in Wilga M. Rivers, ed., *Interactive Language Teaching.* Cambridge, Eng.: Cambridge Univ. Press.

Shrum, Judith L. and Eileen W. Glisan. 1994. *Teacher's Handbook: Contextualized Language Instruction.* Boston, MA: Heinle & Heinle.

Swaffar, Janet K., Katherine M. Arens and Heidi Byrnes. 1991. *Reading for Meaning: An Integrated Approach to Language Learning.* Englewood Cliffs, NJ: Prentice Hall.

Valette, Jean-Paul and Rebecca M. Valette. 1995a. *À Votre Tour: Intermediate French.* Lexington, MA: D.C. Heath.

Valette, Jean-Paul and Rebecca M. Valette. 1995b. *Discovering French -Rouge.* Lexington, MA: D.C. Heath.

Valette, Rebecca M. 1994. *"Teaching, Testing, and Assessment: Conceptualizing the Relationship",* pp. 1-42, in Charles R. Hancock, ed. *Teaching, Testing, and Assessment: Making the Connection* [1994 Northeast Conference Reports]. Lincolnwood, IL: National Textbook.

Valette, Rebecca M. and Joy Renjilian-Burgy. 1993. *Album: Cuentos del mundo hispánico,* 2nd. ed. Lexington, MA: D.C. Heath.

Wiggins, Grant. 1994. *"Toward More Authentic Assessment of Language Performances",* pp. 69-86, in Charles R. Hancock, ed. *Teaching, Testing, and Assessment: Making the Connection* [1994 Northeast Conference Reports]. Lincolnwood, IL: National Textbook.

Reprinted from: Rebecca M. Valette, "Four Approaches to "Authentic" Reading." *Mosaic*, 4, 2 (Winter 1997), pp. 1, 3-7.

36 Teaching Writing in Elementary and Intermediate Language Classes: Suggestions and Activities

Frank Nuessel and Caterina Cicogna

General recommendations to incorporate writing into the curriculum with four specific examples of particular writing tasks.

Introduction

The traditional concept of the four skills (listening/understanding, speaking, reading, and writing) and their conventional classification into the receptive (listening/understanding, reading) and the productive skills (speaking, writing) persists in language teaching today. The prevailing methodological philosophy in vogue has often determined the curricular attention accorded to one or all of these linguistic abilities.

Of the four skills, writing is perhaps the one aptitude that receives the least attention in the elementary and intermediate language class. Magnan (1985:109), for example, observes that "writing has become a neglected skill in language courses." Explanations for the "second-class status" of this skill are varied (see also Dvorak , 1986; Omaggio, 1986; Magnan, 1985, for discussion):

1. a shift in emphasis caused by the advent of audio-lingualism with its stress on oral production;
2. a frequent, albeit erroneous, assumption that this skill will be developed in some other course;
3. the notion that students have already learned how to write in an English composition course, and that they can transfer this knowledge automatically to a language situation (see Dvorak 1986:151-153; Krashen 1984:38 for a discussion that such similarities, in fact, exist);
4. the belief, expressed by some instructors, that they do not know how to develop and enhance their students' writing abilities; and
5. the notion that writing proficiency is not necessary in a language class in the first few years.

Despite a tendency to neglect the skill of writing, this linguistic ability is perhaps more rigorously evaluated than the other three skills because its relative permanency permits the reader to scrutinize every aspect of this form of communication. In this regard, Allen and Valette (1976:285) have observed that:

Writing may well be considered the most difficult of the language skills. People are flattered when a foreigner tries to speak their language, and they tend to tolerate a light accent and occasional awkward expression with good grace. The speaker's personality makes a greater impression than the accuracy of his or her spoken language. But a letter is judged more severely on its purely linguistic merits. Even errors in spelling and grammar are not easily excused, even if the meaning is clear and the handwriting attractive and legible.

Furthermore, Chastain (1976) captures the fact that writing enhances and reinforces the other linguistic skills when he observed that

writing [...] helps to solidify the student's grasp of vocabulary and structure and complements the other language skills.

In a curriculum guideline, the Ontario Ministry of Education (1980) echoes Chastain's remark and comments further

Students should write to practice and consolidate their grasp of structures and vocabulary; they should also write to express their own ideas as early as possible.

The Purposes and Process of Writing

Robert M. Terry (1989:43) cites Magnan (1985) who states that writing has two basic purposes, namely,

- "as a *support skill* (class and homework exercises to practice grammatical forms and structures, vocabulary and spelling) and
- as a *communicative skill* (to inform, relate, question, persuade, etc.)."

Many language instructors continue to focus on the end product of writing, despite the fact that most experts in rhetoric and composition now advocate writing as a process. Process-orientation in composition places emphasis on this skill as a developmental ability which consists of a progressive series of editorial stages of revision, improvement, and, ultimately, a concluding product.

Tricia Hedge (1988:21) views the act of writing as a series of steps in a chain which can be summarized in the following seven stages:

1. Initial motivation
2. Assembly of ideas
3. Planning and outlining
4. Note-taking
5. Preparation of a first draft
6. Revision and replanning of the initial draft
7. Formal presentation of the final product.

According to Hedge (1988:21), the above linear representation of the act of writing amounts to an oversimplification of the writing process. For this reason, Hedge (1988:21) defers to Smith (1982) who describes this task as an unordered set of deletion, substitution, and movement operations that ultimately lead to a finalized version. Hedge (1988:21-23) further notes that many rhetoricians categorize the writing process into to three separate modules:

1. Pre-writing activities.

    A. Determination of the purpose.

    B. Determination of the audience.

  2. Writing and rewriting.

  3. Editing.

These general facets of writing need to be kept in mind when dealing with specific writing assignments in the language class room situation. In fact, time dedicated to an "introduction to writing as process" will ultimately be well-spent since such an orientation will familiarize students with writing and help attenuate fears about this type of assignment.

Types of Writing Tasks

Writing, of course, has many different purposes and functions:

- to persuade
- to inform
- to motivate
- to analyze
- to criticize
- to warn
- and so forth.

In addition, written discourse is varied in its manifestations and may include a wide spectrum of formats, styles, and registers (see Grellet 1981:3-4, cited in Omaggio 1986:125 for a comprehensive listing of written communication formats) exemplified in the following partial enumeration:

Literary pieces

(poems, essays, short stories, drama, and so forth).

Personal communication

- letters
- post cards
- telegrams
- notes

Newspaper and magazine formats

- advertisements
- classified section
- weather forecasts
- and so forth).

Instructions

- recipes
- directions
- and the like).

General Recommendations for the Incorporation of Writing into the Language Curriculum

The following is a series of general suggestions to the instructor to facilitate the development of writing skills in the language classroom. These recommendations will surely contribute to making the subsequent writing task more interesting and more rewarding for all concerned.

1. Make available examples of "authentic" writing samples so that students will become familiar with an appropriate format for the specific assignment given by the instructor.

2. Control the length of the assignment. Short, manageable writing assignments provide students with a sense of accomplishment, especially in the initial writing exercises. Moreover, brief writing tasks make students realize that they can be successful in carrying out writing assignments.

3. Provide students with guided composition tasks. Specify a logically ordered set of individual questions to be answered. This building-block approach to writing may seem simplistic. In the initial stages of writing, however, students will be able to produce short, cohesive writing samples. At a later stage, exercises in sentence-combining activities may be implemented (Cooper, Morain, and Kalivoda 1980) to develop more sophisticated writing techniques.

4. Specify the audience for the particular writing task. The intended audience may be known (communication with a friend, assignment for a course), or unknown (an essay for a publication to be read by a large and unknown readership).

5. Include selected vocabulary related to the writing assignment on a separate sheet of paper.

6. Vary the writing formats. Grellet (1981:3-4, cited in Omaggio 1986:125) has noted the wide variety of writing purposes and functions. Such diversification also helps students to be able to read diverse written communication formats.

7. Synchronize the writing assignment with the appropriate lesson in the textbook with respect to vocabulary and grammar.

8. Avoid the use of a red marking instrument. For revision purposes, use any contrasting colour except red in order to avoid its negative connotations (Semke 1984).

9. Include positive commentary about the well written parts of the writing assignment.

Specific Examples of Writing Tasks

The following four suggestions for types of writing activities contain explicit recommendations designed to facilitate the writing objective with a minimum of difficulty. Each item contains a general account of the specific task together with an ordered list of operations necessary to complete the assignment.

Telegrams

The preparation of a telegram requires students to make very succinct statements about important matters. This type of writing assignment means students must communicate a message quite tersely.

1. Provide students with the following situations or scenarios (Di Pietro 1987):
   a. You are in Rome. You have lost your wallet and you need to have money wired to you immediately.
   b. You send a congratulations notice to your parents for their twenty-fifth wedding anniversary.
   c. You congratulate your sister on the birth of a child.
2. Provide students with a "telegram form" for writing the appropriate message.
3. Provide spaces (underlines) for a message of ten, fifteen, twenty, or thirty words to ensure that students comply with the requirement for conciseness.

Recipes

Food preferences and preparation are important elements of any culture. This assignment is best synchronized with grammar on commands, and food vocabulary, and the basic format is applicable to any culture. This type of assignment also provides students with an opportunity to learn about the culinary habits and preferences of another culture (time of meal, place of meal, types of food, and so forth).

1. Ask students to write a recipe for a specific dish.
2. Review commands.
3. Include a selected sheet of vocabulary for food and the specific verbal activities related to recipes (stir, beat, cut, and so forth)
4. Use the names of specific recipes to provide a sense of the types of dishes possible with attention to the order of presentation in a multi-course meal.

Post Cards

The task of writing a post card to friends or family members can be an interesting activity for students because it involves imagination, fantasy, as well as some research to gather factual information about a particular locale. Moreover, this form of directed writing activity is relatively short, hence students do not perceive it to be an impossible writing exercise.

We advocate the introduction of post cards from various locales to add a realistic dimension to this task. The post cards may be reused by making a photocopy. Assign students as many different post cards as is feasible. The format of this written exercise follows:

Directions to students:

1. Provide exemplary post cards (originals or photocopies).
2. Address the card.
3. Write the date.

4. Write a post card to a friend, family member, parents, boyfriend, girl-friend. Include the appropriate salutation.

5. Indicate where you are.

6. Note the significance of the photograph or other graphic element on the reverse of the card (panorama of city, place of local, national, or inter-national, historical interest).

7. Tell what you are doing (visiting relatives, sightseeing, studying, con-ducting business, and so forth)

8. State your overall reaction to the trip (exciting trip, fast-paced, fun, demanding, and so forth).

9. Mention how the weather is (rain, snow, cold, hot, mild).

10. Indicate when you are returning home (month, date, time).

11. Provide an appropriate closing.

12. Select from items 3-8 above. Be brief since the amount of writing space on a post card is limited.

Directions and map-making

The preparation of a map is a task that everyone does on occasion. One map-making activity that is quite common is the preparation of a map for someone who does not know how to go to your home.

1. Advise students to tell a classmate how to get to their home from the school/university.

2. Prepare an explicit map.

3. Write out clear and comprehensive instructions on how to drive from the school/university to the house/apartment in question.

4. Provide an appropriate vocabulary sheet (cardinal directions, words for street, highway, and so forth.)

5. Advise students to use personal commands, or the second person singular verbal forms.

Conclusion

The suggestions provided in this short article are by no means exhaustive. They do provide, however, a good start for a language skill which is often neglected.

References

Allen, Edward David and Rebecca M. Valette. 1976. *Classroom Techniques: Foreign Language and English as a Second Language*. New York: Harcourt Brace Jovanovich.

Chastain, Kenneth. 1976. *Developing Second-Language Skills: Theory to Practice*. Chicago: Rand McNally.

Cooper, Thomas, G. Morain, and T. Kalivoda. 1980. *Sentence combining in second language instruction*. Language in Education: Theory and Practice Series, Volume 31. Washington, DC: Center for Applied Linguistics.

Di Pietro, Robert J. 1987. *Strategic interaction: learning language through scenarios*. Cambridge: Cambridge University Press.

Dvorak, Trisha. 1986. "Writing in the foreign language." In *Listening. reading and writing analysis and application*, ed. by Barbara Wing, 145-167. Middlebury, VT: Northeast Conference.

Grellet, Françoise. 1981. *Developing reading skills*. Cambridge: Cambridge University Press.

Hedge, Tricia. 1988. *Writing*. Oxford: Oxford University Press.

Krashen, Stephen D. 1984. *Writing research. theory. and applications*. Oxford: Oxford University Press.

Magnan, Sally Sieloff. 1985. "Teaching and testing proficiency in writing: skills to transcend the second-language classroom." In *Proficiency, curriculum, articulation: the ties that bind*, ed. by Alice C. Omaggio, 109-136. Middlebury, VT: Northeast Conference.

Ministry of Education, Ontario. 1980. *French Core Programs 1980*. Toronto: Ministry of Education, Ontario.

Omaggio, Alice C. 1986. *Teaching language in context: proficiency-oriented instruction*. Boston: Heinle and Heinle.

Semke, Harriet D. 1984. "Effects of the red pen." *Foreign Language Annals*, 17:195-202.

Smith, Frank. 1982. *Writing and the writer*. London: Heinemann.

Terry, Robert M. 1989. "Teaching and evaluating writing as a communicative skill." *Foreign Language Annals*, 22:43-54.

Reprinted from: Frank Nuessel and Caterina Cicogna, "Teaching Writing in Elementary and Intermediate Language Classes: Suggestions and Activities," *Mosaic*, 1, 2 (Winter 1993), pp. 9-11.

37 Students' Empowerment: E-mail Exchange and the Development of Writing Skills

Christine Besnard, Charles Elkabas,
and Sylvie Rosienski-Pellerin

The teaching approach described in this paper tries to make second-language learning more attractive to students by placing them at the centre of their own learning experience.

"I was given the possibility of expressing myself in French without being told exactly what to write. Indirectly, I learned a great deal of vocabulary and expressions."

"I had the chance to practise my skills on an informal yet academic basis."

"I wanted to do my best because somebody else rather than my prof would be reading my work."

(Students' comments)

Can we make second-language (henceforth L2) learning more authentically communicative, more interactive and more socially based? As experienced educators, we know for a fact that in spite of the communicative "revolution", the development of writing skills in the foreign language classroom remains artificial, hence the lack of motivation of many students. While teaching a second-year French writing course at the university, we looked into new technologies in order to make language learning socially grounded, experiential, and therefore more meaningful to the students. In 1992-93, we decided to develop a computer-assisted language learning (CALL) writing course in which corresponding via e-mail (i.e., electronic mail) with peers from another institution could turn writing practice and the study of grammar, vocabulary and style into an enriching experience.

Theoretical Background

Research in cognitive psychology, pedagogy and language teaching and learning has placed considerable emphasis on real communication (written and oral) in second language learning. Canale and Swain (1980), Ellis (1990), Guntermann and Phillips (1981), Rivers (1972), Savignon (1983) and Terrell (1984), among others, have all stressed the importance of engaging students in true and meaningful interactions. Indeed, for communication to be authentic, the student needs to communicate with a "real" person (a peer, a friend, the registrar, a journal editor...) and not with the teacher, as it is usually done in language courses. As stressed by Meirieu (1987:57), written practice should not be studied as such, but be a means to an end, and should not have as its sole purpose evaluation and grading by the professor. Littlewood (1984:97) insists that as language teachers,

> we should try to insure that learners are always aware of the communicative value of what they are learning. For example [...] we should create communicative contexts in the classroom; learners should be helped to use the language   for expressing their own personal needs and their own personality...

It has also been reported that most language students at the university level wish to be engaged in a more "experiential approach" to the language that allows them to share their personal experiences and discuss their projects, likes and dislikes (Corbeil, 1992:497). Indeed, the importance of the social aspect of language learning has never been as highly stressed as it has been over the last two decades: researchers agree that social interaction is a key component to language acquisition.

Though computers can jeopardize the establishment of interaction in the classroom (students are hypnotized by the screen, and the computer becomes a physical barrier between students), we believe that computers can still be used as powerful social tools. Even if word-processing and most language softwares do not, as such, lead to interaction in the classroom, when they are integrated in activities that promote interaction, they become most socially effective. As Johnson (1991:62) argues: "it is not computer use that creates social effects, but the way teachers structure classroom interaction involving computer use."

Project Description

When it started in 1992-93, our experimental project involved 8 participants on a voluntary basis. These students (four from the University of Toronto matched with four from York University) had chosen to complement their regular second-year course load by maintaining a bi-weekly e-mail correspondence in French.

Since 1993, this e-mail exchange, along with the use of word-processor and electronic writing tools *(Hugo Plus, Le Correcteur 101, La Disquette linguistique, Collins On-line French-English Dictionary*, etc.), have been fully integrated into the program of our second-year writing courses in both institutions. It involved a total of 20 participants in 1993-94 and now counts more than 30 students. Although the use of e-mail in second language learning and teaching is not new, building a whole course around the interactive use of computers and e-mail is rather original; in our project, e-mail is not a complement to the course (such as bulletin-boards, group discussions around the course content, etc.) but the main component of written language practice. The professors responsible for this exchange do not correspond with the students but are the facilitators for their correspondence. As for the textbooks assigned (composition guides, grammar manuals, etc.), they are mainly used as reference.

Exchange Procedure and Course Content

At the beginning of the academic year, each student is provided not only with the course material but also with a kit which includes:

- the project outline and the protocol to be followed in every exchange
- the technical steps to access university network and to use e-mail
- a summary of basic word-processing features.

As stated in the exchange protocol, in their bi-weekly correspondence, students have to follow these five steps:

1. acknowledge receipt of letter
2. answer partner's questions on various matters
3. react to previous mail and/or ask for clarifications
4. write a content-based composition corresponding to the type of writing studied in class (self-portrait and autobiography, description of urban and natural surroundings, film and book reviews or play critiques, analysis of national and international news, etc.)
5. add a personal note.

To prepare students for each exchange, the professor introduces the linguistic tools (vocabulary, grammar, tips on writing techniques, etc.) needed for specific topics as indicated in step (4) of the protocol. Students are then asked to write a letter to their correspondent focusing on that particular topic. They will type the first draft of their letter at home or in the computer laboratory in order to bring it to the next class where, with the help of the instructor, they will edit it and improve it, using the in-class computers. This second stage is most important since it allows for interaction and cooperation between peers, and between students and teacher; students constantly ask peers for help regarding word-processing as well as grammar, vocabulary and style. It should also be pointed out that in addition to work done during this time slot, some students find it necessary to consult with the professor before or after class. Once the letter is completed and corrected, it is the responsibility of the student to send it by e-mail before the deadline agreed on in the protocol.

As to the receipt of the partner's letter, it is once again the student's responsibility to check his/her mail, retrieve it and print it. Occasionally, students bring their letters to class and willingly share some of the content with peers (photographs, anecdotes, funny stories, "emoticons", etc.).

Research has shown that language learning is facilitated when topics dealt with in the classroom take into consideration students' experience, interests, needs and emotions which, in fact, are part of their daily life. Therefore, exchanges between our students focus on the following subjects or themes in this specific order:

- (auto)biographical information
- family life
- studies and career
- leisure, hobbies and interests

- current affairs (national and international)
- controversial topics

As for grammar, it is not taught for grammar's sake but as a means to achieve better understanding and communication. Thus, we choose topics which we know will generate the need for the study of particular grammatical aspects of the language.

Students' Evaluation of the Exchange Project

During the second year of the project, instructors from both institutions handed out questionnaires to the students who participated in the exchange for its evaluation. Their feedback proved to be most useful. Not only were we encouraged to find out that the project was highly rated, but students' comments also provided us with a better understanding of their learning experience.

To students, the main benefit of this experience was a dramatic improvement of their writing skills which they attributed to the fact that they were writing to fellow students and not for the instructor. Indeed, several of them felt that their work would be scrutinized by their partners and wanted to measure up to their level. They also considered this experience to be a refreshing one since it gave them the opportunity to practise their written French in a more authentic and creative way, thus making learning more challenging than usual. They felt that the project expanded beyond the limits of the classroom and allowed them to exchange personal ideas in an authentic way and to establish new friendships. Students said they also developed more confidence in their computer skills.

Students were stimulated by the fact that their correspondent would enjoy receiving an interesting and well written letter through e-mail. They felt free to express themselves without "being told exactly what to write". They also liked the fact that their textbooks were peripheral rather than central to their learning experience and that the process of letter writing provided them with the opportunity to focus not only on the grammatically correct but also on the importance of expressing themselves clearly.

Though answers were in large part very positive, students pointed out some weaknesses in the project. Technical problems which delayed the processing and the transmission of letters at the beginning of the year received most of the criticism. Another area of disappointment was that they felt left out or ignored when not receiving a letter from their partner. Some students were also frustrated by the lack of time allotted to reply to their correspondent.

When asked whether the work on computer should be done before, during or after class, most students said they favoured working on the computer during classtime because instructors and peers could help; some even suggested that an optional additional hour be offered to compensate for the lack of time. However, others pointed out that doing most of the work outside of the classroom would provide them with more time to consult all sorts of resources (i.e. dictionaries, spell checks, language manuals, etc.) and would thus leave classtime for the correction of errors. This last remark is understandable, considering the fact that the majority of students chose to write first a draft on a piece of paper before typing it and improving it on the computer. Students who elected to type their letters directly on the computer found editing easier; it saved them time and enabled them to do quick spell checks and synonym searches. Most importantly, when asked how this exchange program made them work on their written French differently from the previous years, students mentioned that:

a) editing was not left to the last minute but became a regular practice, thanks to easy access to learning aids;

b) they spent more time correcting their mistakes and organizing their ideas to ensure that their message was properly understood;

c) having a partner to correspond with enabled them to produce very personalized work since they shared their experiences, compared viewpoints, explored different subjects, and related their ideas in a more authentic and direct style;

d) by receiving their partner's letters, they became aware of the latter's writing style which, in turn, influenced their own.

Reflections on Teaching and Learning via E-mail

Three years of observation of students at work with the computers, combined with our analysis of the project, led us to the following conclusions which, we hope, will guide other instructors who wish to embark on a similar venture.

a. Advantages of E-mail

Some advantages of L2 teaching and learning via e-mail are:

- the use of second language is more authentic – learners become aware of its communicative values since they write to a real audience;
- the content of letters is more interesting, dynamic and spontaneous than essays to the professor; students want to write more and do not hesitate to put in extra time;
- L2 learning is done in context;
- students compare their partner's writing skills with their own and try to do better;
- students benefit from facilitated and quicker use of learning aids (electronic dictionary, grammar and spell checks, thesaurus…);
- students familiarize themselves with new technologies;
- the social setting is more congenial and leads to better social interaction between peers;
- motivation is enhanced;
- learning is more autonomous – students take added responsibilities and work on their own in the computer laboratory.

b. Challenges of E-mail

The following are some of the challenges of L2 teaching via e-mail:
technical problems;

- limitations of software (not enough interaction);
- difficulty in adapting this kind of experience to a traditional curriculum;
- difficulty in scheduling exchanges between two institutions with different calendars;
- difficulty in meeting the needs and objectives of two different institutions, two curricula and two groups of learners;
- students not respecting the exchange protocol (not replying to the previous letter);
- students not respecting the time schedule;
- partners feeling left out when not receiving answers;
- possible lack of commitment from students;
- students dropping the course (and leaving their partner);
- danger of unfortunate mismatching of partners.

c. Role of Student

Some new responsibilities of the student will be:

- student becomes more self-disciplined;
- student is more autonomous;
- student must be willing to take more responsibilities (educational commitment);
- student takes more initiatives;
- student has more control over the content of the exchange;
- student is often placed in situations where cooperation with peers is needed (will ask for or provide help);
- student is committed to his/her own learning as well as to his/her partner's learning.

d. Role of Teachers

Teachers will face new responsibilities:

- teachers become facilitators and mediators (learning process is no longer teacher-centred but learner-centred):
- teachers should model the use of learning tools such as grammar books, dictionary, computer-assisted learning material, etc.;
- they should ensure, on a regular basis, that students respect the schedule and protocol;
- they should outline at the beginning of the year the working habits and strategies students are expected to develop in order to maximize this unusual learning experience;
- they should ensure that technical support is provided.
- teachers become consultants both in and out of the classroom;

- they should view themselves as less of an authority figure.

e. Advantages

The main advantages to this new approach to L2 teaching are:
- it generates 3 simultaneous types of interaction:
  - among students (exchange of information, ideas, comments, laughter, etc.);
  - between students and professor (students can instantly and more easily make changes to the text after the professor's critical reading);
  - between students and computer (thanks to computer learning aids such as spell check, thesaurus);
- it is more efficient:
  - instant printing;
  - technical speed;
  - easy deleting, cutting and/or pasting;
- students work at their own speed;
- it brings novelty into the classroom and stimulates learners.

f. Disadvantages

Some disadvantages are:
- technical problems can take too much time away from classroom work;
- exchanging personal letters may make group work impractical;
- corrections by the professor tend to become editorial (pinpointing of details) since the size of the screen prevents the reader from getting an overall picture of the text;
- computers tend to become a physical barrier between the professor and students as well as between students themselves;
- some students and professors may suffer from technophobia;
- the use of technology cannot be imposed on every instructor.

Pre-Test and Post-Test Results

In 1993-1994, students participating in this exchange were given a set of tests at the beginning and at the end of the year. The same tests were also administered to control groups in both institutions. These tests had two components: grammar (fill-in the blanks questions) and style (lexical and syntactical improvement).

Before proceeding with the results, we would like to point out that in our two institutions the second-year writing course focuses on the improvement of style and syntax through intensive writing. We would like to add that we were also fortunate to have two small participating groups in the exchange (12 and 8 students) and that on one campus the course amounted to a total of 33 hours whereas on the other campus it amounted to a total of 60 hours.

The following results represent the average marks received by students who wrote both tests: 24 students in the control group and 17 in the exchange group.

Although the format of the test did not reflect the type of writing the exchange groups practised throughout the year, it was administered with the intention of checking whether the exchange groups acquired the same grammatical, lexical and syntactical skills as the control group. In this respect the project was successful since the exchange group performed better than the control group. (They obtained an average of 63.52% for grammar and 67.35% for style against 61.74% and 60.28%, respectively.) It is worth pointing out that, even though the emphasis was placed on written practice rather than on grammar, test results show that grammar skills improved even more than writing skills. (An increase of 12.40% against an increase of 9.90% for style.)

These good results encouraged us to maintain this second-year writing course centred around an e-mail exchange. We are now in our fourth year, and it is our intention to pursue our testing in order to develop new strategies which could further enrich our experience.

Conclusion

While communicative teaching is difficult to achieve within the limits of the traditional classroom setting, this experience has gone beyond our expectations: students discovered common past experiences, exchanged ideas and advice on various matters, expressed their feelings and moods, and some even sent pictures via e-mail. From a pedagogical point of view, this learner-centred approach highly motivates students from beginning to end and seems to be particularly beneficial to their acquisition of the French language.

As educators conducting this project, we were particularly interested in finding out what led to its success. We believe that the main factors behind the students' renewed interest in the study of a second language are: real communication, social context, integration of technology in the classroom, and interaction between students and between students and the professor.

Our computer-assisted exchange is structured in such a way that all students are involved in a common project which they feel proud of. We also insure that the course is socially based by structuring it around written correspondence dealing with issues which motivate students because they are truly communicative. This project has proven to be particularly enriching from a pedagogical and human point of view.

As confirmed by Nathan (1985), Neu and Scarcella (1991) and Phinney (1989), students using word-processing in writing classes develop positive attitudes and more confidence toward their own writing. Indeed, it is worth noting that in two different surveys (Neu and Scarcella [1991] and the authors of this article), students have indicated that since they can easily access learning tools such as spell checks, thesaurus, etc. they do not hesitate to take risks in writing and editing and therefore become more comfortable with their use of the language. Their motivation leads them to spend considerably more time improving their texts from a linguistic and organizational perspective. As pointed out by Neu and Scarcella (1991:171),

> being able to make changes, to examine the altered work, and quickly to change it back to the original form, if desired, provides a psychological freedom that stimulates students' creativity, their exploration of ideas, and their evaluation and revision of those ideas.

Another source of motivation is the new relationship which is established between students and professor. Indeed, the use of computers is bound to affect the role of the teacher:

> In the computer-based writing class, students come to view the teacher as the consultant, technician, or resource person who can be called upon not only to help them solve writing problems but also to help fix technical problems, such as the failure of the printer. (Neu and Scarcella, 1991:173).

As we have observed in this exchange, this relationship is all the more different in that both students and professor have a common enemy/friend: the computer.

References

Canale, M. and Swain, M. 1980. "Theoretical Bases of Communicative Approaches to Second-Language Teaching and Testing." *Applied Linguistics*, 1 (1):1-47.

Corbeil, G. 1992. "Complémentarité des cours de langue à l'école secondaire et à l'université: existante ou inexistante?" *The Canadian Modern Language Review/La Revue canadienne des langues vivantes*, 48 (3): 497-511.

Ellis, R. 1990. *Instructed Second Language Acquisition – Learning in the Classroom*. Oxford: Basic Blackwell.

Guntermann, G. and J. K. Phillips. 1981. "Communicative Course Design: Developing Functional Ability in All Four Skills." *The Canadian Modern Language Review/La Revue canadienne des langues vivantes*, 37 (2):328-343.

Johnson, D. M. 1991. "Second Language and Content Learning with Computers." In *Computer-Assisted Learning and Testing. Research Issues and Practice*, ed. P. Dunkel, pp. 61-83. New York: Newbury House.

Krashen, S. D. and T. D. Terrell. 1983. *The Natural Approach: Language Acquisition in the Classroom*. New York: Pergamon Press.

Littlewood, W. T. 1984. *Foreign and Second Language Learning – Language Acquisition Research and its Implications for the Classroom*. Cambridge: Cambridge University Press.

Meirieu, P. 1987. *Apprendre... oui mais comment*. Paris: ESF éditeur.

Nathan, J. 1985. *Micro-Myths: Exploring the Limits of Learning with Computers*. Minneapolis: Winston Press.

Neu, J. and R. Scarcella. 1991. "Word Processing in the ESL Writing Classroom – A Survey of Student Attitudes." In *Computer-Assisted Language Learning and Testing. Research Issues and Practice*, ed. P. Dunkel, pp. 169-187. New York: Newbury House Publishers.

Phinney, M. 1989. "Computers, Composition and Second Language Teaching." In *Teaching Languages with Computers: The State of the Art*, ed. M. Pennington, pp. 81-96. La Jolla, Ca: Athelstan.

Rivers, W. 1972. "Talking off the Tops of their Heads." *TESOL Quarterly* 6: 77-81.

Savignon, S. 1983. Communicative Competence: Theory and Classroom Practice. Reading, Mass.: Addison Wesley.

Terrell, T. D. 1984. "The Natural Approach to Language Teaching: An Update." *The Modern Language Journal*, 41 (3): 460-479.

Reprinted from: Christine Besnard, Charles Elkabas, and Sylvie Rosienski-Pellerin "Students' Empowerment: E-mail Exchange and the Development of Writing Skills," *Mosaic*, 3, 2 (Winter 1996), pp. 8-12.

38 Gestures and Language: Fair and Foul in Other Cultures

Joanne Wilcox

Using the correct body language abroad can lessen the risk of failure in personal and business relationships. It's worth careful examination before you pack your bag.

Gestures often communicate faster and better than oral language in getting a point across. The deaf recognize this and transfer ideas and images with grace and beauty, using arms and hands and fingers and here and there a bit of body language thrown in.

A story about the deaf will help make the point. I grew up in the shadow of a tree-laden granite slope called Island View south of Halifax. Island View overlooks St. Margaret's Bay and one of the islands viewed on a clear day is Shut-in Island, along with the nearby community of Peggy's Cove and the most-photographed lighthouse in the world.

Because my uncle suffered total deafness since birth, around our house during his visits, sometimes with friends, lip-reading was our method of conversation. I recall his caution at one point not to "mouth" Island View to a newly-met deaf person at any time, since it might lead to delight or surprise or outright shock. Try it! If you form your lips and say "Island View," your mouth will confuse the lip-reader with three words of considerably greater impact: "I love you."

It's a great lesson why we should not tread on unfamiliar turf without knowing the pitfalls in both oral language and body language. It's important that we pick up the general rules of the new territory. Equally important, it should tell us that any attempt by North American business to establish liaison with peoples in other cultures must be examined with care. Items to be checked would include dress codes, gift-giving and receiving, where to sit at dinner - and at the conference table – where and when your spouse fits in, what days or seasons the government offices are closed and/or the local banks. And much, much more.

And, of course, translation. Faultless translation is essential to a business relationship in most cultures. Even where it is apparently not essential, the passing of a fully translated front-and-back business card is a pleasant and courteous thing to do.

Knowledgeable officials in the export business know this. The President of the Business Council on National Issues, Thomas d'Aquino, summed it up nicely:

Good products and services and vigourous salesmanship are cornerstones of successful exporting. Combine these with knowledge of foreign cultures, languages and business practices, and then you will have the winning edge.

It's sound advice. Yet the truth is North Americans are slow learners when it comes to executive manners and business etiquette abroad. As mentioned, the minimum courtesy when visiting another country on business would seem to be a business card in that country's language, and knowing how to use the body to deliver it. Yet, except for visits to Japan, where in Tokyo some 12 million business cards are exchanged daily, such a courtesy is uncommon with Canadians.

It needs preparation. When you plan your trip, envision your first meeting with your own countrymen at the embassy, and your meeting with your new strategic partner, the bank manager, and the customs people you'll be dealing with. In Tokyo, for example, cards are exchanged in a greeting ceremony of respect and welcome called *aisatsu*. It is important that the card-offering be accompanied by gestures. Here's how it's done:

- Your business card is called *meishi*.
- The seller presents first to the buyer.
- Hold your card Japanese-side up.
- Put the card forward with both hands with your thumbs on the upper side, present it while bowing moderately. Sometimes, the Japanese will receive your card with both hands.
- Cards are presented preferably while standing.
- Receive your contact's card in the same manner.
- When received, read and examine the card carefully. This is an important mark of courtesy; to simply take it and shove it into a pocket or wallet without examining it is offensive to the giver, as would be the case in any culture.

Business cards are winners. Consider this example.

I gave a client some treasured information on Japanese culture a few years ago. He had an international moving company, and was vying with a few large competitors on a job to move a Japanese family from Canada back to Japan. When he arrived at the address, he greeted the lady of the house with a dignified bow from the waist, offering his business card with both hands. As soon as he stepped foot in the home he immediately took off his shoes and put them in order by the door. The woman was so delighted by his efforts to make her comfortable by using her traditions, he got the job.

The point is that being culturally sensitive to body movement as well to language is a pleasant and very civilized way to get the edge on the competition.

When approaching your target market, it is quite natural that the first item to examine is your use of the language. This does not mean that you have to be fluently bilingual; just get to know a few key words like "Hello", "Please", "Thank you" - that kind of thing. You should also have your correspondence translated into the native tongue for ease of understanding. Accentuate the positive.

In making language arrangements, it's always wise to have a reliable source do the work. But to look on the negative side by way of example, executives very often fall into a trap, such as word that the secretary's second cousin took a course in the language seven years ago and that "she'll be able to do it for us." To make this point stick, here are some words that were quite likely put into English by someone like the secretary's second cousin living in another country:

- In a Bangkok cleaning shop is the sign: "Drop your trousers here for best results."
- In an Acapulco hotel: "The Manager has personally passed all the water served here."
- A slogan in China for "Pepsi comes alive" became: "Pepsi brings your dead ancestors back from the grave."
- ... and then there's the folded card that looks like a sandwich board, commonly called a "table-tent", found on the bedroom dresser at a hotel in the Orient. On one side it noted the following: "Our proud bell-captain will be pleased to take your luggage and send it off in all directions" while on the other side the hotel pointed out: "Guests are welcome to take advantage of our chambermaids."*

The point is made. It's risky business to arrange your translation "in-house". To have the prospective buyer or strategic partner in the target market pass it around the office for a good laugh at your expense is surely risk enough.

Most travellers have some notion of the pre-travel checklist. You'll want to think about clothing, gift-giving, where to sit at the conference table, dinner etiquette, and a lengthy list of such matters. But we find that in most cases even those who have thought out some of these needs beforehand have given little thought to a vitally important item: even the world's top politicians have passed by consideration of when and when not to use common North American gestures and body language. Be aware that gestures as well as language goofs can cause a giggle.

Fred Chardtrand, *Canadian Press*
President George Bush's "Thumbs

A few years back, George Bush's presidential visit to Australia was coming to a successful conclusion as he walked up the stairs to his aircraft for the trip home. Then he paused, turned to the crowd and, with a sweeping gesture, gave Aussies something to think about for years: the thumbs-up sign.

North Americans consider this a nice thing to do. In some regions Down Under, however, it's an obscenity worse than giving the finger.

Advice on such body language has been put together in a scholarly work at Oxford University in *Gestures: their origins and meanings* by Desmond Morris, Peter Collett, Peter March and Marie O'Shaughnessy (published by Jonathan Cape). They note that the thumbs-up sign can have this offensive application in certain countries in Europe, while in both Europe and North America it can mean victory or approval.

All countries have sensitive spots. In Indonesian and in some other cultures in southeast Asia, you have a problem if you're left-handed; one never uses the left hand to give or receive anything. The left hand is always kept aside to be brought out for cleaning purposes in the washroom.

In Saudi Arabia, a million dollar deal can be lost if you cross your legs. In the Saudi culture, if the sole of your foot shows, you are telling your host he is beneath a dog. In some parts, the people believe that the dangling foot is the devil pointing at them.

Greg Gibson, *Associated Press*
President Bill Clinton's "OK sign"

The Japanese would much rather you didn't blow your nose anywhere in a public place. To do so in a dining room can put an end to negotiations right away.

Better not scratch your cheek with your forefinger. It may resemble the "cheek screw". When the hand is rotated in this way it means crazy in Germany, and effeminate in Spain. However, in Italy it means good.

In European countries particularly, the forearm jerk can be an aggressive sexual insult or sexual comment. In this display, the clenched fist is jerked forcibly upwards; the jerked arm is bent at the elbow and, as the jerk is performed, the other hand is slapped down on the upper arm, as if something is checking the upward movement.

In a rap session following a seminar on gestures, a Greek person in the audience pointed out that the way we use the head to make a "yes" or "no" is precisely the oppositive in Greece. Over there, the up-and-down nod of the head means "no", while the side-to-side shake means "yes".

Not all gestures are foul. Tap your fingers gently on the table in Taiwan following a meal, and it signals your appreciation of the event.

And some have mixed meanings. The gesture of "pursing the hand" is common in the Mediterranean countries, particularly in Italy. The fingers are straightened and brought together in a point facing upwards. This can be a what-are-you-talking-about query, or praise or approval, or sarcastic criticism.

What is called "The Ring" in some countries is our OK sign, thumb and forefinger forming a circle, with the remaining three fingers aloft. During President Bill Clinton's trip to Russia earlier in 1994, citizens attended a Town Hall meeting in Moscow and got a first hand look at the President's "ring" during an animated oration he was giving at the time. Clinton may have thought it was OK, but to Russians it was a shocker. The OK sign over there, and in a number of other countries, is an "orifice symbol". If the president had been a run-of-the-mill tourist in a Moscow pub, he could have had his nose flattened and ended his evening in a Moscow slammer.

Social gaffes like these can be embarrassing, and a politician or business executive has little room to claim: "Nobody told me." It just won't wash. The President got off lightly. Even a minor miscue can kill a meeting or ruin a deal.

Think you know your international etiquette? If you're planning a trip, try the following quiz. If you do all right, *bon voyage*. If you goof, it's time to bone up.

1. When in Taiwan, you offer thanks for a good meal by:
   (a) Inviting the chef into the dining area with the suggestion that all present raise their glasses to that person's success in marriage.
   (b) Tapping your fingers lightly on the table.
   (c) Lighting a peach-coloured candle that you ask the head waiter to deliver to the table at the conclusion of the meal.

2. A gift of flowers is appropriate in Mexico. The flowers should be in the favourite floral colour of the people, that is:
   (a) Red, symbolizing the great tomato crop.
   (b) White, the international symbol of purity.
   (c) Yellow, for the sun god that has been so kind to Mexico's tourist industry.

3. If offered a drink in the Netherlands prior to a business discussion, you should:
   (a) If you're a woman executive, place it between your knees and hold it there for 30 seconds. If a man, flatten your hand and hold the drink on your upright palm for 30 seconds.
   (b) Accept it without ritual of any kind.
   (c) Decline, stating that you want to carry on with business, and when you've made the sale you'll pick up the tab all around.

4. In the Peoples' Republic of China, a superb gift to offer your host is:
   (a) A T-shirt with the image of your country's leader stamped on it.
   (b) A small clock with white-gloved Mickey Mouse hands pointing the time.
   (c) A vase or basket arrangement from a local florist.

5. When paying a restaurant tab in Japan, be sure to include a tip in this manner:
   (a) Kiss the signed credit card receipt with the tip shown clearly on it and present it to the head waiter.

(b) Put the tip in cash in a decorative envelope and give it to the head waiter, who will then distribute the cash to the appropriate staff.

(c) Ask to see the chef and go to the kitchen to present that person with the tip money in a manila envelope in coins only.

6. When greeting your host/hostess in India, you will:
    (a) Firmly grab his/her right hand in greeting as you would in Canada, and shake it vigorously.
    (b) Click your heels once, then point the toes of your shoes together and bow.
    (c) Press your own two palms together in greeting.

7. When meat or a vegetable on your plate looks somewhat different from what the dining room back home would serve, you would:
    (a) As a conversation opener, show interest by asking whether the dish features an endangered plant or animal species.
    (b) Suggest that you'd like to repay your host's kindness if you could just find a Pizza Delight or a Harvey's in town.
    (c) Cut it into bite-sized pieces and eat the meal placed before you.

8. In Sweden, when asked for your title and the full name of your company:
    (a) Say you'll write the information in English on the place-mat to give it a personal touch.
    (b) Offer to send a fax when you get home.
    (c) Have a business card with you that bears a translation for all pertinent information, including telephone and fax numbers.

9. You've just completed a presentation and the sale looks like a sure thing. You then put your material back in your briefcase and:
    (a) Extend an offer to meet everyone at the bar downstairs and exercise your elbow and wrist to make a drinking gesture.
    (b) Put thumb and forefinger together to form the "okay" circle, and leave the room.
    (c) Say thank you in both your language and theirs, and leave.

10. In Kuwait, when coffee is offered:
    (a) Drink two cups with your right hand, then decline a third by shaking your cup slightly before returning it to the server.
    (b) After each cup, tug at your earlobes in a brief gesture of thanks.
    (c) Take off your right shoe at the start of the coffee service, place it upside down on the floor directly in front of your host until you have finished coffee, and then return it to your foot.

The Answers

1. Avoid A and C. They're apt to start people talking. It's correct to tap your fingers on the table. Choose B.
2. Forget the sun god and the tomato nonsense. To Mexicans, yellow flowers connote death, and red flowers cast spells. On the other hand, white flowers remove spells, so B wins the day.

3. Accept the drink without fuss. B is the choice you'd make, an essential part of business culture in the Netherlands.

4. Try C, the floral arrangement. The gift of a clock is a symbol of bad luck in China, and the T-shirt is, well_a bit Mickey Mouse in its own right.

5. B. The tip in the decorative envelope reflects knowledgeable behaviour and is much appreciated. A and C are out of the question.

6. It's proper to press your own palms together. A and B are in bad taste. Choose C.

7. C might seem like a tough one to handle, but it has to be done. When abroad, eat what's placed in front of you.

8. A and B might lose you some goodwill marks. Go with C, in any country visited, and make sure you have the translation service prepare your cards before you jet away.

9. C wins again. Better stay away from using the "okay" sign in any country; it can be the equivalent of the obscene finger gesture, or just not understood.

10. A is the correct coffee ritual. B is useless, and C is a real loser, since to show the bottom of one's shoe or foot is very rude indeed; this kind of behaviour could result in your early departure from Kuwait.

Next time you plan a trip, somewhere on your checklist between "garments" and "gift-giving", place the reminder: "gestures."

*For additional incorrect translations, read Richard Lederer'anecdotes in Anthony Mollica, *"Traduttore, traditore!:* Beware of Communicative Incompetence!," *Mosaic,* Vol. 3, 4: 19-20. The list is reproduced in the revised and up-dated article, "Language Learning: The Key to Understanding and Harmony", Chapter 1 in this volume.

Photos: Courtesy Canadian Press
Illustrations: George Shane

Reprinted from: Joanne Wilcox, "Gestures and Language:Fair and Foul in Other Cultures," *Mosaic,* 2, 1 (Fall 1994), pp. 10-13.

39 Teaching to the Test: Principles of Authentic Assessment for Second Language Education

Edwin G. Ralph

Educators typically recoil at the phrase, "teach to the test." Yet, this article supports that injunction as being valid for second language teachers - provided that certain conditions are met.

A recent trend that has appeared on the agenda of school reform in several countries is centered on the raising of national educational standards and on the implementation of comprehensive evaluation of students' learning performance. A divisive issue emerging from this movement deals less with whether these assessments will influence classroom teaching and learning – because they will (Marzano, Pickering, and McTighe, 1993; Zessoules and Gardner, 1991) – but more with what types of assessments should be used (Worthen, 1993). A fear is that if these "new" assessments are merely a rehash of the traditional standardized, multiple-choice, norm-referenced type, then teachers will tend to mirror a similar type of instruction in their classroom practice. As a consequence, it is believed that their students' learning will tend to reflect corresponding characteristics, such as low-order thinking, memorization of discrete items, and inability to apply this knowledge in real-world situations (O'Neil, 1993).

The purpose of this article is to demonstrate, however, that the practice of "teaching to the test" is not inappropriate – provided that "the test" is one that meets the criteria of "authentic assessment" as described in the current literature of education reform (Wiggins, 1993). The term "authentic assessment" like many reform notions in education is a new label for an old practice that has been used by good teachers throughout history (Cronin, 1993; Perrone, 1991).

Authentic Assessment: What is it?

Authentic Assessment, "direct assessment", "process testing", or "performance assessment" (Herman, Aschbachers and Winters 1992, Worthen 1993) refers to the otherwise known as "alternative assessment" application of generic formulae, is not considered as revolutionary by current second language educators, as it may be perceived by some other members of the educational establishment. In fact, evidence for the pursuit of such goals as learners' communication competence, language proficiency, and practice in real life situations has been observable in second language education for several years. This evidence has been manifested on several fronts:

- internationally (Girard, Huot, and Lussier-Chasles, 1987);
- nationally, through the establishment of the National Core French Study (Tremblay, 1992);
- provincially, through the formation of several governments' recent second language curriculum policies and guidelines (Diffey, 1991); and
- commercially, through several publishers' dissemination of applicable educational materials (e.g., Jean, 1991).

A further line of support bolstering the fact that the field of second language education has embraced the concept of authentic learning/assessment is the acknowledgment of this phenomenon by recognized experts in the area of authentic learning. Wiggins (1992, 1993), for instance, has complimented second language educators for designing tasks and tests to assist beginning second language students to move progressively from a crude grasp of the complex whole of a communication act to a more sophisticated grasp of the experience. He advocates:

"We need to generalize from [second language] courses, which get the learner speaking and listening in context immediately and working toward the ultimate criterion of fluent contextual performance" (Wiggins, 1993, p. 203).

Thus, this emphasis in current second language education– whether in core or immersion programs of ESL, FSL, Heritage languages, or First Nations' languages – on engaging students in experiential/global learning and assessment activities is a major goal worth pursuing and perfecting. However, for the benefit of second language teachers, who may be entering the profession, or who may be at various stages in their teaching careers, this present paper seeks to identify some of the key principles and practices of authentic assessment as it is applied in the daily practice of second language instruction.

Key Principles of Authentic Assessment

A synthesis of the current research literature related to authentic assessment reveals four key principles characterizing this process (Herman, 1992; Marzano, Pickering, and McTighe, 1993).

Constructivist Learning

Authentic assessment is built on current learning theories espousing cognitivist developmentalist assumptions, whereby learners participate individually and with others in various learning and assessment activities that require personal meaning-making, and reflective and self-regulated interpretation. Students demonstrate their performance by engaging in realistic, motivating communicative tasks.

Although authentic assessment stresses students' production of holistic, unique, and complex linguistic tasks involving a synthesis of higher-order thinking, it does not ignore the performance of lower level skills or discrete linguistic elements. However, the traditional drill skill, mechanical/ algorithmic language activities are used sparingly, and essentially play a supporting role en route to helping learners to progress developmentally toward becoming both accurate (i.e., mechanically correct) and proficient (i.e., communicatively comprehensible) second language users (Valette, 1993). Skilled second language teachers reflectively and effectively supplement students' holistic language experiences (e.g., communicative functions and notions) with occasional language study exercises (e.g., grammatical structure/pronunciation). Moreover, the latter is subordinated to the former, in that the language study component tends to be used to advise learners how to improve the accuracy of their particular second language productive (speaking/writing) skills (Tremblay, 1992).

Communicative Tasks

A learning/assessment task illustrating this cognitive/constructivist principle is one that will engage students in specific functional/notional scenarios appropriate for their age, their interest(s), and their level of linguistic competence. For example, a possible activity for 9 and 10 year old second language students, with 3 to 4 years prior experience in a core second language program, is one that the present author found to be effective in his own teaching practice. Students are requested to prepare and present a role-play, in pairs, of a typical after-school telephone conversation. They would be given clear directions about using recent material presented in class, and everyone would be clear that students would be evaluated on their use of second language, their acting ability, and their creativity "...to make up statements that reflect the intended meaning of the text" (Nemni and Lecerf, 1990, p. 14).

Integration of Teaching/ Learning/Assessment

A second principle of authentic assessment is that the components of teaching, learning, and assessment are considered as an integrated whole. Because the cognitivist-constructivist approach emphasizes learners' performance of tasks that demonstrate what they know and are able to do in real-life situations (or meaningful simulations of the same), then it follows that any of these tasks – whether they take the form of informal practice-sessions, or of more formal performances, projects, portfolios, or tests – are eligible to be evaluated in any second language class period. However, students must be informed of this procedure at the beginning of the course, and periodically throughout the school term (Nemni and Lecerf, 1990). Thus, the traditional distinction between "the test" and "a learning task" is purposefully blurred, so that all classroom activities including individual assignments and group tasks are evaluated and make up part of student grades for reporting purposes.

Regardless whether each second language learning experience is, by nature, formative (ongoing) or summative (terminal), or discrete or integrative, or norm or criterion referenced, or formal or informal, it is crucial that both students and teachers should know clearly what the particular content and performance standards are for each of these tasks (Jean, 1991; Palmer Wolf, LeMahieu, and Eresh, 1992). Moreover, Wiggins (1993) asserts that all authentic assessment whether "task" or "test" should provide enticing, stimulating challenges for learners in which they are engaged in meaningful communicative situations. An example of such a specific second language situation could involve having students conduct and analyze a survey of their peers' typical daily dietary intake, or of their physical activity patterns, and then to present the findings formally to the class via oral and/or project formats in the second language. Again, these tasks would be evaluated according to specific predetermined and clearly stated criteria.

Productions of Unique Simulations

Because of normal logistical constraints that exist in schools, second language teachers may be forced to contrive authentic simulations that are somewhat artificial, but that "feel real" to students (Wiggins, 1992, p. 27). For instance, the present author has had several groups of his former middle-years second language students successfully plan, prepare, and perform the following dramatic skits complete with second language dialogue, taped sound effects and background music, appropriate costumes, and stage props and lighting: "A Missed Aircraft Hijacking," "Fractured Fairy-tales," "Former TV Heros," "Cinderfella and His Godfather," and "At the Movies."

In keeping with authentic performance principles, these students were assessed on both their individual and group use of the second language, their dramatic participation, and their involvement (including their fulfillment of their responsibility to prepare their own costumes and props). Inevitably, this author also found that learner motivation increased toward second language course specifically, and toward the second language generally, as a result of having students to participate in these meaningful but simulated learning tasks (Ralph, 1987, 1989).

Quality and Coverage of Content

A third standard characterizing authentic assessment is that the performance tasks must not only be consistent with the current trends advocated in the curricular field, but that they also must be representative of the key elements of the discipline (Herman, 1992). With respect to second language education in Canada in recent years, the National Core French Study (Lapkin, Harley, and Taylor, 1993) has provided a major impetus both for provincial governments (Lazaruk, 1993), and for publishers (Nemni and Lecerf, 1990) to help revise policies and create materials based on the concept of having students to use language meaningfully in true communicative contexts. Thus, provincial second language guidelines (Diffey, 1991; Saskatchewan, 1988) as well as contemporary published programs (e.g., Jean, 1991; McConnell and Collins, 1989), promote learners' integration of the analytical/technical with the communicative/function aspects of second language acquisition. The goal is that these "communicative situations are made as real as possible in the classroom" (Saskatchewan, 1988, p. 218).

In pursuing the ultimate content objective of helping students to function both fluently *and* accurately in the four second language skills (Valette, 1993), teachers are faced with the perpetual challenge of creating learning and assessment activities that have an appropriate blend of language experience *and* language study. Current experts in the field are agreed that this optimum mix is best reached when second language educators embed learning and assessment activities in units or themes appropriate for specific age groups. Students take part in natural and authentic language experiences as they encounter a variety of interesting tasks related to these broad themes. Thus, learners are actually put into real-life communication situations where they have to use the second language in a personal, direct way – rather than first having to learn several discrete language skills, and then trying to apply them in a new setting (Duplantie, Hullen, and Tremblay, 1992).

Activities Related to Students' Lives

These second language learning and/or testing activities are designed to tap into learners' own life experience and interests. A further example used with middle years students might be to develop (and later to assess) their listening comprehension of actual TV or radio news/ sports/weather reports (or simulations thereof) delivered by a native second language speaker. By answering a set of oral and/or written questions about the report, students would demonstrate several skills: their global understanding of the content, their knowledge of specific facts presented in the broadcast, and their ability to deduce/analyze/interpret these facts. Further, to demonstrate their second language oral production skills they could be assigned to create, prepare, and present a simulated TV or radio report of their own. These resulting role-plays could also be audio or videotaped in the classroom setting and would be assessed not only for the technical aspects of second language grammar and usage, but also for student participation/initiative/creativity.

The present author has found through his 30 years' experience in education from the elementary to adult levels as second language teacher, school principal, school district second language coordinator, university professor, and supervisor of teacher interns – that such stimulating activities meet two key goals. They not only help motivate students and reenergize teachers toward the second language program, but these tasks seem to have an effect on reducing negative attitudes among certain students who may have been formerly categorized either as "reserved, retiring, or recalcitrant," or as "rambunctious, rude, or rebellious" (Ralph, 1982, 1987, 1989, 1993, in press). The positive reinforcement received by students as a result of their participating in a successful authentic performance contributed to an increase in their more favourable acceptance of the second language course.

Quality and Fairness of Standards

A fourth principle of authentic assessments that the assessment process always seeks to produce accurate results upon which to permit fair and sound decisions and conclusions about student performance, teacher effectiveness, and program quality. However, a persistent dilemma for all educators, including those in second language teaching, is to design learning and assessment activities that optimize both the validity (i.e., fidelity to the criterion situations that maximize learners' freedom to respond appropriately in real communicative contexts) and the reliability (i.e., consistency, precision, and standardization of results). Because many traditional assessment formats tend to decontextualize and decompose knowledge into isolated, generic, or simplistic responses, educators advocating the authentic approach seek to reduce these deficiencies by devising alternative standards and tasks that allow for more pluralistic, diverse, and idiosyncratic performance by students (Wiggins, 1993). The latter reflect the complexities involved in confronting ambiguous communication scenarios in the real world of students' lives.

The principle undergirding our best current understanding of second language acquisition and assessment emphasizes the integration of both the analytical *and* the global dimensions of second language learning. Research by Stern (1982), by the National Core French Study (Tremblay, 1992), by provincial ministries of education in Canada (Diffey, 1991), and by the American Council on the Teaching of Foreign Languages (Wiggins, 1993) has resulted in the publication and dissemination of accepted second language proficiency guidelines – empirically grounded in clearly described traits characterizing the performance of learners at various stages of second language abilities.

Moreover, there exists a variety of scoring descriptors, evaluation formats, and assessment frameworks, as well as several actual second language tests that have been piloted and normed on target groups similar to the individuals being tested (Lapkin, Argue, and Foley, 1992). Thus, second language educators currently have a choice among several trustworthy assessment sources, some of which are: the above instruments; materials provided by provincial ministries and/or local school divisions; tests included in the second language programs from commercial publishers; teachers' personally created materials and activities; and combinations of the above.

Quality Assessments

An example of an authentic learning or testing task that seeks to gauge students' second language receptive and productive skills would be for the teacher to arrange time to conduct an oral second language interview with each of the students in a class. Learners would be forewarned, for instance, to be prepared to respond to oral questions from a "TV talk-show host" from another country. The purpose would be for "the interviewer" to record the interview and to take it back for later telecasting in the interviewer's nation, in order to generate interest among similarly aged students to come to visit the interviewee's school in Canada. The interviewee would have been told previously thus to expect to use persuasive and enthusiastic responses in order to motivate these potential viewers to come to Canada.

The interviewer's questions would reflect what Howard (1980) calls a "semi free" format, in that specific topics and/or questions would not be pre-specified for the respondent; and that the interviewee would be expected to make use of previously learned second language material presented and practised in class, such as Canadian geography, descriptions of weather, buildings, families, and school- and home-life. During the activity, respondents would be assessed globally for their integration of the communicative, grammatical, and sociolinguistic dimensions of second language, as well as for their overall knowledge of the topic and their linguistic versatility.

Fairness in the assessment of each of the above learning/testing tasks would be secured if the evaluators ensured that they would incorporate the following criteria:

- to develop and use scoring rubrics based on accepted second language models or templates that would indicate both exemplary and nonexemplary performances (the latter illustrating typical errors for each age/stage of second language development);

- to assess students' grammatical/technical second language skills, such that these mechanical aspects would be regarded as important – but not as sufficient aspects – in learners' demonstrations of their proficiency in realistic and relevant second language communication;

- to delay key decisions regarding learner, teacher, program, and context matters, until a variety of learning/assessment tasks would be collected in order to provide a composite profile of results; and

- to align all such learning/assessment activities with the second language program's objectives, as well as to apply the authentic assessment philosophy, principles, and practices in their daily instructional routines.

Second-Language Education on Track for Authentic Assessment

This article has indicated that our contemporary knowledge of effective second language education is based on the cognitive view of learning, in which learners actively construct personal understanding in a holistic manner as they engage in actual communicative activities. Because the processes of teaching, learning, and assessment of learning are so closely and intimately tied, and because the latter directly affects both of the former processes, then it is essential that second language educators ensure that all of their assessment practices both guide, and are guided by, the specified student-learning tasks for each level, and the accompanying performance standards for these tasks. In the light of this key assumption, Marzano, Pickering, and McTighe (1993) aptly conclude that it is essential that the authentic assessment task "...reflects good instructional practice, so that teaching to the test is desirable" (p. 13).

Thus, "the test" virtually represents any second language activity derived from the experientially-oriented thematic approach that prepares students "for real world language use" (Lapkin, Harley, and Taylor, 1993, p. 486). At this point in time, second language education has already embraced this concept, and may second language educators continue to implement *and* to improve these authentic learning tasks in the daily routines of their classrooms!

References

Cronin, J. 1993. Four misconceptions about authentic learning. *Educational Leadership,* 50, 7: 78-80.

Diffey, N. 1991. Provincial curriculum guidelines in core French. *Canadian Modern Language Review/La Revue canadienne des langues vivantes,* 47: 307-326.

Duplantie, M., J. Hullen, and R. Tremblay. 1992. *Guide pédagogique: Élans 2e. première partie.* Anjou, Québec: Centre Éducatif et Culturel, Inc.

Girard, C., D. Huot, and D. Lussier-Chasles, D. 1987. "L'évaluation de la compétence de communication en classe de langue seconde." In Pierre Calvé and Anthony Mollica, eds., *Le français langue seconde: Des principes à la pratique.* Welland, Ontario: Canadian Modern Language Review.

Herman, J. 1992. "What research tells us about good assessment." *Educational Leadership.* 49, 8: 74-78.

Herman, J., P. Aschbacher, and L. Winters. 1992. *A practical guide to alternative assessment.* Alexandria, VA: Association for Supervision and Curriculum Development.

Howard, F. 1980. "Testing communicative proficiency in French as a second language: A search for procedures." *The Canadian Modern Language Review/La Revue canadienne des langues vivantes,* 36:272-289.

Jean, G. 1991. *Entre amis 1: Teacher's Guide.* Scarborough, Ontario: Prentice-Hall.

Lapkin, S., V. Argue, and D. Foley. 1992. "Annotated lists of French tests: 1991 update." *Canadian Modern Language Review/La Revue canadienne des langues vivantes,* 48:780-807.

Lapkin, S., B. Harley, and S. Taylor. 1993. "Research directions for core French in Canada." *The Canadian Modern Language Review/La Revue canadienne des langues vivantes,* 49:476-513.

Lazaruk, W. 1993. "A multidimensional curriculum model for heritage or international language instruction." *Mosaic.* 1, 1 :13-15.

Marzano, R., D. Pickering, and J. McTighe. 1993. *Assessing student outcomes.* Alexandria, VA: Association for Supervision and Curriculum Development.

McConnell, G., and R. Collins. 1989. *D'accord 2: Teacher's Guide.* Don Mills, Ontario: Addison-Wesley.

Nemni, M., and B. Lecerf. 1990. *Bienvenue 3: C'est parti! Teacher's Guide.* Scarborough, Ontario: Prentice-Hall.

O'Neil, J. 1993. "The promise of portfolios." *ASCD Update.* 35, 7: 1, 5.

Palmer Wolf, D., P. LeMahieu, and J. Eresh. 1992. "Good measure: Assessment as a tool for educational reform." *Educational Leadership.* 49, 8: 8-13.

Perrone, V. 1991. "Introduction." In V. Perrone, ed., *Expanding student assessment*, pp. vii-xi. Alexandria, VA: Association for Supervision and Curriculum Development.

Ralph, E. 1982. "The unmotivated second-language learner: Can students' negative attitudes be changed?" *The Canadian Modern Language Review/La Revue canadienne des langues vivantes*, 38:393-502.

Ralph, E. 1987. "Motivation et étude d'une langue seconde: Peut-on modifier une attitude négative chez les élèves?" In Pierre Calvé and Anthony Mollica, eds., *Le français langue seconde: Des principes à la pratique*. Welland, Ontario: Canadian Modern Language Review.

Ralph, E. 1989. "Research on effective teaching: How can it help second language teachers motivate the unmotivated learner?" *Canadian Modern Language Review/La Revue canadienne des langues vivantes*, 46:135-146.

Ralph, E. 1993. "Beginning teachers and classroom management: Questions from practice, answers from research." *Middle School Journal*. 25, 1: 60-64.

Ralph, E. (in press). "Middle and secondary second language teachers: Meeting classroom management challenges via effective teaching research." *Foreign Language Annals*.

Saskatchewan Education. 1988. *Core French: A curriculum Guide for Grades 7-12*. Regina: Saskatchewan Education.

Tremblay, R. 1992. "Second languages in Canadian education: Curriculum concerns." *The Canadian Modern Language Review/La Revue canadienne des langues vivantes*, 48:811-823.

Valette, R. 1993. "The challenge of the future: Teaching students to speak fluently and accurately." *The Canadian Modern Language Review/La Revue canadienne des langues vivantes*, 50:173-178.

Wiggins, G. 1992. "Creating tests worth taking." *Educational Leadership*. 49, 8: 26-33.

Wiggins, G. 1993. "Assessment: Authenticity, context, and validity." *Phi Delta Kappan*. 75:200-214.

Worthen, B. 1993. "Critical issues that will determine the future of alternative assessment." *Phi Delta Kappan*, 74:444-454.

Zessoules, R., H. Gardner, H. 1991. "Authentic assessment: Beyond the buzzword." In V. Perrone, ed., *Expanding student assessment*, pp. 47-71. Alexandria, VA: Association for Supervision and Curriculum Development.

Reprinted from: Edwin G. Ralph, "Teaching to the Test: Principles of Authentic Assessment for Second Language Education," *Mosaic*, 1, 4 (Summer 1994), pp. 9-13.

40 Teaching Culture in a North American Context:

An Introductory Note

Anthony Mollica

In his widely-read, often-quoted article on "Teaching Culture in the Foreign Language Classroom," Nelson Brooks (1968:204) proposes a list of matters that appear central and critical in the analysis of culture. His list is as follows:

1. Symbolism
2. Value
3. Authority
4. Order
5. Ceremony
6. Love
7. Honour
8. Humour
9. Beauty
10. Spirit

An analysis of *Symbolism*, [suggests Brooks] would tell us not only about a nation's language but also about its literature and art, its politics, and its religion. Under *Value* we would consider personal preferences and rejection, conscience, morality and philosophy. Under *Authority* we would note whose word is accepted and acted upon at various ages in one's life and in various situations and circumstances. Under *Order* we would study what dispositions there are toward a clear, methodical, and harmonious arrangement of thoughts and things in life of both individual and community. *Ceremony* would focus our attention upon the almost excessive human fondness for elaborate dress and complicated ritual, for congregations great and small on occasions gay and solemn. And what analysis of culture could be complete without *Love*, whether it be the attachment of parent and child, of husband and wife, the devotion of one friend toward another, or the attitude of an individual toward a supreme being? Even if we see in love no more than the reciprocal of aggression, it would appear to merit a place in our list. Under *Honour* we would consider the high standards of personal conduct that give evidence of our attitude toward ourselves, our families, our friends, our country. Under *Humour* we would note not only how important and popular is the sense of what is witty, comic and laughable but also what is found to be humorous and how this varies from one age group to another and from one culture to another. Under *Beauty* we would seek for and describe in the products of man's brain and hand that which is over and above the practical and the utilitarian, and marks a striving toward innovation and perfection, and is an indication of the aesthetic sense which man is motivated to express. Finally, under *Spirit* our attention would be turned upon the evidence of man's awareness of himself as man, the special human capacity whereby his thoughts may range in time and space far from the situation in which he finds himself, contemplating both reality and non-reality, and permitting him to pursue the eternal quest of what it is that he is.

For Brooks, then, *ceremony* occupies an important place in the teaching of culture.

"Halloween," "Thanksgiving," "Valentine's Day," "Mother's/Father's Day" are essentially North American celebrations. So why are we trying to impose a North American cultural tradition on a target language other than English? The reason is quite simple. North American students attending English-speaking classes celebrate these festivities by being involved in a number of practical hands-on activities. It seems, therefore, pedagogically sound to draw from this highly motivational source with which the English-speaking students are familiar.

To assist teachers and instructors of various languages who may not be very familiar with these topics, a rubric in *Mosaic*, "Teaching Culture in a North American Context", has been providing background information on a number of these "ceremonial" cultural topics.

The information has been presented in both prose and dialogue format. It is obvious that information presented in dialogue form obviously lends itself much more easily to conversation and discussion than the more intricate narrative or descriptive prose.

The information – whether in prose or in dialogue – is meant to be used as a springboard for further research and activities. The section on "Halloween", for example, provides the background in prose. That same information has been used to recall – in a humorous way – the origins and the reasons for the celebration of "Halloween." Teachers may want to involve their students by having them act out the "interview" or even ask a group of students to videotape it. The latter activity would enlist the participation of a larger group since it would involve "actors," "directors," "stagehands," "producers" in the video production. Students should be encouraged to use the target language during the staging or production of the "interview."

This type of activity will involve not only students who are good language students but also students who – although they may not excel in the target language – feel their participation as being important in the success of the production.

As the late H. H. Stern (1983: 4) pointed out,

> In the last few years a new view of language acquisition has resulted partly from research on second-language learning and partly from the immersion experience. It underlines the fact that a language cannot be learned by formal practice alone. Much of it is learnt in the process of doing something else while using the language.

In essence, Stern is paraphrasing the old adage:

"Tell me and I forget.

Show me and I know.

Involve me and I learn."

Calvé (1985: 278) echoes similar sentiments when he states that "ce n'est qu'en communiquant qu'on peut apprendre à communiquer."

Involvement is the key idea in Stern's quotation, in the adage, and in Calvé's remark. And, if we accept the twin principle that we learn best by doing and that we speak when we want to say something or when we want to obtain information which is of interest to us, then the stimulus proposed above will fulfill these two functions.

Brooks, Nelson. 1968. "Teaching Culture in the Foreign Language Classroom." Foreign Language Annals, 1, 3 (March): 204-217.

Calvé, Pierre. 1985. " Les programmes de base: des principes à la réalité." *The Canadain Modern Language Review/La Revue canadienne des langues vivantes*, 42, 2 (November): 271-287.

Stern, H. H. 1983. "And Cinderella may yet go to the Ball: A personal view of the past, present and future of Core French." *Dialogue. A newsletter on the Teaching of English and French as Second Languages.* Toronto: Council of Ministers of Education, Canada. 2, 1 (November): 1-4.

41 Teaching Culture in a North American Context:

Halloween Revisited

Anthony Mollica, Marjolaine Séguin,
Raffaella Maiguashca, and Natalia Valenzuela

Editor's Note: In Volume 1, No. 1 of *Mosaic*, we published some historical background to *Halloween*. That information is now followed by interviews with a "Witch". The three dialogues which follow, however, contain some interesting "twists":

- the French Witch threatens to turn our intrepid journalist into a rabbit!...
- the Italian witch is in North America as part of an ANSI delegation (the National Associatioon of Italian Witches!)... and complains about the working conditions..
- the Spanish interviewer is ill-at-ease for interviewing a Witch for the first time…

Halloween

Halloween, celebrated every year on the 31st of October, is a custom which dates back more than 2000 years. The current name, which originates from the English expression *All Hallows' eve*, was not coined until much later on. In North America, Irish immigrants introduced several rituals characteristic of this holiday.

Originally, Halloween was celebrated by the Celts who were then living in Great Britain and in northern France. Traditionally, on October 31st which marked the eve of the Celtic new year, the Celts remembered Samhain, the master of Death. They believed that Samhain allowed the dead to return to earth during the ceremony; hence, the notion of ghosts on Halloween.

Marked by superstitions, Halloween has been associated with numerous mysterious rituals. In an attempt to see into the future, the evening was spent practising witchcraft around fires which were destined to scare away evil spirits. In modern times, traces of these beliefs are still noted by the presence of witches.

Pumpkins which are hollowed out, carved and lit are another reminder of this distant era. In fact, an Irish legend relates how Jack, a miser, could not go to Heaven and was even refused entry to Hell because he played tricks on the devil. As a result, Jack was condemned to roam the earth day and night with his lantern. Thus originated the expression *Jack-o'-lantern*.

The custom of going from house to house in search of candy dates back to the beginning of the Christian era. Originally, Irish peasants, in the name of Saint Columba, would call on the neighbouring houses, reminding others to bring pork and lamb meat to the evening's celebrations. Later, the poor began to beg from house to house. Nowadays, children enjoy "trick or treating" their neighbours, asking for candies.

More recently, following UNICEF's initiative, a new custom has been adopted whereby Canadian children collect money for children of under-developed countries. This has proven to be a wonderful way to help those who are less privileged than ourselves.

Over the years, accidents have unfortunately become a part of Hallow-een. Security projects have been launched so that certain dangers would be eliminated in the large cities. For example, children are advised to wear white or light-coloured costumes so that drivers are better able to see them at night. In addition, children are urged to wear make-up on their faces instead of wearing masks which would hinder their vision. Younger children should be accompanied by an adult and should eat only candy which is wrapped in sealed paper.

Entrevue avec une sorcière

Sorcière: C'est bien vous qui m'avez fait voyager sur mon balai magique pour que je vienne vous parler des origines de l'Halloween

Mosaic: C'est exact, très chère sorcière Barbara Cadabra. Merci infiniment d'avoir accepté mon invitation. (Il faut être poli avec les vieilles sorcières pour qu'elles ne nous jettent pas de mauvais sort!)

Sorcière: Chut! Si vous parlez dans mon dos, je vais vous transformer en lapin.

Mosaic: Bon, revenons à nos moutons.

Sorcière: Quoi? Vous préférez devenir un mouton?

Mosaic: Pas du tout! Je disais simplement, revenons au sujet de l'Halloween. Vous en êtes bien la spécialiste, non?

Sorcière: Bien sûr! Commençons par le commencement. Le mot *Halloween* nous vient de l'expression anglaise *All Hallows Eve* qui veut dire Veille de la Toussaint.

Mosaic:: Hum… Toussaint... Toussaint... Il y a le mot *saint* là-dedans, n'est-ce pas?

Sorcière: Mais oui! La Toussaint est une fête catholique en l'honneur de tous les saints.

Mosaic: Alors, si on fête l'Halloween le 31 octobre, cela veut dire qu'on fête la Toussaint le 1er novembre.

Sorcière: C'est bien ça et on fête l'Halloween depuis près de 2000 ans.

Mosaic: Oh! C'est donc bien vieux l'Halloween!

Sorcière: Attention! Du respect pour la vieillesse.

Mosaic: Pardon!

Sorcière: Comme vous disiez tout à l'heure, revenons à nos moutons! Il y a très longtemps, les Celtes qui vivaient en Grande Bretagne et dans le nord de la France célébraient la fin de leur année le 31 octobre.

Mosaic: Le jour de l'Halloween?

Sorcière: Pas tout à fait. À cette époque-là, ils célébraient Samhain, le maître de la mort. Ils croyaient que Samhain avait le pouvoir de faire revenir les morts sur la terre cette nuit-là.

Mosaic: Vous me faites peur avec ces histoires de fantômes!

Sorcière: Hi, hi, hi! Vous comprenez maintenant pourquoi on parle encore de fantômes le soir de l'Halloween.

Mosaic: Et pourquoi alors parle-t-on aussi de sorcières à l'Halloween?

Sorcière: Voyez-vous, mes ancêtres les sorcières ont toujours essayé de prédire l'avenir et plus particulièrement le soir du 31 octobre.

Mosaic: Vous cherchez à me faire peur avec vos histoires de sorcellerie.

Sorcière: Mais non! Je veux juste vous expliquer que mes ancêtres les sorcières effrayaient les mauvais esprits en pratiquant leur magie secrète autour du feu.

Mosaic: Si vous continuez, je ne vais pas sortir de chez moi le soir du 31 octobre.

Sorcière: Tant pis! Vous ne pourrez pas admirer toutes les citrouilles illuminées de votre quartier.

Mosaic: Mais j'aime les citrouilles! Est-ce qu'elles ont une vieille histoire elles aussi?

Sorcière: Avez-vous déjà entendu parler de la légende irlandaise de Jack et sa lanterne?

Mosaic: Jack et sa lanterne... Cela me dit quelque chose.

Sorcière: Et bien voici! Ce Jack était un misérable avare qui avait joué beaucoup de mauvais tours au diable. À sa mort, il n'a pas pu aller ni au Paradis ni en Enfer.

Mosaic: Ne me dites pas qu'on l'a renvoyé sur la terre?

Sorcière: Précisément! Là, il a été obligé d'errer jour et nuit avec sa lanterne à la main.

Mosaic: Si je comprends bien, la lanterne de Jack est l'ancêtre des citrouilles illuminées qui invitent les enfants à aller sonner aux portes des maisons.

Sorcière: C'est ça! Vous savez, il y a très longtemps, les paysans irlandais allaient aussi de maison en maison.

Mosaic: Pour demander des bonbons?

Sorcière: Non, non. Ils allaient chez leurs voisins pour leur rappeler d'apporter du porc et de l'agneau à la fête d'un de leurs saints préférés appelé Saint-Columba. Par la suite, ce sont les pauvres qui se sont mis à mendier de porte en porte.

Mosaic: Alors, c'est sûrement pour cela que les enfants qui sonnent à nos portes aujourd'hui nous disent "La charité s'il vous plaît!"

Sorcière: Et oui, cette courte phrase nous rappelle les mendiants irlandais.

Mosaic: Cela explique donc aussi les petites banques que l'UNICEF distribue dans les écoles pour que les élèves d'ici ramassent de l'argent pour les enfants des pays plus pauvres.

Sorcière: Vous commencez à comprendre bien des choses.

Mosaic: Le soir de l'Halloween, je crois que j'irai faire une promenade en voiture dans les rues pour voir tous les beaux costumes. Peut-être que quelques enfants me donneront des bonbons.

Sorcière: Attention, mangez seulement ceux qui sont enveloppés!

Mosaic: N'ayez crainte, je connais les règles de sécurité pour les bonbons et pour les costumes aussi. Par exemple, il paraît qu'il est préférable de porter un costume de couleur claire et de se maquiller au lieu de porter un masque.

Sorcière: C'est la simple logique, non? De cette façon les automobilistes peuvent mieux voir les enfants dans la rue et les enfants peuvent mieux voir autour d'eux.

Mosaic: Mais vous, sorcière Barbara Cadabra, vous portez une robe, une cape et un chapeau tout noirs. Si je me promène en voiture, je ne pourrai pas bien vous voir.

Sorcière: Cela ne fait rien. Hi, hi, hi. Moi, je suis une vraie sorcière et vous, *abracadabra*, si vous ne me respectez pas, je vais vous changer en lapin..

Mosaic: Non!

Intervista con una Strega

Mosaic: Buonasera, Signora Strega!

Strega: Buonasera!

Mosaic: Innanzitutto vorrei ringraziarla per averci concesso questa intervista. Per noi lettori di *Mosaic*, questa è un'occasione molto speciale. Non capita tutti i giorni di poter parlare a una strega...

Strega: Anche a me non capita spesso di parlare con studenti e docenti di lingua italiana. Il piacere è tutto mio!

Mosaic: Beh, noi vorremmo farle alcune domande sulla festa di Halloween... Ormai la festa si avvicina. È alla fine di ottobre, no?

Strega: Sì, certo. Il 31 ottobre per essere esatti. Io sono arrivata qui dall'Italia con qualche giorno di anticipo... e mi sto appunto preparando per la grande serata.

Mosaic: Dall'Italia? Ma è venuta da sola?

Strega: No, faccio parte di una delegazione inviata dall'ANSI (Associazione Nazionale Streghe Italiane) per partecipare a questo Halloween 1996. Siamo in tredici a rappresentare l'Italia.

Mosaic: Ma, scusi, in Italia non si festeggia Halloween?

Strega: No, da noi non esiste questa festa! C'è una ricorrenza simile in questo periodo, il giorno dei morti, il 2 novembre... Però è molto diverso: la gente va al cimitero a visitare i morti, poi la sera c'è la tradizione di mangiare le castagne arrosto, di pregare insieme per i morti, di ricordarli... Ma noi streghe non interveniamo in queste attività.

Mosaic: Ma allora, scusi, Signora Strega, Lei non conosce bene la tradizione di Halloween...

Strega: Come no, la conosco benissimo! Prima di venire qui ci hanno fatto seguire un corso intensivo di lingua e cultura inglese. E poi ci hanno fatto anche un "training" speciale per poter partecipare alle attività che si svolgeranno qui, in Nord America.

Mosaic: Ah, ho capito. Bene, allora, per cominciare vorremmo farle una domanda di tipo linguistico. Da dove viene la parola *Halloween*?

Strega: Viene dall'espressione inglese *All Hallows' Eve*. Questa tradizione è stata introdotta in Nord America dagli immigranti irlandesi ma risale a un periodo molto più antico. Infatti originariamente Halloween era un rituale celebrato dai celti, un popolo antico che viveva in Gran Bretagna e nella Francia del nord. Durante la notte del 31 ottobre, che per loro segnava la vigilia di capodanno, si credeva che le anime dei morti tornassero sulla terra. Ecco perché ci sono i fantasmi, le streghe... Capisce?

Mosaic: Sì, capisco. Però mi deve spiegare una cosa: le streghe esistevano anche in passato?

Strega: Ma certo che esistevano! Anzi, le dirò, in passato noi streghe avevamo un ruolo molto più importante di adesso. La notte di Halloween ci riunivamo intorno al fuoco, passavamo tutta la notte a ballare, a fare incantesimi e magie... Eravamo molto potenti allora: gli spiriti maligni avevano paura di noi... *(sospiro)* Quelli sì che erano bei tempi!

Mosaic: Beh, anche oggi ci sono rimaste tracce di questi riti antichi...

Strega: Sì, è vero... Per esempio, l'abitudine di svuotare le zucche e ritagliare una faccia che assomiglia a una strega, e poi illuminarle dal di dentro con una candela o con una lampadina. Questo ricorda la leggenda inglese di *Jack-o'-lantern*, il fantasma di un uomo avaro che, dopo la morte, è stato condannato per sempre a vagare sulla terra con la sua lanterna.

Mosaic: Ah sì, questa storia me la ricordo...

Strega: Jack era un tipo molto avaro e per questo non era stato ammesso in Paradiso. Però anche all'Inferno non l'avevano accettato perché aveva fatto dei brutti scherzi al diavolo...

Mosaic: Sì, proprio così...

Strega: E poi c'è anche "Trick or treat"... I bambini mascherati vanno di casa in casa chiedendo dolci e caramelle... o minacciando di fare brutti scherzi se rimangono a mani vuote. Sono sicura che questa è la parte più divertente per loro... Credo che piacerebbe molto ai bambini italiani!

Mosaic: Ma qual è l'origine di questa usanza?

Strega: Anche questa deriva da un antico costume irlandese. I contadini la sera andavano dai loro vicini a chiedere cibo e bevande per la festa della notte.

Mosaic: L'unica parte nuova, allora, è la raccolta dei soldi per l'UNICEF, non è vero?

Strega: Sì, questa è un'iniziativa moderna. Mi sembra molto bella perché i bambini, mentre si divertono, sanno di aiutare altri bambini meno fortunati di loro.

Mosaic: E mi dica, Signora, cosa ne pensa, Lei, dei brutti episodi che si sono verificati negli ultimi anni durante la notte di Halloween?

Strega: Penso che sia un vero peccato. Comunque, sono state proposte delle regole di sicurezza che dovrebbero diminuire il pericolo. Per esempio, i bambini più piccoli devono essere accompagnati da un adulto, i dolci devono essere controllati accuratamente, e così via. Io suggerirei anche ai bambini di truccarsi invece di mettersi una maschera.. Le maschere possono impedire di vedere chiaramente, specialmente di notte.

Mosaic: Certamente! Dunque, Signora Strega, Lei rimarrà qui in Nord America con le sue colleghe fino alla notte di Halloween. E dopo, mi dica, ha intenzione di trattenersi ancora qualche giorno?

Strega: Eh, purtroppo non possiamo assolutamente permetter-celo. Per ragioni professionali dobbiamo rientrare in Italia al più presto. Abbiamo molto da fare nei prossimi due mesi...

Mosaic: Come mai?

Strega: Beh, ci sono soltanto due mesi prima di Natale, e poi arriva subito il 6 gennaio, il giorno della *Befana*... Noi streghe italiane siamo molto occupate in quel periodo.

Mosaic: Perché? Cosa succede il 6 gennaio? Chi è la Befana?

Strega: Il 6 gennaio è appunto al festa della Befana, cioè dell'Epifania. È una festa molto im- portante per noi streghe, e per i bambini naturalmente. Vede, la Befana è una donna vecchia e brutta, una strega insomma, che va in giro per le case, scendendo per il camino, a cavallo di una scopa, e porta i regali ai bambini...

Mosaic: Ma i regali, scusi, non li porta Babbo Natale?

Strega: Sì, certo. Però in certe parti d'Italia, a Roma per esempio, la tradizione della Befana è ancora molto sentita. La sera precedente la gente sta alzata fino a tardi, la città è tutta illuminata, c'è chiasso per le strade... E poi il 6 gennaio è un giorno festivo in Italia. Non c'è scuola. Non si lavora...

Mosaic: Ah! Beati voi! Da noi invece il 6 gennaio non è festa. Dunque, Signora Strega, vedo che Lei e le Sue colleghe siete molto occupate...

Strega: Altro che occupate! E per stipendi bassissimi, mi creda. Infatti è molto probabile che facciamo sciopero...

Mosaic: (incredulo) Sciopero? Ma avete un sindacato?

Strega: Eccome! Il SINSI (Sindacato Nazionale Streghe Italiane) al momento è in trattative per gli aumenti salariali...

Mosaic: Veramente?!

Strega: Eh sì. Anche le condizioni di lavoro sono inaccettabili: orari quasi sempre notturni, il fumo e l'aria sporca dei camini, e poi queste scope così scomode... Non le dico il mal di schiena durante il volo Roma-Toronto!

Mosaic: Eh, capisco...

Strega: Alle soglie del 2000, nel boom della tecnologia, giriamo ancora con queste scope antiquate: senza telefonino... senza stereo... Insomma è una vita da cani!

Mosaic: Beh, noi le auguriamo tutto il successo professionale possibile, Signora Strega. E poi le facciamo doppi auguri: *Buon Halloween* e *Buona Befana!*

Strega: Grazie!

Mosaic: Grazie a Lei, Signora, per essere venuta e per averci detto tante cose interessanti. Speriamo di rivederci...

Strega: Sì, arrivederci!

Entrevista con una Bruja

Mosaic: Muchas gracias, estimada señora Bruja, por consentir en darnos esta entrevista con *Mosaic:*. Sé que está haciendo frío y entiendo que ha venido en su escoba. ¿Está tiritando? *(Preguntado con cara de preocupación.)*

Bruja: No, no, no... No tienen que preocuparse. El placer es mío. Tengo la costumbre de viajar en escoba hasta cuando nieva, no me molesta. Así me da la oportunidad de presentarles informaciones sobre la historia y las tradiciones de la fiesta de Halloween.

Mosaic: De acuerdo. Ahora quiero preguntarle... Perdóneme, señora Bruja, por mirarle así con tanta curiosidad; es que nunca he visto una verdadera bruja de tan cerca.

Bruja: (sonrisa tímida) Sí, entiendo... todos los mortales suelen mirarme así.

Mosaic: Me imagino que estará muy ocupada preparándose para esta gran fiesta. ¿Podría decirme por qué sólo le vemos una vez al año?

Bruja: Pues la verdad es que las brujas siempre estamos merodeando allí, lo que pasa es que recibimos una mayor publicidad en fines de octubre, hasta en día de Halloween que es el día 31.

Mosaic: Se estarán preparando las brujas por todo el mundo, ¿verdad?

Bruja: No. la fiesta de Halloween es esencialmente una tradición norteamericana, aunque nació en Europa hace más de 2000 años. Lo que se celebra todavía en España, en Italia y en Francia es el día de los muertos, el día 2 de noviembre. Pero es algo distinto. La gente suele ir a visitar a sus muertos en cementerios para recordarlos. Pero las brujas no entramos en esta costumbre.

Mosaic: Bueno, interesante saberlo. ¿Qué significa la palabra *Halloween*?

Bruja: Se originó de la expresión inglesa *All Hallows' Eve*.

Mosaic: Y ¿quiénes fueron los que iniciaron esta costumbre en Norte América?

Bruja: Fueron los inmigrantes irlandeses que introdujeron en Norte América varios rituales característicos de la fiesta. Pero al principio el día de Halloween fue celebrado por los Célticos que vivían en Gran Bretaña y en el norte de Francia.

Mosaic: ¿Qué celebraban los Célticos?

Bruja: El día 31 de octubre era el día de la noche vieja para los Célticos. Veneraban a Samhain, el patrón de la muerte. Creían que gracias a Samhain, durante la ceremonia de la noche vieja, reaparecían los muertos. De allí vino la noción de fantasmas el día de Halloween.

Mosaic: ¿Entonces nos dice que existían brujas en aquella época?

Bruja: Si, como no. El día 31 de octubre, las brujas – mis abuelas y mis bisabuelas – se reunían al rededor del fuego para tratar de ver el futuro, utilizando brujería. Se creía que el fuego asustaba a los espíritus del mal. Hoy los rastros de esta creencia se manifiestan en el surgimiento de la popularidad de brujas la noche de Halloween.

Mosaic: Pero si las brujas no hacían más que ver el futuro, ¿por qué en Norte América le tenemos tanto susto?

Bruja: Me alegra de que usted me haya hecho esta pregunta. Las brujas tenemos una mala reputación, gracias a las películas de Hollywood. Claro que existen algunas que tienen mal carácter pero no todas somos tan irritables.

Mosaic: Me dices que Usted nunca ha transformado algún desgraciado en sapo por haberla molestado?

Bruja: Lo mejor hubo unas ocasiones en las cuales he tenido que enseñarles una lección a algunos granujas que me molestaban. Pero a mí no me gustan los sapos. Cuando tengo que cambiarles en algo, les cambio en murciélagos. Pero no tengo malas intenciones. Mis encantos no duran más de diez minutos. Pero dejemos de hablar de estas tonterías. No quiero asustarla.

Mosaic: Ha, ha, ha... yo no me asusto *(cara blanca de miedo)*. Bien pues entonces *(aclarandóse la garganta)* ¿Cómo se daría cuenta un turista de que el día de Halloween es una gran fiesta en Norteamérica?

Bruja: Existen decoraciones características de la fiesta. La más popular es el *jack-o'-lantern* que la gente exhibe en sus casas. Son calabazas vaciadas, limpiadas, talladas e iluminadas de dentro con bombillas o candelas.

Mosaic: ¿Qué tiene que ver esta costumbre con fantasmas?

Bruja: Según una leyenda irlandesa, había una vez un avaro llamado Jack. Al morir, le negaron la entrada al cielo por su avaricia; y tampoco le admitieron en el infierno por haberse burlado del diablo. Resultó que el espíritu del difunto Jack fue condenado a rodear el mundo eternamente con su linterna, sin poder jamás descansar. De allí nació la expresión *Jack-o'-lantern*.

Mosaic: ¿Qué nos puede decir acerca de la costumbre de *"Trick or treat"*?

Bruja: Esta es una costumbre para los niños. Van de casa en casa, disfrazados y pidiendo dulces. A principios de la época cristiana, los campesinos irlandeses visitaban a sus vecinos para recordarles traer carne de puerco y de cordero a las celebraciones de la noche. Después, los pobres empezaron a mendigar de casa en casa pidiendo limosna. Hoy, en Norte América, niños van vestidos de brujas, fantasmas y personajes populares, de casa en casa pidiendo caramelos.

Mosaic: ¿Ha cambiado esta tradición desde que empezó en Norte América?

Bruja: Sí. Recientemente, gracias a una iniciativa de UNICEF, la tradición adoptó una nueva costumbre. Además de caramelos, los niños piden dinero para países menos afortunados. Así los niños se divierten mientras ayudan a los que más lo necesitan.

Mosaic: ¿Nos puede ofrecer más informaciones acerca de la fiesta de Halloween que no le he preguntado?

Bruja: Sí. Hay algo muy importante que le quiero decir. Desafortunadamente, resulta que varios accidentes también forman parte de la fiesta e iniciativas de seguridad han sido presentadas para eliminar ciertos peligros. Aquí tiene unos consejos que les ayudarán a los niños a divertirse y a evitar accidentes: Niños que van disfrazados deben llevar ropa de color blanco o claro para que los motoristas les puedan ver fácilmente... En vez de llevar máscaras, es mejor que los niños se disfrazen pintándose la cara. Así, no se impide su vista, y pueden evitar situaciones peligrosas... Niños pequeños deben ser acompañados por un adulto en caso de emergencia imprevisto... Se debe comer sólo caramelos que son bien envueltos y sellados, y se debe examinar minuciosamente toda la fruta que reciben.

Mosaic: Muchísimas gracias, Señora Bruja. Le agradecemos su tiempo y sus informaciones.

Bruja: No hay de que. Espero que todos los niños pasen un día de fiesta divertidos.

Pedagogical Suggestions

The following are some suggested activities for Halloween. They are not presented in any order or difficulty. Teachers will know the linguistic background of the students and will select only those activities appropriate to the age and linguistic level of the class. The suggestions are by no means exhaustive; the teacher will undoubtedly think of others!

Follow-up Activities

Teacher-initiated Activities:

1. Identify and explain any difficult vocabulary found in the text. Use synonyms, antonyms, cognates, definitions and illustrations to do so.

2. Ask comprehension questions based on the text. Use the following key words (known in English as the five "W"s):

   - *Who...?*
   - *What...?*
   - *Where...?*
   - *When...?*
   - *Why...?*

Student-initiated Activities:

1. You have been asked to prepare a poster on "Safety on Halloween." Prepare a list of suggestions you will give to children going out "trick-or-treating" on Halloween. (This will be a good review of the imperative.) For example:

   - Wear light-coloured clothing.
   - Paint your face instead of wearing a mask. (Masks often block your vision.)
   - Have an adult accompany you when "trick-or-treating."
   - Examine apples, pears and other fruit very carefully before eating it.
   - Eat only wrapped candies.
   - etc.
   - Illustrate the poster.

2. Ask one of your classmates to play the role of the witch. Imagine you are a reporter. Interview the "witch" and obtain from her as much information as possible on the origin of Halloween. (For an effective interview, the "witch" will have to be familiar with the historical information about Halloween provided in the above paragraphs.)

3. Interview Jack-o'-lantern. Try to find out what trick he played on the devil. Make the interview as humourous as possible.

4. You have been given a pumpkin. Draw the pumpkin on a sheet of paper. Then draw on the pumpkin a face which is happy, sad, angry or scary. Colour it accordingly.

5. Tell your classmates or write about the first time you went out "trick-or-treating" in your neighbourhood.

6. Write an imaginary story entitled, "The Haunted House." Tape the story and use spooky sounds to obtain the desired effect.

7. Imagine someone has sent you one of the photographs which appear on this page. Describe it to your classmates.

Photo: Wanda Goodwin, *Canada Wide*   Photo: Wanda Goodwin, *Canada Wide*

8. Some people are superstitious. What superstitions exist in your target culture? List them. What superstitions exist here in Canada? The following are some examples:
   - Walking under a ladder.
   - Black cat crossing your path.
   - Breaking a mirror.
   - Spilling salt.
   - Friday, the 13th.
   - Giving knives as gifts (if you do, you generally give a penny for good luck with the gift).

   Some superstitions, symbols of good luck:
   - Breaking china.
   - Rabbit's foot.
   - Horseshoe.
   - Four-leaf clover.

9. Draw a mask you would like to wear at a Halloween party.

10. Prepare a bulletin board on "Halloween."

11. Prepare a pumpkin pie from a recipe you find in a book.

12. Have you ever read a ghost story? Have you ever heard one? Tell your classmates about it.

13. The suffix *phobia* comes from the Greek word *phobos* meaning *fear*. Find the equivalent suffix in your language and explain the fear. Here are some irrational fears some people have:
    - *agoraphobia* = fear of public or open spaces.
    - *claustrophobia* = a morbid fear of being in confined spaces.
    - *arachnaphobia* = fear of spiders.
    - *xenophobia* = fear or dislike of strangers or foreigners.

    What other fears do you know? List them.

14. Do a research project and find out more about the Celts.

15. Have you ever played a trick on someone? Tell your classmates about it. If you have never played a trick on anyone, tell about a trick someone played on the TV program, *TV Bloopers and Practical Jokes*.

Editor's Note: The Pedagogical Suggestions included in this article have been drawn from Anthony Mollica, "Teaching Culture in a North American Context: Halloween." *Mosaic*, 1, 1 (Fall 1993): 20-21.

Reprinted from: Anthony Mollica, Marjolaine Séguin, Raffaella Maiguashca, and Natalia Valenzuela, "Teaching Language in a North American Context: Halloween Revisited." *Mosaic*, 4, 1 (Fall 1996), pp. 18-22.

42 Teaching Culture in a North American Context:

Thanksgiving

Anthony Mollica

Through a "time-machine" interview, we were able to reach a Pilgrim and ask him a few questions about Thanksgiving Day.

Mosaic: The tradition of a Thanksgiving festival at harvest time is an ancient custom. We know that the oldest harvest festival is that of the Succoth, the Jewish Feast of the Tabernacles. The Romans held a nine-day feast dedicated to Demeter, the goddess of agriculture. The pre-Christian Druid priests of Britain held a "harvest home" celebration, a feast after the last crops were reaped and stored for the long winter months ahead.

Pilgrim: Yes, that's true. And so did the people in Egypt, China, Japan, India, and Africa. They even gave some of their best foods to their gods as part of their celebration.

Mosaic: Our modern-day Thanksgiving, however, originated with you, the Pilgrims.

Pilgrim: Yes, the first American Thanksgiving was celebrated in 1621 at the Plymouth Colony in Massachusetts.

Mosaic: Who initiated the custom of this celebration?

Pilgrim: It was William Bradford's idea. Mr. Bradford was the Governor of our colony at that time.

Mosaic: What was the reason for this celebration?

Pilgrim: Governor Bradford ordered a day of Thanksgiving for surviving the very hard times the new settlers had gone through.

Mosaic: To what hard times are you referring?

Pilgrim: Less than a year before, we had landed on the shores far from our native England. During the first winter, half of the group died. For a time it looked as if no one would survive.

Mosaic: You led a somewhat comfortable life in England. What reasons led you to leave that country?

Pilgrim: It was mostly for religious reasons.

Mosaic: Kindly explain.

Pilgrim: As you know, at that time, the Church of England stood between Catholic and Protestant religions. The Anglican services were filled with ritual. We were told what to believe.

Mosaic: And you opposed the Church's views?

Pilgrim: We wanted to study the Bible and decide for ourselves what to believe. Some people made fun of us for wanting to "purify the church" and they nicknamed us "Puritans." Many of us still went to the Church of England, but also met secretly in homes to study the Bible and listen to sermons. Some of us were prepared to leave the Church right away.

Mosaic: What did you do?

Pilgrim: Some with enough courage did break away. One such group had been meeting in William Brewster's home in the village of Scrooby. When eventually we did separate from the Church, life became harder and harder for us.

Mosaic: What steps did you take to alleviate your hardships?

Pilgrim: In 1607 we decided to move to Holland, where we could worship as we pleased. But leaving England was a real problem.

Mosaic: Why a problem?

Pilgrim: England would not issue passports to "traitors", and the voyage would be expensive. No one, except William Brewster, had much money. In spite of such obstacles, by 1608 about 125 of us had reached Holland.

Mosaic: Why Holland?

Pilgrim: The Dutch were tolerant, peace-loving, and kind. In Holland we could worship as we pleased.

Mosaic: Where did you first settle?

Pilgrim: We first settled in Amsterdam, but then moved to Leyden, a centre for the spinning and weaving of woollen cloth. We managed to make a living and support our new church. But after more than ten years of this life, we became restless.

Mosaic: Why the restlessness?

Pilgrim: In England most of us had been farmers. In Holland, farmland was scarce and expensive. What's more, our children were forgetting the English language and the English ways. Some of our children were even losing respect for the Sabbath. And at this time, a war was also brewing between the Dutch and the Spanish.

Mosaic: And so you decided to leave Holland for the New World?

Pilgrim: Precisely. In September 1620, we set sail on the *Mayflower*, and after almost three months at sea we spotted land. We landed at last on the rock-bound shores of a strange and lonely coast and named the land New England. I still recall that cold December day very vividly.

Mosaic: Life must have been very difficult in the New World.

Pilgrim: Yes. During the first winter, many of my friends died. But in spite of the hardships, we survived as a colony and our gratitude led us to hold a time of Thanksgiving.

Mosaic: Who was invited to this first celebration?

Pilgrim: All the colonists and the native Americans who lived nearby shared this great feast.

Mosaic: What had the native Americans done for you?

Pilgrim: They had helped us to survive, showing us new and wonderful foods so we wouldn't starve. They even taught us to gather cranberries, to plant corn, to hunt wild turkeys, and to dig for clams. Of particular help was Chief Massassoit and his tribe.

Mosaic: Was he invited to the celebration?

Pilgrim: Of course! He came with ninety of his fellow tribesmen. It was a larger crowd than we had expected but we welcomed them. Four of our marksmen had been sent out to hunt game for the occasion and they had returned laden with wild turkeys, quail and other game. Chief Massasoit had sent his best hunters into the forest and they had shot five deer. We had plenty of food for everyone.

Mosaic: Did this Thanksgiving immediately become a yearly celebration as we know of it today?

Pilgrim: No, it took many years for Thanksgiving Day in America to become the permanent and regularly observed holiday we know today. In 1789, President George Washington issued a proclamation urging Americans to celebrate Thanksgiving. But, it was Sara Josepha Hale who is credited with the establishment of this national holiday.

Mosaic: What did Mrs. Hale do?

Pilgrim: She wrote thousands of letters to those who, she felt, would be of help to her cause. She wrote to governors of states urging them to make Thanksgiving an annual holiday in their states. She even wrote to President Abraham Lincoln, sending him a copy of President Washington's original declaration. As a result of this campaign, Mrs. Hale was granted an interview with President Lincoln in 1863. The President subsequently declared the last Thursday in November an annual, Thanksgiving Day.

Mosaic: Was this date widely accepted?

Pilgrim: The custom since 1863 has been for the President to issue a proclamation setting the day of Thanksgiving. The date was set for the fourth Thursday in November. Some of the New England States had opted to celebrate it the last Thursday in November (whenever November had five Thursdays). It was 1941 when a joint resolution of Congress proclaimed that after the year 1941, the last Thursday of November would be set aside to celebrate Thanksgiving.

Mosaic: The situation is different in Canada, isn't it?

Pilgrim: You're right. In Canada the first Thanksgiving was celebrated by the city of Halifax in 1763. Its citizens wanted to express their gratitude for the Treaty of Paris whereby France yielded Canada to Great Britain. On October 9, 1879, the Canadian Government proclaimed the first Thanksgiving as we know it to-day. Canadians celebrated it for the first time on November 6, 1879.

Mosaic: As you well know, our Canadian Thanksgiving falls in October. What is the explanation?

Pilgrim: Following World War I, Thanksgiving and Armistice Day were both celebrated on the same day. In 1931, "Armistice Day" was changed into "Remembrance Day" and so it was decided to celebrate Thanksgiving in October to avoid two major holidays in the same month.

Mosaic: And so Canadians celebrate Thanksgiving in October?

Pilgrim: As of 1953, Thanksgiving is celebrated the second Monday in October.

Mosaic: How do the United States and Canada celebrate Thanksgiving?

Pilgrim: Canadians celebrate it the same way as Americans. There is a dinner to which family and friends are invited. But we in the United States hold parades, and watch football games.

Mosaic: Thank you. You've been very helpful with your information on Thanksgiving.

Reprinted from: Anthony Mollica, "Teaching Culture in a North AmericanContext: Thanksgiving." *Mosaic*, 2, 1 (Fall 1994), pp. 21-22.

Pedagogical Suggestions

1. Illustrate all the key words from the text either by bringing into class illustrations or by drawing them yourself.
2. Write a short paragraph about what Thanksgiving means to you.
3. Research and speak briefly on the following:
   (a) President George Washington
   (b) President Abraham Lincoln
   (c) Sara Josepha Hale.
4. Mosaic was able to record a soliloquy by a turkey... Create a similar monologue from the point of view of
   (a) a Pilgrim
   (b) a native American.

Le soliloque du dindon

Être ou ne pas être rôti:
voilà la question!
Depuis 1621,
mes ancêtres et toute ma famille tremblons
dès qu'approche l'automne...
glou... glou, glou... glou,
«Et pourquoi donc?»
À cause du massacre
de l'Action de grâce,
qui se célèbre
le deuxième lundi d'octobre
au Canada,
et le dernier jeudi de novembre
aux États-Unis.
Lors de la première célébration
de la fête de l'Action de grâce,
nos ancêtres sauvages
ont été décimés
par les Indiens;
mais depuis l'arrivée des Pèlerins,
on nous élève pour nous sacrifier
en ce jour funeste.
Dès l'heure de notre naissance,
glou... glou...
nous connaissons notre sort
tragique,
notre destin fatal
et l'heure exacte de notre
exécution...
La guillotine,

malheureusement,
nous attend.
On nous coupe la tête.
On nous plume.
On nous congèle.
Quelle coutume barbare!
Avant de nous manger,
ces inexorables êtres humains
nous farcissent
et trempent notre chair
dans la sauce de canneberges.
Puis, ils se gavent
à s'en rendre malades.
Quelle honte!
 Quel scandale!
Quelle horreur!
Mais pourquoi toujours nous?
Pourquoi pas les canards?
Ou même les sales vautours?
glou... glou...
Quand je pense que nous sommes
d'innocents végétariens...
Quel outrage!
je suis bien d'accord...
Il faut remercier Dieu
pour toutes les bénédictions
reçues pendant l'année
et pour la bonne récolte...
mais pourquoi ne pas fêter
cet événement
le 32 octobre?

43 Teaching Culture in a North American Context:

Hannukka

Louise Lewin and Perla Riesenbach

The Story of Hannukka

About 2100 years ago, the land of Israel, then called Judea, was ruled by the Greeks. Their king, Antiochus, tried to force the Jews in his kingdom to worship his people's Greek gods. It was forbidden to practise the Jewish religion. Those who were caught were killed. Antiochus had a powerful army who punished those who disobeyed his orders.

A spiritual leader named Mattatias, together with his five sons and other brave Jews, formed a small army to fight for their rights and freedom to practise the Jewish religion. The Jewish people were ready to risk their lives rather than give up the right to worship their God.

Upon Mattatias' death, his son Judah became the leader of the revolt. The Jews continued the battle against Antiochus and his army. Judah is considered the hero of Hannukka because his blows were hard and strong like those of a hammer. This is the reason he was given the name Judah Maccabbee. (Maccabbee means hammer in Hebrew.)

After many battles, the Jews were finally victorious. After their victory, Judah and his army returned to the Temple in Jerusalem. The Jews had to clean and purify the Temple. They had to remove the statues of Greek gods that Antiochus had placed there. Only then was the Temple restored to its former beauty.

It was the 25th day of the Hebrew month of Kislev when the Jews were finally able to pray in their Temple. They needed some oil to light the Menorah to start their prayers. They found a small amount of oil which appeared to be enough for only one day. To their amazement, this small amount of oil continued to burn for eight days. This is considered a miracle of Hannukka.

The Jews were grateful for several reasons. With a small army, they defeated Antiochus' powerful army. They recaptured their Temple and they regained their freedom to worship their God. For these reasons, Hannukka is considered a celebration of liberty and heroism.

To commemorate the miracle of the oil which lasted eight days, every year the Jews light candles during the eight days of Hannukka. This is the reason Hannukka is referred to as the Festival of Lights.

The Celebration of Hannukka

Hannukka is celebrated every year for eight days according to the date on the Jewish calendar (25 Kislev to 2 Tevet). This usually corresponds to a date in late November or December. This year, 1994, Hannukka will begin on November 28. The hannukka candles are placed in a special type of candelabra called Hannukkia in Hebrew. This Hannukkia is more commonly referred to as a Menorah. It has nine candle holders. The first candle is lit on the eve of the first day. The candle-lighting takes place every night after dark, except on Friday night. A servant-candle, (called *shamash* in Hebrew), always placed higher than the others is used to light the other candles. The first night, the *shamash* lights one candle; the second night, the *shamash* lights two candles and so on until the eighth night when the *shamash* and all the eight candles are lit. The lit Hannukka candles are meant to be placed in the window or other spots where they may be seen by others, who will be reminded of the tale they tell.

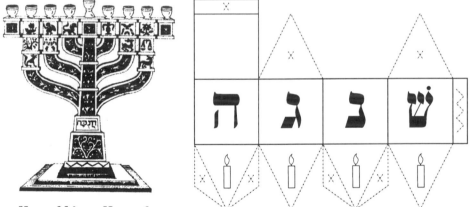

Hannukkia or Menorah

Hannukka is very much a celebration that involves the children. They play with a special spinning top called *dreidel* which has four sides. Each side has a Hebrew letter on it: Nun, Gimel, Heh, Shin. The Hebrew letters stand for the words: "A great miracle happened there". ("There" refers to Israel.). The children play with raisins, pennies, toothpicks or any other collection of small items. The children take turns spinning the Dreidel and usually play by the following rules:

- if the *dreidel* falls on Nun, the player gets nothing.
- if the *dreidel* falls on Gimmel, the player takes the whole pot.
- if the *dreidel* falls on Hay, the player takes half the pot.
- if the *dreidel* falls on Shin, the player puts in one.

Food

No celebration is complete without food, and Hannukka is no exception. As "oil" is the important symbol of Hannukka, the foods that are eaten have been fried in oil. A very popular dish is potato pancakes, *latkes*, in Yiddish.

(See recipe below). The pancakes are eaten with sour cream and apple sauce. The other traditional dish is jelly doughnuts, which have also been fried in oil, thus continuing the theme of oil.

Gifts

The children traditionally receive a small sum of money at this time. The Yiddish term for this is "Hannukka gelt". Little packs of chocolate coins are also popular at this time. These days, in many families, the children receive gifts for Hannukka.

Hannukka is a time for celebration. Parties with families and friends are held throughout the holiday. Hannukka can easily be incorporated into a language class activity at this festive time.

Suggestions for Activities

1. Draw a Hannukkia.

   Place the left hand on the left side and trace along the four fingers. Repeat with the right hand. To obtain flame, the students can draw and colour each flame.

2. Make a *dreidel*.

   Cut along the dots. Fold along the lines and glue where marked X. See illustration below.

3. Draw and send a postcard to a Jewish friend. The card can have the drawing of a Hannukkia or a dreidel on the front. The message can be as simple as "Happy Hannukka".

4. Riddles

   I am small. I produce flames. I can be lit. What am I?

   I was found in the Temple. I burned for eight days. What am I?

   The children play with me during Hannukka. I can turn. What am I?

   I am delicious. I am served with apple sauce. What am I?

5. The following is a recipe for latkes that can easily be made at school. Note that since hot oil is required to make this recipe, the students should be closely supervised.

   Ingredients:

2 large potatoes	half cup of flour
half of an onion	oil (enough to coat the pan)
1 (beaten) egg	apple sauce and/or sour cream
1/2 teaspoon of salt	

   Method:

   Peel and grate the potatoes. Peel and grate the onion. Stir the beaten egg and salt. Add the flour, a bit at a time, mixing well. Coat the pan with the oil and heat it until it sizzles. Pour the mixture into the pan. Brown one side, then the other. Serve with apple sauce and/or sour cream and enjoy!

6. **For intermediate and senior levels.**

Hannukka falls at a time of year when values and feelings such as hope, charity and friendship surround our everyday life. It is a good opportunity to share during Hannukka the values that are attached to this Jewish holiday, but more importantly to relate these values to other religions, faiths, and cultures. The following suggestions for group activities attempt to do so.

Hope:

Terry Fox and Rick Hansen are Canadian heroes today because they did not lose hope. In small groups, students can talk about these heroes and can think of other people that they consider as heroes. They can tell each other the stories of these people who did not lose hope.

Charity:

It is important to give. One can give many things such as clothing, money, food, and time. In small groups, students can list what can be given, what organizations, organized charities (UNICEF, etc.) are available. Given the time allotted for such activities, in a secondary school class small groups can organize, with the help of their teacher, a charity project in their class and/or in their school.

Friendship:

Many questions need to be answered when it comes to friendship. How can one make friends? What are the characteristics of a good friend? Of a best friend? How does it feel when one is rejected by a group? Students can share their experiences with this complex relationship.

Peace:

After discussing the meaning of the concept of peace, students can find the word peace in as many languages as possible.

Tradition:

There are many traditions associated with Hannukka. Every person has traditions, whether it be a family, religious, or food tradition. The students can share

a. one of their traditions

b. a recipe that represents their own culture. (*Latkes* is the one which is related to Hannukka.)

c. The class can compile the recipes brought by each student and publish a multicultural recipe book.

Reprinted from: Louise Lewin and Perla Riesenbach, "Teaching Culture in a North American Context: Hannukka." *Mosaic*, 1, 2 (Winter 1993): pp. 20-21.

44 Teaching Culture in a North American Context:

The Chinese New Year

Cheng Luo

Introduction

One of the most significant developments in second language (SL) learning in recent years has been the recognition of the close relationship between language and culture. Among the questions that are often asked by teachers regarding the teaching of culture are: *what* to teach and *how* to teach it. The answer, especially to the first question, depends, among other things, upon how we define *culture*. According to Brooks (1982: 20-21), culture may be defined as the *best* of everything in human life, e.g. the observable Culture MLA (music, letters, and arts); or as *everything* in human life, that is, the nonobservable Culture BBV (belief, behaviour and values). While neither perspective is sufficient for giving a full definition of culture, many SL teachers seem to emphasize MLA more than BBV. If this is indeed the case, then it appears that a more balanced approach is needed in teaching culture, such that both MLA and BBV receive due attention in the SL teaching/learning process.

This article addresses the above issue by looking at a particular cultural event: the Chinese New Year. The reason for selecting this event is twofold:

- major cultural festivals like the Chinese New Year encompass both MLA and BBV;
- some festivals manifest the close relationship between language and culture.

In addition, ethnographic description on the Chinese New Year and how people celebrate it will be provided, both for information purposes and as the basis of suggested language and cultural activities for the Chinese as a second language class.

The Chinese New Year

Of all the Chinese festivals, the Chinese New Year, also known as the Spring Festival, is the most important and most celebrated. It is the first day of the year according to the Chinese lunar calendar, which works somewhat differently from the Christian Gregorian (solar) calendar. Because of this, the exact date of the Chinese New Year varies from year to year: somewhere between January 15 and February 20 on the solar calendar. For 1995, it falls on January 31.

Origin

The Chinese have celebrated their New Year for about 5,000 years. The traditional term for the event is 過年 *Guo Nian*, literally "to get over Nian". According to an ancient Chinese legend, *Nian* was a fierce animal that came out to devour people on the last night of the year. Once *Nian* went to a village where someone was cracking a whip. At the sound, *Nian* ran away. When it got to the next village, *Nian* saw some red clothes that had been hung out to dry. Again, it was scared away. At the third village, the sight of a fire once again kept *Nian* from the villagers. Now that people knew what *Nian* was afraid of, they set off firecrackers, put up red spring couplets on doors (see Suggested Activities, section 4), and hung out lanterns on the same night every year, in order to "get over Nian". This practice, together with the people's ever-renewing wish for a better life in the new year, formed the tradition of Chinese New Year celebrations.

The Chinese Zodiac

Celebration of a particular New Year is based on a 12-year cycle on the Chinese zodiac, with each year named after an animal that represents an Earthly Branch. 1995 marks the year of the Pig. The animal ruling the year of one's birth becomes that person's animal sign and is believed to influence his or her character and destiny. For example, those born in the year of the Pig (1947, 1959, 1971, 1983, 1995) are said to be honest and brave. Traditionally, decisions about marriage, friendship, business, etc. are made according to the guidelines of one's animal sign. The Appendix shows a horoscope of the Chinese Zodiac. Beginning with the Mouse, the cycle reads counter-clockwise.

Stories about the zodiac animals abound. According to one, the Heavenly Jade Emperor once invited twelve earthly animals to his palace the next day to become zodiac animals. Among the invited was the Cat, who at the time was a good friend of the Mouse. Early the next morning, the Mouse, who had not been invited, went with the other animals without waking up the Cat. Just before they entered the Heavenly Gate, the Mouse jumped onto the horn of the Ox, who happened to lead the team, and was the first to be seen and appointed by the Jade Emperor. By the time the Cat woke up and hurried to the Heavenly Palace, all the zodiac animals had already been named. Furious, the Cat vowed to revenge itself on the Mouse who has since been its arch enemy.

Preparations

Household preparations for the New Year start about one week before the New Year. These include house cleaning, festival shopping, making new clothes, window decoration (with paper cuttings), hanging New Year pictures, writing spring scrolls, and preparing festival food, including *jiaozi* and New Year cakes. It is a common practice to put on the door an upside down character 福 (*fu* "happiness"), because "upside down" (倒 *dao*) in Chinese sounds the same as the word for "arrive" (到 *dao*). The intention is to elicit 福倒了 *Fu dao le* "The *happiness* is upside down", which is interpreted as "Happiness has arrived."

New Year's Eve

The New Year's Eve is the time for all the family members, including those away from home, to come together to share a sumptuous feast, to drink a toast to each other's happiness, to give out "lucky money" in red envelopes to children and to stay up throughout the night chatting, playing games or watching special TV programs. When the clock strikes midnight, a new round of firecrackers is set off, people bid farewell to the old year, cheer the coming of the new, and eat 餃子 *jiaozi*, a kind of stuffed dumplings whose pronunciation comes from the phrase 交子 *jiao zi* "reach midnight", and which symbolizes smooth transition into the new year.

New Year's Day

On New Year's Day, people put on new clothes, offer ritual homage and thanksgiving to their ancestors and gods, pay respects to senior members of the family, wish each other good luck, and exchange gifts. Then they go out to bring New Year greetings to their friends and relatives. Favoured greetings include 恭喜發財 *Gongxi facai* "Wish you great fortune" and 新年好 *Xin nian hao* "Happy New Year". The New Year feast, which is shared with visiting relatives and friends, is as sumptuous as the New Year's Eve feast, and must include a course of whole fish to symbolize a surplus year to come, because, again, "fish" (魚 *yu*) sounds like "surplus" (餘 *yu*).

Throughout the festival, the crackling of firecrackers continues, and dragon and lion dances are performed on the streets. In some areas, the festivities last about two weeks till the Lantern Festival.

Suggested Activities

1. Stories

Stories about the Chinese New Year, such as "Guo Nian" and "How the Mouse became a zodiac animal", may be told to the students, who may then roleplay the story. Advanced students may, under the teacher's guidance, write down their own version of the story in the form of a short play and then act it out.

2. The Lunar Calendar

A Chinese lunar year consists of 12 months, five of which have 29 days and seven have 30 days. There is a leap year about every three years which contains an extra month. 1995 happens to be a leap year with an extra August. Students may compare the different ways the Chinese lunar calendar and the western solar calendar work and, in small groups, work out the corresponding dates of the Chinese New Year on the solar calendar for the next two or three years.

3. The Chinese Zodiac

Using the horoscope (see Appendix), students may work in groups to find out each other's animal sign, alleged character and destiny, as well as the do's and don'ts for individual students according to the Chinese zodiac. It should be pointed out to the students, however, that the alleged do's and don'ts, as well as the characterization, are merely cultural beliefs and do not have to be taken literally. In addition, students may also discuss and compare animal images in Chinese and other cultures.

4. Spring Couplets

These are the poetic couplets written vertically on red scrolls in strictly symmetrical forms, with a short phrase written horizontally as a conclusion. The content expresses such themes as thanksgiving, prosperity, newness, goodwill and social or natural harmony. These couplets are a good source of folk literature that may be appreciated by advanced students through guided analysis of sample couplets such as:

The right scroll:

五　　谷　　　豐登辭　　　舊　歲
wu　　gu　　　feng-deng ci　　jiu　sui

five crop abound　　farewell-to　　old　year

"Farewell to the old year in bumper harvest of the five crops."

The left scroll:

六畜　　　興 旺 迎　　　新　　春
liu xu　　xing-wang ying　　xin　　chun

six animal　　　thrive　　　welcome new spring

"Welcome in the new spring with thriving prospect of the six animals."

The horizontal scroll:

年　　年　　有　　餘
nian　　nian　　you　　yu

year　　year　　have　　surplus

"(There's) surplus year after year."

5. Colours

Colours have culture-specific symbolic meanings. For example, *red* in Chinese symbolizes happiness, luck or success, and is the favoured colour for festivals, weddings, opening ceremonies, etc. Students may discuss the symbolic meanings of different colours in Chinese and compare them to those of other cultures they are familiar with. The following is a short list of common colour terms and their symbolic meaning in Chinese (Luo 1992). Other colour-meaning correspondences can be elicited from the students.

Colour	Meaning	Example
red	happiness	wedding dress
	luck	*"red luck"* 紅運

yellow	noble	royal colour
white	purity	"innocent" 清白
	sadness	funeral dress
green	life	
black	wickedness	"black gang" 黑幫

6. Linguistic Preferisms

These are socio-psychologically favoured expressions, especially at festival times, for example:

* 恭喜發財 Gongxi fa cai "Wish you great fortune"
* 萬事如意 Wan shi ruyi "Everything as you wish", 福到了 *Fu dao le* "Happiness has arrived", and
* 年年有餘 *Nian nian you yu* "Surplus year after year."

Also to be noted is the number "eight" (八 *ba*), which rhymes with the word for "(fortune) expansion" (發 *fa*) and therefore gains popularity among Chinese. These and other similar expressions tell about cultural beliefs and values of the Chinese, and should be made known to the students, who can then use them, first in simulated, and then in real, communicative situations.

7. Window Decoration

The traditional art of paper cutting is most popularly used in New Year window decoration. Students may learn to paper cut simple patterns from demonstrations by invited folk artists or by following instructions in relevant books.

8. Making *jiaozi*

There is no festival without food. A popular food for the New Year is *jiaozi*, whose symbolic meaning is explained under New Year's Eve, above. The teacher may give a demo on how to make *jiaozi* and ask the students to make some on their own. Where feasible, tasting of other New Year food such as the New Year cake and spring rolls will also enrich students' cultural experience.

Conclusion

The major themes of the Chinese New Year include thanksgiving, wish for prosperity, newness, and social cohesiveness (kinship, friendship, etc.), which reflect the cultural belief, behaviour, and values (BBV) of the Chinese. On the other hand, music, letters and arts (MLA) are reflected in such festival elements as dragon or lion dances, spring couplets, and paper cut window decoration. Such a balance provides not only rich input of cultural content (i.e. what to teach) for the language classroom, but also an appropriate source for enriched language learning activities (i.e. how to teach).

Appendix

Horoscope of the Chinese Zodiac

The Chinese Zodiac consists of a 12-year cycle, with each year named after a different animal that distinctly characterizes its year. Many Chinese believe that the year of a person's birth is the primary factor determining that person's personality throughout his lifetime. To learn about your Animal Sign, find the year of your birth in the sequence below.

Mouse/Rat

1936, 1948, 1960, 1972, 1984, 1996.

You are ambitious yet honest. You like to invent things and are a good artist. Prone to spend freely. Most compatible with Dragons and Monkeys; least compatible with Horses.

Ox

1937, 1949, 1961, 1973, 1985, 1997.

You are dependable, patient, and bright, with strong ideas to inspire others. You can be happy by yourself, yet make an outstanding parent. Marry a Snake or a Rooster. The Sheep will bring trouble.

Tiger

1938, 1950, 1962, 1974, 1986, 1998.

You are aggressive, courageous, candid, and sensitive. People respect you for your deep thoughts and courageous actions. Look to the Horse and Dog for happiness. Beware of the Monkey.

Rabbit

1939, 1951, 1963, 1975, 1987, 1999.

Luckiest of all signs, you are talented, good-natured and articulate. Affectionate yet shy, you seek peace throughout your life. Marry a Sheep or Pig. Your opponent is the Rooster.

Dragon

1940, 1952, 1964, 1976, 1988, 2000.

Healthy, energetic, and passionate, you make a good friend because you listen to others carefully. Your life is complex. Marry a Monkey or Rabbit late in life. Avoid the Dog.

Snake

1941, 1953, 1965, 1977, 1989, 2001.

You are wise and a passionate lover of good books, food, music and plays. Though lucky with money, you are vain and high tempered. The Rooster or the Ox is your best sign.

Horse

1942, 1954, 1966, 1978, 1990, 2002.

You are hard-working, cheerful, popular and attractive to the opposite sex. Yet you are often ostentatious and impatient. You need people. Marry a Tiger or a Dog early, but never a Mouse.

Sheep

1943, 1955, 1967, 1979, 1991, 2003.

Elegant, inquisitive, and creative, you have good taste and make a good artist. Yet you are timid and prefer anonymity. You are most compatible with the Pig and the Rabbit, but never the Ox.

Monkey

1944, 1956, 1968, 1980, 1992, 2004.

An enthusiastic achiever, you are intelligent, funny and good at solving problems. But you are easily discouraged and confused. Avoid Tigers. Seek a Dragon or a Mouse.

Rooster

1945, 1957, 1969, 1981, 1993, 2005.

A pioneer in spirit, you are talented, hard-working, and a deep thinker in questing after knowledge. You are selfish and eccentric. Rabbits are trouble.

Dog

1946, 1958, 1970, 1982, 1994, 2006.

Loyal, honest and a good secret-keeper, you work well with others. You are generous yet stubborn, and sometimes selfish. Look to the Horse or Tiger. Watch out for Dragons.

Pig

1947, 1959, 1971, 1983, 1995, 2007.

Noble, chivalrous and honest, you make a good student for always finishing projects or assignments. Your friends will be lifelong, yet you are prone to marital strife. Avoid other Pigs. Marry a Rabbit or a Sheep.

References

Brooks, N. 1982. "The analysis of foreign and familiar cultures," in R.C. Lafayette, H.B. Altman and R. Schulz, eds., *The Culture Revolution in Foreign Language Teaching*, 19-31. Skokie, Ill.: National Textbook Co.

Cheng, H-T. 1976. *The Chinese New Year*. New York: Holt, Rinehart & Winston.

Luo, C. 1992. "Culture in vocabulary," in G. Irons and T.S. Paribakht, eds., *Make Changes, Make a Difference*, 171-186. Welland, Ontario: éditions Soleil publishing inc.

Robinson, G.N. 1985. *Crosscultural Understanding*. New York: Pergamon.

Modern Chinese: Beginner's Course, Vol. 3. Beijing: Beijing Language Institute Press.

Traditional Chinese Culture in Taiwan (2nd ed.), 1991. Taipei: Kwang Hwa Publishing Co.

Reprinted from: Cheng Luo, "Teaching Culture in a North American Context: The Chinese New Year." *Mosaic*, 2, 2 (Winter 1994), pp. 23-26.

45 Teaching Culture in a North American Context:

Ukrainian Easter

Tania Onyschuk

Background

Khrystos Voskres! (Christ is risen!) then *"Voistynu Voskres!"* (Indeed He is risen!) are the joyous greetings heard on Ukrainian Easter morning and throughout the Easter season. It is a happy time when families and the community join together to celebrate Christ's Resurrection.

This year Ukrainian Easter will fall on May 1. Most other Christian churches will already have celebrated Easter a month earlier. The difference occurs because Ukrainian religious holidays follow the Julian calendar and not our present-day Gregorian one. Thus, Ukrainian Easter can be on the same day or up to five weeks later than Easter of other churches.

Ukrainian Easter has many rich traditions that have developed over a long period of history. Some of these date back to pre-Christian rites greeting spring. In springtime people saw re-growth and re-birth everywhere. The earliest signs of spring were the returning birds, which built nests and laid eggs that hatched into new birds. People believed birds brought spring on their wings. This is why the egg became an important part of spring festivities.

With the coming of Christianity in the tenth century, the spring rituals were transformed into Easter traditions and given Christian meaning. Today's Ukrainian Easter traditions, while deeply religious, contain many elements that can be traced back to the joyous greeting of spring.

The Sunday before Easter (Palm Sunday) is known as Willow Sunday. There are no palm trees in Ukraine, so the willow was chosen because it was thought to have healing powers. After the pussy willows are blessed in church, people, and children in particular, tap each other with the willows saying, "Be as tall as the willow, as healthy as water, and as rich as the earth". The blessed willows are then placed behind religious pictures in the home or planted. They are never thrown away.

The week before Easter is spent in preparation. On the evening of "Pure" Thursday, Ukrainians attend a special Passion service and return home with lighted candles, which are used in the Easter celebrations. On "Passion" (Good) Friday a special shroud is laid out in church. Everyone fasts during Friday and Saturday in remembrance of Christ's fast.

Paska

During these days special Easter breads are baked, *krashanky* (one-coloured eggs) and Easter baskets are prepared. *"Babka"* is a tall, round bread that is light, sweet and rich. *"Paska"* is a round bread topped with symbolic decorations in the form of a cross or a circle symbolizing eternal life.

Pysanka Symbols

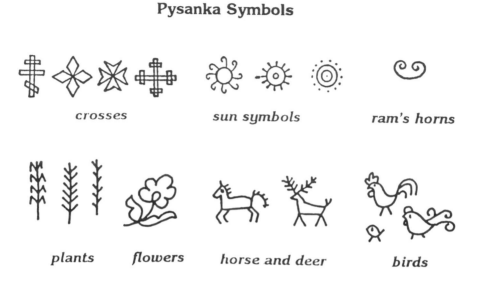

crosses   sun symbols   ram's horns

plants   flowers   horse and deer   birds

On Easter morning, there is a sunrise service, after which all the Easter baskets containing the special breads, butter, cheese, ham, sausage, horse-radish, salt, *krashanky* and Easter eggs are blessed. The rows of baskets containing embroidered cloths, artistically arranged food, colourful Easter eggs and candles are a lovely sight. Each family then hurries home to break the fast. The meal starts with the family sharing one blessed egg, as a symbol of family strength and unity. The food in the Easter basket is only part of the meal that includes cheesecakes and many baked sweets.

In the afternoon, families gather in the church yard or parish hall for Easter games and *hahilky. Hahilky* are choral dances performed by girls and young children. The children then play games using *krashanky* in egg rolling contests or tests of the eggs' strength. The winners get to keep the coloured eggs. On Easter Sunday everyone tries to give and receive a beautifully decorated Easter egg.

Easter Monday is called "Wet" Monday. After the church service, young people squirt or drench each other with water. This commemorates the persecution suffered by early Christians. Traditionally, girls presented each boy that doused them with water with an Easter egg.

Ukrainian Easter eggs - Pysanky

The most famous of Ukrainian Easter traditions are the lovely and intricate *pysanky.* What may seem like decorations on the eggs, are actually symbols with special meanings. If you know the meaning of these symbols, you can read the respective meaning of each egg. That is why in Ukrainian you don't make *pysanky*, you "write" them.

The oldest symbols are circles that represent the sun and symbolize eternal life. Crosses represent the four corners of the world and Christ's Resurrection. Horses and deer symbolize wealth, birds, a fulfilment of wishes. Flowers and plants symbolize growth. Ram's horns represent strength.

Colours also have symbolic meanings. Red symbolizes love, green - health, youth and spring. Yellow brings with it the warmth of the sun and represents happiness. Orange is symbolic of strength. Brown depicts the wealth of the earth. Black is a sad colour, but when combined with white, symbolizes safety. Purple suggests patience and trust.

Pysanky are "written" using hot bees' wax, dyes, and a special writing tool, which is a small metal cone attached to a stick. The melted wax flows through the tip of the cone onto the egg. The parts of the egg that are covered in wax will remain white. The egg is next dipped into the lightest dye, usually yellow. Then parts of the yellow egg are drawn upon with wax. These parts will stay yellow. Afterwards, the egg is dipped in orange dye and the process is repeated to the final colour. The egg is placed in a heated oven to melt the wax. The result is a multicoloured *pysanka*.

Suggestions for activities
a. General Activities

Since Ukrainian Easter is a time of joy and renewal, the suggested activities can be incorporated into language classes as part of an "Easter-around-the-world-theme" or as part of a unit on spring.

1. Make a *krashanka*.

   Use hard-boiled white eggs. Prepare food colouring or special dyes in glass jars. Add a tablespoon of vinegar to each jar of dye. Dye each egg a different colour. Use the *krashanky* in games or as decorations.

2. Make a natural green dye.

   Use a young branch from an apple tree (don't destroy more branches than necessary).
   Shave the bark from the branches to make about 2 cups of bark shavings.
   Cover with water, add 1 tsp. of alum and simmer gently for 1 hour.
   Cool and add 2 tbsps. of vinegar. Place an egg for about 2 hours in the dye. The egg will be light purple. After the egg is removed from the dye, it will start turning light green.

3. Make an Easter card.

   Use Ukrainian *pysanka* symbols to make a card with special wishes for a friend. Remember that the symbols and colours have certain meanings. Explain the meaning of your wishes inside the card.

4. Play Ukrainian Easter games.

Each child will need a *krashanka*. Set up races in groups of four to see whose egg rolls the farthest. Have the finalists race each other. The child whose egg rolls the farthest is the winner.

5. Write a story.

Long ago, people did not know the scientific reason for changes from season to season. Imagine you are a person living long ago. Write a story about how and why spring comes.

b. Activities for higher levels

6. Write a *pysanka*.

Invite to class someone who is experienced in writing Easter eggs to instruct and help the students. This person should be able to obtain all the necessary materials. Set aside at least 2 hours for this class.

7. Traditions and beliefs associated with Ukrainian Easter can be used as the starting point for group activities and discussions that share and compare traditions and beliefs of other cultures, faiths and religions.

Calendar

Many cultures make use of different calendars to determine the time of religious or cultural celebrations. Ukrainians use the Julian calendar. Small groups of students can research a calendar that may be relevant in their lives. A display can be set up of the various calendars.

Symbols

Symbols appear in many aspects of our lives. They also play an important part in most celebrations, rituals, religious and cultural holidays. Each student can share a symbol from his/her experience and explain its meaning or significance. This sharing may lead to a discussion of humanity's need for symbols and how their use affects our lives.

The egg is an important symbol of Ukrainian Easter. Is the egg also a symbol in other cultures? Students can list cultures, celebrations or festivals where the egg is used as a symbol. If there is interest, they can make charts comparing and contrasting the various symbolic meanings of eggs.

Spring

The coming of spring and the rebirth and regeneration of nature is an important part of the celebration of Ukrainian Easter. Today our planet has difficulty in regenerating itself. The class can list various reasons why our planet may be in danger. The students may also wish to organize a spring project that will help nature regenerate itself, for example, tree planting, recycling or clean-up projects.

Reprinted from: Tania Onyschuk, "Teaching Culture in a North American Context: Ukrainian Easter." *Mosaic*, 1, 3 (Spring 1994), pp. 21-22.

46 Teaching Culture in a North American Context:

Valentine's Day

Anthony Mollica, Marjolaine Séguin
and Natalia Valenzuela

Through a "time machine" interview, we were able to reach Cupid, the Roman God of Love, and ask him a few questions about St. Valentine's Day.

Mosaic: I am delighted that you've accepted to be interviewed…As the mythological Roman God of Love, you should be able to provide our readers with a wealth of background information about St. Valentine's day.

Cupid: Yes, of course. This is a celebration which began in Rome more than 2000 years ago with the feast of Lupercalia, celebrated every February 15 to ensure protection from wolves.

Mosaic: Why was this feast so important to the Romans?

Cupid: The celebration was in honour of the God Lupercus, the Roman shepherd's protector against ravaging wolves. These fierce, hungry animals lived in the woods that covered most of the land. They killed sheep and goats. The wolves were so bold that even the farmers and their families were not always safe.

Mosaic: And so each year the Romans had feasts to honour Lupercus and thank him for his protection. But what has this to do with Valentine's Day?

Cupid: At the time of the *Lupercalia* – as the feast to honour Lupercus was called – the people feasted and danced and played games. When the young men wanted partners for the dances and games, they drew the names of the girls out of a bowl. These girls would be their partners. Often these girls became the young men's sweethearts.

Mosaic: I understand that these festivities changed with the advent of Christianity.

Cupid: Correct! With the advent of Christianity, the Romans no longer believed in Gods such as Lupercus, and priests tried to do away with this pagan ritual. The people did not want to give up this celebration, however, and so the church fathers decided to keep this holiday in the middle of February…with some changes.

Mosaic: To what changes are you referring?

Cupid: At these feasts, the people were asked to honour a man of the church, St. Valentine, who was beheaded on February 14.

Mosaic: Who was this Valentine?

Cupid: Valentine – or rather *Valentinus* – was a priest who lived in pagan Rome around the year 270 A.D. He was imprisoned for defying the laws of Emperor Claudius.

Mosaic: What laws did he defy?

Cupid: Claudius had considerable difficulty in recruiting men to serve as soldiers in his wars. The men preferred not to leave their wives, families and sweethearts to fight in foreign lands. And so Claudius declared that no more marriages could be performed and that all engagements were to be cancelled. Valentine believed that this edict was against the laws of God and nature, so he performed Christian marriage ceremonies secretly. When Emperor Claudius discovered what Valentine was doing, he had the priest arrested and sentenced to death.

Mosaic: There is another legend surrounding this incident…

Cupid: Ah, yes! One legend tells that while Valentine was in prison, he restored the sight of the jailer's blind daughter, who brought him food and tried to cheer him up. Legend has it that before dawn on the morning of his execution, he wrote her a farewell note in which he spoke of the bond of affection between people, and he signed the message, "From your Valentine."

Mosaic: I understand that there is a possible third source for the origin of the feast.

Cupid: Yes… Another possibility for the naming of February 14 as a courtship day may have come from an old belief that birds choose their mates on that day, and that man, whose thoughts generally turn to love about the same time of the year, would do well to imitate the birds. Doves and pigeons mate for life and therefore were used as a symbol of "fidelity".

Mosaic: And so, through the centuries, these rituals all merged together?

Cupid: Yes. The modern St. Valentine's Day is a day dedicated to lovers, a time to exchange sentimental greeting cards and love words of never-ending adoration.

Mosaic: February 14 was designated as a feast day by the Catholic Church, was it not?

Cupid: Yes. In 496 A.D. Pope Gelanius named February 14 as St. Valentine's Day. In fact, St. Valentine became the patron saint of lovers; but in 1969 this celebration was dropped from the Roman Catholic calendar.

Mosaic: True. But, nevertheless, the exchange of cards and some traditions continued throughout the years…

Cupid: Some historians trace the custom of sending verses on Valentine's Day to a Frenchman named Charles, Duke of Orléans. Charles was captured by the English during the Battle of Agincourt in 1415. He was taken to England and thrown in prison. It is believed that on Valentine's Day he sent his wife a rhymed love letter from his cell in the Tower of London.

Mosaic: Sending Valentine cards to-day is a common occurrence…

Cupid: Quite right… The custom of sending Valentine cards began in the early 1800s. In fact, it was Esther A. Howland, a Mount Holyoke College student in Worcester, Massachussetts, to craft the first cards in the United States. Her idea was an immediate success; so much so, that she hired a staff of young women and set up an assembly line to produce the cards. Miss Howland's business was so successful that she is reported to have built it into a $100,000 a year business! Some cards were hand painted...others were decorated with dried flowers, lace, feathers, imitation jewels. Some even featured a fat Cupid or showed arrows piercing a heart. Needless to say, I was not pleased with the way I was portrayed... (smiling) being fat, I mean...

Mosaic: I've seen several illustrations of you represented as a chubby, naked, winged boy with a mischievous smile. You appear with a bow and a quiver of arrows by which you transfix the hearts of youths and maidens. I am sure you are probably responsible for the union of many famous couples.

Cupid: I should like to take credit for their union and not for their separation! I certainly do not want to be held responsible for the separation of royal couples... or for the many divorces taking place in the entertainment world...

Mosaic: I can appreciate your point of view. We all want to appear successful in our line of work. And, certainly, your line of work has created many jobs... particularly in the production of Valentine cards which are manufactured on an enormous scale today...

Cupid: Yes... There is a Valentine for everyone – sweetheart, spouse, children, parents, teachers. In terms of the number of greeting cards sent, Valentine's Day ranks second only to Christmas!

Mosaic: That reminds me... I have a lot of cards to send I appreciate your taking the time out during your busy schedule to talk to us about the background for this important celebration. (seeing Cupid getting ready to place an arrow in his bow) Please don't... hope that on this occasion I can remain unscathed from your arrow...

Cupid: All right. On this occasion, I'll let you get along with your work and not have your thoughts turn to love. But next year!...

Entrevue avec Cupidon

Cher Jean,

le directeur de la revue Mosaic me demande de vous informer que nous allons travailler ensemble pour interviewer Cupidon au sujet de la Saint-Valentin. Je vous donne donc rendez-vous à 16 heures demain après-midi à l'entrée du Pavillon des crocus du Jardin Botanique. Vous pourrez facilement me reconnaître. Je porterai une rose à la boutonnière. Au plaisir de faire votre connaissance.

Marie.

Numéro de télécopieur [222] 222-2222

Le lendemain à 16 heures.

Jean arrive au Pavillon des crocus et voit une femme qui porte une rose à la boutonnière. C'est sûrement elle! Elle est assise sur un banc, élégamment vêtue. Il s'approche d'elle et, tout à coup, il sent comme une piqûre dans sa poitrine.

Jean: (timidement) Pardon, Mademoiselle,... vous êtes bien...

Marie: (toute souriante) Marie. Oui, c'est moi. Merci d'être à l'heure. Je suis un peu pressée cet après-midi et je n'ai pas encore repéré notre ami Cupidon mais il ne devrait pas tarder.

Cupidon: (caché derrière les crocus, rit tout bas) Les gens croient toujours que je suis en retard mais, en réalité, j'arrive toujours avant eux. Il le faut bien si je veux utiliser mes flèches discrètement. J'attendrai encore un peu pour voir l'effet de celle que je viens juste de lancer dans le coeur de ce jeune homme.

Jean: Hum!... C'est un beau Pavillon... *(à part:* et Marie est une belle fille)

Marie: Oui, notre ami Cupidon l'a choisi car les crocus sont les fleurs officielles de la Saint-Valentin.

Jean: Je croyais que les roses étaient les fleurs de prédilection de la Saint-Valentin.

Marie: Les roses ont toujours été le choix par excellence de plusieurs amoureux dans le monde entier, mais les crocus sont les fleurs officielles de la Saint-Valentin car elles annoncent l'arrivée du printemps.

Cupidon: (sortant de sa cachette) Les crocus sont aussi un rappel de l'histoire de Valentin lui-même!

Marie: Cupidon, te voilà enfin! Mais d'où viens-tu? Je ne t'ai pas vu arriver.

Cupidon: (taquin) Ah, je ne révèle pas tous mes secrets! Je m'excuse d'être en retard. J'avais un autre rendez-vous avec Radio-Canada. Que veux-tu, en février, je suis très occupé. Tu n'es pas seule aujourd'hui, Marie?

Marie: Tu as un bon sens de l'observation, Cupidon! Je te présente Jean, un nouveau rédacteur de la revue *Mosaic*. Le directeur nous envoie faire une recherche sur la Saint-Valentin et j'ai pensé que tu serais la meilleure personne pour nous aider.

Cupidon: Très bon choix en effet! Écoute, il faut d'abord que je finisse ce que j'ai commencé à te dire au sujet de Valentin. C'était un très bon médecin de la Rome Antique et il paraît qu'il a guéri miraculeusement une jeune fille aveugle un jour avant son exécution.

Jean: L'exécution de la jeune fille aveugle?

Cupidon: Vous êtes bien impatient, jeune homme! Non, l'exécution de Valentin lui-même. L'Empereur Claudius lui a fait couper la tête car il mariait des jeunes gens en cachette.

Marie: Les médecins mariaient les gens dans la Rome Antique?

Cupidon: Tu es impatiente, toi aussi, Marie. *(à part:* L'impatience est un ingrédient qui se marie très bien avec mes flèches!) J'ai oublié de te dire que Valentin était prêtre en plus d'être médecin.

Marie: Mais je ne pouvais pas deviner cela, moi.

Cupidon: Bien sûr que non, Marie. Excuse-moi.

Jean: Très bien, mais pourquoi alors mariait-il les gens en cachette?

Cupidon: Il faut savoir qu'à cette époque, l'Empereur de Rome avait besoin de beaucoup de soldats et il avait remarqué que ceux qui étaient mariés préféraient rester à la maison avec leur épouse et leur famille. Il avait donc interdit les fiançailles et les mariages.

Jean: (offusqué) Mais cela n'a pas de sens d'empêcher les coeurs de s'aimer!

Cupidon: Je suis bien d'accord avec vous!

Marie: Alors l'empereur s'est fâché et a fait tuer Valentin pour cette raison-là?

Cupidon: C'est une des versions que nous a laissées l'histoire mais il paraît qu'il y aurait eu sept personnes nommées Valentin.

Marie: Six autres Valentins?

Cupidon: Et oui, mais je suis pressé aujourd'hui. Je ne crois pas que j'aurai le temps de tout vous raconter. *(Il regarde la porte d'entrée.)* D'ailleurs je dois m'absenter pendant deux secondes. À tout de suite! Ne bougez pas d'ici!

Jean reste interloqué. Marie sourit.

Jean: Mais où est-ce qu'il va comme ça?

Marie: Tu ne connais pas encore notre cher Cupidon. Tu vois le couple qui vient de rentrer?

Jean: Les jeunes habillés en jeans?

Marie: Oui.

Jean: Mais je ne vois pas Cupidon.

Marie: C'est ça son astuce! Il se cache toujours pour lancer ses flèches d'amour.

Cupidon: (de retour) Bon, excusez-moi, mais les affaires urgentes ne peuvent jamais attendre. Ce charmant petit couple avait besoin d'un philtre d'amour. Grâce à moi, ils seront irrésistiblement attirés l'un vers l'autre.

Marie: Dis donc, Cupidon, toi aussi tu travailles en cachette, comme notre ami Valentin?

Cupidon: Tu sais, tout ce que je fais c'est de lancer la première flèche. Le reste, je n'en suis pas responsable. *(à part: heureuse-ment!...)*

Jean: Bon, écoutez, tous les deux. Nous sommes venus ici pour faire une entrevue et il nous reste très peu de temps. Cupidon, laissons faire les six autres Valentin mais dis-moi une chose. Je croyais que la Fête de la Saint-Valentin venait de traditions païennes, bien avant Jésus Christ.

Cupidon: Dis-donc Marie, ton copain est bien informé! En effet, dans la Rome Antique, on célébrait à la mi-février une fête païenne appelée Lupercales.

Marie: Et quelle est la relation avec la fête des amoureux?

Cupidon: Bonne question! Ce jour-là, on mettait le nom de jeunes filles dans une boîte et celui de jeunes hommes dans une autre boîte et on tirait au sort deux noms.

Jean: Qu'est-ce qui arrivait aux deux personnes?

Cupidon: Ils sortaient souvent ensemble pendant le reste de l'année.

Marie: Cupidon, est-ce qu'il y a aussi une histoire à propos des oiseaux?

Cupidon: Bien sûr, Marie! Au Moyen-Âge, on pensait que c'était le 14 février que les oiseaux s'accouplaient et construisaient leur nid.

Marie: Il me semble qu'il fait encore bien froid en février pour s'accoupler. Enfin...

Jean: Cupidon, tous ces faits historiques sont bien intéressants mais que peux-tu nous dire ton rôle à toi dans cette Fête de la Saint-Valentin?

Cupidon: Je ne peux pas vous révéler tous mes secrets, mais si je vous dis que mon nom vient d'un mot latin qui veut dire "désir", vous pourrez tirer vos propres conclusions.

Marie: Cupidon, la Saint-Valentin, ce n'est pas seulement pour les amoureux. Si j'ai envie d'exprimer mon amitié ou mon appréciation pour des personnes que j'aime bien, comme ma soeur, ma mère ou mon professeur, ça me semble l'occasion appropriée.

Cupidon: Et oui, de nos jours, on envoie des cartes aux personnes qu'on aime et ce ne sont pas nécessairement des demandes en mariage comme c'était le cas dans le passé. Oh, Oh! Je vois des jeunes coeurs tout prêts à être transpercés. Vous m'excuserez, mais je dois voler au devant de ces jeunes gens. Merci pour l'invitation. À bientôt!

Jean: Il ne va pas revenir?

Marie: Cette fois-ci, je ne pense pas. Il faudra attendre à l'année prochaine pour lui parler à nouveau.

Jean: (un peu nerveux) En attendant, on pourrait peut-être aller quelque part pour rédiger notre article sur la Saint-Valentin. Au restaurant du Jardin Botanique peut-être.

Marie: C'est que…je n'ai pas beaucoup de temps…

Cupidon, caché derrière elle, lui lance une flèche invisible.

Marie: Ahï!

Jean: Qu'est-ce qu'il y a?

Marie: Rien. Une piqûre de moustique probablement.

Jean: Alors, le restaurant?

Una entrevista con Cupido

Mosaic: Buenos días y bienvenido, Señor Cupido. Me alegro mucho de tenerle aquí para hablarnos de la fiesta de San Valentín.

Cupido: El gusto es mío, señora. Si me hubieran dicho que estaría hablando con una mujer tan guapa *(dándole una mirada de arriba a abajo)* habría traído mis flechas amorosas…

Mosaic: Gracias, pues a mí, sí, me advirtieron que Ud. es muy encantador y que le gusta coquetear con las mujeres.

Cupido: Así es. Me gusta todo lo romántico. *(acercándose a la mujer)*

Mosaic: Dígame Sr. Cupido lo que lo que significa su nombre.

Cupido: Soy uno de los dioses mitológicos y la palabra "cupido" significa "deseo" *(tomando la mano de la mujer)*.

Mosaic: (extricando calmamente la mano y aclarándose la garganta) Hablamos de otra cosa. ¿Cuál es el origen del día de San Valentín?

Cupido: Pues la verdad es que hay varias interpretaciones acerca del origen de esta fiesta. Su espíritu romántico decidirá la que más le guste.

Mosaic: Sí, de acuerdo. Me parece que es una fiesta antigua, ¿no?

Cupido: Sí, el día de San Valentín que celebramos hoy nació de una tradición pagana de la Roma antigua. Se celebraba entonces la fiesta de *Lupercalia*. La gente honraba al dios Lupercus, el cual era responsable de proteger a los pastores y a su rebaño de lobos afamados que rodeaban por las afueras de Roma.

Mosaic: Entonces… ¿era más bien una fiesta pastoral?

Cupido: De una parte, sí, pero también se celebraba la fertilidad y veneraban a los dioses romanos *Juno y Pan*.

Mosaic: ¿Cuáles eran las costumbres asociadas a la fiesta de Lupercalia?

Cupido: Había una tradición muy simpática. Cada doncella escribía su nombre y un mensaje romántico en una carta. Luego, ponían todas las cartas en un gran cacharro. Después los mancebos del pueblo, uno a uno, escojían una carta. Así, los jóvenes se juntaban. Claro que yo tuve que ayudarles a enamorarse.

Mosaic: Es una tradición lindísima, hasta sería divertido hacerlo hoy día; pero ¿quién fue San Valentín?

Cupido: En tiempos romanos, durante el reino del Emperador Claudius II Gothicus, había un curandero cristiano muy conocido llamado San Valentín, que también era uno de los primeros sacerdotes cristianos. El ser cristiano era algo de valiente puesto que en esa época perseguían a los cristianos por sus creencias.

Mosaic: ¿Y nada más que por ser cristiano le encarcelaron?

Cupido: No era tan sencillo. El Emperador Claudius buscaba desesperadamente a soldados para luchas en sus guerras, pero los hombres no cumplían porque no querían dejar a sus mujeres o a sus novias. Claudius se enojó y declaró que no habría más bodas. Era ilegal casarse. Todos los noviazgos fueron cancelados.

Mosaic: ¡Que triste! Me imagino que los enamorados se desesperaron...

Cupido: (Diciendo "no" de la cabeza) No necesariamente. El padre Valentín creía que la nueva ley era injusta y por lo tanto, en secreto, él casó a varias parejas.

Mosaic: Eso sí que es romántico. Y por eso le encarcelaron a San Valentín ¿verdad?

Cupido: Según una versión de la historia, sí, cuando Claudius se enteró que le esteban engañando, le encarceló y le condenaron a muerte; pero también hay otra leyenda... la de la hija del encarcelero.

Mosaic: Sí, conozco esta leyenda. La niña estaba ciega, ¿verdad?

Cupido: Así era. Un día vino un carcelero a visitar a Valentín, para ver si él pudiera ayudar a su hija y devolverle la vista. Valentín trató de sanar a la niña y, mientras tanto el rumor de su cristiandad, su reputación de curandero, y el hecho de que seguía casando a la gente, llegó a oídos de Claudius. Valentín fue condenado a muerte.

Mosaic: ¿Y por eso le santificaron a Valentín?

Cupido: Paciencia...hay más. Unas horas antes de morir, Valentín le mandó una carta a la niña ciega. Al abrir la carta hubo un milagro. ¡Ella la leyó! Le había vuelto la vista. Pronto todos se enteraron y Valentín fue considerado un santo. El mismo día le asesinaron. Era el día 14 de febrero.

Mosaic: Increíble. ¡Qué emocionante! Hasta me trae lágrimas a los ojos. *(tirando de su bolsa un pañuelo).*

Cupido: Sí. Santificaron a San Valentín y en 496 D.C el Papa Gelasius declaró el día 14 de febrero día de San Valentín. El cristianismo ya era aceptado, y querían depaganizar la fiesta de Lupercalia.

Mosaic: He oído que en 1969 el día 14 de febrero fue dejado del calendario litúrgico. ¿Es cierto?

Cupido: Sí es cierto. Pero aunque no es una fecha religiosa sigue siendo una fiesta popular.

Mosaic: ¿Cuáles son las costumbres del día de San Valentín hoy día?

Cupido: Es el día de los amantes y de los enamorados. Se suele enviar cartas románticas, flores, mensajes de amor y chocolate a la persona da la que estamos enamorados.

Mosaic: Ud debe de estar muy ocupado puesto que se acerca el día 14 de febrero.

Cupido: Estoy siempre ocupado. No olvide que la gente no se enamora del un día al otro. Hasta me parece que hoy la gente tarde aun más en enamorarse.

Mosaic: ¿Porque dice eso?

Cupido: Tuve recientemente a un hombre que cuando le percé el corazón de una de mis flechas amorosas, en vez de alegrarse ¡se fue al médico quejándose de indigestación! ¡Y fíjese que mis flechas son de mayor calidad!

Mosaic: No sabía que había diferentes grados de flechas.

Cupido: Sí, hay que tener mucho cuidado. Sino la gente se enamora pero de pronto dejan de amarse. Con las flechas de mayor calidad, la gente sigue amándose por toda la vida.

Mosaic: Veo la importancia de la calidad de las flechas. Y aunque podré hablar con Ud. todo el día, no tenemos más tiempo. Muchísimas gracias por la visita y le deseo un día de San Valentín estupendo.

Cupido: (besándole la mano) Señora, ha sido un encanto conocerla y compartir estas informaciones con Ud. Espero que la próxima vez que nos encontramos que yo tenga mis flechas... *(tirándole un besito).**

*The Authors wish to express their appreciation to Daphne Tunks for researching some of the background information contained in this "interview".

Reprinted from: Anthony Mollica, Marjolaine Séguin, and Natalia Valenzuela "Teaching Culture in a North American Context: Valentine's Day." *Mosaic*, 4, 2 (Winter 1997), pp. 23-26.

47 Teaching Culture in a North American Context:

Mother's/Father's Day

Anthony Mollica

Through a "time-machine" interview, we were able to reach Anna Jarvis and ask her a few questions about Mother's Day.

Mosaic: Miss Jarvis, you are credited as being the driving force behind Mother's Day which is celebrated in the United States, in Canada and in many other parts of the world. How did this idea originate?

Anna Jarvis: As you probably know, the custom of holding a festival in honour of motherhood is very old. The ancient Greeks worshipped the goddess Cybele, the mother of the gods. The custom was later introduced into Rome about 250 B.C., and on the Ides of March the festival continued for three days. But these festivals were entirely different from the one I proposed in honour of mothers.

Mosaic: How was your suggestion different?

Anna Jarvis: I felt that at least one day a year should be identified when sons and daughters should pay a tribute to their mothers.

Mosaic: What steps did you take to achieve this?

Anna Jarvis: As you know, my mother died on May 9, 1905. In succeeding years, I held memorial services and encouraged other sons and daughters to remember their mothers in a similar way. I arranged for a special mother's day service in one of the churches and everyone was asked to wear a white carnation.

Mosaic: I understand that the custom of wearing a white carnation was later modified...

Anna Jarvis: Yes, that's true. There were so many requests for white carnations that florists could not meet the demand... Florists soon discovered that people wanted something more colourful...

Mosaic: What was the solution?

Anna Jarvis: Eventually a distinction was made between those whose mothers were still alive and those whose mothers were dead. The red carnation was worn by sons and daughters whose mothers were still alive, while the white carnation was worn by sons and daughters whose mothers had passed away.

Mosaic: Was the idea of celebrating Mother's Day readily acceptable?

Anna Jarvis: It appears so. The suggestion of honouring one's mother appealed to the imagination of others, and services were held in more churches the next year. As you know, the city of Philadelphia where I was born, was the first city to observe formally the celebration on May 10, 1908. But I wanted to make this day a national holiday and lobbied with our politicians...

Mosaic: How did you go about it?

Anna Jarvis: I wrote thousands of letters to influential persons suggesting that a day be chosen to honour and remember our mothers.

Mosaic: How did the various politicians respond to your request?

Anna Jarvis: They were quite positive and encouraging. President Woodrow Wilson was so enthusiastic about it that on May 9, 1914, following the adoption of a resolution by Congress, he issued a proclamation declaring that the second Sunday in May be observed as Mother's Day.

Mosaic: Yes. I recall President Wilson stating that this day was to be regarded "as a public expression of our love and reverence for the mothers of our country."

Anna Jarvis: The idea spread like wild fire to countries such as Afghanistan, Costa Rica, Spain, Italy, England, Sweden, Denmark, China, Mexico to mention only a few. In India, for example, Mother's Day was established as a memorial to the wife of the political and spiritual leader Mohandas K. Gandhi.

Mosaic: You must be very pleased with the dissemination of this celebration which had humble origins.

Anna Jarvis: I was particularly pleased that sons and daughters soon got into the habit of making little gifts on this day to their mothers. I do emphatically deplore, however, the commercialism which eventually infested this day of tribute.

Mosaic: I would like to move on to another tribute: the one established to honour fathers. Could you provide us with some background information?

Anna Jarvis: I'd be very pleased to. You know, however, that I had nothing to do with this. The idea was originated by Mrs. John Bruce Dodd from Spokane, Washington, in 1909.

Mosaic: Were Mrs. Dodd's reasons in wanting to establish a day to honour her parent similar to yours?

Anna Jarvis: There are some minor differences. Mrs. Dodd wanted to honour her father who had successfully reared a family of children after the death of their mother.

Mosaic: How did she go about it?

Anna Jarvis: I am told that she wrote to the Rev. Conrad Bluhm, president of the Spokane Ministerial Association and proposed that the third Sunday in June be set apart for honouring fathers.

Mosaic: What was the reaction?

Anna Jarvis: The congregation immediately approved the proposal, and the first celebration was held in Spokane in June 1910.

Mosaic: Was there any difference between the celebration of Father's Day and Mother's Day?

Anna Jarvis: The only major difference that immediately comes to mind is the flower used. Sons and daughters were asked to wear a red rose if their father was alive and a white one if he was deceased. You will recall that the carnation is the symbol for Mother's Day.

Mosaic: Was the rose the first choice as the symbol?

Anna Jarvis: Actually, members of the Martin W. Callener Bible class of Wilkinsburg, PA, had suggested the dandelion in 1924, as "the more it is trampled on, the more it grows," but its use did not become general.

Mosaic: Did the Father's Day celebration spread as quickly as Mother's Day?

Anna Jarvis: Not quite. In 1911, the celebration was discussed in Chicago as if the idea was new. A dispatch from Vancouver, Washington appearing in the Portland *Oregonian* in 1913 believed that the celebration for Father's Day had originated there.

Mosaic: When did the celebration officially come into general use?

Anna Jarvis: If I am not mistaken, it was in 1934.

Mosaic: Thank you, Miss Jarvis, for all this useful information.

Pedagogical Suggestions

Following are some suggested activities for Mother's Day/Father's Day. They are not presented in any specific order of difficulty. Teachers will know the linguistic background of their students and will select only those activities appropriate to the age and linguistic level of the class. These suggestions are by no means exhaustive; teachers will undoubtedly think of others.

1. Send a singing telegram to your Mother/Father expressing your best wishes for the Day. (The telegram may be live or pre-recorded on audiotape.)
2. Send a balloon-o-gram (with a secret message inside the balloon).
3. Create a menu and take your parent breakfast in bed.
4. Design a ticket and mail it to your parent inviting him/her to attend a scene (or scenes) you will perform at your house depicting why your parent is so special to you.
5. Imagine that the idea of Mother's/Father's Day originated with you. Write a letter to a politician urging him/her to lobby to have it declared a national holiday.
6. Your local newspaper is having a contest for the Best Mom/Best Dad. Write a short paragraph about the qualities of your parent and submit it to the contest.
7. Write a poem for your parent expressing your love and your gratitude for what he/she has done for you.
8. Make a placemat and get it laminated for the kitchen table.
9. Design a Best Mother/Best Father Certificate. List at least three reasons for this "award".
10. Using the information from the Jarvis "interview" printed above, write in your own words a short paragraph about the origins of Mother's Day/Father's Day.
11. Write an Editorial indicating reasons why sons and daughters should celebrate Mother's Day/Father's Day.
12. Interview several people (on audiotape, if possible) and ask them what they think of Mother's Day/Father's Day celebrations.

13. Design a Happy Mother's/Father's Day card and write a message in one of the languages you are currently studying.
14. List a dozen adjectives which best describe your parent.
15. Make a series of drawings illustrating the activities in which your parent is frequently involved.
16. Imagine that you are Anna Jarvis and have the opportunity to meet President Wilson. Select a partner to play the role of the President and try to persuade him to establish a day to celebrate Mother's/Father's Day.

[Text by Anthony Mollica; Pedagogical Suggestions by Tania Sterling.]

Reprinted from: Anthony Mollica and Tania Sterling, "Teaching Culture in a North American Context: Mother's Day/Father's Day." *Mosaic*, 1, 4 (Summer 1994): pp. 22-23.

Contributors

Janis L. Antonek is Assistant Professor, Department of Curriculum and Instruction, University of North Carolina at Greensboro, where she teaches and oversees the FL and ESL methodology programs.

W. Jane Bancroft is Associate Professor of French and Humanities at the Scarborough Campus, University of Toronto.

Jill Bell is Assistant Professor in the Faculty of Education, York University, where she teaches courses on language and literacy.

Christine Besnard is Associate Professor of French. She teaches at Glendon College, York University, North York, Ontario.

Paul Cankar, MA, is instructor of Spanish at St. Michael's High School in Austin, Texas. His interests include learner strategies and the development of proficiency-based materials.

Kenneth Chastain is Professor of Spanish, Department of Spanish, Italian and Portuguese, University of Virginia, Charlottesville, Virginia

Caterina Cicogna is Education Officer, Office of the Consulate General of Italy, Toronto, Ontario.

Rebecca Constantino is adjunct Assistant Professor, School of Education, University of Southern California. She is also a Reading

teacher, Los Angeles City College.

Marcel Danesi is Professor of Semiotics and Applied Linguistics ,Victoria College, University of Toronto and Adjunct Professor at the Università della Svizzera Italiana of Lugano, Switzerland.

Richard Donato is Associate Professor of Foreign Languages in the School of Education at the University of Pittsburgh, Pennsylvania.

Philip Donley Ph.D., has taught Spanish at the University of Texas at Austin, Southwestern University, and Austin Community College. His interests include language anxiety and teaching critical thinking skills. He often conducts seminars in anxiety-reduction and critical thinking.

Charles Elkabas is Associate Professor of French at Erindale College, University of Toronto.

Hector Hammerly is Professor of Applied Linguistics and teaches in the Linguistic Department, Simon Fraser University, Burnaby, British Columbia.

Cher Evans Harvey is Assistant Professor, Faculty of Education, Nipissing University, where she teaches courses in methodology for French as a second language.

Peter J. Heffernan is Professor of Education at the Faculty of Education, University of Lethbridge, Alberta, with primary responsibility for second-language teacher preparation.

Fred Howlett is a former Head of Moderns with the North York Board of Education, North York, Ontario.

Stephen D. Krashen is Professor of Education at the University of Southern California. It has always been his desire to write a paper in which both the footnotes and the references were longer than the actual article.

J. Clarence LeBlanc is a retired high school and university second-language teacher who maintains his passion for teaching, and its administrative and political dimensions. He was a member of the National Core French Study and chaired the Culture Syllabus Task Group

Louise Lewin teaches methodology courses in French as a second language at the Faculty of Education, Glendon College, York University.

Cheng Luo holds a Ph.D. in Linguistca and TESL from the University of Manitoba. He is currently teaching at Brock University.

Domenico Maceri teaches in the Foreign Language Program, Allan Hancock College, Santa Maria, California.

Raffaella Maiguashca is Associate Lecturer at York University where she teaches Italian language and methodology courses.

Keith Mason Ph.D. is a teacher of Spanish and Italian in the New Providence School District, New Providence, NJ.

Anthony Mollica is Professor of Education, Faculty of Education, Brock University, St. Catharines, Ontario and Adjunct Professor, University of Toronto at Mississauga.

Frank Nuessel is Professor of Linguistics at the University of Louisville, Louisville, Kentucky.

Tania Onyschuk is an instructor in charge and co-ordinator of Ukrainian classes at Our Lady of Sorrows, Metropolitan Separate School Board, Toronto.

Anthony Papalia was a former Chair, Faculty of Educational Studies, SUNY, Buffalo. At the time of his death in 1988, he was Professor in the Faculty of Educational Studies, SUNY, Buffalo.

Alain Péchon is a former French teacher with the North York Board of Education, North York, Ontario.

Edwin G. Ralph is Associate Professor of Education, College of Education, University of Saskatchewan, Saskatoon, Saskatchewan.

Merle Richards is Associate Professor of Education, Faculty of Education, Brock University, St. Catharines, Ontario.

Perla Riesenbach teaches French as a second language at Leo Baeck Day School, Board of Jewish Education, Toronto.

Sylvie Rosienski-Pellerin is Associate Professor of French and teaches at Glendon College, York University, North York, Ontario.

Roseann Runte, professor, author, and poet is President of Victoria University, University of Toronto. She has published widely in national and international journals.

Herbert Schutz is Professor of German and Chair, Department of Slavic Studies, Brock University, St. Catharines, Ontario.

Marjolaine Séguin is a teacher currently enrolled in the French as a second language program, Brock University.

Tania Sterling teaches French as a second language at Canadian Martyrs, Burlington, Ontario.

Karen Tessar is a student completing her B.Ed. at the Faculty of Education, Brock University, St. Catharines, Ontario.

G. Richard Tucker is professor of Applied Linguistics at Carnegie Mellon University, Pittsburgh, Pennsylvania.

Natalia Valenzuela is completing her B.Ed at the Faculty of Education, Brock University.

Rebecca M. Valette is Professor of Romance Languages at Boston College. She is past President of the American Association of Teachers of French.

Joanne Wilcox is President of Multilingual Communications for Management (MCM), Manotick, Ontario. MCM specializes in translation and cross-culture business etiquette.